OLD AGE IN PREINDUSTRIAL SOCIETY

Old Age in Preindustrial Society

Edited by Peter N. Stearns

Holmes & Meier
Publishers, Inc.
New York　　　　London

First published in the United States of America 1982 by
Holmes & Meier Publishers, Inc.
30 Irving Place
New York, N.Y. 10003

Great Britain:
Holmes & Meier Publishers, Ltd.
131 Trafalgar Road
Greenwich, London SE10 9TX

Book design by Rose Jacobowitz

Library of Congress Cataloging in Publication Data
Main entry under title:

Old age in preindustrial society.

  Includes index.
  1. Old age—History—Addresses, essays, lectures.
2. Aged—History—Addresses, essays, lectures.
I. Stearns, Peter N.
HQ1061.038 1982   305.2′6   81-6874
ISBN 0-8419-0645-9   AACR2

Manufactured in the United States of America

For Clio-Elizabeth
less a muse than amusing

Contents

CHAPTER ONE—INTRODUCTION

PETER N. STEARNS

O ld age, as a field of history, remains shockingly untended. It is doubtless symptomatic of the shaky esteem the elderly command in contemporary society that, of all the major "inarticulate" groups, the aged have been taken up last and least by historians. Anthropologists have done better, and a flourishing network of gerontological specialists exists in this discipline.[1] Historians, comparatively alert to the need for historical perspective on women and several ethnic minorities, have approached the elderly much more gingerly.

Nevertheless, a small band of old age historians does now exist. They have already uncovered some interesting data and unleashed some still more interesting hypotheses. Their focus, understandably, has been primarily on the elderly during the past two centuries, and in Western society. The impact of industrialization on old people, and the nature and impact of more recent social legislation in their regard have, along with trends of residence and family affiliation, begun to produce something of a perspective on the position of the elderly today.[2]

Research on the position of old people in preindustrial society, aside from the sweeping effort of Simone de Beauvoir, has lagged.[3] Work on family history or on the history of the poor has provided some soundings, largely indirectly. It is, clearly, possible to offer more.[4] Even de Beauvoir's survey, largely an exercise in intellectual history with a few confusing concrete indicators (see the contradictions as to whether or not the elderly were rare in France before 1780), has not been followed up, though it offers the beginnings of a corrective against some common misimpressions of the elderly before modernity's onset.

Preindustrial old age is thus, from the historian's standpoint, almost virgin territory, a gap to be filled. One can envision, with only a slight shudder, a goodly number of theses on various aspects of the subject, if imaginative doctoral dissertations survive the present crisis of the discipline. The subject has some intrinsic fascination, besides virginity: of all the inarticulate groups social historians have turned to, the elderly may prove the greatest challenge, clothed as they were with official respect and buried, as they often were, in reality.

However, the purpose of a collection of essays on various aspects of the preindustrial elderly is not, primarily, to plug an empirical gap merely because it exists. There are two additional reasons to take the subject up, the second with a further subset.

A rather silly French doctor commented, early in the present century, that the treatment of the elderly was a measure of the quality of a society.[5] His purpose was to urge a patronizing kind of charity, and he ignored the burden a growing percentage of elderly could place on even a prosperous modern society, or the burdens a modern society could place on the elderly. But his remark has some merit. As with the history of women and other "inarticulate" groups, a concentration on the situation of old people may prove to be something of a window on larger aspects of a past society's functioning. We already know that the position of old people looms large in the emotional and power relationships of preindustrial families;[6] we are beginning to understand the impact of old people on poor relief institutions.[7] And we have generalizations aplenty, if little hard data, on the role of the elderly in directing the larger outlook of societies that stressed veneration and obedience.[8] What was said about the old, and what was done, and the gap between may provide significant insight into the way preindustrial societies operated.

The second reason to open the subject of preindustrial old age is that we cannot readily evaluate even more modern history of the subject without some sense of what the elderly are moving from. Thus the two leading histories of American old age have begun with an examination, possibly too facile, of the colonial period, in an attempt to show a deterioration from a once-solid base.[9] (The two works differ considerably in dating and evaluating the deterioration, but they both share the starting point.) Similarly the more thoughtful gerontologists have long posited a "golden age of age" in the preindustrial past, as a framework for what they typically see as a peculiarly modern set of problems for their subjects.[10] Conclusions about preindustrial old age thus bear inescapably on modern judgments. This connection may wane a bit as further details of the modern history are uncovered, and as a more complex internal periodization for the modern period is established. But a considerable linkage is inevitable: we cannot judge the quality, much less the trend, of modern characteristics of the elderly without some basis for comparison across time. In a very real sense, a few biological givens aside, we are not yet sure what features of the social position of old people are new, what are rather typical of any civilization, and what, perhaps, are not new but distinctively Western.

This temporal baseline has implications even for present policy concerns about the elderly. Because of the need to have some historical referents despite real historical ignorance, a good many policy stances bear at least an implicit set of assumptions about the relationship between modern and premodern old age. We grow troubled about the predominant retirement experience for the contemporary elderly. Our reasons are partly very new, as we face a literally unprecedented percentage of older people in our society. But some sense of trouble existed earlier, even before the sheer cost of retirement emerged as a problem. Gerontologists have thus long worried about the impact of cessation of work on the orientation, the basic sense of worth, of retirees. Their concerns, and even the more recent ones, could be embellished if it could be shown that before retirement became common, that is, in preindustrial society, the elderly had greater dignity as well as greater function. There is an almost direct appeal, in some gerontologists' recommendations, for a return to the policies and values of preindustrial society, for old people if for no other group.[11] If this kind of thinking even remotely influences present policymakers, or justifies their policies after the fact, it surely behooves us to know whereof we speak. Which is where some history comes in.

Inevitably, of course, history complicates. We have already moved through two stages of viewing preindustrial old age (both stages developed in advance of much information)—although public and even some expert opinion has yet to catch up even with the second stage.

Until historians began to contribute to the discussion, the golden age theory predominated. Those gerontologists who invoked a historical frame of reference at all certainly subscribed to it, and often still do. In some cases "premodern" is extended in fact to the later nineteenth century, because of the convenience of a dramatic contrast with present ills. Confused periodization aside, the basic approach resulted in part from a belief that, since various modern practices toward old people were bad, premodern practices, known to have been different, must have been better. Retirement is an obvious case in point. If seen as bad, because of loss of function and power, an era in which it could rarely be afforded and in which the practice was certainly not mandated might easily be viewed with a certain admiration. The same temptation holds for residential patterns. Gerontologists who bemoan the present age-segregation—with older people living largely separate from younger kin, and sometimes in groupings with other elderly—could easily posit that a presumed preindustrial pattern of coresidence with kin was preferable. Often these assumptions fit larger beliefs about the superiority of pre-industrial family structure to present structure.

This basis for an evaluation of preindustrial society is obviously, upon any reflection, faulty. In some respects it has simply been inaccurate, as in the common assumption of a total contrast in residential patterns. Even the belief that the preindustrial elderly retained the dignity of work proves partially wrong, as retirement or partial retirement was both a need and a goal of many agriculturalists. Equally important, where contrasts do exist, they do not automatically redound in favor of the preindustrial. Retirement may be bad for the elderly—a highly debatable point about modern society—but that does not mean nonretirement was good. (And, though voluntarily, the elderly did retire sometimes in preindustrial society, which led to derisive comments on their decrepitude.)[12] One of the key points to guide an inquiry into preindustrial old age is in fact the need to find out whether problems in the social state of the elderly do not run far deeper than mere modernity. That many gerontologists hoped not, and therefore conjured a pleasant golden age in the past, is admirable, but it may be wrong and therefore, in the long run, unhelpful.

But of course there was more to the golden age approach than a mere assumption of contrast. Knowledge of societies that are preindustrial today, or nearly so, and in which the old are venerated, not surprisingly encouraged a belief that our own preindustrial past was similarly constructed—especially since some practices and also some cultural tag words, such as *respect* and *filial duty*, did indeed overlap.[13] Again, it is obvious that there is no necessary logic in this kind of overlap. While preindustrial societies do have certain very general points in common, deriving mainly from their common base in agriculture, they cannot serve as a generic unit of analysis. A comparative approach is always called for, in which differences are sought as eagerly as similarities. In the case of old age, even assuming a revered place for the elderly in some agricultural societies, it is both logically and empirically possible that a Western tradition was distinctive. We know that the West had a distinctive family pattern overall, in the centuries between the Middle Ages and industrializa-tion;[14] it is certainly valid to look for the role of these distinctions in the life of the elderly.

But the golden age advocate could grant even the need for further inquiry, and the possibility of diversity, and still claim some general basis for believing that the situation of the preindustrial elderly had to be better than that of their modern counterparts, at least in terms of community status. Two key arguments here, which if valid might indeed apply across the board in preindustrial societies, are scarcity value and educational role.

Old people formed a small percentage of the total population of any preindustrial society. This is unquestionably true. High birth and child mortality rates guaranteed a percentage preponderance of the very young far above any modern level.[15] After this is said, however, the argument often wanders. Some, for example, point to low longevity rates as proof of the rarity of old age (indeed, almost the impossibility of attaining that state). With life expectancy at birth around twenty-eight years, in preindustrial Europe, surely the rare sixty-year-old must have been a cause for godlike wonder. Of course, this misconstrues preindustrial demography.[16] If one lived through early childhood, life expectancy was not radically different from modern levels (although it did differ to an extent); twenty-year-olds could expect to live into their later fifties on average. And this in turn meant that, in the adult population, old people were not exactly collectors' items. They were rarer than today, and their relative rarity, compared to contemporary levels, increased with each year of life, but they were hardly unknown. David Troyansky's essay in this volume shows that the over-sixties could be a sizable percentage of a village population. Further, we cannot assume that what we rank as old was so regarded in the past. Classical wisdom held sixty to be the beginning of male old age, a bit earlier than the common belief holds today, while women were in many respects old upon menopause.[17] Culturally appropriate definitions of old age are elusive, and historians still largely assume a conventional, and rather modern, point of reference. But it is really possible that, everything considered, those considered "old people" loomed just as large among adults as they do today — and that it was the adult frame of reference, not the percentage of the total population, that really served to orient attitudes toward, and treatment of, the elderly. The point about percentage differences need not be rejected, but it cannot be assumed.

The educational role of the elderly is more attractive, and it is worth getting ahead of our argument to note that debunking historians have largely neglected this staple of the golden age approach. Preindustrial society was largely illiterate; learning depended on word of mouth; the elderly (problems of senility are conveniently forgotten) know most because their memories run longest; and so they serve as society's mentors. The Silverman/ Maxwell essay, in this collection, stresses the importance of the information control function of the elderly in determining their position in preindustrial society. Correspondingly, with modern literacy, learning is stored in books—not old minds—and so the elderly automatically lose status and function (at least over the long haul, not necessarily quickly).

Surely this was sometimes true. One thinks of tribes in which old men served as storytellers; situations in which old women were founts of medical lore; priests whose educational role was enhanced by their venerability. Key preindustrial institutions did indeed assume wisdom with age (although this more clearly involved age limits that excluded the young than guarantees that the really old would prevail).[18]

But the assumption of a pervasive educational role for old people cannot be made; it sets an empirical problem, not a conclusion. Most learning, for most people, involved work training, and this was often conducted by the middle-aged rather than by less active older people. A minority of literate clerks could displace the venerable memory, as the Troyansky essay suggests. In West European society, an additional problem emerges. We tend to assume, in invoking an educational role, a function for grandparents with their grandchildren. But, uniquely among major societies, the European marriage pattern inhibited this kind of contact. Not marrying until about twenty-seven, with their children later doing likewise, and with an adult life expectancy of roughly fifty-six, the average person would overlap the firstborn grandchild by only a year or so—hardly time enough to do much educating. Obviously averages must allow for exceptions; David Troyansky shows considerable grandparenting in his eighteenth-century French village. Obviously also even grandchild-less older people may have played a more general storytelling role. But, attractive as the oral transmission hypothesis is, it requires investigation, particularly in the Western context.

In addition to questionable specifics, the golden age of age approach relies on our sense of the deference and respect urged upon preindustrial people—European and other—by the major religions and by family culture. We think in terms of honored patriarchs, perhaps on the somewhat Cartesian assumption that since we have the concept of patriarchs, and since we find few of them around today, they must have existed sometime. It is, certainly, hard to suggest jettisoning this view. In power terms, an elderly property holder did have the legal and economic basis for wielding considerable power over younger kin. Keith Thomas has noted how widows could gain in status when they had a business to take over through inheritance.[19] In cultural terms, the premodern emphasis on duties owed to parents are an undeniable feature of the family ethic. And, individually,, patriarchs, and more subtly powerful older women, there undoubtedly were.

Yet again what we have is in fact a subject for inquiry, not a firm conclusion. Propertied power—not the lot of all older people in any event—was fully useful for most people only if accompanied by sufficient work ability to make the property pay. If this ability declined, property would have to be used to dicker, not to control, for only a small minority had enough property to pay others to do the work without diminishing the property—and therefore the familial authority—itself.[20] Without economic power, it may be doubted the cultural ascendancy could normally be maintained. The vigorous injunctions to honor one's parents may suggest constant tension, the need to repeat given actual behavior, rather than a smooth age hierarchy.[21] And it may be that it was the authority of middle-aged parents over teen-agers, not the elderly over adult children, that was being touted in any event.

With one important category of exceptions, historians who have begun to take up the theme of old age in preindustrial Western society have attempted to debunk the golden age of age approach.[22] They stress the number of poor and abandoned older people in almshouses and city hospitals, and the absence of any policy to deal with older people as such. They grant that the elderly who flooded the charitable institutions were a minority of the whole, but they stress that their isolation follows from still more typical problems. Instead of the honored patriarch, the revisionists emphasize the tensions between adult generations, as younger adults chafed at the very existence of their older, owning parents. Hence the need for old people, who had to surrender all or part of their property because they could no longer work it, to stipulate in the greatest detail what support their children would owe them in return for their concessions. A culture of veneration gives way, in other words, to a power relationship in which many old people could not really hold their own, and to the material suffering that resulted.[23]

Adding to the revisionist picture is the realization that in Western society, at any rate, the culture itself was as often harsh as mellow to the elderly even in principle. Preindustrial society might ridicule youth—in marked contrast to the nineteenth century—but it did not therefore venerate age. Thus in court the testimony of witnesses might be impeached if they were young, *or* if they were old. Mature adulthood, but not old age, was best. Although the virtues of filial respect need not be forgotten, and a classical strand, from Cicero, emphasized the special wisdom and objectivity of the elderly, an important current of thought stressed the degeneration, even the ugliness, of the old.[24] The old might be held wise, but they were just as often judged miserly, selfish, libidinous—indeed, unpleasant figures of fun. The concept "No fool like an old fool" is not a modern invention. Without pressing the imagery too far, at an opposite extreme to the idea that veneration described reality, there was some correspondence between the harsh view and what many older people actually faced. Accusations of avarice obviously reflected tensions over property between the fearful elderly and the aspiring young. The idea of the old as ugly, even dangerous, could take concrete shape in attacks on old people as witches. Small wonder that Lawrence Stone has concluded that, whatever the continued or novel problems of the old in modern society, the elderly are better off than ever before.[25]

There remain some difficulties even with the revisionist view. If the simplest kind of nostalgia for a golden age is now ridiculous, in light of available evidence, it is true that not all of the points raised in the earlier scheme have been refuted. The educative role of the elderly, although not as automatic as once assumed, has not really been investigated from a revisionist standpoint. Nor, as already suggested, can we deny all claims of venerable patriarchy. Related cultural issues are unclear. The impact of the decline of religion on the position of the modern elderly, particularly as its values are displaced by youth-dominated celebrations such as athletic contests, has not been integrated into a revisionist picture.[26] Nor have the elderly as the only age group prone to frequent death—since the decline of infant mortality in 1900—in an antideath society[27] been seriously taken up in old age history. We may, as we newly fear death, have new reasons to isolate and fear old people—just as preindustrial society feared infants, the "death group" in the society.

Further, historians dealing with one special case of a preindustrial Western society, that of colonial America, have produced a picture far more similar to the idea of a golden age than that currently admitted by Europeanists. David Hackett Fischer and Andrew Achenbaum both qualify the simplest kind of nostalgia.[28] They note laments from colonial elderly themselves, particularly about their distinctive problems of health and physical decline. Achenbaum, particularly, also stresses the economic hardship that befell any older person who had no property to bargain with. But they stress that many older people really were revered by their children; that property settlements were often amicable; that even coresidence with younger kin was more common than in Europe, where the old were typically shunted into separate cottages. Above all, they stress a public esteem for the old, both in the general culture and in specific practices such as preferential church seating. They conclude, although quite diversely in specific terms, that in America the modern period would see a deterioration of the lot of old people in many respects.

It is of course possible to reconcile the American and European impressions. Colonial America, blessed with more abundant property, more easily avoided generational tensions. Older parents could settle a handsome property on their children and still have something left over.[29] Earlier marriage, itself the result of greater abundance, meant that old people in colonial America typically overlapped their grandchildren, and might in some cases help with them: the European family pattern did not apply. America, then, may be the exception that proves the revisionist rule, in that the causes of normal hardships of the elderly were attenuated, and therefore the behavior altered. And even Fischer, who produces the rosiest impression, carefully notes that the elderly still depended on their propertied position, that their family role was not surrounded with real affection.

And yet the American exception (however great it may prove to be with further study), and the sheer gaps in our information about the preindustrial elderly, do suggest that possibly the revisionists have gone overboard in their turn, stimulated by the simplistic quality of the golden age model. It is time for more serious work and, with it, a third stage in our approach to the elderly in preindustrial society. In various ways the essays in this volume, and the small amount of careful research elsewhere available, represent an approach to this stage, in which the starkest contrast between preindustrial and modern — whether to the advantage of the former or of the latter — will be downplayed in favor of a more subtle balance sheet.

For even aside from the American anomaly, what is striking about the two existing pictures available is that neither fully addresses the other. This means, in the first place, an emphasis on different groups of old people. Class distinctions have not been carefully considered in dealing with the preindustrial elderly. The golden age approach implicitly emphasizes those elderly who had enough property or physical vigor to retain some real control over their lot—as seems to have been disproportionately the case in colonial America. The debunkers stress those who had to surrender their property or the significant group who never had property, or even family of their own, in the first place. Greater coherence can be introduced into the assessment of preindustrial old age by pursuing these basic distinctions—and greater precision by undertaking the difficult task of determining how many and what kinds of people fell into each category. Fuller attention to gender will also help. The optimistic assessment of preindustrial old age works best for men, though some individual women need not be excluded. Problems of property control and the clear cultural bias against older women made the fate of this group far shakier. Aside from specific attacks on older women—not only witch hunts but also charivaris against an older woman whose behavior seemed out of line[30]—the fact that widows past menopause could rarely remarry, in contrast to widowers of the same age, combined with the economic value of remarriage, suggests the real difficulty of living old and female.[31]

In addition to developing a set of generalizations supple enough to include various groupings within the old age category, historians must begin integrating the various aspects of life of a given group, even a given individual, once old age was reached. Although disputes over the nature of preindustrial old age have zeroed in on some common issues—economic power and cultural prestige—there is a distressing tendency to ignore the total picture. Optimists deal with the putative educational and storytelling role, which deserves assessment. Pessimists mention health concerns, and the question of who could care for a partially disabled older person, and in what spirit. They also deal with the issue of familial affection.

A final balance sheet on preindustrial old age and its qualities compared with those of the modern counterpart must surely take into account a variety of plusses and minuses, not the simplest kind of good/bad contrast. Almost certainly, a larger proportion of older people in 1700 had some property to bargain with for services and assistance that would allow a reduction of the workload than was true in the industrial societies of 1900. Less certainly, but possibly, an older person in 1700 could retain a sense of attunement with his society, which in principle, at least, was immune to basic change; in contrast, the 1900 counterpart could realistically develop the old person's lament that social change left the elderly confused and out of touch. On the other hand the oldster of 1900 might benefit from a bit of relevant medical attention, including hospital facilities that were beginning to be something more than deathtraps or even the humbler possibility of acquiring a set of false teeth. He or she might benefit also from a greater amount of familial affection and from the sense of function provided by the possibility of caring for grandchildren. Again, we need an integrated picture of both preindustrial and modern old age before the full mix of improvement and deterioration involved in the passage from one period to the next can be realistically grasped.[32] We need, in sum, a richer texture in the historical analysis.

This analysis must also, as we move beyond the first reactions of historians to the simplicities of nostalgic generalizations, provide a clearer sense of regional factors. The debunking approach of Europeanists has been based primarily on English and French data, although strictly demographic statements—attacking the idea of the coresident extended family for example—have utilized Scandinavian and Central European material as well.[33] We know too little about the experience of old age in other parts of Europe; it is even premature to assume that there was a "Western" form of old age, although distinctive family patterns do suggest its high probability.

Finally, the evaluation of preindustrial old age must come to grips more seriously with issues of periodization. How far back in time, once established with suitable sophistication, can a model of preindustrial old age reach—even in Western Europe? Are there key periods of old age history within Western agricultural society? Presumably, the late medieval centuries that marked the beginnings of the European family type and the distinctive attachment of the family to property marked also a change in the old age experience. But it would be useful to have greater detail about the nature of the change. Here, indeed, is a case where attention to old age history might provide the kind of entrée into broader social dynamics suggested previously in more general terms. Were there other significant changes in the situation of the elderly between the advent of the European family type and the industrial revolution itself? Seventeenth-century alterations in the view and organization of charity and the definition of deviance suggest a possible subject for further inquiry,[34] and demographic and intellectual shifts in the eighteenth century produced greater and more diverse concern for old age; but again, in terms of existing literature, the key issues of periodization are far from resolution: we are only beginning to be able to state them properly.

And when does the preindustrial situation end, as far as old age history is concerned? Almost surely in two phases.[35] The advent of industrialization had a somewhat muted impact on the elderly, partly because the old were less quickly drawn into the newer economic processes than was the rest of the population. For many old people, left behind in the villages, industrialization created a sense of family disruption, but it did not bring direct, immediate change in style of life. Thus demographers point out that the decisive change in the household structure of the elderly in modern society is a twentieth-century change, involving fully separate residence; nineteenth-century industrialization only mildly altered preindustrial household patterns.[36] Sylvia Vatuk, in her essay on India in this volume, confirms the persistence of basic preindustrial arrangements in an industrializing context. Similarly, in Europe, many key attitudes about old age deterioration remained unaltered into the twentieth century; they were at most deepened and more widely publicized via new medical discoveries about the process of senescence.[37] Continuities of this sort cause some historians to argue that the whole preindustrial/industrial distinction is inapplicable to old age history, preferring a more recent, less clearly labeled periodization.

Nevertheless, the industrial revolution did have an impact. Most important was the fact that the old became relatively less significant economically, declining as a percentage of the work force, unable to offer the most up-to-date skills. Above all, this lack of significance held true for the proletariat, devoid of property. Everywhere, the elderly swelled the ranks of unskilled labor; everywhere they were disproportionately unemployed or degraded in pay and skill levels.[38] In the economic sense, at least for the urban working class, preindustrial society had ended; or at least the conditions previously applicable to the propertyless group extended to a much larger category—certainly by the mid-nineteenth century in Western Europe. To this was added the problem of a clearer sense of the economic inappropriateness of the old to the modern economy. In the United States, industrialization (or Fischer would argue, its cultural preconditions around 1800) reversed the favorable culture of the colonial period, with a new emphasis on youth, thus compounding the clearer changes in economic situation.[39] Possibly compensating, at least in small part, were new family functions in the industrial cities, as in caring for grandchildren, and perhaps a new level of familial affection as tension over property transmission perforce declined. In India, industrialization to date has brought improvement in family structure affecting the elderly, notably greater likelihood that an adult son will survive to support older parents; here a preindustrial support pattern that was often defective is actually aided by early industrial development.

The Indian case notwithstanding, the emphasis in Western society remains on some unsettling features of early industrialization. Even in the West, however, it is true that the impact of industrialization was incomplete, particularly in terms of the reactive power of the elderly themselves. In the Western world, the preindustrial culture of old age began to yield more decisively only in the first half of the twentieth century. It was only then that the elderly began to appear explicitly as the subject of public policy—with a lag symptomatic of the preindustrial unwillingness (or lack of need) to admit that all was not well with the old that had persisted despite new problems through most of the nineteenth century. Furthermore, during the first third of the twentieth century, groups of old people, aided by retirement support and improved health (particularly with the advent of sulpha drugs in the 1930s), began to cultivate more active leisure patterns, new associational efforts, even a new appearance and image.[40] Old age in the most literal—preindustrial—sense might still be disdained, but an increasing number of old people were bent on showing that, by these same preindustrial standards, they were not old. Objective changes in the twentieth century included residential separation from kin; new longevity levels; the growing percentage of old people in the population at large; and mass, virtually mandatory, retirement. As noted, the elderly were for the first time viewed as a group for which explicit public policy must be designed.[41]

The prolonged impact of preindustrial values and behaviors toward old age and the lag between the impact of modernized economic structures and any thorough modernization of old people as a group—or modernization of policy toward the elderly—lends further value to a careful inquiry into what preindustrial old age was. The fact is, of course, that some of the tensions that a careful inquiry into preindustrial old age reveals are still with us, even if many of the structural features of the life stage have yielded to more modern forms. Society did not move neatly from veneration to scorn for the elderly, in shifting from a preindustrial to an industrial base.[42] Even twentieth-century modernization of outlook, toward a more activist definition of old age, develops against a backdrop of more traditional uncertainties about the value of the elderly. In seeking to understand preindustrial old age, we learn of ourselves not only by contrast, but also through continuity.

The essays that follow treat various facets of preindustrial old age, and from various vantage points. A survey of Western literary images adds new insight into the important issue of stereotypes and intellectual presentations of the elderly, which continues to inform this aspect of social history, along with material and demographic criteria. Historians of old age weigh the cultural factor quite heavily, and while this may prove to be a way station toward a more quantifiable structural analysis, the linkage between literary images and real behaviors, as in family and policy contexts, suggests that beliefs about the elderly may have had—and may still have— unusual power. (David Herlihy's contribution on Renaissance Florence, a bit later, more directly links attitudes and demographic structure.) Two essays by anthropologists follow the literary survey, conveying some approaches that historians have not yet been able to test so thoroughly, as well as an explicit comparative sense. More strictly socio-historical essays comprise the bulk of the volume, ranging in time from the Renaissance to the late nineteenth century, in place from the United States through Western Europe to Russia. The socio-historical essays convey a state-of-the-art survey for demography, as it bears on old age history, and for preindustrial England, which is a particularly well-developed national case. The treatment of eighteenth century Provence provides the kind of local case study sorely needed to advance knowledge in this area. The essays on Russia and on the Florentine Orbatello have more specific— policy or institutional—foci, while that on witchcraft imaginatively ties a familiar historical landmark of preindustrial Europe to old age history.

The reader must judge, of course, the extent to which the essays in this volume stimulate a new, more sophisticated generation of old age history. The collection is at least free from the full constraint of the golden age imagery. Admittedly, several of the authors feel compelled to combat pervasive "golden age" errors, such as the exaggerated view of the rarity of old age in preindustrial society; certainly we are not too removed from the simplest formulas. Indeed the Silverman/Maxwell essay, using a very broad definition of modernization, at points suggests a return to the golden age approach, though the essay complicates any simple dichotomy by showing that modern media, for example, dislodge varied traditional patterns only slowly. Nor, on the other hand, are the essays bent toward single-minded refutation of the golden age imagery. Steven Smith's discussion of seventeenth-century England indeed reintroduces a balance into the evaluation of the culture toward old people, while David Troyansky revives emphasis on the familial framework. Richard Trexler's essay on Florence demonstrates a "surprisingly" early case even of semiformal official policy toward the elderly, though a policy that proved vulnerable to priority for other age groups over the long haul.

The essays are collectively designed to introduce a desirable comparative dimension to old age history, and the overall impression of the experience of later age clearly varies with the area considered. The comparison involves an admittedly loose definition of the preindustrial periodization, with aspects of the Western pattern discussed into the eighteenth century; Steven Smith's essay specifically emphasizes continuity in the experience of old age, however, even when a preindustrial society was changing rapidly in other respects. India and Russia are treated considerably later, after the advent of serious beginnings of modernization, however defined. Adele Lindenmeyr's essay on Russia explicitly deals with the stresses early industrialization placed on the limitations of preindustrial concepts of the elderly, while Sylvia Vatuk notes some changes—indeed, possibly improvements—increased urbanization has brought in India amid continuity of basic family values. Daniel Scott Smith's essay, ranging wide geographically, indeed elaborates the challenge to a preindustrial/industrial periodization in this field by contrasting twentieth-century data with those of the nineteenth as well as earlier centuries. Clearly, it remains necessary to approach the temporal framework of old age history with real flexibility. This granted, the geographically comparative dimension remains promising for all the areas here considered. Certain peculiar features of the Western experience do seem indicated, not only in family relationships but in both formal- and popular-cultural outlook; Russia seems confirmed as a non-Western case in some key respects; India, treated within a comparative framework, emerges as in some ways closer to the conventional impression of preindustrial old age than does the West; while other anthropological findings suggest further diversity among preindustrial cultures.

The essays, again collectively, suggest a useful range of facets of the old age experience. Their interdisciplinary provenance—from literature to history through anthropology—enhances this range. Edward Bever's essay, though historical, integrates gerontological and medical findings within its own compass. Some are deliberately designed to evoke attention to cultural factors, others emphasize demographic materials and so the role of the elderly in family and household, still others a social-policy dimension. Richard Trexler's discussion of the Ortabello offers policy implications, but also individual portraits of old women in an unusual institutional setting—a useful counterweight to the generalizing propensity of most historians of the subject. The result is not a full integration of the old age experience. If we have entered a new stage of old age history, we are at the beginnings of it. But the emphasis on the variety of angles from which the subject must be viewed is a significant step forward. Some of the basic framework of preindustrial old age is now established, with demographic data at one end and literary and philosophical views at the other. We are moving toward filling in the middle area, in terms of the role of the elderly in social institutions, the experience of growing old, and special but revealing episodes such as witchcraft persecutions, and the quality as well as the structure of family life in later age. If this volume contributes more precise questions in these areas, as well as a number of important findings, its purpose will have been amply served.

NOTES

1. See "Directory of Anthropologists Interested in Aging," 2nd ed. (Ms. compiled by Christine L. Fry, Department of Anthropology, Loyola University of Chicago and John M. Peterson, Department of Elder Affairs, State of Massachusetts, 1977.)

2. Carole Haber, "Mandatory Retirement in 19th Century America: The Conceptual Basis for a Work Cycle," *Journal of Social History* 12 (1979): 77–97; David Van Tassel, ed., *Aging, Death and the Completion of Being* (Philadelphia: University of Pennsylvania Press, 1979); David Van Tassel, Stuart Spicker, and Kathleen Woodward, *Aging and the Elderly: Humanistic Perspectives in Gerontology* (Atlantic Highlands, N.J.: Humanities Press, 1978); Peter N. Stearns, *Old Age in European Society: The Case of France* (New York: Holmes & Meier, 1978); W. Andrew Achenbaum, *Old Age in the New Land: The American Experience since 1790* (Baltimore: Johns Hopkins University Press, 1978); David Hackett Fischer, *Growing Old in America* (New York: Oxford University Press, 1977).

3. Simone de Beauvoir, *The Coming of Age*, trans. P. O'Brien (New York: G.P. Putnam's, 1972); Keith Thomas, "Age and Authority in Early Modern England," *Proceedings of the British Academy* 62 (1976): 233–248.

4. Lawrence Stone, *Family, Sex and Marriage in England 1500–1800* (New York: Harper and Row, 1977); Peter Laslett, "A History of Aging and the Aged," in Laslett, *Family Life and Illicit Love in Earlier Generations* (Cambridge: Cambridge University Press, 1977), pp. 174–213; Olwen Hufton, *The Poor of Eighteenth Century France* (New York: Oxford University Press, 1975).

5. J. Grasset, *La Fin de la vie* (La Chapelle-Montligeon: Lonquet, 1903), p. 20.

6. Philip J. Greven, Jr., *Four Generations: Population, Land, and Family in Colonial Andover, Massachusetts* (Ithaca: Cornell University Press, 1970).

7. Hufton, *The Poor*; Cissie Fairchilds, *Poverty and Charity in Aix-en-Provence, 1640–1789* (Baltimore: Johns Hopkins University Press, 1976); Haber, "Mandatory Retirement."

8. Fischer, *Growing Old*, pp. 23ff.

9. Achenbaum, *Old Age*; Fischer, *Growing Old*.

10. Jerome Kaplan and G. J. Aldridge, eds., *Social Welfare of the Aging* (New York: Columbia University Press, 1962), p. 350; Bryan Wilson, *The Youth Culture and the Universities* (London: Faber and Faber, 1970), p. 219; D. Cowgill and L. D. Holmes, *Aging and Modernization* (New York: Appleton-Century-Crofts, 1972); M. Clark and B. G. Anderson, *Culture and Aging* (Springfield, Mass.: Charles Thomas, 1967). See, for a somewhat more balanced view, Jon Hendricks and C. Davis Hendricks, *Aging in Mass Society: Myths and Realities* (Cambridge, Mass.: Winthrop, 1977), pp. 26–50.

11. Denis F. Johnston, "The Future of Work: Three Possible Alternatives," *Monthly Labor Review* 32 (1972): 3–11; Zena Blau, *Old Age in a Changing Society* (New York: New Viewpoints, 1973), pp. 21–36, 133–146.

12. Gail Buchwalter King and Peter N. Stearns, "The Retirement Experience as a Policy Factor: An Applied History Approach," *Journal of Social History* 14 (1981): 589–626; Thomas, "Age and Authority," p. 237.

13. Erdman Padmore, *The Honorable Elders: A Cross-Cultural Analysis of Aging in Japan* (Durham, N.C.: Duke University Press, 1975).

14. J. Hajnal, "European Marriage Patterns in Perspective," in D. V. Glass and D. E. C. Eversley, eds., *Population in History* (Chicago: Aldine, 1965), pp. 101–143.

15. E. A. Wrigley, *Population in History* (New York: McGraw-Hill, 1969).

16. De Beauvoir, *Coming of Age*.

17. Stearns, *Old Age*, ch. 1; Peter N. Stearns, "Old Women: Some Historical Observations," *Family History* 5 (1980): 44–57.

18. Fischer, *Growing Old*, pp. 23ff.

19. Thomas, "Age and Authority."

20. Lutz Berkner, "The Stem Family and the Developmental Cycle: An 18th-Century Austrian Example," *American Historical Review* 77 (1972): 398–414; Thomas, "Age and Authority," p. 236.

21. Jean-Louis Flandrin, *Families in Former Times: Kinship, Household and Sexuality*, trans. R. Southern (Cambridge: Cambridge University Press, 1979).

22. Lawrence Stone, "Walking Over Grandma," *New York Review of Books* 24 (1977): 10–16.

23. Berkner, "Stem Family," 398–414.

24. Stearns, *Old Age*, ch. 1; de Beauvoir, *Coming of Age*; Thomas, "Age and Authority," pp. 244–248.

25. Stone, "Walking Over Grandma."

26. Michael Novak, *The Joy of Sports* (New York: Basic Books, 1976).

27. Philippe Ariès, *Western Attitudes toward Death*, trans. P. Ranum (Baltimore: Johns Hopkins University Press, 1974), pp. 85–108.

28. Fischer, *Growing Old*; Achenbaum, *Old Age*.

29. Greven, *Four Generations*.

30. Natalie Z. Davis, *Society and Culture in Early Modern France* (Stanford: Stanford University Press, 1975), pp. 116–117.

31. Stearns, "Old Women"; Alain Bideau, "A Demographic and Social Analysis of Remarriage; the example of the Castellany of Thoissey-en-Daubes, 1670–1840," *Family History* 5 (1980): 28–43.

32. W. Andrew Achenbaum and Peter N. Stearns, "Modernization and the History of Old Age," *Gerontologist* 18 (1978): 306–313.

33. Michael Anderson, *Family Structure in Nineteenth Century Lancashire* (Cambridge: Cambridge University Press, 1971); A. Plakans, "The Familial Contexts of Old Age in a Serf Society" (paper presented to the Social Science History Association, Columbus, Ohio, 1978); H. C. Johansen, "Some Aspects of Danish Rural Population Structure in 1787," *Scandinavian Economic History Review* 20 (1972): 61–70; H. C. Johansen, "The Position of the Old in the Rural Household in a Traditional Society," in S. Akerman and others, eds., *Chance and Change: Social and Economic Studies in Historical Demography in the Baltic Area* (Odense, Denmark: Christiansen, 1978), pp. 122–130; J. Zitomersky, "From Prestan to Herdenreichstein to Sweden: Approaching Intergenerational Propinquity in the Swedish Past" (paper presented to the 9th World Congress of Sociology, Uppsala, 1978).

34. George Rosen, *Madness in Society* (New York: Harper and Row, 1968), pp. 151–165.

35. Peter N. Stearns, "The Modernization of Old Age in France: Approaches through History," *International Journal of Aging and Human Development*, in press.

36. Daniel Scott Smith, "Historical Change in the Household Structure of the Elderly" (paper presented to the Workshop on the Elderly of the Future, Committee on Aging, National Research Council, Annapolis, 1979).

37. De Beauvoir, *Coming of Age*; Stearns, *Old Age*.

38. Haber, "Mandatory Retirement"; Peter N. Stearns, *Lives of Labor: Work in Mature Industrial Society* (New York: Holmes & Meier, 1975), pp. 85–108.

39. Fischer, *Growing Old*.

40. Stearns, "Modernization"; Achenbaum and Stearns, "Modernization."

41. William Graebner, *A History of Retirement* (New Haven: Yale University Press, 1980).

42. Smith, "Historical Change."

CHAPTER TWO—THEMES OF OLD AGE IN PREINDUSTRIAL WESTERN LITERATURE

DAVID H. FOWLER, LOIS JOSEPHS FOWLER, AND LOIS LAMDIN

> *Old age is full of death and full of life. It is a tolerable achievement and it is a disaster. It transcends desire and it taunts it. It is long enough and it is far from being long enough . . .* [1]

To grow old, in literature of the preindustrial Western world, was usually to endure an unhappy fate.[2] For three thousand years bards and writers lamented the losses of power and competence that age inflicted on the wellborn or mighty, while mocking the senile vagaries and time-ravaged faces and forms of the lesser. There were, to be sure, some brighter notes. Traditional tales from ruder societies sometimes celebrated the aged leader as hero, while later authors—usually elderly themselves—occasionally offered glimpses of peace and wisdom in old age. Variants of all these themes added depth and complexity to the subject. Yet the dominant purposes of those who sang or wrote about aging throughout the premodern era were to convey either sadness or ridicule.

Their imagery, shadowed, bitter, or cruel as most of it was, fell far short of reflecting accurately the even darker reality of life. Most literature before the nineteenth century was composed for and about the favored upper classes; the multitude, who did not read, furnished mainly the stuff for occasional comedy. Had writers dealt more fully with aging in the grim circumstances of the lowly, their pictures would have been far gloomier.

While growing old recurred persistently as a topic in Western literature—it was, after all, an experience universal to those who lived long enough—it never became a major theme. This was probably not because those who lived long enough were so few, for they may well have formed a substantial part of the surviving adults.[3] Growing old was a rather passive, sometimes painful business, far less attractive to a writer than themes having to do with the active living of life. The subject of death was likewise more compelling than that of aging. With death for both youth and adult a constant presence through those centuries of hunger, disease, and pestilence, the trials of old age may have seemed comparatively trivial to writers, most themselves not old. And, in dealing with death, a writer might envision transcendence, salvation, eternal life; in that scheme old age could hardly seem other than a tedious set of preliminaries for purgatory.

In neither literature nor life, then, was there ever a golden age for the aged in the preindustrial West. Such a dream—of times when old age was honored, its wisdom acknowledged, its mental failings forgiven, its ailments nursed with affection—appeared in the popular culture of the nineteenth century, fed by some romantic prose and poetry. In time the illusion succumbed to literary and social realism.

Modern writers, avoiding such utopianism, have found more substantial and lasting ways to modify traditional treatments of old age. They have narrowed the psychological gap which their forerunners placed between themselves and the aged. They have accepted less stereotyped patterns of aging. Most important, they have substituted compassion for ridicule. These shifts of perception, feeling, and taste have marked the ending of the preindustrial world's characteristic views of old age.

In these pages we cannot survey comprehensively the topic of old age in the literature of the West. We offer instead, as an introduction to the subject, a glance at old age in our oldest literatures—biblical, Greek, and Roman—and a tracing of the tragic, hopeful, and comic views of aging in English literature from its earliest times to the recent past.

The first chapters of the Bible, with their emphases on the longevity and continuing sexual potency of the patriarchs, offer tributes to ancestors by a tribal society. Adam lives 930 years, begetting Seth at 130; his great-grandson Methusaleh fathers a child at 187 and lives to the age of 969. On a more modest scale, Abraham is 86 when he begets Ishmael of the servant girl Hagar, but at 100, when his wife Sarah is 90 and well beyond menopause, he has with her the son that God has promised him in his covenant. Noah lives on for 350 years after the Flood; Moses dies at 120, "his eye . . . not dim, nor his natural force abated."[4] Whatever the precise meaning of these claims to longevity and potency, there can be no denying their stress on the accomplishments of age.

This oral tradition of ancestral feats came eventually to be written down by scribes, embedding miracles—or confusions—in our literary traditions. While to celebrate the patriarch in a patriarchal society is the norm, these descendants of herdsmen, living in a land torn by strife, were also intent on establishing their lineage as matters of personal identity, social prestige, and claims to property.

In other and later episodes of the history of the Hebrews the woes of age become central matters. After the Flood, Noah "drank of the wine, and was drunken; and he was uncovered within his tent."[5] In his senility his power falls to his sons Shem and Japheth. The Bible depicts the loss of power in old age of the two great kings Saul and David. Saul, furious in his realization that he must yield his kingdom to David, tries to destroy the younger man, fights with his own son Jonathan, suffers depression to the point of illness, and kills himself on the battlefield when defeat seems imminent. There is a poignant picture of David's old age. "Now King David was old and stricken in years; and they covered him with clothes, but he gat no heat."[6] His servants find for him a young virgin to lie against for warmth, but though she is fair and cherishes him, "the king knew her not."[7]

While some of the patriarchs retain their political power and, like Jacob and Joseph, die in relative peace, with age and wisdom respected and prophecies heard if not heeded, others are tricked by those who take advantage of their vulnerability. Isaac, old and blind, is manipulated by his wife, Rebekah, on behalf of their second son, Jacob, thus cutting Esau off from his heritage. Similarly, Bathsheba conspires with the prophet Nathan against her husband, the aged King David, to thwart the succession of Adonijah. The senile David is easily persuaded that he has promised the throne to Bathsheba's son Solomon, who even before the death of David, seems to have assumed both the name and the substance of kingship.

The poet of Ecclesiastes assures us that the elderly in biblical times were no strangers to the ravages of age and accompanying despair. He exhorts the young man:

> *Remember now thy Creator in the days of thy youth,*
> *while the evil days come not,*
> *nor the years draw nigh,*
> *when thou shalt say, I have no pleasure in them . . .*

In the "evil days" to come, the senses will die, physical and intellectual pleasures will wane, "fears shall be in the way . . . and desire shall fail," in that brief space of time before "the dust return to the earth as it was."[8]

In the Apocrypha appears the beginning of laughter at those whose desire seems inappropriate to their age. The two elders who spy on Susannah in her garden "so that their lust was inflamed toward her," and then attempt to force themselves upon her in the bath, anticipate the lecherous old men who serve as a staple for comedy in later ages.[9]

As the literature of Hellenic Greece broadens the imaginative view of the human condition, these several themes reappear in enlarged and more dramatic form, with the tragic view dominant. With the Greek emphasis on the joy of free exercise of mind and body, old age could not but be seen as a time of tragic wasting. Most simple and pointed is the riddle of the Sphinx: "What creature . . . goes on four feet in the morning, on two at noonday, on three in the evening?"[10] This thought is echoed and expanded by the chorus in Aeschylus' *Agamemnon*, bewailing their aged state:

> *But we; dishonored, old in our bones,*
> *cast off even then from the gathering horde,*
> *stay here, to prop up*
> *on staves the strength of a baby.*
> *Since the young vigor that urges*
> *inward to the heart*
> *is frail as age, no warcraft yet perfect,*
> *while beyond age, leaf*
> *withered, man goes three footed*
> *no stronger than a child is,*
> *a dream that falters in daylight.*[11]

The myth of Tithonus, to whom Zeus gave immortality without the accompanying gift of everlasting youth, is a hideous representation of the physical decay of old age. Tithonus grows so senescent that he is unable even to move arms and legs, and lives on, babbling words without meaning, until he is mercifully turned into a grasshopper.

Although old age could hardly be regarded as beautiful in a culture that worshipped the beauty of youth, it might still be found impressive or pathetic.[12] The elderly might contribute in memory and experience what they lacked in health and strength, for the Greeks "saw that the passage of years transforms experience into something which is even more worth having" than the golden time of youth.[13] The ideal was to maintain one's mental faculties through exercising them unremittingly. The longevity, with mental powers sustained, of some of the greatest Greek writers and philosophers gave substance to that ideal. Plato died at eighty-two, Sophocles and Democritus at ninety, while Xenophanes was over ninety-two and Gorgias over one hundred.[14]

Homer's Nestor, the old charioteer, the tamer of horses, who by the time of the Trojan War had already begun to suffer losses of bodily powers, is a magnificent example of the homage the Greeks paid to the man who aged well. Though Nestor complains to Achilles:

I am infirm of limb. My feet are not so steady now, my friend, and my arms no longer swing out lightly from the shoulder as they did . . . Now I must leave this sort of thing [participation in the funeral games] to younger men and take the painful lessons of old age to heart.[15]

Yet he is respected as "the oldest among the chieftains and therefore the wisest,"[16] known for his "good sense and ripe judgment."[17] In the words of Odysseus' son Telemachus, who has come to consult Nestor about the whereabouts of his father, the old man's

knowledge of men's ways and thoughts is unrivalled. For they tell me he has been king through three generations, and when I look at him, I seem to gaze on immortality itself.[18]

Old age could also be a time of pain and mental anguish. Even Teiresias, the blind prophet, the holy man of Thebes, is frequently treated as a garrulous and tiresome old man by those he would warn of impending disaster. Euripides is uncompromising in his dismissal of the compensations of age:

> Youth is always dear to me;
> Old age is a load that lies
> More heavily on the head
> Than the rocks of Etna.[19]

Perhaps the most affecting portrait of age is that of Oedipus, the self-blinded king, purified through his great suffering, arriving in Athens on the arm of his daughter Antigone, bereft of his kingly power, having lost almost everyone and everything dear to him, without even the strength to "creep unaided or without a guide." Yet there remain courage, pride, and a hint of optimism:

> . . . Who shall receive to-day
> With stinted alms the wanderer Oedipus? –
> Asking but little; than that little still
> Obtaining less; and yet enough for me
> For my afflictions and the weight of years
> And something, too, of my own dignity
> Teach me contentment.[20]

The chorus, considering his plight, passes over the note of hope, insisting that

> *Whoso thinks average years a paltry thing*
> *Choosing prolonged old age,*
> *He, to my mind, will be found treasuring*
> *A foolish heritage.* [21]

Plato and Aristotle illustrate the schism running through literature between acceptance and rejection of the diminishments of old age. Plato stresses preparation for old age through living the good life, having the wisdom to anticipate what is to come. Because his reality is noumenal rather than phenomenal, the decay of the body means less to him than does the preservation of the soul. Cephalus in *The Republic*, though not scorning the usefulness of money in assuring comfort in one's old age, says that men's character and temper are more important. When the passions relax their hold, old age can be a time of "calm and freedom,"[22] and if the man has led a sin-free life, then he need not spend his last years tormented by fears of death and the afterlife.

Aristotle, whose reality is more physical, finds old age a time when men's normal failings are magnified, when the body loses its inward heat and physical decline depresses the spirit. "For old age and every disability is thought to make men mean," he says.[23]

Greek comedy takes its stand with Aristotle on the subject of senescence. The elderly in the plays of Aristophanes are objects of fun, their physical and mental failings a source of cruel humor. The treatment of Plutus, the god of wealth in the play that bears his name, is a prime example of antigeriatric attitudes. He is described as

. . . a disgusting old fellow, all bent and wrinkled, with a most pitiful appearance, bald and toothless; upon my word, I even believe he is circumcised like some vile barbarian.[24]

An old woman in the play has been keeping her young lover faithful by giving him lavish gifts. When Plutus makes the young man wealthy, however, the latter is suddenly repelled by his mistress's wrinkles, gray hair, and toothlessness, and taunts her about the tatters of her face beneath the white lead paint. Similarly, in *Clouds*, *Wasps*, and *Lysistrata*, the elderly are treated as almost subhuman, mocked for wanting to live full lives, made the target of jests.

The literature of Augustan Rome, while closely imitating that of Greece, nevertheless provides what is perhaps the best known statement of man's hopes for fruitfulness in old age, Cicero's essay *De*

Senectute (On Old Age). It is a highly idealized picture, as suggested by his observation that "the composition of this book has been so delightful that it has not only wiped away all the annoyances of old age, but has even made it an easy and a happy state."[25] Himself sixty-two at the time of writing, Cicero, like Plato, dismisses sensual pleasures as insignificant, congratulating himself on the waning of fleshly desires with "the absence of longing is more pleasant." All that is necessary to enjoy one's declining years is to employ "the principles and practices of the virtues" for the character, "moderate exercise" and temperance for the body, and "intellectual activity" for the mind.[26]

In the essay, Cicero puts his opinions into the mouth of Cato the Elder, who has as companions Laelius and Scipio Africanus the Younger. They challenge Cato. Scipio, paraphrasing Euripides (without an attribution by Cicero), wonders why " . . . old age is never burdensome to you, though it is so vexatious to most old men that they declare it to be a load heavier than Aetna." Laelius remarks to Cato that " . . . perhaps some one may reply that old age seems more tolerable to you because of your resources, means, and social position, and that these are advantages which cannot fall to the lot of many."[27]

"There is something in that objection, Laelius, but not everything," Cicero has Cato say. The author then goes on to fill his essay with examples of men who enjoy and profit from their golden years. Of these, the poet Ennius is poor and the statesman Appius Claudius blind, but the many others share wealth, power, and good fortune.[28] The moralist keeps tragedy at a distance; only old men "who are weak in mind and will" in their earlier lives are subject to "senile folly—usually called imbecility."[29] In the end the reservations of Laelius seem confirmed, to the modern reader, by Cicero's hazy moralizing and the biased selection of his examples.

Cicero's evocation of the dignity of the elders of the state squares precisely with the ideals of patriarchal society as imposed by the cultures of both Hellenic Greece—especially the Spartan version as it appeared in Athenian literature—and Republican Rome. In his tribute to old age, however, Cicero refers to a contrasting tradition in quoting a description of " 'the old fools of the comic stage,' . . . characterized by credulity, forgetfulness, and carelessness."[30] These are figures of the comic theater of the earlier playwrights Terence and Plautus, the Roman heirs of Aristophanes. Plautus was especially popular; his situations and characters furnished raw materials for comic playwrights down to Shakespeare and beyond.

Plautus lampoons all that is conventionally sacred in Republican Rome; the old are favorite targets, no doubt, because the crowd at the popular theater welcomed relief from the *gravitas* of official patriarchal morality. In contrast to the conventionally crusty elders of Terence, who oppose the schemes of the young out of conservatism, the old men of Plautus behave less as foils than as comedians in their own right. As Erich Segal observes, "If a Plautine father does actively oppose his son's love affair, it is usually because the old codger is a *senex amator*, fighting for the same girl."[31]

The poet Horace, in his youthful prime and struggling for recognition, urges living life to the full:

> *My friends, we'll seize the hour*
> *While youth yet revels in our veins,*
> *And unimpaired our strength remains*[32]

and then again:

> *Use today, and trust as little*
> *As thou mayst tomorrow's light.*[33]

While these lines speak more of the certainty of death than the possibility of decay, the realities of decay—in women, rather than in men—alarm and offend Horace. He offers many caustic images of hags and witches, but it is his own mistress, an older woman, whose aging appearance and importunate manner provoke him to taunt her:

> *What are you up to, you woman, most fit*
> *For dark-swarthy elephants? Why do you send*
> *Letters and gifts to me? Why would it not*
> *Be better a youth with no nose to offend? . . .*
> *What a sweat, what a stench from her withered limbs rise*
> *All about, when her passion she seeks to assuage—*
> *Without moist cosmetics, and smeared with the dyes*
> *Of crocodile's dung!*[34]

and again to an older woman, who has stung him with a criticism of his sexual prowess:

> *How dare you, withered as you are*
> *With years, ask me what saps my strength?*
> *Your teeth are black and furrows scar*
> *With wrinkles all your forehead's length!*

> *Your filthy private gapes between*
> *Shrunk buttocks like a scrawny cow's;*
> *Your chest and wizened breasts are seen*
> *Like horse's teats, and flabby shows*
>
> *Your belly, and your lank thighs strung*
> *To swollen calves, provoke my wrath! . . .* [35]

In his forties, enjoying good health on his tranquil Sabine farm, secure in the friendship of Augustus and the patronage of Maecaenas, Horace gives a few passing thoughts to his own aging:

> *. . . Our years*
> *Glide silently away. No tears,*
> *No loving orisons repair*
> *The wrinkled cheek, the whitening hair*
> *That drop forgotten to the tomb.* [36]

He has achieved calmness of spirit:

> *Hairs growing gray compose a mind*
> *To feuds and quarrels once inclined. . .* [37]

He has also—or so he claims—found freedom from fleshly passions. With wry whimsy he congratulates a friend on the latter's love for a pretty maid:

> *I extol with free heart, and with fancy as free,*
> *Her sweet face, fine ankles, and tapering arms.*
> *How? Jealous? Nay, trust an old fellow like me,*
> *Who can feel, but not follow, where loveliness charms.* [38]

While Horace's work suggests that as he grows into his fifties, he endeavors with some success to practice what Cicero preached, he nevertheless experiences one of the classic ironies of aging:

> *"Why, when in early years I shone,*
> *Wore not my mind its present tone?*
> *Or why, since now such tone is mine*
> *Wear not my cheeks their youthful shine?"* [39]

He gloats at the attrition of age on a woman who had earlier scorned him:

But now — the young men lightly
Laugh at your wrinkled brow.
The torch that burned so brightly
Is only ashes now,
A charred and blackened bough. [40]

And in the end he weeps for his lost powers of love:

Venus, again thou mov'st a war
Long intermitted; pray thee, pray thee spare!
I am not such, as in the reign
Of the good Cynara I was: refrain
Sour mother of sweet Loves, forbear
To bend a man, now at his fiftieth year
Too stubborn for commands so slack:
Go where youth's soft entreaties call thee back. . . .
Me now, nor girl, nor wanton boy,
Delights, nor credulous hope of mutual joy;
Nor care I now healths to propound
Or with fresh flowers to gird my temples round.
But why, oh why, my Ligurine,
Flow my thin tears down these pale cheeks of mine?
Or why my well-graced words among,
With an uncomely silence, fails my tongue? . . . [41]

To move from the refinements of Roman literature to the bleak, windswept landscapes of Old English poetry is to move from an ordered, intellectually comprehensible universe to one that is sensing anew the tragic brevity of life, and its deprivations and sorrows, including that of old age. Poised between Germanic paganism and emerging Christianity, Old English poetry frequently reflects a wistful yearning for what has been. "Deor's Lament," a dramatic monologue spoken by a former court singer who has been ousted from his lord's favor by a rival, recites a series of historical woes, compares them to his own, and concludes in a repetitive refrain, "That evil ended. So also may this!"[42] The old bard, bereft of his power and place in the community, longs for the death that will release him from sorrow. In "The Wanderer," the theme is again one of passing time. It is the lament of another old man who has lost his lord, whose old comrades are all dead, and who travels alone on frigid seas, enduring the sorrows of age when honor and companionship are no more. The poem mourns the inevitable decay of earthly beauty and pleasure in a series of wintry, storm-riven images, bemoaning the evanescence and mutability of life:

> *Here wealth is fleeting, friends are fleeting,*
> *Man is fleeting, maid is fleeting;*
> *All the foundation of earth shall fail.*[43]

The Christian conclusion of the poem, that the man who seeks mercy from God will be happy, is totally at odds with the pessimistic tone of the rest, which takes a dour view of age, and indeed, of life.

That same sense of loss in the passing of years, in the draining of a man's strengths, gives a powerful thrust to the epic poem *Beowulf*. The aging hero has ruled his people for fifty years, protecting them by his strength from surrounding perils. Now, on the eve of battle with the fire-breathing dragon, Beowulf knows, although his courage has not failed, that he has lost his strength and that this will be his last adventure. Before the battle he reminisces, as the old do, about his childhood, when he was adopted by King Hrethel, and about his early sorrows and triumphs. Then, girding himself for battle, he goes, brave as ever, to seek the dragon. The fight is unequal; Beowulf lacks the strength to kill the beast and even his sword, "old and steel-gray," betrays him.[44] Although his younger companions have hung back out of fear, his loyal thane Wiglaf comes to the rescue. Together they slay the dragon, but the old king has suffered mortal wounds. As he lies dying he asks Wiglaf to bring from the cave the dragon's hidden hoard of gold, so that he may gaze on this, his final gift to his people.

Beowulf passes on the succession to Wiglaf, gives directions for his funeral pyre, and dies peacefully. The old must pass away so the young may inherit and such a death is better than a life of weakness. An aged woman, toothless and withered, sings a song of lament for Beowulf. Ironically, she lives on because her life is made up of daily survival; the king, whose greatness lies in his physical prowess and courage, cannot live beyond his loss of strength. But his death is the death of the hero, and the triumph of his deeds illuminates the darkness far more than the two previous poems.

In the Middle Ages, although life remained harsh and brief, there was a resurgence of humor, much of it directed against the elderly. Some of this comic treatment of the old, picking up where the Greeks and Romans had left off, is found in the fabliaux, the short bawdy stories of lower-middle-class life. These are replete with examples of elderly greed and lust, old men tricked by the young wives they marry, a theme adapted by Chaucer in "The Merchant's Tale." In Chaucer's version, January, a sixty-year-old rich bachelor, marries May, a beautiful young woman. Fortified by liberal amounts of claret, potions, and drugs, he manages to consummate their union on the wedding night. After this achievement he sits up singing, the wattles of his neck quivering in his joy. However, his wife takes a young lover; and when January comes upon them making love in a pear tree, they succeed in convincing him that he is not seeing what he sees. The dotard, ashamed by his apparent error, apologizes to them both.

Chaucer further develops the comic plight of the old in the Wife of Bath's Prologue and Tale. In the Prologue, the Wife describes graphically her first three husbands, "good, and rich and olde," — and impotent.[45] By flattering them into thinking she is jealous of their affairs, she manages to get a great deal of money from them. In the meantime she enjoys her own affairs; to be old apparently means to be cuckolded. As she herself grows older the tables are turned; her fifth husband, the first she has truly loved, is only twenty, and she is the target of jibes and laughter. And whereas she easily managed her husbands when she was young and they were old, she now must struggle for the upper hand in marriage.

The Tale enlarges on the plight of the old. A handsome knight, on a quest to discover what women want most, encounters an old hag who promises to reveal that secret if he will marry her. But she gives him a choice: he can have her old and ugly and faithful, or young and fair and take his chances on her fidelity. Faced with this dilemma, the knight adroitly avoids either horn. He leaves the decision to his bride-to-be, for he understands that what women really want is sovereignty. The old woman is then transformed into a lovely young maiden who is also faithful. The story gives insight into both women and the old, who desire to regain youth and its power.

Comic treatment of the elderly appears often in the theater that evolved out of church ritual in the Middle Ages in England. Traveling companies performed Bible-based stories, which were shaped in part by what the players thought audiences would like. In the "Second Shepherd's Play," though it treats the birth of the Christ Child seriously, the shepherds are played as comical old men. Their wives are shrews; younger men steal their sheep; they creak with age: "I am near-hand dold, so long have I napped; My legs they fold, my fingers are chapped."[46] In the Noah play his wife is carried screaming and protesting onto the Ark by her three sons, who think her a foolish old lady because she does not wish to leave her friends. And although

Balaam in the Bible was not old, he is played in medieval drama by an older man, who is jeered and taunted by the audience when his ass speaks to him with the voice of God. In these instances, comedy grows from the inability of the old to maintain control. These distortions of the Bible pander to the crowd's delight in the foibles of the elderly, who clearly deserve to be tricked or overpowered.

And yet the famous morality play *Everyman* gives an ironic turn to this comic view of aged impotency. In the drama the characters who represent Wealth, Power, and Strength falter at the gates of Heaven. Wisdom has some influence, but Good Deeds, old and weak, limping along because Everyman's good deeds have been few, makes the only significant impression on Death. The play, arguing the ultimate worthlessness of the things the world values, hints symbolically that the elderly meek may inherit heaven if not earth.

In Malory's *Morte D'Arthur*, even wise Merlin, who has been adviser and seer to King Arthur from the beginning of the latter's reign, falls victim to the troubles of age. In his later days he succumbs to the wiles of a beautiful young woman, Vivian, who is an enemy to the king, and gives her all his secrets. Merlin's treachery, resulting from his senility, symbolizes the growing decadence of the court.

Thus in early English literature, as in the earlier traditions, aged heroes of the tribe appear and vanish, to be replaced by the elderly, whose appearance is primarily woeful or ridiculous. There is yet little to suggest wise and honored and comfortable old age, even among the mighty and the wealthy. Nor does the evolution of Renaissance humanism at first bring any change in conventions.

To assign the Renaissance scholar Erasmus to the English literary tradition is to take a liberty but perhaps not an excessive one. In his frequent visits to England and his intimate friendships with its scholars, churchmen, and other persons of importance, the Dutch-born humanist, a truly international figure, exercised great influence on literature there. In his *The Praise of Folly*, written in London at the home of his friend Thomas More, and dedicated to him, Erasmus spares no one; his scathing caricatures of the pretentious old, of both sexes, recalls the treatment of hags and old mistresses by Horace. Folly, his allegorical creation, rants about what men do in her name; some of Erasmus' examples may well have come from his observations of London life. Of old men, Folly jibes that some no longer even look like men:

driveling, doting, toothless, whitehaired, bald, (in the words of Aristophanes) "filthy, crook-backed, wretched, shriveled, bald, toothless, and lame of their best limb"; but yet they are so in love with life and 'have such young ideas' that one of them will dye his hair, another will hide his baldness with a toupee, another will wear false teeth (borrowed perhaps from some hog), another will fall head over heels in love with some young girl and outdo any beardless youth in amorous idiocy. In fact, to see old codgers with one foot in the grave marry some sweet young thing—with no dowry at that, and of far more use to other men than to him—this sort of thing happens so often that people almost consider it praiseworthy.[47]

And Folly has more to say of old women who are

so ancient they might as well be dead and so cadaverous they look as if they had returned from the grave, yet they are always mouthing the proverb 'life is sweet.' They are as hot as bitches in heat, or (as the Greeks say) they rut like goats. They never cease smearing their faces with makeup. They can't tear themselves away from the mirror. They pluck and thin their pubic bush. They show off their withered and flabby breasts. They whip up their languid lust with quavering whines and whimpers. They drink a lot. They mingle with the young girls on the dance floor. They write billets-doux. Everyone laughs at these things as utterly foolish (and indeed they are), but the old bags themselves are perfectly self-satisfied.[48]

Shakespeare offers a broader and more humane vision of old age. In the famous speech on the seven ages of man from *As You Like It*, he approaches the physical and intellectual losses of age in a serio-comic mode:

> . . . the sixth age shifts
> Into the lean and slipper'd pantaloon,
> With spectacles on nose and pouch on side;
> His youthful hose, well sav'd, a world too wide
> For his shrunk shank, and his big manly voice,
> Turning again toward childish treble, pipes
> And whistles in his sound. Last scene of all,
> That ends this strange eventful history,
> Is second childishness, and mere oblivion,
> Sans teeth, sans eyes, sans taste, sans everything.[49]

Here, underlying the humor, is an uncompromising realism, refusing to cover over the deterioration of age with sentimental pieties about wisdom and fulfillment, but avoiding the tone of scorn.

Nor does Shakespeare long sustain the light-hearted view of the old man as a figure of fun. Falstaff, one of his finest comic creations, the butt of jokes because of his inappropriate behavior, becomes ultimately a figure of tragedy. One of the moments in literature that best captures the loss of power that accompanies old age is the scene in *Henry IV, Part II* where the newly crowned Henry V turns his back on his old drinking companion Falstaff. The poignancy of the scene is less in what is said than in the audience's realization that Falstaff's expectations of favor, built on his old friendship, are doomed. The aged roisterer, confident in the influence and power that Henry's continued friendship will bring him, has staved off importunate creditors and has promised favors. In his joy at the news of the old king's death, Falstaff calls himself "Fortune's steward" and, proclaiming that "the laws of England are at my commandment," rushes off to London to join his new sovereign. Henry V, however, has vowed to abandon his feckless ways, and in the interest of making clear to all his reform, greets his erstwhile friend with the chilling words

> *I know thee not, old man: fall to thy prayers;*
> *How ill white hairs become a fool and jester!*[50]

In his shock and bewilderment at the sudden collapse of his pretensions, Falstaff feigns assurance that Henry will send for him in private, but Shallow's immediate call for repayment of half of the debt of a thousand pounds gives the old man a bitter foretaste of the collapse of all his hopes.

Shakespeare's *King Lear* gives the Western world its most memorable picture of agonized old age, the antithesis of Platonic contentment. The eighty-year-old Lear, foolishly ignoring the claims of his faithful daughter Cordelia, gives his power and wealth to his ungrateful older daughters and then finds himself suddenly facing the loss of all that has sustained him. Shakespeare's genius allows us to see that the traits of old age have deep roots; apparently Lear has always had a passionate, impulsive temper. His daughter Goneril reflects that

> *The best and soundest of his time hath been but rash.*
> *Then must we look from his age to receive*
> *not alone the imperfections of long-engraffed condition,*
> *but therewithal the unruly waywardness*
> *that infirm and choleric years bring with them.*[51]

In the end Lear is stripped of his illusions, crying "I am a very foolish fond old man," a victim not of fate but of himself.[52] In two images that haunt the imagination: the old king alone on a heath swept by storm, mad, naked, almost blind, conversing with an idiot, and later, with the dead Cordelia in his arms, howling his rage and anguish to the heavens, the poet has endowed us with a terrible vision of the suffering and bitterness of old age.

In a calmer vein Shakespeare turns to the *carpe diem* (seize the day) theme defined by Horace, urging in one of his sonnets the young Earl of Southhampton to marry and beget children as a way of cheating age. Only by creating another young face like his own can he call back the April of his prime before wrinkles appear and "winter's ragged hand" defaces his beauty. [53]

This theme of "seize the day," in which the speaker is most commonly a lover exhorting his mistress to make haste to bed with him to thwart their enemy, Time, found its greatest popularity among poets of the sixteenth and seventeenth centuries. It is, of course, a point of view which ignores any possible compensations of aging. In a classic statement of its kind, Robert Herrick pleads with virgins to

> *Gather ye rose-buds while ye may,*
>   *Old Time is still a-flying:*
> *And this same flower that smiles today,*
>   *To morrow will be dying.*
> . . . .
> *Then be not coy, but use your time;*
>   *And while ye may, goe marry:*
> *For having lost but once your prime,*
>   *You may for ever tarry.* [54]

In a more somber mood, Herrick chides his mistress for despising him for his gray hair; in time she too will look in the mirror to find her hair frosted and cheeks faded.

> *Ah! then too late, close in your chamber keeping,*
>   *It will be told*
>   *That you are old*
> *By those true teares y'are weeping.* [55]

Andrew Marvell in "To His Coy Mistress" is even more direct, insisting that although it might be pleasant to draw out their courtship, time is fleeting.

> *And yonder all before us lie*
> *Deserts of vast eternity.*
> *Thy beauty shall no more be found,*
> *Nor, in thy marble vault shall sound*
> *My echoing song; then worms shall try*
> *That long preserved virginity,*

And your quaint honor turn to dust,
And into ashes all my lust. [56]

John Dryden, in much the same vein, sighs for love and laments that year by year the price of love's gifts increases:

Ah how sweet it is to love!
Ah how gay is young desire!
. . . .
Love, like spring-tides full and high,
Swells in every youthful vein;
But each tide does less supply
Till they quite shrink in again:
  If a flow in age appear,
  'Tis but rain, and runs not clear. [57]

In all these many poems the seducer or speaker urges the inevitability of senescence in order to create sexual tension. He assumes that sensual love is the exclusive possession of the young and will be extinguished by the onset of age. A startling exception to this conventional view is found in John Donne's Elegy IX, "The Autumnal," in which the poet finds a beauty richer than the superficialities of youth in the face of his older mistress.

No spring, nor summer beauty hath such grace,
As I have seen in one autumnal face. [58]

Donne praises the wrinkles of his beloved, at fifty less voluptuous but wiser than before, superior in her conversation, possessing in her maturity the quality of "gold oft tried and ever new." While he distinguishes between age's "glory" and "winter-faces," slack-skinned, toothless, "not ancient, but antique," he will, forced to the choice, prefer tombs to cradles. [59]

Yet Donne's reputation as an eccentric occasionally given to outrageous sentiments cautions us not to accept this more benign vision of age as typical. In the great bulk of literature written before the nineteenth century it is assumed that old age for both sexes means sexual indifference, and for men, impotence. Lewd comic figures constitute exceptions to be scorned. The act of love, beautiful in the young, becomes lecherous, animal-like in the old. For them, marriage exists only for companionship; elderly lovers are an affront to the dignity of love. The fate decreed for those aging lovers in myth, Philemon and Baucis, who were given immortality as neighboring trees, may have been an attempt to resolve the perceived anomaly of sexuality in age.

In Restoration comedy the comic treatment of the aged flowers anew. Although this comedy is attuned to the moral indulgence of the aristocracy, it satirizes those who cannot manage their sensuality and greed with good taste. Women in particular are treated unmercifully when they pretend to youth in order to satisfy unseemly lust. Although typically they engage in manhunts, they conceal their yearnings beneath coyness and pretended morality. When the elderly leave their places to engage in flirtation or to attempt witty repartee, they invariably become targets of ridicule. Lady Wishfort in Congreve's *The Way of the World* is such an example. In *Volpone*, Ben Jonson satirizes the avarice of those old men who, still in possession of their intellects, use them to satisfy their lust for riches. Volpone himself has become wealthy as a charlatan selling a spurious elixir of youth:

" . . . wherever it but touches in youth it perpetually preserves, in age restores the complexion; seats your teeth, did they dance like virginal jacks, firm as a wall; makes them white as ivory, that were black as——."[60]

The miser feigns illness to expose the hypocrisy of those friends who hope to inherit his estate. But the satire is a double one: Volpone laughs at the greed of those he tricks and so does the reader, who is entertained by his cunning as well, but Volpone's own miserly qualities furnish much of the occasion for mirth.

The spirit of reason, which informs so much of eighteenth century thought and writing, does relatively little to affect long-standing views of aging and the elderly. The comic tradition remains unchanged. Mrs. Malaprop, in Sheridan's *The Rivals*, is a descendant of Lady Wishfort; she vies with her beautiful young niece for beaux but loses despite her wiles, wigs, and cosmetics. In the new and growing literary form of the novel, Lady Booby, in Henry Fielding's *Joseph Andrews*, tries and fails to woo the hero away from her young maid.

Nor does the era's more serious and penetrating writing provide new insights into age and its circumstances. Henry St. John, Viscount Bolingbroke, close friend to Pope and Swift, at the end of a long life spent actively in politics and letters, echoes Plato and Cicero in his essay "Of the True Use of Retirement and Study." Age and leisure offer the chance to break the bonds of authority and custom and to live one's last years in "a state of freedom, under the laws of reason." Constant exercise of the mind will keep it fresh:

It fares with the mind just as it does with the body. He who was born with a texture of brain as strong as that of Newton, may become unable to perform the common rules of arithmetic: just as he who has the same elasticity in his muscles, the same suppleness in his joints, . . . may become a fat, unwieldly sluggard.[61]

For the true man of reason, the passing of sensual pleasure will not be mourned if it is replaced by the pleasures of the mind, "for he who jogs forward on a battered horse, in the right way, may get to the end of his journey; which he cannot do, who gallops the fleetest courser of Newmarket, out of it."[62]

While Pope takes a less sanguine view of age, one tinged with the wryness of Shakespeare's seven ages of man, he speaks with the detached voice of reason. In "An Essay on Man," he finds a measure of comfort in each stage of life, each age having an appropriate passion and pride, each its reason to hope:

> And beads and prayer-books are the toys of age:
> Pleased with this bauble still, as that before;
> 'Til tired he sleeps, and Life's poor play is o'er.[63]

In "Moral Essays," Pope returns to the metaphor of toys:

> See how the World its Veterans rewards!
> A Youth of Frolics, an old Age of Cards;
> Fair to no purpose, artful to no end,
> Young without Lovers, old without a Friend.[64]

If old age appears faintly ridiculous, it is no more ridiculous than youth.

To Samuel Johnson the prospect of age is much darker. In "The Vanity of Human Wishes," he takes as an antitext the prayer "Enlarge my life with multitude of days" and goes on to prove, in sonorous voice and telling images, that "life protracted is protracted woe." Time steals from man his ability to enjoy nature's bounty: meats are tasteless, wine gives no joy, neither visual beauty nor music nor the luxuries available to the wealthy bring pleasure. The old man grows garrulous, short-tempered, prey to various pains, while those who should care for him are primarily interested in the disposal of his wealth. Although the nobler emotions are extinguished

> . . . unextinguished Av'rice still remains,
> And dreaded losses aggravate his pains:
> He turns, with anxious heart and crippled hands,
> His bonds of debt, and mortgages of lands;
> Or views his coffers with suspicious eyes,
> Unlocks his gold, and counts it till he dies.[65]

Even in the happiest of conditions one still must endure the sickness and death of those one loves; inevitable decay takes its toll; new ideas and forms of society make one's thinking anachronistic. Johnson points to the aging of some of his contemporaries as horrifying examples of what awaits us:

> *From Marlb'rough's eyes the streams of dotage flow,*
> *And Swift expires a Driv'ller and a show.*[66]

No one can count himself happy until the end, says Johnson, and what we might pray for rather than a "multitude of days" is a "healthful mind," for love, patience, a resigned will and a faith that can accept death as "kind Nature's signal of retreat."[67]

Ten years later, in *Rasselas*, Johnson enlarges upon this gloomy picture. The book strips away systematically the delusion of worldly enjoyments, including the possibility of a serene old age. When, in search of a way of life, Prince Rasselas and his retinue visit an old man, they are at first delighted to find him cheerful and talkative. This is, however, but a superficial state induced by the momentary diversion of their company; the old man tells them that for him "the world has lost its novelty." Although still in possession of his senses, he cannot take much delight in physical truth, "for what have I to do with those things which I am soon to leave?" He no longer has a mother or wife who might gain joy from the praise he receives. He takes little interest in much beyond himself, has nothing to hope for, but much to regret. His existence is an attenuated wait for death, a state like life itself, in which "much is to be endured and little to be enjoyed."[68]

No one in the eighteenth century or since has depicted the horrors of the dark side of old age as does Jonathan Swift in *Gulliver's Travels*. In his description of the mythical Struldbruggs of Luggnagg, Swift extends his nightmare to the ultimate point: perpetual old age. The Struldbruggs, marked from birth as immortal, are loathed and despised by their countrymen, who see in them all of man's mortal ills and degeneration expanded to monstrous proportions: "Besides the usual Deformities in extreme old Age, they acquired an additional Ghastliness in Proportion to their Number of Years, which is not to be described." They are subject to all the physical and mental deterioration of extreme old age, being spared none of its degradations, all described in excruciating detail. They are, in addition, acutely depressed by their inability to die. When they reach the age of eighty, their estates are confiscated and they are considered dead legally, stripped of all rights and privileges. Far from being repositories of wisdom, their fading memories make it impossible for them to read or even to converse. Some of them retain some knowledge, but it does not extend past the events of their earlier years. Gulliver, his appetite for immortality extinguished, says, "no Tyrant could invent a Death into which I would not run with Pleasure from such a Life."[69] Swift's vision is an epitome, a caricature, but it rests firmly in the tragic mode. It is a latter-day Inferno for the aged.

These images, created by English writers in a slowly modernizing society about to experience an industrial revolution, fail to bring the aged alive as individual human beings. Whether they represent Bolingbroke's or Pope's serene or ironic reflections, or Johnson's or Swift's melancholy or despair, they remain abstractions or stock figures, ideas rather than persons. In that sense the light of the Age of Reason illuminates their fates less clearly than Shakespeare's passion did for his characters. Yet there are intimations of change. It is worth noting that Pope, Johnson, and Swift, masters of clever irony and caustic satire, avoid ridiculing the elderly, instead giving realistic or grimly exaggerated portrayals of the very real fates that so many of them face. Moreover, their images, whether real or exaggerated, are designed to tell unflinchingly the truth about both the aged and the way they are treated.

Clearer beginnings of change in traditional literary presentation of the old appear in the feminine world of Jane Austen, a world which is both rational and sentimental. With all her puncturing of the pretensions of those in authority, Austen nevertheless holds firm to the principle of respect for their positions. Among the obligations to authority on which she insists most firmly is that of the respect owed by the young to their elders. She goes further. The young must not only respect their elders but also, if at all possible and appropriate, must maintain and show affection for them.

In her novel *Emma* these matters are well defined. Emma Woodhouse, a bright but impulsive young woman, impatiently ridicules and affronts her gentle, middle-aged neighbor, Miss Bates. While Miss Bates is not old, having an aged mother of her own, the failings for which Emma mocks her are associated with aging: garrulity, disorganized thought, inability to recognize one's own boringness. Mr. Knightley, Emma's voice of conscience (and future husband), chastises her:

Her situation should secure your compassion. It was badly done, indeed! You, whom she had known from an infant, whom she had seen grow up from a period when her notice was an honour—to have you now, in thoughtless spirits and the pride of the moment, laugh at her, humble her. . . [70]

Austen's portrayal of Emma's father, a widower, gives striking evidence of the interest and ability of writers in these new times to treat the aged as individuals rather than as representatives of abstract ideas. Mr. Woodhouse's age is nowhere given, but despite Emma's youth, he is old whatever his years. He is altogether the valetudinarian, increasingly alarmed at any change in his shrinking world. Yet Austen's humor is gentle; she explores his kindness and genuine concern for others while satirizing his eccentricities and growing self-centeredness. Here is sympathy as well as deft rationality. Mr. Woodhouse is neither the philosopher in command of his mind, and hence his fate, nor the agonized victim of degeneration, but rather an individual in a set of circumstances peculiar to him. That these circumstances are comfortable is incidental, for Austen makes old Mrs. Bates, a minor character in some financial need, also appear an individual rather than a caricature.

In telling the story of Emma's increasing maturity the novel defines further the due of youth to age. She learns to do her duty by the Bateses, whose need is as much to be listened to as to be given charity. Her tribute to age, in the end, is to decide that she cannot marry Mr. Knightley while her father lives. Mr. Woodhouse, so dependent on Emma, would be agitated and unhappy if she left their home of Hartfield; he would be even more disturbed if he had to follow her, even to the comfort of Knightley's Donwell Abbey. It happens, for the proper resolution of things, that Mr. Knightley is ingenious and adaptable as well as smitten by Emma, so he forsakes his estate temporarily to live with her, and to help care for her father, at the lesser mansion of Hartfield. It is fortunate that love, which is secondary, can be so conveniently reconciled with duty, which is primary.

> The impossibility of her quitting her father Mr. Knightley felt as strongly as herself; . . . . He had at first hoped to induce Mr. Woodhouse to remove with her to Donwell; he had wanted to believe it feasible; but his knowledge of Mr. Woodhouse would not suffer him to deceive himself long; and now he confessed his persuasion that such a transplantation would be a risk of her father's comfort, perhaps even of his life, which must not be hazarded. Mr. Woodhouse taken from Hartfield! No, he felt that it ought not to be attempted.[71]

In her insight into age and aging, as in so many other ways, Jane Austen furnishes a bridge between the lost world of preindustrial England and the newer views of a rapidly changing society. Her successors of the nineteenth century help to shift literary perceptions of age further. Some sentimentalize their humane feelings. One of the most benign visions of old age in all of literature is that of Robert Browning in "Rabbi Ben Ezra." It begins on a singing note of optimism:

> *Grow old along with me!*
> *The best is yet to be,*
> *The last of life for which the first was made. . .*

In this dramatic monologue, the speaker, a Spanish rabbi who believes deeply in immortality, professes to find God's plan perfect, from the physical perfection of youth to the thoughtfulness of age. One need not seize the day because, like the potter's wheel, time runs back or stops, but "potter and clay endure."

> *All that is, at all,*
> *Lasts ever, past recall;*
> *Earth changes, but thy soul and God stand sure.* [72]

For other writers, sentimentalism fails to cloud clear visions of realism, irony, and tragedy. In "Growing Old," Matthew Arnold provides yet another catalogue of the deprivations of age. The poem warns that to grow old is not only to lose beauty, strength, and the dream of golden days, but is also to forget that one was ever young, to be imprisoned in a present of pain without even emotion or the memory of what it was to be alive. In Tennyson's poem "Ulysses," the writer recalls not the hero of war and voyaging but rather the aged, impotent man who continues, in futile fashion, to gather again his old crew so they may embark on further adventures.

Perhaps most important of all, ridicule, like the crude stereotyping of characters, begins to disappear in portrayals of the old. It survives longest in the theater's low comedy, where its remnants may be found to this day, but seems increasingly in bad taste in serious literature and drama. In a biographical sketch of the nineteenth-century actor William Farren, the author notes that Farren's impersonations of comic old men turn by the 1840s into "poignant and realistic" portrayals. It is what audiences have come to want and expect. [73]

By the time of Charles Dickens, master of showing the advent of ugly industrialism and unbridled commerce into rural Old England, readers are accustomed to old people's calls upon their sympathy and empathy. They accept old people as individuals with individual fates, who cannot so easily as before be rigidly categorized. Aunt Betsy Trotwood and Mr. Dick in *David Copperfield*, Wemmick's Aged Parent in *Great Expectations*, Dr. Manette in *A Tale of Two Cities*, John Jarndyce in *Bleak House*, and a host of others inhabit a world of new perceptions of the aged and aging.

One of the most imaginatively drawn and sharply delineated of these characters is Nell's grandfather in *The Old Curiosity Shop*. Here is a perceptive study of approaching senility in a man who has hitherto lived an effective life. As the destitute old man and the child struggle from the squalor of one newly industrialized city to that of another, he turns to gambling to try to rescue her from poverty. Dickens depicts the sharp alteration of personality that accompanies his obsession, the avidity and cupidity with which he pursues luck at cards, the deceptions he practices. He steals Nell's last coin from the hem of her dress. When she succeeds at last in removing the old man from temptation, he subsides into childish dependency, allowing the girl to lead him where she will, to sacrifice her food and rest for him. Oblivious to her needs, he does not recognize her growing weakness and approaching death. When Nell dies, their friends conspire to shield him from immediate knowledge. We last glimpse him as he sits absently by her grave, even his grief dulled by his senility.

This humane, sentimental, individualized portrait of a plebian would have aroused little sympathy or interest, perhaps even little recognition, in literature of the preindustrial world. Preindustrial writers would have taken account of the grandfather, if at all, only to ridicule or to scorn him. Now the reader grieves, not only for Nell, but also for the bringing low of this cantankerous, energetic, affectionate old man. The reader has joined him in sympathy and understanding; he is not the embodiment of wealth, power, wisdom, or virtue, nor the representation of an idea, principle, class, or category, nor a mere shadow figure—but a realistic person, representing himself alone. He bursts through the genteel world's categorizations of humble folk; he violates the conventional world's expectations of proper behavior for a character with whom one has sympathy. He is doomed to his individual fate. The literature which has created him grows from a consciousness new to Western society.

NOTES

1. Roland Blythe, *The View in Winter: Reflections on Old Age* (New York and London: Harcourt, Brace, Jovanovich, 1979), p. 29. Blythe is valuable for his insights. See also Simone de Beauvoir, *The Coming of Age* (New York: G. P. Putnam's Sons, 1972), the best and most extensive treatment to date of old age in society, its value only slightly lessened by the Marxist flavor of her comments on literature. Also valuable for our purposes have been Leslie A. Fiedler, "Eros and Thanatos: Old Age in Love," in David

D. Van Tassel, ed., *Aging, Death, and the Completion of Being* (Philadelphia: University of Pennsylvania Press, 1979), pp. 235–254; and two articles which parallel in some ways the argument here, Harold M. Stahmer, "The Aged in Two Ancient Oral Cultures: The Ancient Hebrews and Homeric Greece" and Richard Freedman, "Sufficiently Decayed: Gerontophobia in English Literature" in Stuart F. Spicker et al., eds., *Aging and the Elderly: Humanistic Perspectives in Gerontology* (Atlantic Highlands, N.J.: Humanities Press, 1978), pp. 23–36, 49–61. Other articles in these two compendia have also been useful.

2. The age at which "old age" begins is quite uncertain in premodern times. In both folktales and literature one might be called "old" if one had children of an age to be married. Here we avoid numerical definitions of old age, depending instead on the sense of the writer.

3. Peter Laslett, *The World We Have Lost*, 2nd ed. (New York: Charles Scribner's Sons, 1973), p. 108, offers five samples of English populations ranging from 1599 to 1821 which show people over sixty constituting from one-fourth to one-seventh of people over twenty. See E. A. Wrigley, *Population and History* (New York and Toronto: McGraw-Hill, 1969), p. 25, for age pyramids of two modern preindustrial societies with similar proportions of people over sixty, but see Laslett, *World We Have Lost*, p. 108 for one with a smaller proportion of elderly. Our intent here is simply to indicate that evidence exists that preindustrial authors who dealt with age and aging were speaking of significant, rather than insignificant, fractions of their populations.

4. Deuteronomy 34:4. This and the four following references are to Roy B. Chamberlin and Herman Feldman, eds., *The Dartmouth Bible* (Boston: Houghton Mifflin Co., 1961).

5. Genesis 9:21.

6. I Kings 1:1.

7. Ibid., 1:4.

8. Ecclesiastes 12:1–7, passim.

9. From the Apocrypha, in Ernest Sutherland Bates, arr. and ed., *The Bible, Designed to be Read as Living Literature: The Old and the New Testaments in the King James Version* (New York: Simon and Schuster, 1936), p. 858.

10. Edith Hamilton, *Mythology* (New York: New American Library, 1942), p. 257.

11. Aeschylus, *Agamemnon*, trans. Richmond Lattimore, in David Grene and Richmond Lattimore, eds. *The Complete Greek Tragedies*, I (Chicago: University of Chicago Press, 1959), 37.

12. C. M. Bowra, *The Greek Experience* (New York: New American Library, 1957), p. 106.

13. Ibid., p. 112.

14. Ibid.

15. Homer, *The Iliad*, trans. E. V. Rieu (London: Penguin, 1977), p. 429.

16. Edith Hamilton, *The Greek Way* (New York: Avon Books, 1973), p. 187.

17. Homer, *The Odyssey*, trans. E. V. Rieu (London: Penguin, 1976), p. 53.

18. Ibid., pp. 56–57.

19. Euripides, *Heracles*, trans. William Arrowsmith, in *The Complete Greek Tragedies*, III, 306.

20. Sophocles, *Oedipus Coloneus*, in *Poetic Drama*, ed. Alfred Kreymbourg (New York: Modern Age Books, 1941), p. 70.

21. Ibid., p. 86.

22. Plato, *The Republic*, trans. Benjamin Jowett (New York: World Publishing, 1946), p. 17.

23. Aristotle, *Ethics*, trans. W. D. Ross (London: Oxford University Press, 1942), 1121b: 13–14.

24. Aristophanes, *Plutus*, in *The Complete Greek Drama*, ed. Whitney J. Oates and Eugene O'Neill, Jr. (New York: Random House, 1938), II, 1075.

25. Cicero, *De Senectute, De Amicitia, De Divinatione*, trans. W. A. Falconer: Cicero, vol. XX (Cambridge, Mass.: Harvard University Press, 1923), 11. (Loeb Classical Library)

26. Ibid., 59, 17, 45.

27. Ibid., 13, 17.

28. Ibid., 17, 25.

29. Ibid., 45.

30. Ibid.

31. Erich Segal, *Roman Laughter; The Comedy of Plautus* (Cambridge, Mass.: Harvard University Press, 1968), p. 93.

32. Epode 13, trans. John Duncombe, in *The Complete Works of Horace*, ed. and intro. Caspar J. Kraemer, Jr. (New York: Modern Library, 1936), p. 113. Succeeding references are to this source.

33. Odes, I, 11, trans. Thomas Charles Baring, p. 143.

34. Epode 12, trans. Hubert Wetmore Wells, p. 111.

35. Epode 8, trans. Hubert Wetmore Wells, p. 103.

36. Odes, II, 14, trans. Stephen Edward De Vere, p. 200.

37. Odes, III, 14, trans. William Sinclair Marris, p. 246.

38. Odes, II, 4, trans. Theodore Martin, p. 187.

39. Odes, IV, 10, trans. Francis Wrangham, p. 291.

40. Odes, IV, 13, trans. Louis Untermeyer, p. 297.

41. Odes, IV, 1, trans. Ben Jonson, pp. 272–273.

42. *An Anthology of Old English Poetry*, ed. and trans. Charles W. Kennedy (New York: Oxford University Press, 1960), pp. 57–58.

43. Ibid., p. 7.

44. *Beowulf*, trans. Edwin Morgan (Berkeley and Los Angeles: University of California Press, 1964), p. 75.

45. Donald R. Howard, ed. and intro., *The Canterbury Tales, A Selection* (New York: New American Library, 1969), p. 267.

46. Sylvan Barnet, Morton Berman, and William Burto, eds. and intro., *The Genius of the Early English Theater* (New York: New American Library, 1962), p. 43.

47. Desiderius Erasmus, *The Praise of Folly*, trans. Clarence H. Miller (New Haven: Yale University Press, 1979), pp. 48–49.

48. Ibid.

49. *As You Like It*, II, vii, 11. 157–165. This and subsequent Shakespeare citations are to the Yale Shakespeare, rev. ed., 1954.

50. *King Henry the Fourth, Part II*, V, v, 11. 51–53.

51. *The Tragedy of King Lear*, I, i, 11. 298–302.

52. Ibid., IV, vii, 1. 59.

53. *Sonnets*, no. 6, 1. 1.

54. "To the Virgins, to make much of Time," *Herrick*, ed. William J. Smith (New York: Dell Publishing Co., 1962), pp. 63–64.

55. "To a Gentlewoman, objecting to him his gray haires," *Herrick*, p. 48.

56. "To His Coy Mistress" in Hazelton Spencer, Beverly J. Layman, and David Ferry, eds., *British Literature*, 3rd ed. (Lexington, Mass.: Heath, 1974), I, 645.

57. "Song from Tyrranic Love," *Selected Works of John Dryden*, ed. William Frost (New York: Rinehart & Co., 1955), pp. 84–85.

58. A. L. Clements, ed., *John Donne's Poetry* (New York: W. W. Norton & Co., 1966), p. 48.

59. Ibid., p. 49.

60. *Volpone*, in *British Literature*, II, ii, 11. 283–287.

61. "Of the True use of Retirement and Study," in *English Prose and Poetry 1660–1800*, eds. Odell Shepard and Paul Spencer Wood (Cambridge, Mass.: Houghton Mifflin Co., 1934), p. 387.

62. Ibid., p. 391.

63. *Alexander Pope*, intro. John Bailey (London and Edinburgh: Thomas Nelson and Sons Ltd., n.d.), Epistle II, vi, p. 133.

64. Ibid., p. 172.

65. *English Prose and Poetry 1660–1800*, p. 610, 11. 285–290.

66. Ibid., 11. 317–318.

67. Ibid., p. 611, 1. 364.

68. *The History of Rasselas*, ed. Warren Fleischauer (New York: Barron's Educational Series, 1962), p. 55.

69. *Gulliver's Travels*, ed. Philip Dinkus (New York: Odyssey Press, 1968), p. 207.

70. *Emma* (Boston: Houghton Mifflin Co., 1957), p. 294.

71. Ibid., p. 352.

72. *Poems of Robert Browning*, ed. Donald Smalley (Boston: Houghton Mifflin Co., 1956), pp. 281–287.

73. David L. Rinear, "From the Artificial Toward the Real: The Acting of William Farren," *Theatre Notebook* 31, no. 1 (1977): 21–28.

CHAPTER THREE—CROSS-CULTURAL VARIATION IN THE STATUS OF OLD PEOPLE*

PHILIP SILVERMAN AND ROBERT J. MAXWELL

INTRODUCTION

In all societies for which we have any information, at least two distinctions are always made in defining social categories—age and sex. Further, with respect to age, every society distinguishes at least three levels—childhood, adulthood, and old age—and, in all the cases we have come across, these levels are invariably represented by a distinct term in the language. Obviously, the chronological boundary between one age level and the next may vary considerably across societies, but these fundamental distinctions remain one of the true cultural universals uncovered by anthropologists.

Nevertheless, as a discrete body of knowledge, with distinctive theoretical insights, an anthropology of aging hardly exists. Despite the considerable attention given to age categories, especially the earliest stages in the human life cycle, interest in aging has been surprisingly rare. For example, psychoanalytic ideas from Freud and his more culturally minded disciples have been particularly influential in fostering studies of child-training practices. But Freud's own lack of interest in, and markedly pejorative view of, old age surely contributed to the intellectual indifference toward the final stages of the life cycle.

Only with the very recent growth in interest during the last decade or so can one recognize a subdiscipline dealing with the anthropology of aging. Pragmatic considerations have been an important stimulus to this growth in interest. The social problems created by the dramatic demographic shift taking place in the industrial societies have aroused considerable concern and beg for

*The cross-cultural research presented in this paper was supported by the National Institute on Aging Grant #AG-00482. Eleanor K. Maxwell has made crucial contributions to this study.

adequate solution. It is not surprising, perhaps, that one of the first anthropologists to devote a career to the study of the aged is Margaret Clark, of the University of California in San Francisco, who has concentrated on urban and ethnic America rather than on some exotic non-Western culture.

When one considers the characteristic way anthropologists go about their studies, the paucity of information on the aged is even more astonishing. Although supplemented by various techniques, participant observation typically is employed as the primary data-gathering strategy. This requires the researcher (occasionally a team) to live among a people, usually a specific community, over an extended period of time. He or she observes and participates in a range of cultural settings, employs at times structured interview schedules or other formal data-gathering techniques, but most usually interviews key informants in a more or less unstructured way.

For various reasons these key informants are more likely than not to be older people. They are often the ones who are considered most knowledgeable about various aspects of the culture. After all, experience is a valuable attribute for most endeavors, and that is usually one thing the elders may be expected to possess in greater abundance than their more youthful contemporaries. And perhaps even more importantly, it is likely that the older people enjoy the leisure time to spend responding to the anthropologists' questions, many of which must surely have seemed curious and irrelevant to any normal member of the culture. Yet, these questions are typically concerned with the activities of the young and middle-aged adults rather than the elderly, and usually the males rather than the females.

The reasons for this age and sex bias in the available data are no doubt many and complex. Aside from the theoretical bias mentioned above, at least three other factors must have contributed to the problem, although it is impossible to determine precisely the extent of their influence. Nevertheless, it is instructive to mention them briefly.

First, field workers usually have been young males who, as more or less typical Westerners, probably found rapport with age-mates more congenial than with the elderly. Second, again as Westerners, they may have been more likely to minimize or ignore the importance of the elderly, reflecting the latter's role in the researcher's culture. And third, the small proportion of elderly in the nonindustrial societies normally studied by anthropologists tended to make less salient the significance of old people within their culture.

Despite these limitations, there is much to be found on the role and treatment of the aged in the enormous corpus of data available in the ethnographic literature. The seemingly endless variety of cultural systems which have existed and continue to exist throughout the world provide the data base of primary interest to anthropology. And it is within this data context that anthropology has a unique role to play in answering crucial questions regarding the nature of old age. Some questions of particular interest are:

1. What is the range of cultural variation found in the world with respect to the role of the aged and their treatment by other members of the society? Concerning the second part of this question, which is the more typical situation, a sympathetic attitude and concern for their welfare, or the neglect and mistreatment of old people?

2. Has there been any evolution in the position of the aged? Are there any recognizable developmental changes through the various stages postulated by those who give emphasis to evolutionary theories?

3. To what extent are there differences to be found over major geographical areas in the world? How, if at all, do ecological factors affect the treatment of the aged?

4. What aspects of cultural life or social organization appear to be most important in determining the role and treatment of the aged? More specifically, what conditions appear to be most conducive for providing the aged with a relatively rich, varied, and dignified way of life?

No one study can hope to embrace all of these in a definitive way at this time. However, in the presentation of data which follows, we shall address several of these issues based on some of the results obtained from an ongoing cross-cultural study. Preliminary to the discussion of these results, we first present a detailed comparison of the role and treatment of the aged in two distinct and contrasting cultural contexts.

A COMPARISON OF TWO CULTURES

As mentioned earlier, the typical data-collection technique employed in anthropology is participant observation. The results of such studies are published as ethnographies, monographs describing the way of life of a particular people. These are very frequently so detailed that the task of reading them is far too forbidding except for the hardy specialist. To allow readers a minimal test of their stamina, we have chosen two very different societies to examine closely. In this way some appreciation may be gained of the range of cultural situations to which old people must adapt. Although two cases provide a limited data base, this should be helpful in considering the generalizations which have emerged from the large-scale, cross-cultural study we have undertaken over the past several years. Thus, in addition to the information on old people, we also present data on cultural beliefs and social organization which will aid us in understanding their position in the society.

We have chosen each society to represent contrasting situations for the elderly. In the first case, the Samburu of East Africa, the aged enjoy a particularly advantageous position. In the second case, the Tibetans of the Himalayan highlands, the aged must often adjust to circumstances less favorable to their well-being. In choosing these two societies for closer examination, we have consciously avoided the extremes that could be found in the literature with respect to the situation of the aged, for we are less interested in ethnographic curiosities than in gaining some appreciation of the circumstances under which most people live. Thus, the Samburu do not represent the extreme situation of, say, the traditional Chinese (or at least some of the Chinese), where the aged enjoyed a form of veneration perhaps unequaled by any other culture. Nor may the Tibetans be thought of in the same depressing terms, as, say, the Siriono, a hunting and gathering tribe of the Amazonian basin of Bolivia, where the neglect of the aged can best be compared with the attitude toward excess baggage which other members of the society seem relieved to unload.

Samburu

A gerontocracy is a society in which power is essentially in the hands of old people. In the anthropological literature this power most frequently revolves around the control old men have over marriageable women. This is certainly the case among the Samburu, a nomadic tribe living in the harsh, semidesert environment of northern Kenya. The Samburu are closely related to the more famous Massai, the tall, graceful-looking pastoralists of East Africa who are often chosen to provide an exotic touch to the photography books on Africa. Like many other cattle-herding societies in this area, the Samburu have remained aloof from most of the changes brought about by British colonial rule in the twentieth century and have succeeded in maintaining a firm commitment to their traditional involvements. When the anthropologist Paul Spencer began his fieldwork among them in 1957,[1] he decided it was possible to understand the essentials of Samburu culture while ignoring the colonial administration which held ultimate authority in Kenya. He found that the British interfered little in the affairs of these people living in a remote and, for outsiders, inhospitable region. Even the momentous independence movement, which would achieve its goal a few years later, had minimal impact on the Samburu. Ironically, the end of British rule was welcome not because of their identity with the new nation but, instead, as an opportunity to revive the tradition of raiding other groups for cattle.

The Samburu live in independent homesteads comprising an extended family of about eleven or twelve people and supported by a large herd of cattle (averaging eighty head) and other domestic animals. The senior male in each homestead is the owner of all stock and the undisputed director of all activities within the household unit. The Samburu prefer polygyny (the marriage of one man to more than one woman simultaneously) and are able to maintain a remarkably high rate of such marriages for reasons that will be discussed. Thus, a typical homestead consists of a male head, his co-wives located respectively in separate huts arranged according to seniority, all children including any married sons and their in-marrying wives, and the children of their sons. Married daughters typically move to their husband's homestead.

Although the ideal of the Samburu is to set up a separate homestead at marriage and manage an independent herd of cattle, the most valued commodity, it is more typical for younger married men to remain within the homestead of their father until they have built up the economic resources needed to strike out on their own. In such situations the father retains ultimate ownership of all cattle until his death or possible senility. No cattle can be dispersed, nor any other important matter decided, without first consulting, and gaining the approval of, the father. Even if a married son living in the homestead has taken over many of the responsibilities from an elderly father, there can be no question of the old man's prerogative to interfere in all the affairs of the homestead. Upon the death of the father all stock that has not been allotted to the individual wives for their use must be inherited by the eldest son of the senior wife.

Several homesteads combine together to form small settlements. These consist of a group of closely related kinsmen who are in day-to-day contact with one another and cooperate extensively in subsistence activities such as tending the large herds. Settlements may vary in size from four to ten independent homesteads and they typically move together on the average of once every five weeks. But there is great flexibility in the size of a given settlement over time, since each homestead is free to move wherever it appears most advantageous for grazing and watering the stock, and this may well involve joining other kinsmen who are located in various settlements throughout the area.

Most people living in the settlement are members of the same clan, an extended kinship group of varying size, all of whose members consider themselves related to one another through males. Thus, a clan is a patrilineal descent group, plus all in-marrying wives. Not all sections of the clan, the patrilineages, can actually trace their relations to one another. In fact, often these sections have very diverse origins, but this historical diversity does not affect the unity and solidarity of all clan members. Although adjacent settlements will tend to consist of people from the same clan, it is not a local group. Members of the same clan may be dispersed over a large area and intermingled with members of other clans, yet it is in terms of links with fellow-clansmen spread over a wide geographic area that decisions are made regarding movement of stock and homesteads.

As a result, members of the same clan are brought together by their strong reliance on one another and by their common interests. Given that political influence rarely extends beyond one's clan, the elders of the clan living in the same area represent the rulers of the Samburu. Clan elders may intervene in any matter concerning their fellow clansmen, even reversing decisions made by the head of a constituent homestead if it is considered inimical to the interests of the clan or in violation of accepted custom.

Clans are exogamous and marriage requires the giving of cattle and other stock as bridewealth to the elders in the bride's clan. Since this property must be obtained from the elders in the bridegroom's clan, the support of the oldest clan members is always crucial in order to contract a marriage. Elders from either clan involved in marriage negotiations have the right to veto the arrangement, and this must be respected even if it conflicts with the wishes not only of the couple involved, but also their parents.

Nevertheless, any disputes that arise within the clan are usually settled without any great difficulty as a consequence of the spirit of compromise and cooperation that prevails among fellow clansmen. But this same spirit is not the same in dealings with members of other clans, for the obverse of clan solidarity is the relative absence of close relations with members of other clans. In general, contact between clans is characterized by suspicion and mistrust, and it is unlikely that members of one clan ever become privy to the intimate affairs of another, or indeed are even interested in such affairs. Yet, in spite of the hostility that frequently exists, the necessity of seeking a spouse outside the clan renders a certain advantage to those who maintain friendly relations with those considered outsiders.

The key to Samburu social organization, the institution that provides the structure for gerontocratic rule in the society, is the age-grade system. An age-grade is simply a stage through which everyone passes at some period during the life cycle, and it is defined as broadly or narrowly as the particular society considers relevant. All individuals who pass through the various age-grades together compromise an age-set. Since it is the age-grading of males that dominates this distinctively androcentric society, we leave for subsequent consideration the position of females.

The Samburu recognize three major age-grades: boyhood, lasting until adolescence; warriorhood, lasting from the circumcision of all boys during adolescence until they are about thirty years old; and elderhood, all males who have moved beyond the warrior status as marked by their being allowed to marry. It should be made clear that the warrior age-set has not engaged in military exploits since the coming of British rule toward the end of the nineteenth century; but the ethos associated with warlike activities and the circumstances under which the warriors live remain very much alive, so that it is not inappropriate to use this terminology.

It should also be clear at this point that the term "elders" refers to a much broader cohort than what would normally be considered "old people"; indeed, any male who is married, upon leaving the warrior age-grade at the approximate age of thirty, is considered an elder. Given that a new age-set of warriors is initiated every twelve or fourteen years, thus requiring everyone in the senior age-sets to move up one notch, there are always several age-sets simultaneously in the elder age-grade. In fact, at the time of Spencer's fieldwork, the very oldest men still alive were five age-sets removed from the warriors; they had been circumcised some time before the turn of the century. In general, however, there are three more or less intact age-sets senior to the warrior age-grade, and the oldest of these (who are called senior elders) range in age from fifty-eight to seventy-one. Thus, anyone at least three age-grades removed from the warrior status is a senior elder and generally considered an old person. Given the relatively late age that a man may marry, whenever a homestead consists of an older male head and married sons, a not uncommon family structure, then the older male must at least be a senior elder.

Furthermore, it is unlikely that any elder begins to have influence and can contribute to the discussions of important matters until he approaches the senior elder status. Given the rather rigid separation from the rest of society imposed during the warrior period, it is not possible for junior elders to have obtained the experience and the economic resources to become influential. And given that seniority is always deferred to, the older an elder is, the more elaborate will be the displays of respect. Thus, we continue to use the term "elders" as a synonym for the aged unless greater specificity is warranted.

Once a youth becomes circumcised and assumes warrior status, his most exciting and carefree period begins, although it is a period with many frustrations as well. Despite physical maturity the warriors remain, in the eyes of the elders, socially immature and undisciplined. They must go through a long period of training under the tutelage of the elders, who will gather the warriors together frequently and harangue them about their lack of proper conduct. Finally, after the warriors participate in several solemn rituals marking their progress towards elderhood, the elders may decide that it is time to initiate a new warrior group and thus allow the incumbent warrior set to marry and join them as elders.

Despite the authority held by elders, it is the warriors' life-style that is of primary interest among the Samburu. Warriors form clubs consisting of all their age-mates in the clan, and the members of each club develop a strong feeling of solidarity and a keen sense of competition towards the peer clubs of other clans. Many customs function to keep the warriors separate from the rest of society. They are expected to spend a great deal of time outside the settlements living together in the bush or herding the cattle. Normally they are expected to eat and drink only in the company of their age-mates, and during rituals they must often remain physically separate from the others. Strictly forbidden is the eating of any meat that has been seen by a married woman, including one's own mother. The utility of this last taboo is rather transparent, given that the most common topic of gossip—and the behavior that is clearly most irritating to the elders—is the adulterous relations established frequently between the warriors and the elders' wives, many of whom are of the same age cohort as the warriors.

Despite the enforced bachelorhood and the danger of establishing a liaison with the wife of an elder, warriors need not remain abstemious, a notion that would be quite foreign to the Samburu. Warriors are free to have sexual relations with the young females of their own clan, although not with those within their own lineage section. The competition in finding a lover is intense and can easily lead to feuds. But the attempt of warriors to display their courage (often provoked by the females), and to defend their easily wounded sense of honor, is never allowed to get out of hand by the elders, who may interfere whenever they consider it necessary. Over time the frustration of the warriors increases as they must witness their lovers, whom as members of the same clan they may not marry, taken away as wives by the elders of other clans.

Elders explain the delay in marriage for the warriors as necessary until they are able to learn respect and the traditions of the tribe. Until a warrior behaves maturely and with restraint, elders will not associate with him. That this system allows elders to maintain a monopoly over marriageable females and to marry as many wives as their economic resources will allow is not openly discussed by the Samburu (at least, not with the ethnographer). But the consequences are clear: most women must marry a man much older, typically twice as old but not infrequently three times as old, a situation the young women clearly detest in many cases.

The position of females in this male-oriented society is not a terribly enviable one. Girls are brought up to avoid the male elders at all times—and that includes one's own father. A girl should never be in the same hut as an elder, unless it is her father, and should never initiate conversations with him. When it is time to be married, it is possible for a girl, having recently attained puberty, to experience a dramatic and anxiety-filled transformation in her life within the brief period of about forty-eight hours: (1) she must break off her relationship with her lover; (2) she is circumcised (cliterodectomy) in preparation for marriage; (3) she is married to someone usually much older who has been chosen by her clan elders; (4) she must leave her natal home, undertaking in some cases a long and exhausting walk shortly after undergoing the genital operation; and (5) she must now live in close association with virtual strangers, including elders she had been taught all her life to avoid.

With age a woman can also acquire seniority and respect from others. An older woman with married sons enjoys an honored position on the homestead. She has a certain authority over her daughters-in-law and, if a senior wife, also her junior co-wives. They may be expected to help her with her tasks, especially when it comes to moving the settlement and rebuilding the huts elsewhere, a complex of chores performed essentially by the women. Older women are allowed to build their huts toward the center of the settlement, the area considered most desirable. Within the hut they have a sleeping area advantageously located close to the hearth. And as she becomes incapacitated because of sickness or decrepitude, an old woman can always expect her youngest son to look after her.

Despite the increase in rights won by women as they grow older, the control of the society remains very much in the hands of the male elders. Their control over the most important economic resource, cattle, allows them to acquire as many wives as they can afford and also to regulate the marriages of the younger members of their family who need cattle for the bridewealth payments. Supernaturally, elders can impose their will through the mechanisms of powerful curses they may utter against younger members of the society who do not conform. They preside over all important social transitions, which are given dramatic resonance by customs such as genital mutilations. To inculcate respect for social values they use devices such as haranguing, blessing, and insisting on the meticulous performance of complex rituals. And although elders admire the life of a warrior and view their own physical decline with great sorrow, in no way does this compromise the control they are able to exercise and the capacity they have for overawing other members of the society.

The ethical principle which dominates Samburu social life, and from their point of view the characteristic that distinguishes them from all neighboring tribes, is their strong sense of respect. This pervasive theme operates most clearly in regard to seniority, for age must invariably be given deference. In secular and ritual settings, the oldest people may be expected to have a place of honor. During ceremonial feasts the elders are provided with the choicest pieces of meat. Aged parents can be assured of both respect and care from their children, and in any case younger people must be prepared to help all their elders whenever they need it.

Despite this sincere attitude of respect that pervades the society, tensions exist due to the ambivalent attitude that warriors have toward the elders. The firm control under which they must live for many years is resented, and on rare occasions it leads to fights with the elders. A more typical and less disruptive outlet for this frustration involves the singing of songs and the telling of stories about the greed, selfishness, and weakness of the elders. Normally, however, even this mechanism must not be directed at the senior elders.

In presenting this overview of Samburu culture, it has been necessary to ignore some of the complex features of their society, particularly the details of the age-grade system. Nevertheless, this window into Samburu life should allow some appreciation of the dominant position enjoyed by old people. After presenting the Tibetan case, those aspects of social organization that seem particularly relevant to the position of the aged will be drawn together by means of a comparison of the two cases before going on to a consideration of the cross-cultural study.

In conclusion, it should be made clear that gerontocratic principles can operate in societies very different from the Samburu, albeit not always with such encompassing effects. Near the end of his ethnography, Spencer[2] draws many interesting analogies between the warrior status of the Samburu and the life of boys in the public schools of England during the first half of the nineteenth century. These boys were subjected to strict control and prevented from taking part in a variety of social settings through their isolation in these total institutions. In effect, the upper class and upper middle-class families were able to delay their marriages to suitable females and to prevent competition in family matters as long as possible.

Finally, it is also worth mentioning that the marriage of young, socially desirable women to considerably older men has always been the prerogative of the exceptionally successful or wealthy in Western society. It would not be difficult to compile a rather extensive list that would include such illustrious figures as the immortal Charlie Chaplin, the late Associate Justice William O. Douglas, and the still very active Senator Strom Thurmond of South Carolina. In 1966, at the age of sixty-six, Senator Thurmond married the twenty-two-year-old Nancy Moore, a former Miss South Carolina. Twelve years later the senator was waging a vigorous, and ultimately successful, campaign for reelection with the aid of his wife and four young children.

Tibetans

There is no single ethnography available on Tibetan life that adequately covers both the social organization and the position of the aged. Tibetan "culture" is a complex notion involving many people dispersed over a formidable and mostly inaccessible area, living in several independent nations. They have succeeded in distilling a unique set of traditions by syncretizing elements from very different civilizations. Most of our data will come from a kingdom in Western Tibet called Ladak, since, in one cross-cultural study of twenty-four societies,[3] these were the people rated among the lowest with respect to the positive treatment received by the aged from the other members of the society. However, we shall not hesitate to bring in information from other regions of Tibetan culture, for there is good reason to believe considerable cultural homogeneity exists throughout this vast area.

All Tibetans live on the high plateaus of the Himalayas, from India in the west, where the kingdom of Ladak is located in the state of Kashmir; through Nepal, where the southern Tibetan groups live in the northern regions of this mountain kingdom; to China in the east, where the most famous Tibetan center is found at Lhasa. This area is the highest inhabited region in the world, where some people have never been below twelve thousand feet. In other parts of Asia there is a sharp demarcation between the spheres of influences of the two great cultures of the continent, India and China. But in Tibet these two competitive civilizations were joined into a rich mixture, with political and legal institutions coming essentially from China and religious ideas deriving from India—especially Buddhism, which became a pervasive force throughout so much of Tibetan life.

From the very earliest report available on Tibet as recorded in the Chinese chronicles of the fifth through the seventh centuries A.D., there is evidence of the low esteem in which the aged are held. Later, when Marco Polo made his incredible voyage through Asia in the thirteenth century, he reported that the Tibetans still engaged in the strangling of the elderly and subsequent eating of them with lamb's meat.[4] Presumably the relatives waited until their departing kinsman was close to death before invoking this macabre custom.[5] Again, in the nineteenth century, we have reports of the aged receiving little respect and being killed by their sons when they became a bother.[6]

In the nineteenth century, the Tibetan kingdom of Ladak became a part of the British Empire, and was then passed on to an independent India in 1947. Through the changes in political hegemony the kingdom always remained closely tied to the center of Tibetan culture at Lhasa, at least until the takeover of this later area by the People's Republic of China in 1951. The predominantly agricultural Ladakhi must sustain themselves in the arid mountain valleys of poor soil and fierce winters. Although there is little arable land, certainly less than five acres per family unit, and grain varieties must be vigorous to survive at these altitudes, the Ladakhi harvest enough crops and obtain sufficient products from their sheep and goats so that they enjoy a reputation of being well fed. This is even more remarkable, given the need to support a large, nonproductive proportion of the population—estimated to be anywhere from one-sixth to one-third of the total—living a spiritual life in lamaseries and convents.[7] The Lamaist Church is, of course, such a unique and intellectually rich tradition that other equally fascinating aspects of Tibetan life have been neglected by scholars due to the focus on ritual and religious art.

The population of Ladak is so widely dispersed that the approximately two hundred thousand inhabitants average only about four persons per square mile. Yet, difficult terrain and great distances have not imposed undue social isolation upon the Lakakhi or other Tibetans. Traveling primarily on horseback, they have frequent commercial contacts with people hundreds, even thousands, of miles away. Leh, the capital of the kingdom, has been a great religious and trading center, a major nexus in the caravan route between India and Tibet proper, and a town where people of diverse cultures live in close proximity. Indeed, the importance of commercial activities throughout all sections of Tibetan society has led some to characterize Tibet as a nation of traders.[8]

A striking feature of social organization among Tibetans is the flexibility allowed people in choosing a marital relationship compatible with their interests and desires. Although all forms of marriage can be found, the Ladakhi are predominantly polyandrous (the marriage of one woman to more than one man simultaneously). If no children result from this union, cohusbands, who are usually brothers, may decide to bring in an outside male as an additional cohusband or to add a second wife to the household, thus forming group marriage, the rarest marital form known in the ethnographic literature.

The key event in the domestic cycle of the polyandrous household is the marriage of the eldest male child. This requires the parents to turn over immediately all property to the younger couple, often forcing parents not much past middle age to leave the household and retire from all responsibilities. A small portion of the property, including lodgings, is given to the parents for their use, but this portion is frequently inadequate. The younger members of the family may help the elderly parents in cultivating the field allocated to this small portion, but this support is by no means automatic and as a result old people are forced at times to lead destitute lives.

Like the Samburu, the Ladakhi are also organized into exogamous patrilineal clans which are not localized. The exact function of these clans is not clear,[9] and they are thus considered to play a rather minor role in Tibetan life. However, all clansmen worship a common "father-god" and gather together for all important life-cycle events to participate in carefully regulated rituals. The elderly also participate in these rituals and in the other recurring religious festivals which are so important to Tibetan Buddhism, but they no longer assume any responsibility for carrying out these rituals once they have been replaced in the household by a married son.

There is some evidence that the political organization of the Ladakhi villages included officials designated as "elders," but it is not clear that these men were necessarily old. The most important village official is the headman, who has multiple functions including the administration of justice, which is carried out apparently with the assistance of a council of five to seven elders.[10] Beyond the three or four elders who act as lower-level councillors in the king's court, there is no evidence that old people play any active role in the society.

Returning to more general features of Ladakhi social organization, there is a remarkable lack of rigidity which characterizes social relations in a variety of cultural settings. Even the practice of polyandry is described as promiscuous in comparison with other polyandrous societies. No fixed rules regulate access to the wife (or wives), and cohusbands may even observe one another having intercourse with their common spouse. Ladakhi are generally considered to be easygoing, friendly, and nonquarrelsome. Women are not the least bit shy and mix freely with men in many settings. Many tasks are done by both sexes in common. Even the settlement pattern reflects a preference for frequent and easy communication in the villages, where houses are built in wall-to-wall proximity to one another. And the extensive involvement in religious ritual has not led to an inflexible, dogmatic view of the world. Instead, Tibetans remain in general, receptive to new religious ideas and are without bigotry.[11]

These same characteristics have been remarked upon by researchers who have worked in very different regions of the Tibetan culture area. In a relatively recent ethnography of the Sherpas, a Tibetan people of Nepal who are famous for their prowess as mountaineers, Fuerer-Haimendorf devotes a whole chapter to what he calls the "open society." Although the Sherpa live in a country with a closed caste system, they can easily tolerate and assimilate different peoples and ideas. Yet, again this openness occurs in a context which can also include a repugnant negligence of the elderly:

An occasional casualness towards aged parents, though by no means frequent, mars to some extent, the otherwise pleasant picture of Sherpa family life. The most shocking instance of really callous treatment of an old father occurred a generation ago in Khumjung. A once exceedingly rich but spendthrift man, who in his old age became somewhat eccentric and was dispossessed of his house by a ruthless [headman] for failure to pay the revenue, lived the last year of his life in a cave above the village temple and died destitute, though a son of his lived in reasonably comfortable circumstances in Kunde, and his sister's son was one of the two richest men of Khumjung. This was no doubt a very exceptional case, but there are nevertheless societies in which such indifference to the plight of an aged father would be considered so disgraceful that, if nothing else, the fear of public condemnation would induce the sons to adopt a more charitable attitude. Wealthy old people sometimes avoid the possibility of friction with grown-up sons and daughters-in-law by leaving their home and spending the last years of their life in a religious retreat such as a nuns' settlement of Devuche. [12]

Coming back to Ladak, we might summarize the insecurity of old age in Tibetan culture by including a comment made by Prince Peter, [13] one of the world's experts on polyandrous societies, who claims one informant admitted that parents are reluctant to be strict with their children for fear of how they will be treated after turning over their property. Clearly, under such conditions the position of elderly people cannot be considered a particularly commanding one.

Conclusions

The Samburu and Tibetans provide us with contrasting cultural settings within which old people must adapt. Whereas the Samburu aged remain active, powerful members of the society as long as they are mentally alert and physically capable, the Tibetans appear to be extruded from most important activities prematurely. Among the Samburu, all ritual involvements are under the direction of the elderly, who also may invoke powerful supernatural curses to support their authority; in contrast, the ritual life of the Tibetans is mostly in the hands of an elaborately organized monastic order. Samburu men maintain control of their resources and dependents until they die, but Tibetans must give them up upon the marriage of their eldest son.

Turning to the treatment elderly people receive from other members of society, the Samburu emphasis on respect and deference to age, despite the universal admiration for the life of the young warriors, is absent among the Tibetans. Whereas the Samburu allow the aged the most advantageous allocation of space within the household and the settlement, the Tibetans can expect to be relegated to the less desirable portion of the household property as early as middle age. Finally, the Samburu can invariably anticipate receiving loving care from younger family members when and if the infirmities accompanying old age occur, whereas this remains rather problematic for the Tibetan elderly.

It is possible to consider at least two features of social life which may be influential in determining the position of the aged. First, the Samburu have been much more isolated from the outside world and the diverse effects that can be expected in a colonial situation; thus, they have held firmly to traditional patterns while maintaining a pejorative attitude towards outsiders and their ways. On the other hand, the Tibetans have had a long history of contact with the outside world despite living in an inaccessible area. As a buffer between the Indian and Chinese civilizations, they have been involved in wide-ranging economic, political, and religious contacts with their own dispersed communities and many outsiders.

Second, we find a contrast between the relative social rigidity of Samburu in comparison with the openness and flexibility of the Tibetans. The Samburu maintain very strict boundaries which hinder communication between the sexes and differing age cohorts. These barriers support a system which defines normative behavior very narrowly and also function to overawe the less powerful members of society, particularly the women. No such barriers can be found among the Tibetans. Men and women intermingle freely and acceptable behavior provides for a variety of options in many spheres of life. One is left with the impression of a society all of whose subgroups tend to intercommunicate freely with one another.

Thus, based on the comparison of these two cases, tentatively we can consider the following broad propositions:

1. Where old people tend to play an active and nontrivial role in the affairs of a culture, they will enjoy greater esteem from the nonaged members of the society. "Active" and "esteem" are very broad concepts, and it will be necessary to operationalize them more precisely in the subsequent discussion.

2. Where a society is characterized by relative community isolation and social rigidity, the role of the aged will be more active and thus they will enjoy greater esteem. This is consistent with the hypothesis that the prestige of the elderly varies inversely with modernization,[14] a process which can be viewed as the obverse of community isolation. These and other relationships will be covered in considering the large-scale, cross-cultural study in the next section.

SYSTEMATIC CROSS-CULTURAL COMPARISONS

Considerations of space preclude a presentation of the precise definitions and methodological details of our study of preindustrial society,[15] which are, in any case, retrievable from our Manual for

Coders.[16] A statistical analysis of some of the most important findings thus far has been published recently.[17] Here, the generalizations which emerged from our study will be couched in qualitative terms. When we describe an association as strong or significant, we mean that it is technically established as unlikely to have occurred by chance.

We have proposed that where old people play an active role in cultural affairs, they will enjoy greater esteem from younger members of the community. Our study has investigated the exact nature of the active roles that old people play in nonindustrial societies. Briefly, these active roles can be divided into two broad types: (1) information processing, and (2) exercising control over valuable resources.

By "information processing," we mean simply that old people give useful information to younger people in the form of advice, counseling, settling disputes, teaching, telling members of work or other groups how to coordinate their labors, reciting myths, and so forth. We have already seen some instances of information processing among the Samburu, where the elders inculcate respect for social values by using such devices as haranguing, blessing and insisting on the meticulous performance of complex rituals.

"Control over valuable resources," on the other hand, refers to (1) the ownership of real or movable property, (2) the ownership of goods that are valued for their ritual significance, (3) prerogatives concerning the acquisition of spouses, children, or other subordinate laborers, and (4) supernatural resources such as the ability to cause or cure human misfortune. We have also seen instances of the control of supernatural resources among the Samburu, where the elders can impose their will through the mechanism of powerful curses they may utter against younger members of the society who do not conform.

Information processing and the control of valuable resources are the two main ways in which old people actively participate in community affairs. Together they represent the sources of power individuals may employ in dealing with others. Esteem, on the other hand, is not something old people do, but rather something that other members of the community do for old people. By "esteem," we mean any activity of community members which enhances the physical well-being of old people or is designed to maximize their self-image or to dramatize in some fashion the respect and appreciation they enjoy from others.[18] Among the Samburu, for instance, we found many examples of the deference given age. In secular and ritual settings the oldest people may be expected to have a place of honor. During ceremonial feasts the elders are provided with the choicest pieces of meat. Aged parents can be assured of respect and care from their children, and in any case younger people must be prepared to help all their elders whenever they need it.

Our study, then, dealt with the relationships between three concepts: information processing, resource control, and esteem. We predicted that active social roles, as indicated by information processing and resource control, would lead to greater esteem being expressed toward old people.

We did in fact find an extremely strong relationship between information processing and esteem, one which virtually precludes the possibility of a chance association. How you are treated when you are old clearly depends a great deal upon exactly what useful information and advice you have to give to younger community members. The old men, however, tend to receive this positive treatment more frequently than old women, especially if the esteem involves symbolic or ritual expressions rather than the more usual custodial care. [19]

As for the second component of active roles for the aged, however, we did not find a direct relationship between the overall exercise of control over valuable resources and esteem. There *is* actually a relationship, but it is not a simple one.

Before exploring this relationship, it must be mentioned that control over valuable resources, as a determinant of esteem for whatever age group, has an extremely important place in socio-historical theory. Marx and Engels, and their various modern progeny, are likely to view all sorts of mass social effects as consequences of the operation of this sort of power. Our earlier work on the importance of information processing frequently generated a set of related criticisms which we came to call "the Rockefeller objection." How, indeed, did the Rockefellers come by all that information they were processing? It is a serious issue, not to be lightly dismissed.

Fortunately, we were able to examine the relationship between these various sources of power and esteem more closely. We had categorized control over resources into four types, as has been mentioned: material goods, symbolic goods, social resources, and supernatural resources. Marxist theories focus on the first type, ownership of valuable material goods, as the most important. And, indeed, we found that none of the other types of power resulted in an increase in esteem for old people.

When we eliminated the other types of power from the analysis, we did find that control of material resources was significant, but only for old men. And even then it does not have a great deal of explanatory power, since only about one-third of the ninety-five societies we examined showed any appreciable accumulation of material goods in the hands of old people. This is not to denigrate a materialist explanation of esteem, but it does indicate that such theories are perhaps more likely to be heuristic in understanding the socio-historical dynamics of industrial and postindustrial societies than of preindustrial ones. Marx was concerned primarily with the obvious horrors of the industrial revolution. And there has been no industrial revolution among such societies as the Samburu and Western Tibetans. The ownership of material goods by old men still exerts a noticeable effect, but it occurs only in a minority of our societies. In most preindustrial societies, joint control of material goods may be exercised — or there may simply be no significant material goods worth speaking of. The all-too-obvious unequal distribution of wealth we see around us appears to be the result of a particular kind of society which occurred rather late in the course of social evolution.

Still, old men do benefit from the ownership of valuable goods, even in preindustrial society; and, in addition, old people of both sexes reap some reward in less tangible ways. Our analysis disclosed that a concentration of wealth in the hands of old people leads to an increase in the intensity of ancestor worship, as measured by the number of ceremonial elements involved. Further, an increase in ancestor worship is strongly linked to the elaborateness of funeral ceremonies, indicating that we have uncovered a complex of death-related rituals which tend to appear, or not appear, as a single package.

We may now turn from an examination of the relationships between active roles and esteem to an analysis of the antecedent conditions promoting those relationships. That is, if old people taking an active role in community affairs leads to greater esteem for them, then what is it that leads to their taking active roles in the first place?

We have proposed that one of these conditions is social rigidity, by which we mean the division of the community into several cohesive subcommunities, such as families, clans, or neighborhoods. The theoretical justification for this is that subcommunities may be something like seminars, in which the person who has attended the seminar the longest is in the best position to evaluate novel informational input. He is also in some ways more likely to be the most judicious, disinclined to endorse radical ideas or aggressive solutions to resolving differences. Dr. Spock and Bertrand Russell notwithstanding, it is rather well established that old people tend to contribute to the continuity of traditional social values and thus provide the necessary ideological framework for maintaining subgroup solidarity.[20]

We have seen an example of how social rigidity operates among the Samburu, in that the obverse of clan solidarity is the relative absence of close relations with members of other clans. In other words, there is a null point in information exchanged between clans, which illustrates fairly clearly why we consider rigidity to be so important. Each subcommunity is to some extent an information pool unto itself. And where societies are characterized by such a low level of social mobility that stable subcommunities emerge, then old people are more likely to be the guardians of traditions and secrets.

The second antecedent condition we have posited, community isolation, simply refers to the exchange of information between a given community and its neighbors. This was measured by noting the presence or absence of such things as trading relationships, government officials in the community, mass transportation, and mass media. Community isolation, as a concept, was about as close as we could come to achieving an index of modernization. Modernization is an idea that has been so bandied about in social science literature as to be almost bereft of meaning. It is an obviously multidimensional concept, involving such community features as industrialization, social complexity, permanency and elaborateness of settlement, and literacy. Our investigation categorized the concept into discrete elements and measured each one. We presumed that an isolated community was a slow-changing one, and that a slow rate of information turnover was likely to enhance the value of traditional ideas and so promote the position of old people within the community. The proposition is elementary enough. In a totally static society, information would rarely become obsolete, and knowledge, once acquired, would remain indefinitely valuable.

Turning now to the results obtained from consideration of these antecedent variables, we discovered that social rigidity was significantly related to information processing. This is a strong relationship, with the likelihood of its occurring by chance being in the neighborhood of one in one hundred. Community isolation, rather surprisingly, was not related to information processing—nor to esteem.

In other words, as far as our first proposed antecedent condition—social rigidity—is concerned, the results support our hypothesis strongly. The more a community is divided into subgroups or social categories which tend to guard their informational pool with some jealousy, the more old people are involved in managing that information, and the greater the esteem they enjoy.

As far as our second antecedent condition is concerned, old people process no more information in socially isolated societies than in societies fully articulated with their circumjacent communities. Moreover, if we drop all the measures of isolation from the analysis except the mass media, we encounter a rather surprising finding. The general idea was that the presence of the mass media would undermine the position of old people as information processors, since books and other archives would replace old people as repositories of knowledge. Instead, we find that the increasing presence of mass media and the involvement of old people in information processing tend to co-occur. Old people remain important conveyors of information in communities where there is *increasing* penetration of such mass media as newspapers, books, movies, radio, and television.

That this should be true is, we suspect, a function of the sorts of communities we examined. This is, after all, a preindustrial sample of communities; they range in terms of subsistence techniques from hunters and gatherers to rural, traditional agricultural communities in otherwise industrialized nations, such as Japan in the 1950s. A diachronic perspective suggests that perhaps in these communities not enough time has elapsed between the introduction of the mass media and their maximal impact on the community to erode the position of old people. We did not, for instance, examine such communities as Akron, Ohio. The generalization nevertheless holds true for preindustrial, or early industrializing, societies.

Several other important relationships that we have uncovered thus far deserve brief mention. In addition to esteem, the positive treatment received by the aged, we also took note of all instances of disparaging or contemptible treatment received by the elderly. Among the most severe forms of ill-treatment recorded is the abandonment or killing of the aged by younger members of the community. We found either one or both of these to be present in twenty of the ninety-five societies in our sample.[21] Our initial suspicion, based on previous suggestions, that such acts are associated with the severity of the climate was only partially confirmed. However, further analysis was able to demonstrate that the presence of the abandonment and/or killing of the aged was related to societies which tended to lack permanent settlements. Interestingly enough, the highest proportion of societies where these customs are found are not those with the least permanent settlement, the ones with fully nomadic bands typical of hunting and gathering societies, but instead those having seminomadic communities. Fully 50 percent of the fourteen such societies in our sample had at least one of these customs present.

Finally, a previous report dealt with the explanations given in the ethnographies for any kind of ill-treatment received by the elderly.[22] The explanation that occurred most prominently was the absence of closely related family kinsmen, a finding that perhaps would little surprise social workers in our contemporary society. Yet, this finding provided persuasive confirmation for the universal importance of an effective family support system to ensure the well-being of people who have become infirm and decrepit during old age.

There are obviously many causal threads running through this analysis of active roles, esteem, and type of society. However difficult it may seem to tie them up into a neat theoretical bundle, they have the virtue of being founded not on speculation but on careful scrutiny of an extensive body of data. The cross-cultural approach in anthropology provides a unique opportunity to say something about the enormous range of human experiments about which we now have reasonably adequate information. The extent to which there are fundamental insights into the constraints and potentials of human behavior to be gained by this approach cannot be easily predicted. Our ongoing study of the final stages in the life-cycle suggest that there still remains a rich crop to harvest.

NOTES

1. Paul Spencer, *The Samburu: A Study of Gerontocracy in a Nomadic Tribe* (Berkeley: University of California Press, 1965).

2. Spencer, *Samburu*, pp. 308–312.

3. Robert J. Maxwell and Philip Silverman, "Information and Esteem: Cultural Considerations in the Treatment of the Aged," *Aging and Human Development* 1 (1970): 361–392.

4. John Koty, *Die Behandlung der Alten und Kranken Bei Den Naturvoelken* (Stuttgart: W. Kohlhammer, 1933), p. 59.

5. Tsung-lieu Shen and Shen-chi Liu, *Tibet and the Tibetans* (Stanford: Stanford University Press, 1953).

6. Koty, *Die Behandlung der Alten und Kranken*, p. 59.

7. A. Reeve Heber and Kathleen M. Heber, *In Himalayan Tibet* (Philadelphia: J. B. Lippincott Company, 1926).

8. Pedro Carrasco Pizana, *Land and Polity in Tibet* (Seattle: University of Washington Press, 1959).

68 _Philip Silverman and Robert J. Maxwell_

9. Carrasco, _Land and Polity_, p. 38.

10. Carrasco, _Land and Polity_, p. 43.

11. H. Ramsey, _A Practical Dictionary of the Language and Customs of the Districts Included in the Ladak Wazarat_ (Lahore: Ball and Company, 1890), p. 36.

12. Christoph von Fuerer-Haimendorf, _The Sherpas of Nepal: Buddhist Highlanders_ (Berkeley: University of California Press, 1964), p. 87.

13. H. R. H. Prince Peter of Greece and Denmark, _A Study of Polyandry_ (The Hague: Mouton & Co., 1963).

14. Donald O. Cowgill and Lowell D. Holmes, eds., _Aging and Modernization_ (New York: Appleton, Century, Crofts, 1972).

15. This sample is derived from George P. Murdock and Douglas R. White, "Standard Cross-Cultural Sample," _Ethnology_ 8 (1969): 321–369. It consists of 186 societies from throughout the world, both contemporary and historical. The societies are carefully selected, based on a specific set of criteria designed to maximize their independence. The literature of each society is pinpointed according to time and locality so that there is both temporal and spatial control over the data used. In case any one society has inadequate data on a particular subject, it is possible to select an alternative society within the same "sampling province," as delineated by Murdock and his colleagues. We selected a 55 percent random subsample from the Standard Cross-Cultural Sample, and were able to find adequate data on 95 societies, slightly above the 50 percent we had hoped to achieve. The societies in our subsample, listed in the order they appear in Murdock and White, are: !Kung Bushmen, Lozi, Bakongo, Yao, Kikuyu, Mbuti, Bamileke, Ibo, Fon, Mende, Bambara, Songhai, Hausa, Massa, Fur, Shilluk, Lango, Amhara, Teda, Riffians, Hebrews, Rwala, Turks, Irish, Samoyed, Abhaz, Kurds, Basseri, Gond, Santal, Burusho, Mongols, Lepcha, Garo, North Vietnamese, Khmer, Semang, Andamanese, Tanala, Negri Sembilan, Balinese, Badjau, Tobelorese, Tiwi, Orokaiva, Kimam, Kwoma, Lesu, Siaui, Tikopia, Fiji, Maori, Samoans, Marshallese, Yapese, Ifugao, Manchu, Japanese, Gilyak, Chukchee, Ingalik, Copper Eskimo, Micmac, Slave, Eyak, Bellacoola, Twana, Pomo, Ute, Kutenai, Hidatsa, Pawnee, Huron, Natchez, Apache, Havasupai, Huichol, Aztec, Quiche, Bribri, Goajiro, Callinago, Yanomamo, Carib, Mundurucu, Cayapa, Amahuaca, Aymara, Siriono, Trumai, Tupinamba, Shavante, Abipone, Mapuche, Yahgan.

16. Robert J. Maxwell, Eleanor Krassen-Maxwell, and Philip Silverman, _The Cross-Cultural Study of Aging: A Manual for Coders_ (New Haven: Human Relations Area Files, HRAFlex Books, 1978).

17. Philip Silverman and Robert J. Maxwell, "The Significance of Information and Power in the Comparative Study of the Aged," in Jay Sokolovsky, ed., _Growing Old in Different Societies: Cross-Cultural Perspectives_ (Belmont: Wadsworth Publishing Co., n.d.).

18. A more detailed consideration of the various categories of esteem can be found in Philip Silverman and Robert J. Maxwell, "How Do I Respect Thee? Let Me Count the Ways: Deference Towards Elderly Men and Women," _Behavior Science Research_ 13 (1978): 91–108.

19. Silverman and Maxwell, "How Do I Respect Thee? Let Me Count the Ways," p. 104.

20. On the role played by the elderly in providing continuity with the past, see Matilda White Riley and Anne Foner, _Aging and Society_ vol. 1 (New York: Russell Sage Foundation, 1968), p. 5. On the role played by the elderly in providing commitment to

subcultural identifications, see Linda Cool, "Ethnicity and Aging: Continuity through Change for Elderly Corsicans," in Christine Fry, ed., *Aging in Culture and Society* (New York: J. F. Bergin Publishers, 1980).

21. The twenty societies for which there is evidence for the abandonment and/or killing of the aged are: !Kung Bushmen, Bakongo, Kikuyu, Shilluk, Khalka Mongols, Kiman, Fijian, Ifugao, Chukchee, Ingalik, Copper Eskimo, Micmac, Pomo, Shoshone, Natchez, Callinago, Aymara, Siriono, Tupinamba, and Yahgan.

22. Eleanor Krassen Maxwell and Robert J. Maxwell, "Contempt for the Elderly: A Cross-Cultural Analysis," *Current Anthropology* 24 (1980): 569–570.

CHAPTER FOUR—OLD AGE IN INDIA

SYLVIA VATUK

I n recent years, research in social gerontology has made us increasingly aware of the special social problems facing the aged
in contemporary Western societies, and considerable thought is being
given to whether these problems are an inevitable consequence of
industrialization. A widely accepted thesis holds that in preindustrial
societies the aged are generally better provided for, and retain a more
central and active role in family and community life. It is suggested,
thus, that as one moves from this type of society, through the
transitional stages of industrialization, to the kind of fully industrial
society most familiar to us in the United States and Europe, there
occurs a consistent decline for older people in terms of overall social
well-being.[1] In attempting to assess the validity of this thesis,
historians have begun to look more closely at evidence concerning the
actual situation of the elderly in preindustrial Europe and during the
industrial revolution. Cross-cultural studies have been less numerous, although they are potentially of great significance in terms of
enabling one to separate out the effects of a particular cultural
tradition from those of a set of similar economic transformations.
Furthermore, since many non-Western societies are currently passing
through a stage of development comparable to that which we in the
West experienced centuries earlier, such studies enable us to observe
these processes in action, instead of being limited to reconstructing
them from the incomplete evidence which has survived.

India, as a developing country, quite well advanced in the twin
processes of industrialization and urbanization, cannot, of course,
serve as a type specimen of the "preindustrial" society for the
purpose of testing theories of aging and modernization. Nevertheless, as a country still predominantly agrarian, with over 80 percent of
its population living in rural areas and 70 percent of its work force
directly engaged in agriculture and related occupations, its
preindustrial past still strongly colors not only its present
demographic profile, but also the cultural and social-structural

context within which the roles and statuses of its older population must be understood. It is a society which is frequently cited in the literature as having traditionally conformed to the idealized "preindustrial" pattern of providing the aged a secure place—both physically and emotionally—within their families. A body of ancient religious literature prescribes respect and obedience to one's elders, and buttresses a family system in which adult sons are enjoined to remain in the parental home after marriage and repay with loving care the sacrifices of their mother and father in giving them birth and raising them from infancy. The scriptural tradition furthermore provides for an orderly transmission of responsibility and effective management of the household from the senior to the junior generation in the context of an idealized model of life stages (*āshrama*) for the individual.[2] But India is a country which is currently undergoing rapid social change, and it is reasonable to expect that the positions and roles of the older person in the family and community would feel the impact of such change.

The most serious hindrance to an effective test of received theory on aging and modernization in the Indian case is a paucity of concrete evidence concerning the actual—as contrasted to the idealized— situation of the elderly in former times. And even in respect to the contemporary period, there is very little published material which bears directly upon the question of the status and roles of the elderly. Of course, it is possible from literary evidence, and from the ethnographic record (largely from studies of rural communities), to discern the broad patterns of the life paths of older Indians. And a few recent sociological surveys of sample populations of the aged—most of these undertaken in urban centers—have begun to highlight some of the contemporary problems of older people, in terms of their support, housing, and health needs. For the past, however, one has little more than the data on older age groups provided in the decennial Census of India since 1881, and some scattered local censuses for earlier periods, some of which have been examined in recent years and described in the literature by historians and sociologists. The kinds of historical questions to which we can expect to find answers are consequently limited. In the following pages I will concentrate on the question of how well old people in India, over the past century, have been able to meet their needs for shelter and support within the framework of the traditional family system—a concrete and relatively manageable focus for some of the larger questions about the elderly in traditional society.

THE INDIAN FAMILY AND OLD AGE SECURITY

In India it is universally expected—or, at least, hoped—that the elderly person will be provided shelter and care by his or her adult offspring, in the setting of home and family. The provision of a home, and of care in time of illness or incapacity, is considered by most Indians to be the responsibility of adult sons and their wives. Daughters are by custom regarded as being free of this duty, unless their parents have no one else to whom to turn. In fact, there is among many Indians a strong element of shame associated with having to rely upon one's daughter for support or for personal services of any kind. Persons without sons, it is felt, ought to be able to find a home with some other close male relative. In fact, it is recognized that the responsibility to house and care for an aging aunt or uncle is much less keenly felt than is the corresponding responsibility for one's own parents, and for this reason the fate in old age of a sonless—and particularly of a childless—man or woman is considered to be uncertain at best. Extrafamilial, or institutional, facilities for the support and care of the aged are lacking in India on any substantial scale, and pension levels, for that small minority of the population included within such schemes, are generally quite insufficient for subsistence. In such a setting, preparation for old age security must begin for most people quite early in life, as it hinges in a crucial sense upon their reproductive success in youth and early middle age, and upon their ability to raise children—particularly sons—to maturity, acquiring spouses for them at the appropriate time, and inculcating in them strong emotional attachments and a compelling sense of obligation and duty to their parents.

Care for the aged is seen as ideally taking place in the context of a multigenerational family, which is initially formed when a wife is brought into the household for a young man by his parents. If a couple has daughters, but no sons, they may seek a young man who is willing to join their household as a resident son-in-law. In either case, the young married couple is not expected to set up an independent home of their own, but to remain, at least for a number of years after their marriage, and ideally until the parents' death, part of a larger household, contributing their labor (and their income, if any) to the family pool.

These cultural expectations for meeting one's needs in old age within an extended family contribute to the continued persistence into the contemporary period of a system of arranged marriages. In spite of the increasing incidence in recent years, especially among the educated elite, of so-called "love marriages," the extent to which most young people have the opportunity to choose their own spouse—or to choose to remain single—is extremely small. Parental arrangement of the marriages of their offspring is an important mechanism ensuring that few men, and virtually no women, fail to marry. Today in India almost all females, and most males, are married

TABLE 4.1

Marital Status of Persons 60 Years of Age and Over, 1881–1971

(Percentage of total in age–sex category)

		NEVER-MARRIED	MARRIED	WIDOWED	DIVORCED/ SEPARATED*
1881	M	3.2	69.3	27.5	–
	F	.5	14.9	84.4	–
1891	M	2.8	68.7	28.5	–
	F	.8	14.3	84.9	–
1901	M	3.9	66.9	29.2	–
	F	1.2	16.3	82.5	–
1911	M	3.8	66.0	30.2	–
	F	1.2	15.8	83.0	–
1921	M	3.7	64.1	32.2	–
	F	1.2	17.4	81.4	–
1931	M	3.2	64.6	32.2	–
	F	1.0	18.8	80.2	–
1941**		NA	NA	NA	–
1951***	M	3.1	70.0	26.9	–
	F	1.0	33.4	65.6	–
1961	M	2.9	69.1	27.4	.6
	F	.4	23.7	75.4	.5
1971	M	2.4	74.7	22.4	.5
	F	.4	30.0	69.2	.4

Source: Census of India, 1921, 1931, 1951, 1961, 1971.

  *Divorced and separated persons are reported as "widowed" in Census tables through 1951.

 **Figures on age and marital status were not published in the Census of India, 1941.

***Due to differences in the manner of tabulating age and marital status data in the 1951 Census, figures in this row apply to persons 55 and over, and are based on a 10 percent sample of the population.

TABLE 4.2
Sex Ratio of Population 60 Years and Over, 1881-1971
(Males per 100 females)

1881	1891	1901	1911	1921	1931	1941	1951	1961	1971
81.4	82.0	83.9	88.5	92.6	95.6	97.2	97.3	100.0	106.6

Source: Calculated after S. B. Mukherjee, *The Age Distribution of the Indian Population: A Reconstruction for the States and Territories, 1881-1961* (Honolulu: East-West Center, 1976), Basic Table 1.

by the age of thirty. This pattern of universal marriage is probably of great antiquity, and census figures attest to it from 1881 to the present. The trend, in fact, has even been for a slight decline in the numbers of never-married persons over the age of thirty during the past century. The reasons for this trend are probably demographic rather than a matter of changing marriage norms (see tables 4.1, 4.2, and 4.3).

An early age at first marriage is another concomitant of the traditional Indian family system. There is no strong impediment to legitimizing a youthful union when a couple's emotional maturity or their ability to be self-supporting are not at issue. Nor must one wait until a share of the parental estate can be handed over to the children, as in societies in which readiness to marry presupposes readiness to live independent of parental support and direction. While there is, of

TABLE 4.3
Marital Status at Various Ages, 1971*
(Percentage of age group)

Age Group	NEVER-MARRIED		MARRIED		WIDOWED		DIVORCED/SEPARATED	
	M	F	M	F	M	F	M	F
10-14	95.31	88.24	4.49	11.53	0.04	0.05	0.01	0.04
15-19	81.42	43.70	18.11	55.41	0.18	0.33	0.09	0.44
20-24	49.90	9.52	49.02	88.83	0.58	0.88	0.32	0.71
25-29	18.62	2.29	79.45	94.95	1.25	1.94	0.54	0.76
30-34	6.97	1.02	90.38	94.06	1.99	4.09	0.56	0.79
35-39	4.02	0.78	92.71	91.35	2.66	7.03	0.53	0.80

Source: Census of India, 1971
*In the 1971 Census, all persons under age 10 were assumed to be never-married.

course, a religious justification for strikingly low marriage ages in India (especially for females), this is a phenomenon which is clearly deeply embedded in the structure of the traditional domestic economy. In historical perspective, there has been a distinct rise in the average age of marriage since 1881, and this trend is most marked for females. But it is largely due to a fairly sharp decline since the 1930s in the incidence of infant and child marriage, as a result of government fiat.[3] It is still customary throughout India to begin making arrangements for the marriage of a daughter around or shortly after the onset of puberty (see table 4.4).

It should be clear from the foregoing that in the Indian context marriage strategies are best viewed as strategies pursued by the parents of young men and women, rather than by the young people themselves, although obviously what the parents perceive to be the interests of their son or daughter are taken into account in their decision. But such matters as the timing of the marriage—within the young person's own life course, on the one hand, and with reference to the marriages of others in the sibling group, on the other—are often best understood within the context of a set of goals and motivations held by the parental generation. An important component of these motivations is preparation for the parents' old age security; other more immediate motives may be financial (for marriages involve substantial transfers of cash and goods between the families of a marrying pair), or relate to current labor requirements in the household or to less pragmatic emotional or religious purposes.

As a consequence of these marriage patterns, an older person in India is not only almost certain to have been married himself, but also to have had the opportunity to see that his children—if any—have made matches suitable in terms of his own desires and needs,

TABLE 4.4
Mean Age at Marriage for Decade, Synthetic Cohorts, 1891–1971

	1891–1901	1901–1911	1911–1921	1921–1931	1931–1941	1941–1951	1951–1961	1961–1971
Male*	21.01	20.44	20.74	18.45	20.34	19.93	21.76	22.70
Female**	12.77	13.04	13.52	12.50	14.39	15.38	15.43	17.20

Source: S. N. Agarwala, *India's Population Problems,* 2nd ed. (Bombay: Tata McGraw-Hill, 1977), Table 6.3.
*For those married up to age 50.
**For those married up to age 35.

including his needs for security and care in old age. The same, of course, applies to the older woman.

Today well over 97 percent of Indians over sixty years of age are either currently married or widowed (table 4.1). This total has risen only slightly since a century ago, but the relative proportions in each marital status have altered appreciably during this period, as I shall discuss below. The number of persons of any age group reported in the Census of India as divorced or separated is extremely small. For aged women it is about the same as the number of never-married, namely .4 percent of the total. Figures on the divorced and separated have in fact been tabulated separately from those on the widowed only since 1961. In the absence of a comprehensive system of marriage registration in India, it is impossible to determine actual divorce rates, and there is considerable evidence of underreporting in the Census because of the strong cultural stigma attaching to the divorced person. Only since 1955 has there even been a legal provision, on an all-India basis, for the formal dissolution of a Hindu marriage, and court records indicate that there has been relatively little resort to this law since its inception.[4] It is clear, however, from sociological surveys and the ethnographic record that broken unions are quite infrequent in India by Western standards. However, the informal separation of elderly parents between the homes of different sons is a not uncommon solution to the problem of apportioning the responsibility for support among one's offspring—and perhaps incidentally to problems of marital incompatibility between elderly spouses. The partners to such arrangements do not, of course, show up in census statistics as separated or divorced, and it is impossible to know whether or not this observed phenomenon is of recent development.

Just as in Western industrial countries, most elderly widowed persons are women, and this has been so as long as we have records to document it. While almost 70 percent of Indian women today in the over-sixty age cohort are currently widowed, only one quarter of their male peers are in the same status. Over the span of time with which we are concerned, the trend has been toward an increase in the relative numbers of persons of both sexes who are still married in the sixth decade of life and beyond, but the differences between the sexes are still very large.

Most striking is the fact that, even in the seventy-and-over age cohort, over 60 percent of males still have a living spouse. In Europe and in the United States today, a major reason for a parallel difference in the incidences of widowhood and widowerhood among the aged is the markedly longer life-expectancy of women, which contributes to a highly unbalanced sex ratio in their favor at the older ages. The situation in India is quite different. In fact, despite lower survival rates for males than for females starting in late middle age, men continue to outnumber women in every age cohort up to the age of eighty. It is of particular historical interest—and, to many, of concern—that rather than approaching a balance, or a more "normal" excess of women, India's sex ratio has, over the past one hundred years, been moving toward ever-increasing proportions of males relative to females, at all ages (see tables 4.2 and 4.5). This trend is especially marked in the elderly age cohorts, in which a century ago men were significantly outnumbered by women. While the reasons for this trend are not fully understood, it is doubtless related to cultural preferences which have ensured better care and nutrition for males than for females. In the past several decades of greatly improved public health conditions and a wider availability of modern medical treatment, it is apparent that these cultural dispositions have allowed the male population to benefit disproportionately.

Certain cultural factors help to explain the much higher incidence of widowhood among elderly Indian women than of widowerhood among men. First, there is the usual age difference between husband

TABLE 4.5
Sex Ratio for India and Major Zones, 1881-1971
(Males per 100 females)

	ALL-INDIA	EASTERN	CENTRAL	SOUTHERN	WESTERN	NORTHERN
1881	103.8	99.2	108.7	99.5	105.4	118.6
1891	103.9	98.8	107.0	99.3	105.2	114.9
1901	102.8	99.0	105.2	99.4	103.1	114.6
1911	103.7	99.9	107.0	99.2	104.2	117.0
1921	104.6	101.5	107.9	99.8	105.5	117.2
1931	105.2	103.4	108.2	100.0	105.7	115.9
1941	105.7	105.2	108.1	100.8	105.7	114.8
1951	105.6	105.8	108.0	100.5	105.9	113.2
1961	106.2	105.9	108.5	101.4	106.7	113.6
1971	107.5	107.3	111.3	102.2	107.3	113.0

Source: S. B. Muhkerjee, *The Age Distribution of the Indian Population: A Reconstruction for the States and Territories, 1881-1961* (Honolulu: East-West Center, 1976), Table 7.12 and Basic Table 1.

and wife, which is significant in first marriages, and even greater, on the average, in subsequent unions. This disparity has been somewhat reduced over the past one hundred years, but is still significant (see table 4.4). Furthermore, men who lose a spouse are far more likely than are widows to remarry. While there are no all-India figures to substantiate this, a recent survey in some rural communities in northern India has shown, for example, a remarriage rate for widowed males of 61 percent. Rates were far higher for those whose wives had died when they were in their youth or middle age. Since the sample included current widowers, it is to be expected that the rate of eventual remarriage among these men would be even higher than that reported in this study (see table 4.6).[5]

Widows do not remarry at anything approaching male rates, although the limited quantitative evidence we do have demonstrates that the common impression that widows in India are universally condemned either to die on the funeral pyre of their husbands (by the practice of ritual suicide, *sati*) or to remain forever celibate, is misleading and greatly exaggerated.[6] Orthodox Hinduism does prescribe lifelong chastity for widows, even for those whose husbands may have died before consummating their marriages. Among the higher castes severe disabilities were imposed on widows in the past, restricting their participation in ritual and social activities and enforcing an ascetic life-style, and to some extent these continue today. However, those castes which adhere to the orthodox proscription against widow remarriage nowhere make up more than a minority of the population.[7] The Muslim religion does not set up any religious or cultural barriers to the remarriage of widows, and most Hindu castes have in fact traditionally permitted widows to remarry as well, particularly if they are young and have no children. In many low and middle-ranking castes, widows in their

TABLE 4.6
Remarriage of Widowers in Six Villages of North India

TOTAL MALES IN SAMPLE	NUMBER EVER WIDOWERED	PERCENTAGE REMARRIED BY AGE AT WIDOWERHOOD			
		Under 30	*30–40*	*Over 40*	*All Ages*
1386	318	91	85	10	61

Source: S. N. Agarwala, *A Demographic Study of Six Urbanising Villages* (Bombay: Asia Publishing House, 1970), pp. 77–78.

reproductive years are almost routinely remarried, often to a brother or other close male relative of the deceased.[8]

Table 4.7 shows the results of several studies of widow remarriage rates in different parts of India. More detailed data in these studies show that age at widowhood is a key variable. For example, in his survey of Hindu women in Delhi area villages, Agarwala found that 94.4 percent of those widowed at fourteen years of age and under, and 87.5 percent of those widowed between the ages of fifteen and nineteen, had remarried. On the other hand, no woman past the age of forty-five had done so.[9] Furthermore, his data show that a widow with no children, or with only one child, is far more likely to remarry than is one with several children.[10] Of course, the variables of age at widowhood and number of children are closely associated, but the author does not provide sufficient information to enable one to separate out their independent effects on rates of remarriage.

CHILDBEARING AND OLD-AGE SECURITY

Childbearing in India tends to begin very shortly after cohabitation commences, and to continue thereafter over a relatively

TABLE 4.7
Widow Remarriage in India

LOCALE	NUMBER OF EVER-MARRIED FEMALES	NUMBER OF EVER-WIDOWED	PERCENTAGE REMARRIED OF EVER-WIDOWED
Western India (rural) [1]	10,420	3,131	25.7
Delhi (rural) [2]	1,447	255	40.9
Rohtak (rural) [3]	2,903	380	25.3
Mathura (rural) [3]	2,382	331	18.7
Saharanpur (rural) [3]	3,526	453	34.2
Madhya Pradesh (rural) [4]	252	80	45.0

Sources: 1. K. Dandekar, "Widow Remarriages in Rural Communities in Western India," *Medical Digest* 30 (1962): 69–78.
2. S. N. Agarwala, *A Demographic Study of Six Urbanising Villages* (Bombay: Asia Publishing House, 1970), pp. 77–78.
3. S. N. Agarwala, *India's Population Problems*, 2nd ed. (Bombay: Tata McGraw-Hill, 1977), pp. 116–118.
4. B. R. Dubey, "Widow Remarriage in Madhya Pradesh," *Man in India* 45 (1965): 50–52.

lengthy span of years, with large birth intervals in comparison with those typical of the industrial West.[11] The length of the typical period of active childbearing in India has important implications, not only for the couple's ability to provide themselves with adequate numbers of potential caretakers in their old age, but also for the overall profile of the individual and family life cycles in India. As Collver has so clearly demonstrated, the Indian family cycle is not clearly divided into distinct stages, as it is in the United States and Western Europe, but is rather "a continuous flow, with little to mark off the transition from one stage to another. Each stage of life . . . overlaps the previous one. . . ."[12] In the contemporary Western industrial setting, siblings, their births having been close together and concentrated within the early years of their parents' marriage, tend themselves to marry within a relatively compact time period and to leave their parents for a distinct and fairly long "empty nest" phase, before it eventually becomes necessary for the parents to become dependents, in turn, of their adult children. In India, on the other hand, there is commonly no clear break between the phases of childrearing and dependent old age. While a man in his sixties may have adolescent grandchildren, he frequently also has unmarried sons and daughters dependent upon him for support and requiring to be educated and married off.

Students of Indian fertility patterns, and of family planning efforts in India, generally agree that an important factor in India's high rate of fertility is the positive desire for children—and particularly for sons—both to meet current labor force needs in the family production unit and to ensure shelter and support for themselves in old age.[13] As one would expect in a society in which one depends on one's grown children to provide care in old age, couples childless by design are almost unknown in India. The natural sterility rate is also very low, insofar as it is possible to determine this on the basis of sample fertility studies, and compares very favorably with that of Western industrial countries. A comparison of a number of studies which cite the incidence of childlessness in women in predominantly rural samples in different parts of India provides estimates ranging from a low of 1.3 percent to a high of 7.5 percent of women with completed fertility who have had no live-born children.[14]

Furthermore, fertile couples whose marriages remain intact until the woman reaches menopause tend to have many children. For example, in the course of a long-term study of fertility patterns in a rural area of northwestern India, Wyon and Gordon found an average completed family size of 7.5, with a range of from zero to eighteen live births. Other studies report figures very close to this.[15]

It might appear from these data, then, that most people in India could without difficulty arrange for their old age security through childbearing. But this would not take into account the matter of survival—not only the survival of whatever children are born to a couple, but survival of the spouses themselves to the time when sufficient children of the appropriate sex have been born to ensure a home for the remaining parent in old age. While tables 4.1, 4.8, and 4.9 confirm that over the past century the likelihood that a couple will jointly survive to the end of the woman's reproductive period has steadily increased, it has, nevertheless, been estimated that even in the contemporary period more than half of all marriages in India are broken by the death of one of the pair before the wife reaches the end of her fecund period.[16]

Uncertainties of this sort make it difficult to establish very precisely what the typical Indian man's or woman's chances for old age security actually are, in terms of his or her likelihood of being able to bear and raise children to adulthood, who will in turn survive at least until the time of the parents' deaths. It is even more difficult, if not impossible, to estimate this historically, although an examination of age-specific mortality trends would clearly confirm the impression that over the past century, at least, the potential for attaining this form of old age security has on the average dramatically improved.

Some attention has been given in the literature on Indian fertility to the question of "son survivorship," in the context of attempts to find an explanatory model for existing high levels of fertility in India,

TABLE 4.8
Expectation of Life at Birth, Age 10 and Age 50, 1881–1971

	BIRTH		AGE 10		AGE 50	
	M	F	M	F	M	F
1881	23.67	25.58	34.00	33.42	13.93	14.96
1891	24.59	25.54	35.46	34.40	14.28	15.59
1901	23.63	23.96	34.73	33.86	13.59	14.50
1911	22.59	23.32	33.36	33.74	13.97	14.28
1921	19.40	20.90	29.60	29.20	14.30	15.00
1931	26.91	26.36	36.38	33.61	14.31	14.65
1941	32.10	31.40	41.20	38.60	17.80	18.20
1951	32.45	31.66	38.97	39.45	14.89	16.15
1961	41.89	40.55	45.21	43.78	16.45	17.46
1971	46.40	44.70	48.80	47.70	19.20	19.70

Source: Census of India, 1971.

TABLE 4.9

Birth and Death Rates for India, France, Sweden, United States, and Great Britain—1901, 1941, 1961

		1901		1941		1961	
		Male	Female	Male	Female	Male	Female
INDIA	BR	49.00	47.00	45.00	45.00	44.00	45.00
	DR	49.00	45.00	32.00	33.00	25.00	27.00
FRANCE	BR	22.65	21.09	16.49	14.64	19.03	17.17
	DR	21.74	19.57	17.21	14.37	11.91	10.76
SWEDEN	BR	28.20	25.43	16.32	15.20	14.48	13.56
	DR	16.63	15.78	11.22	11.06	10.36	9.26
UNITED	BR	23.62	23.22	18.54	17.60	24.59	22.74
STATES	DR	12.91	12.04	11.87	9.41	10.85	7.97
GREAT	BR	30.05	27.06	17.24	13.11	18.70	16.53
BRITAIN	DR	18.11	15.79	15.69	11.81	12.46	11.20

Source: S. B. Mukherjee, *The Age Distribution of the Indian Population: A Reconstruction for the States and Territories, 1881–1961* (Honolulu: East-West Center, 1976), Table 9.9.

and for the failure of most family planning programs to achieve notable success. For example, using available mortality estimates for India as a whole, May and Heer have determined through computer simulation that the average Indian mother must bear five children if the couple is to be 95 percent certain that one son will survive until the father's sixty-fifth birthday. [17]

In order for such calculations to be usefully applied to the problem of clarifying the current and past demographic pictures for those hoping to be able to rely upon a male child or children for support in old age, the question must be phrased in another way. Given present (or past) conditions of fertility and mortality, what proportions of old people in India do (or did at some particular time in the past) have a son available to support them? There have been some computer simulations which are methodologically suggestive: for example, assuming zero population growth, or a population with a very low rate of increase, Wrigley has determined that only 60 percent of families, under typical "preindustrial" mortality conditions, would have a male heir. [18] To use such a model for contemporary India would, of course, require adjusting the assumptions to a regime of rapidly increasing population growth and far lower mortality rates.

Two recent fertility studies provide data for small samples of rural Indians which are suggestive of the prevalence of sonlessness in old age in this society. Collver, using data from a sample survey of 2,380 couples in sixty villages in northern India, found that "despite the high rate of reproduction [mean completed family size of 6.1 for *all* women forty-five and over], 22 percent of all parents reached the end of the reproductive period without a living son."[19] And in another study of a much smaller rural sample, Montgomery provides longitudinal data on the marital and reproductive histories of 119 men of three generations in a Karnataka village. Of those in the original group of 72 men of senior generation who themselves survived to marriageable age—and did marry—25 percent never had a son, and 31 percent had no living son by the time of the study in 1969. A similar pattern was found in the second generation, although some of the wives of the latter men were still in their reproductive years when the survey was undertaken.[20]

It would be important, in trying to calculate an Indian parent's chances of being survived by a child now, or in the past, to distinguish between males and females, since a childless—or sonless—man has the option of remarriage, while a childless married woman does not. A couple's infertility tends to be blamed on the woman's inability to conceive; rarely is it contemplated that the husband may be sterile. Thus a man who finds himself, after a number of years of marriage with no living children, commonly tries to achieve fatherhood with another woman, either abandoning his present wife or simply bringing an additional wife into his household, in a polygamous union.[21]

Adoption or fosterage is another option for a childless man—and under certain circumstances to the childless widow as well—who is concerned about old age security. According to traditional Hindu law only males could be formally adopted, although the Hindu Adoption and Maintenance Act of 1956 permits the adoption of girls as well. But regardless of the modern official legal position on the matter, it is in practice extremely rare in India for females—of any religion—to be adopted. As Goody has pointed out, adoption may serve one of two primary social functions: to provide a home for an orphan or to provide an heir—and a home in old age—for childless parents.[22] In India, although orphaned children are typically taken into the home of relatives on an informal basis, the formal institution of adoption is traditionally intended to serve the needs of sonless men for heirs—to inherit property, to perform the prescribed death rituals and thereafter make annual ancestral offerings, and to provide a home and care for the adoptive father (and mother) in their old age.

The choice of an adoptee is almost always made within the circle of a man's close relatives and often involves a boy or young man whose own parents are still living. Other things being equal, a patrilineal relative, such as a brother's son, is usually preferred. However, a sister's son may be chosen, or a daughter's son, or nephew of the wife. Consistent with the primary motives of adoption, it is not uncommon for the adoptee to be an adult or a young man in late adolescence. In such cases an explicit bargain may be struck between adopter and adoptee: the latter agrees to reside with and "serve" his adoptive parents until their death, in return for an eventual inheritance. To adopt a grown man is clearly an option most readily available to those with an independent source of income. Otherwise, a couple can more effectively arrange to take in a small child and socialize him as they would a son of their own, inclining him to remain with them and care for them in old age out of love and a sense of obligation.

FAMILY STRUCTURE AND LIVING ARRANGEMENTS OF THE ELDERLY

I have outlined the prevailing cultural expectations for old age within Indian society, and the social and demographic constraints within which an individual must operate in order to realize them. Now I will turn to a discussion of what we know about the actual — as opposed to the ideal — patterns of family organization in India, and about their implications for the living situations of older people in that society.

Much of the large body of sociological and anthropological research on Indian family structure which has been carried out during the past three decades has focused on the hypothesis that the traditional Indian "joint family" is in the process of disintegrating under the impact of modernization, industrialization, and urbanization. Replacing it, according to this hypothesis, is a system of predominantly nuclear families, on the Western European and American pattern.[23] Although, for the most part, students of the Indian family have not directly addressed the issue of the welfare of the elderly in the context of the changing family, it is clear that if the pattern of change were as postulated, increasing numbers of older people must now be living alone, with a spouse, or with unmarried children, rather than with married sons and grandchildren. In fact, however, the results of many studies of rural communities and surveys of urban and suburban sample populations have failed to support the hypothesis of a marked decline in the incidence of extended family households, and have instead documented the fact that the extended family system is alive and well among many different segments of the Indian population. Firm conclusions about historical trends have been impossible to draw because of the difficulty of establishing a satisfactory base line in comparable data for measuring change over any significant span of time. We are limited for all practical purposes to considering in this context only the contemporary period, for there is very little information of a quantitative kind on Indian household composition prior to the past twenty-five or thirty years. Here even the Indian Census reports are not very helpful, for the information they present on households does not, in most Census years, go beyond figures on average household size, and on numbers of men and women of each marital status per household. In the 1951 and 1961 Censuses, in contrast to earlier years, respondents from a special sample group were classified in terms of their relationship to the head of their household. But family members other than spouse, son, and daughter of head are listed only by sex and (in 1961) by marital status. In none of the household tables are the data broken down by age of respondent.

Household size certainly bears some relationship to the degree of complexity of household composition. All other things being equal, one would expect to find households of larger average size in a society in which it was customary for parents and other elderly relatives to share a household with adult offspring and grandchildren. Furthermore, any decline in the prevalence of such a system might be expected to be reflected in smaller households, on the average. It has been noted, however, that—contrary to popular beliefs about the supposed breakdown of the traditional Indian family system in the wake of industrialization—Census figures provide no evidence either of a decline in average household size in India since the late nineteenth century—this has remained close to five persons throughout—or of a decrease in the numbers of married and widowed males per household. In fact, in most regions of the country both indices have shown a slight rise during the period.[24] One might be tempted to conclude from this that there has been in fact little change in the structure of the Indian household over the past century, and that, concomitantly, living arrangements for older people in India have probably remained essentially unchanged. However, there are so many pitfalls in trying to use data on household size to make deductions about household composition, so many factors other than changing patterns of residence for the elderly which may influence household size, and so many problems with the interpretation of the household data provided in the Census, that it is impossible to be at all confident of the validity of such a conclusion.[25]

As for Census data on relationship to head of household, it is certainly possible to derive from these some estimates of the prevalence of complex or extended, households in India, and to generalize to some extent about regional variations. But no historical speculation is possible because of the recency of the inclusion of this datum in the special sample Census. Those households which include "married sons" and "married daughters" of the head clearly conform structurally to some kind of extended family pattern in which parents are coresiding with their married offspring, and many of those households with "other married males or females" may be assumed to be made up of a couple with the husband's (or wife's) aging parents. But it is of course impossible even to begin to estimate on a national basis from these figures what proportions of elderly *persons* live with married offspring, how many live with a spouse and/or with unmarried children, and how many live alone. The only thing we can say which is of relevance here is that these data show a great deal of regional variation, from one district and state of India to another, in the percentages of persons in the sample population who are classified as married relatives of the head of their respective households. For example, Kolenda's analysis shows a range from a high of 9 percent married sons and 31 percent other married relatives, to a low of 0.7 percent married sons and 5.6 other married relatives, according to district-wide figures. If these percentages are mapped, they show a clear belt of high incidence of complex households reaching across northern India, and two distinct and widely separated areas of low incidence, in the far northeastern hill area and along the southwest coast.[26] Such evidence of regional variation in the prevalence of complex households would lead one to predict a parallel pattern of variation from one region of India to another in the extent to which aged parents are sheltered and cared for within the households of their adult sons. Future research on the situation of the aged in India might usefully choose to focus on this question of regional variation, attempting to establish its form and possible causes.

In recent years a small number of sociological studies have been published which deal specifically with the problems of the elderly in India, in terms of living arrangements, financial support, health, and social participation. For the most part these have been carried out in urban areas—one of the largest sample surveys of the elderly was undertaken in metropolitan Delhi, while others have been done in Bombay and in Lucknow in northern India. There is one fairly intensive study by an anthropologist of the aged in a village in southern India, and several brief reports of similar studies carried out in other rural communities in different parts of the country.[27] None of these studies is precisely comparable to the others, but most of them do include information on the family life of the elderly, and quantitative data on their living arrangements. As table 4.10 indicates, all of these studies have found a very high proportion of the elderly residing with relatives of some kind, comparatively few living alone, and only a negligible number living with nonkin. According to those studies for which detailed information is available, the preferred relatives are married sons: between 54.4 and 78 percent of the elderly in these samples live with these, while the remainder live either with the spouse alone, with a married daughter, with unmarried children, or with some other relative. It is by and large the younger segment of the elderly group who live with unmarried children, and most of those living with a spouse alone are the younger males. These commonly have wives who do not themselves fall into the "aged" category.

The percentages of elderly persons reported in these surveys to be living with married sons are not inconsistent with the provisional estimates from village studies cited above of from 22 to 31 percent of persons in their sixties having no surviving son. It may be suggested, then, that most of those persons who have sons probably do in fact reside with one or more of them. But in some of these studies considerably fewer than 70 percent of the aged are living with *married* sons. This may only mean the presence of significant numbers of older persons whose sons are still unmarried. But an alternative interpretation would suggest that, for some reason, up to one-third of those who could conceivably live with a married son do not do so. Furthermore, we cannot discount the possibility that the cited evidence on sonlessness provided from the above-mentioned fertility studies is not applicable to the samples of elderly persons surveyed here. We cannot choose definitively among these interpretations of the data because the relevant information about the sample

TABLE 4.10
Living Arrangements of the Elderly

	SAMPLE NUMBER	*PERCENTAGE OF TOTAL WHO ARE LIVING:*				
		Alone	*With Spouse Only*	*With Ever-Married Son*	*With Ever-Married Daughter*	*With All Relatives Combined*
Desai and Naik [1]	600	3.0	8.0	N.A.	N.A.	96.0
Soodan [2]	390	7.2	10.5	73.3	4.6	92.8
Marulasiddaiah [3]	154	13.6	10.4	64.9	3.9	86.4
Raj and Prasad [4]	327	7.6	N.A.	N.A.	N.A.	92.4
Bose and Saxena [5]	821	1.3	1.7	N.A.	N.A.	97.0
Delhi School of Social Work [6]	2,000	5.9	7.8	61.6	5.7	94.1
Vatuk [7]	59	0.0	3.4	78.0	3.4	100.0
Vatuk [8]	60	1.7	11.7	58.3	3.3	98.3
Vatuk [9]	57	5.3	0.0	54.4	1.8	94.7

Sources: 1. K. G. Desai and R. D. Naik, *Problems of Retired People in Greater Bombay* (Bombay: Tata Institute of Social Sciences, n.d.). Based on a sample of 573 male and 27 female retirees in the Bombay area—mostly over fifty-five years of age. See pp. 24–29, especially Table 4.4.

2. Kirpal Singh Soodan, *Aging in India* (Calcutta: Minerva Associates, 1975). A random area sampling of 214 male and 176 female residents of Lucknow, all over fifty-five years of age. See pp. 48–53, especially Table 3.7.

3. H. M. Marulasiddaiah, *Old People of Makunti* (Dharwar: Kamatak University, 1969). Total aged population, over fifty-five years old, in a Karnataka village, including eighty-one males and seventy-three females (pp. 102–114, Table 7).

4. B. Raj and B. G. Prasad, "A Study of Rural Aged Persons in Social Profile," *The Indian Journal of Social Work* 32 (1971): 155–162. A survey of 188 male and 139 female residents of three villages near Lucknow. Sample represents the total over-fifty population of these villages, less forty-one persons who refused to cooperate. See pp. 158–159, Table 5.

5. A. B. Bose and P. C. Saxena, "Characteristics of Aged Population in Rural Society," *Journal of Family Welfare (India)* 10, no. 4 (1964): 33–39. Twenty percent random sample of households in seventy-eight villages in Rajasthan, containing 459 male and 372 females over fifty-five years of age. See p. 36, especially Table 5.

6. Delhi School of Social Work, *A Study of the Aged in Delhi* (Delhi, University of Delhi, 1977). Random sampling, through voter registration lists, of 1,092 male and 908 female residents of metropolitan Delhi, all over sixty years of age.

TABLE 4.10 *(Continued)*

7. Unpublished data from a study of sixty-and-over native inhabitants of an urbanized village in the city of Delhi.
8. Unpublished data from a study of urbanization and family change in a white-collar neighborhood in Meerut, U.P., of residents sixty years of age and above. (See my *Kinship and Urbanization* [Berkeley, University of California Press, 1972] .
9. Unpublished data from a survey of aged persons, sixty years and over, in a village north of Delhi.

Note: The final column includes those who live with unmarried children or with other relatives, hence it is not in every case a total of the previous three columns.

populations on numbers of living offspring, their sex, and their marital status, is either not available or has not been published. This difficulty in interpretation highlights the importance in future studies of aging populations in India of including detailed fertility and marital histories and information on the survival and whereabouts of any offspring. Without the possibility of cross-referencing information on living arrangements with these kinds of data it is impossible to fully appreciate the significance of the reported residence patterns.

Despite these uncertainties, it is quite clear that all our evidence indicates that the overwhelming majority of older people in India live with relatives. The percentage of those living alone is quite small by Western standards. However, the various studies display a rather wide range of varation: from no residential isolates in the group of elderly former landowners in Delhi, to 13.6 percent of the aged in single-person households in the southern Indian village studied by Marulasiddaiah. The number of cases is small, and sample size in most cases is also small, but it seems likely that, as I have suggested above, this variation reflects real differences from one region and social group to another in terms of the extent to which elderly people are found to be living alone.

But the data from Marulasiddaiah's Karnataka village point up a serious problem in interpreting data of this kind on the living arrangements of the elderly. Generally in gerontological studies, as in the Census of India and in most sociological and anthropological studies of the Indian family, the convention is followed of defining the household in terms of the "cooking hearth." That is, a person is assigned to a household on the basis of his or her eating from a common stove with other people. One who prepares his or her own food, not shared with others on a regular basis, is considered to constitute a single-person household. For most purposes this kind of definition is consistent and reasonably adequate. But it may be misleading in studies of the aged to consider such a person as "living alone," when in fact he or she may share other household activities with, and live under the same roof as, his offspring or other relatives. The following passage from the Marulasiddaiah study illustrates this problem:

Mathada Sivamma is, for example, staying in a small room on the verandah of her house, and she cooks her food. Inside the house two of her sons are living separately with their wives and children, while another son . . . stays . . . across the street. . . . Sivamma gets her water with the help of her granddaughters. . . . She sweeps the floor, not only of her room, but of the entire verandah. She feeds her grandchildren with whatever she has cooked and she gets one dish or the other from her sons' families. She looks after the infants of her sons. Given these circumstances it becomes rather difficult to say that Sivamma is living alone.[28]

But the author goes on to say that, consistent with his definition of the household as coterminous with the cooking hearth, he will so classify her. Similar decisions, not so explicitly noted, certainly underlie the assignment of respondents to this category by other researchers as well.

Leaving aside this issue of what "living alone" actually means for the aged in the Indian context, we should place these data in perspective by pointing out that single-person households of any age cohort are in fact very rare in India. Whether one is dealing with rural or urban populations, they seldom total more than 10 percent of all households. For example, a review of twenty-six studies of family structure in various parts of India shows the percentage of single-person households to range between extremes of 1 and 14 percent. However, the percentage of *persons* living alone nowhere exceeds 3 percent.[29] Those who live alone fall by and large into one of two main categories: young unmarried males or married men living apart from their wives (these are especially prevalent in urban or industrial centers), or aged widows and widowers.

For example, Shah reports 33 persons living alone in the Gujarat village of Radhavanaj, out of a total of 1,305 inhabitants. Of these, 21 are "either old widows or widowers," and another is an elderly man separated from his wife. The rest are young or middle-aged men.[30] In a different kind of setting, Mukherjee's survey of five thousand households in West Bengal and Calcutta revealed a total of 815, or 13.4 percent, single-person households. Over four-fifths of those persons living alone were males; most were living apart from their families for employment reasons. The residentially isolated women were largely widows and divorcees, and—in contrast to the men—90 percent reported that they had no family.[31]

While an analysis of these and other reports on single-person households in India shows that, overall, males predominate among those persons who live alone, when we look at samples of *aged* persons, we find that this pattern of sex distribution is reversed. For example, according to the Delhi School of Social Work survey of two thousand persons over the age of sixty, well over half of the 117 persons living alone were women, even though males were more numerous in the total sample, as they are in this age group in the population at large.[32] Marulasiddaiah's rural data show an even more marked preponderance of women among his 21 residential isolates, only 2 of whom were men.[33] Marital status is of course also a key variable, and, as one would expect, the widowed account for most of those living alone. This is particularly true in the case of females, the bulk of whom are of course widows by this age. In the Delhi study almost all of the residentially isolated *women* were widowed, whereas close to one-half of the men living alone were either separated or divorced, or were currently married but with wives living elsewhere.[34] In Marulasiddaiah's village, similarly, 16 out of the 19 aged women living alone were widows.[35]

One would also expect that childlessness—or the absence of sons—would be positively associated with single living for the aged, but it is difficult to establish this empirically on the basis of the available published data. While only 61.6 percent of those in the total Delhi sample reportedly live with married sons, it is clear from the authors' discussion that a significant proportion of those in other living arrangements do have married sons who reside elsewhere, and/or have *unmarried* sons with whom they are currently living. Over one-half of the residential isolates have one or more living sons, and in some cases these sons support the respondent financially.[36] An indeterminate number of those with no sons have living daughters.

CONCLUSIONS

Putting all of these data together, what is it possible to say about the past and present situation of the aged in India, and about the impact of the various forces of modernization on their overall well-being? The demographic information relating to the aged—their life chances in terms of marriage, childbearing, survival of spouses and children, and the like—provides a basis for estimating trends over the past century in the ability of Indians to provide old age security for themselves in the traditionally expected manner. And recent research findings concerning family structure and living arrangements of the present-day elderly give us some notion of the extent to which, within these demographic constraints, the traditional forms of old age security operate in practice. Now I will try to relate these data to some of the theoretical assumptions underlying the thesis that the position of the aged declines under the impact of industrialization and urbanization.

We have seen that over the past century conditions of mortality have greatly improved in India, thus increasing the chances that an elderly person of either sex will have a living spouse, and that any children born to the couple will have survived to maturity. In this respect, the fundamental demographic conditions for the realization of the ideal three-generation extended family are significantly more favorable than they were in the past. On the other hand, declining mortality has also brought about a rapid increase in India's population, especially during the last several decades, so that the numbers of old people in the country have approximately tripled.

One of the demographic variables which has commonly been cited as having important consequences for the "social status" of older people is their numbers proportionate to the total population of the country or society in which they live. It has been suggested by one observer, for example, that

the number and proportion of older people are, in themselves, among the determinants of their role and prestige. In the little community, the scarcity value of older persons undoubtedly contributed to the age deference patterns which characterize it. In contrast, . . . [when] one in seven persons is 65 or older . . . the scarcity value of older people is lost, and their prestige is accordingly diminished.[37]

This hypothesis would seem, at least, consistent with current comparative modernization theory as applied to the historical development of the Western countries, for in Europe and the United States the advance of industrialization has gone hand in hand with the aging of the population. But it is not yet even testable for India at current levels of industrial growth, because the proportions of the elderly in the population have not increased markedly over the past one hundred years. In comparison with most industrialized countries, and even in comparison with many developing countries, India's is still a relatively young population (see figure 4.1). It is perhaps somewhat less generally realized that in historical perspective the age structure, overall, has changed very little since 1881 — as far back as we have documented evidence. The percentage

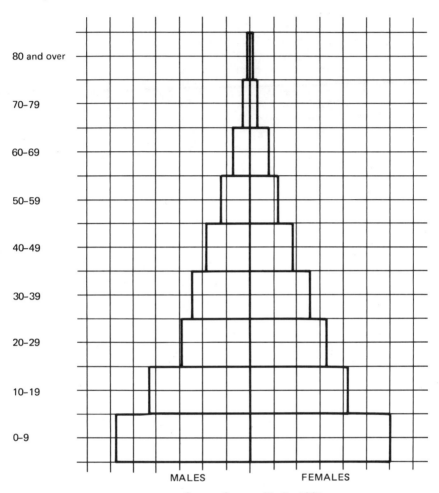

Source: Census of India, 1971.

of the population sixty years and over has risen over the past century by only .72 percent, from 5.25 percent of the total in 1881 to 5.97 percent in 1971, with periodic downward fluctuations in some of the intervening Census years (see table 4.11). This is so despite the dramatic increase in India's population from approximately 193 million in 1881 to almost 550 million in 1971, and despite notable advances in the reduction of mortality over this period (see tables 4.9 and 4.12).

TABLE 4.11
Percentage of Population 60 Years of Age
and Over, 1881–1971

	Male	Female	Total
1881	4.62	5.90	5.25
1891	4.63	5.86	5.23
1901	4.57	5.60	5.07
1911	4.83	5.67	5.24
1921	5.06	5.72	5.38
1931	4.87	5.36	5.11
1941	5.45	5.94	5.69
1951	5.28	5.73	5.50
1961	5.47	5.81	5.63
1971	5.94	5.99	5.97

Source: S. B. Mukherjee, *The Age Distribution of
the Indian Population: A Reconstruction for the
States and Territories, 1881–1961* (Honolulu: East-
West Center, 1976), Tables 1 & 2.

The nearly static age structure of India's population is primarily a consequence of consistently high rates of fertility (see table 4.9). Until these begin to drop markedly, and to remain low for a considerable period of time, the percentage of older persons in the population will not even begin to approach that of Western industrial nations.[38] And the prognosis for such a development within the next few decades is doubtful, even if current attempts to encourage the use of contraception and other methods of birth limitation begin to succeed dramatically. Therefore, it would seem reasonable to suggest that the kinds of social problems accompanying a shift in the dependency ratio to include relatively greater numbers of nonproductive older persons are not going to face India in the immediate future, and it is not to the age structure that we must look for the source of any present problems which may become evident in the course of our further investigations.

In view of the kinds of data we have access to, it is useful to compare rural and urban areas in India, under the assumption that some of the differences may indicate the differential impact of modernization between the two. However, we must be careful not to take a simplistic view in such a comparison, and to assume that the more severe impact of urbanization on the conditions of older people

TABLE 4.12
Population Growth, India, 1881–1971

	MALE	FEMALE	TOTAL	PERCENTAGE INCREASE
1881	98,646,260	94,962,339	193,608,600	
1891	118,892,784	114,429,444	233,322,228	20.5
1901	120,473,501	117,041,255	237,513,756	1.8
1911	127,925,442	123,241,471	251,166,913	5.8
1921	128,112,399	122,319,293	251,431,692	.1
1931	142,598,899	135,452,234	278,051,113	10.6
1941	162,986,100	154,055,800	317,041,900	14.0
1951	183,263,837	173,523,462	356,787,299	12.5
1961	225,989,740	212,664,033	438,653,773	23.0
1971	283,936,614	264,013,195	547,949,809	24.9

Source: S. B. Mukherjee, *The Age Distribution of the Indian Population: A Reconstruction for the States and Territories, 1881–1961* (Honolulu: East-West Center, 1976), Basic Table 1.

should be observed within the urban areas. Some of the evidence in fact suggests the contrary. The aged population is more heavily concentrated in rural than in urban localities—the latter defined by the Census of India as places of over five thousand population. While in the country as a whole just under 6 persons out of every 100 were sixty years of age or over in 1971, in rural areas 6.21 percent fell into this age group. Representation of the aged in urban places, on the other hand, was only 4.97 percent.[39] The difference is not very large, but it is a difference which is consistent in direction throughout, and is probably, therefore, significant. In fact, if we disaggregate these data by district, the differences in some parts of the country, particularly those containing large urban centers, are revealed to be far greater than the aggregate ones.

The most important reason for such a pattern of rural-urban contrast in age structure is age-selective migration from the villages to urban areas. For example, Connell and his colleagues, reporting on the findings of surveys of sixteen northern Indian villages in the 1950s and 1960s, show that 60 percent of all adult emigrants were between the ages of fifteen and thirty. In twelve of these villages there were no out-migrants at all in the sixty-and-over age group.[40] Furthermore, not only do the young leave rural areas in larger numbers than do their elders, but return migration by older persons who have spent their working life in the city is a common phenomenon. Rural-urban migration in India is also highly sex-selective: migrants are predominantly either unmarried young men, or married men who leave their wives behind in the village home. There is some regional variation in this respect: migration of women, with or without the male members of their families, is more prevalent in southern India, for example, than in the north, doubtless primarily for cultural reasons having to do with the overall status of women in these different areas of the country. In the northern Indian villages surveyed by Connell *et al.*, emigration was 88 percent male.[41] Female out-migration for purposes other than marriage was somewhat greater than this in the Punjab villages surveyed by Wyon and Gordon, but males still outnumbered females three to two. The greatest net loss to migration from these villages was in the category of males fifteen to twenty-four years of age, while over the age of forty-five, there was no appreciable loss of population to migration among either sex.[42]

For these reasons, it is in the rural areas, rather than in the cities, that one might expect to begin to see the earliest sociological effects of an aging of the population pyramid in India. Not only are there relatively more older people in village India, but—because of the predominantly young male composition of the out-migrating groups—these old people are being left behind by those whose responsibility it is, ideally, to live with and care for them. And yet there is no clear evidence from the figures we have on family organization and living arrangements that residential isolation and/or abandonment of the old has become, or is becoming, a significant phenomenon, numerically, in rural India. The family literature I have referred to above does not reveal a clear and consistent pattern of rural–urban differences in the incidence of "joint" and nuclear family households, nor does the limited information in the Census of India indicate any observable changes over time in the more indirect indices of family structure, namely household size and composition. Most surveys of household composition which include rural and urban samples from the same general cultural region have revealed proportions of complex households in each setting which are within the range of variation of one another. Similarly, the studies of living arrangements of the elderly which I have reviewed do not show any clear relationship either way, between level of urbanization of the community surveyed and incidence of older people living alone. The community with the highest frequency of residentially isolated older persons, as cited in table 4.10, is a rural village, but there is no *consistent* pattern of this kind for the remaining samples. Certainly this does not mean that no such process is under way, and the extent to which it is occurring—and what the ultimate outcome will be—is still an open question for future field research.

However, we know a number of things about contemporary Indian family organization which may help to explain why such a pattern does not show up very clearly, if at all, in the available statistics on living arrangements of the elderly. First, when sons migrate to urban areas, it is usual—if there are two or more sons—for at least one to remain in the village. Furthermore, even if all sons migrate, their wives—or at least one wife—will typically be left in the village, not only to care for the elderly parents, but to enable the sons to save money for the family as a whole and to protect their wives and children from the "unwholesome" conditions and influences of city life. Other accommodations are also being made to mitigate the effects of migration on elderly rural parents: for example, it is common for those who reach a point where they are unable to live alone to join the urban household of their son at an advanced age. Or elderly parents will split up, each moving in with a different son (who may be located in different cities or towns away from the home village). Some old persons are "shared" among their sons, spending several months in the home of each. Clearly these novel arrangements create very different social and psychological environments for the old person who—in "traditional" times—would have expected to have his sons living in *his* home, or close by, for all of their adult lives. But they do not have a noticeable impact on the kinds of statistics that are collected and published on family living arrangements. Households formed in these new ways conform outwardly in structure and composition to the traditional "joint family" pattern, even though internally the assignment of social roles and the balance of power and authority relations have been altered drastically. The implications of this kind of social change for the quality of life of the elderly cannot effectively be measured by quantitative analysis alone—and without considerably more refined techniques of data collection and analysis will not even become evident as social phenomena in need of explanation.

The evidence I have been able to gather together here seems to suggest that traditional cultural arrangements for old age security continue—even under rapidly changing social and economic conditions—to provide fairly adequately for the shelter and support needs of most aged Indians, within a family setting. Individual life development strategies continue, by and large, to be constructed in terms of the cultural expectation that a son is the appropriate provider of old age security. However, even though the majority of older Indians find a place in old age with their sons and daughters-in-law, there are many who can not do so. Among the latter are certain categories of elderly people who seem to be especially vulnerable in this social system to insecurity and even isolation and destitution. Unmarried persons are one such category, although their numbers are not large. Almost all never-married persons in the aged cohorts are males, and the typical solution for them is to attach themselves to the family of a brother or agnatic nephew; this is usually done long before old age commences. However, old bachelors, particularly among the poorer segments of the population, are certainly at high risk of being obliged to live alone.

Widowed persons are also a vulnerable category, although many, of course, have adult children to assume the responsibilities of their care just as if their spouse were still alive. Among these, it is the widowed *woman* who seems, from the evidence cited, to be most exposed to the likelihood of residential isolation in old age. Whether this apparent circumstance is simply a reflection of the fact that most widowed persons are females, or whether there is a real difference between widows and widowers in their relative ability to make arrangements for a secure old age, is something I have not been able to determine from the evidence available. One thing is clear, at least from the results of the Delhi study: that the available alternatives for widowed males and females, in terms of living arrangements, are somewhat different. In the Delhi sample, as many as 10 percent of all widows lived by themselves (even though half of these had living sons). Furthermore, in spite of cultural norms prescribing that a widow remain with her husband's family after his death, this study shows only three sonless widows to be living with relatives of their late husband. The rest resided either with a married daughter, with their own brother or sister, with grandchildren, or alone. Men in the same situation were most likely to be living with a brother or other patrilineal kinsman. Few sonless widowers lived with daughters, even if they had daughters. These data point up the somewhat anomalous position in Indian society of a woman who has no currently viable connection with a living male householder—either as daughter, wife, or dependent mother. A woman's rights to maintenance are in such a circumstance rather clearly specified in customary law, but inasmuch as she is by definition an economic dependent, if she has no male to enforce these rights for her she is at risk of being left to fend for herself. A man's rights, on the other hand, to ownership of a share in his patrimony, however meager, and therefore to a place in the family home, is virtually incontrovertible. Therefore, aging bachelors and widowers tend to remain with agnatic relatives, while widows may have to seek refuge—often grudgingly given—with natal kin or assume the shame of depending on a daughter, as the only viable alternatives to a solitary existence.

Women as a group are in overall terms more vulnerable to old age insecurity than are men, because they have a three-to-one chance of being bereft of a spouse by the time they reach sixty years of age, and as they grow older these chances rapidly multiply. Older men, on the other hand, generally have a younger wife to care for their needs. Furthermore, an older man who loses his spouse toward the latter years of his life is still eligible for remarriage and if he has any kind of resources can make such an arrangement for companionship and care in old age if he so wishes. An older man can adopt a young man to care for him, in return for a promise of an inheritance. A woman is seldom in a position to strike such a bargain, as she rarely owns property, and does not normally inherit it either from her father or husband. Furthermore, it is not customary, except among the poorest classes, for women to be employed outside of the home, and one who must support herself alone in old age has access only to the most marginal and menial of occupations. All of these culturally structured circumstances compound the woman's difficulties of providing for herself when the traditional mechanisms of old age support fail.

The evidence from these surveys of living arrangements of the elderly also suggests that, although most old persons *who have sons* find a place with them in old age, there are others who do not. There is no clear indication in any of these studies of a pattern in these failures for particular old people. In some cases, geographical mobility may be responsible: the relatively low percentage of old people living with married sons in the Delhi sample may reflect the movement of young men out of Delhi for employment purposes. (The hypothesis is given some support by the cited fact that some of the residentially isolated elderly persons are being supported financially by their married sons who live elsewhere.) But this is purely speculative, since we do not have sufficient information to test it. An intensive study of old persons who live alone should reward one with the discovery of certain social patterns in these variable circumstances, and with some further insight into the possible association of these phenomena with changing social conditions under India's modernization.

It would still be premature to conclude from what has been said that India's case generally supports the notion that the elderly there have had a secure and favored social status, and that this is changing slowly, if at all. The fact that most aged persons have been shown to be living with sons or other relatives does not necessarily mean that their overall status in society, or even their status within the family, is "high." Quantitative data on living arrangements and household structure cannot show what the quality of life is like in this setting, and cannot clarify the nature of the material and psychological deprivation, and the role conflicts, which the dependent older person may be subjected to, even within a cultural setting in which high value is placed on the display of respect and consideration for one's aged parents. While it is not possible to go into these issues in any detail here, there is considerable evidence in the literature that the reality is much less agreeable than the ideal. This is one area which, to my mind, should be emphasized in future investigations of the role of the aged in India.

Finally, in assessing the kinds of changes which have been and will be occurring in India with respect to the aged, one must also consider the impact of governmental policy for the provision of social services to the aged. Up to the present time, the guiding philosophy seems to have been to rely on the family to fulfill this function for its aged members, rather than, on any extensive scale, to replace the family or to supplement the resources of the family for supporting and sheltering the old and infirm. Economic constraints in this developing nation will certainly dictate continued adherence to this policy for many decades to come, and the family will therefore receive official encouragement to continue to provide for the aged according to the traditional mode. Few ready alternatives will be provided. While the context of such arrangements may indeed alter with changing social conditions, there does not seem to be any compelling evidence that the family in India is abandoning—or will soon begin to abandon—its responsibility for providing at least a minimal level of security for the aged as industrialization progresses.

NOTES

1. For some examples of statements of this theory, see L. W. Simmons, *The Role of the Aged in Primitive Society* (New Haven: Yale University Press, 1945); D. Cowgill and L. Holmes, eds., *Aging and Modernization* (New York: Appleton-Century-Crofts, 1972); and P. Laslett, "Societal Development and Aging," in R. Binstock and E. Shanas, eds., *Handbook of Aging and the Social Sciences* (New York: Van Nostrand Reinhold, 1976), pp. 89–92.

2. See my "Withdrawal and Disengagement as a Cultural Response to Aging in India," in C. Fry, ed., *Aging in Culture and Society,* (New York: J. Bergin, 1980),

pp. 126–148. Also "The Aging Woman in India: Self Perceptions and Changing Roles," in A. deSouza, ed., *Women in Contemporary India* (New Delhi: Manohar, 1975), pp. 142–163.

3. See the extended discussion in S. N. Agarwala, *Age at Marriage in India* (Allahabad: Kitab Mahal, 1962), and *India's Population Problems*, 2nd ed. (New Delhi: Tata, McGraw-Hill, 1977), pp. 87–105. Note in table 4.4 the marked, but temporary, decline in the mean marriage age in the 1931 Census. This was apparently due to the widespread rush to solemnize the marriages of children before the Child Marriage Restraint Act of 1929 took effect. It should also be noted that Census figures are not the best source of data on marriage age, since tables must be extrapolated from figures on marital status at various ages, and are therefore subject to inaccuracies in the reporting of current ages (and current marital status) in the Census. Furthermore, "married," for Census purposes, means that the respondent has undergone the formal marriage ceremony. Since the usual practice in India is for child brides to remain with their parents until physically mature, the age of effective marriage in India is in fact considerably higher than these figures would suggest.

4. For a full discussion of Hindu law pertaining to marriage and divorce, from earliest times to the present, see J. D. M. Derrett, *The Death of a Marriage Law: Epitaph for the Rishis* (Durham: Carolina Academic Press, 1978).

5. S. N. Agarwala, *A Demographic Study of Six Urbanising Villages* (Bombay: Asia Publishing House, 1970), pp. 77–78.

6. See, for example, a recent discussion of widowhood in cross-cultural perspective by H. Lopata, "Role Changes in Widowhood: A World Perspective," in Cowgill and Holmes, eds., *Aging and Modernization*, pp. 285–290.

7. The Committee on the Status of Women in India, in its *Report* (New Delhi: Dept. of Social Welfare, Government of India, 1974) estimates that in 1931 approximately 86 percent of the Hindu population belonged to castes in which widow remarriage was either allowed or preferred. Since the Census of India no longer provides data on caste membership, this estimate is of course only roughly applicable to present conditions. See the discussion, ibid., p. 77.

8. See, for example. B. R. Dubey, "Widow Remarriage in Madhya Pradesh," *Man in India* 45 (1965): 50–56; S. N. Agarwala, "Widow Remarriages in Some Rural Areas of Northern India," *Demography* 4 (1967): 126–134; Jean-Luc Chambard, "Mariages Secondaires et Foires aux Femmes en Inde Centrale," *L'Homme* 1, no. 2 (1961): 51–88.

9. Agarwala, *A Demographic Study of Six Urbanising Villages*, p. 83. See also the figures cited by John B. Wyon and John E. Gordon for a Punjab village, in which 60 percent of women widowed before the age of thirty-five remarried, and 50 percent of those widowed between thirty-five and forty did so. See *The Khanna Study: Population Problems in the Rural Punjab* (Cambridge, Mass.: Harvard University Press, 1971), pp. 164–165.

10. Agarwala, ibid., pp. 84–85.

11. A. Das Gupta et al., *Couple Fertility*, The National Sample Survey, No. 7 (New Delhi: Dept. of Economic Affairs, Government of India, 1955), pp. 48–53.

12. A. Collver, "The Family Cycle in India and the United States," *American Sociological Review* 28 (1963): 86.

13. For example, see M. Mamdani, *The Myth of Population Control* (New York: Monthly Review Press, 1972); D. Mandelbaum, *Human Fertility in India* (Berkeley: University of California Press, 1974), pp. 17–23; J. R. Rele, "Some Aspects of Family and Fertility in India," *Population Studies* 15 (1962): 8–9.

14. Wyon and Gordon, *Khanna Study*, pp. 163–164; Das Gupta, *Couple Fertility*, p. 45.

15. Wyon and Gordon, p. 161. See also F. Lorimer, *Culture and Human Fertility* (Paris: UNESCO, 1954), p. 31 and Das Gupta, *Couple Fertility*, p. 46.

16. Collver, "Family Cycle," p. 87.

17. D. A. May and D. M. Heer, "Son Survivorship Motivation and Family Size in India: A Computer Simulation," *Population Studies* 22 (1968): 199–210. See also, D. M. Heer and D. O. Smith, "Mortality Level, Desired Family Size, and Population Increase," *Demography* 5 (1968): 104–121; Heer and Smith, "Mortality Level, Desired Family Size and Population Increase: Further Variations on a Basic Model," *Demography* 6 (1969): 141–149; G. E. Immerwahr, "Survivorship of Sons under Conditions of Improving Mortality," *Demography* 4 (1967): 710–720; S. Krishnamoorthy, "Mortality Level, Desire for Surviving Son and Rate of Population Increase," *Population Studies* 33 (1979): 565–571.

18. E. A. Wrigley, "Fertility Strategy for the Individual and the Group," in C. Tilly, ed., *Historical Studies of Changing Fertility* (Princeton: Princeton University Press, 1978), pp. 135–153.

19. Collver, "Family Cycle," pp. 95–96.

20. E. Montgomery, "The Relationship between Natality and Family Form: A Case Study from Southern India," in J. F. Marshall and S. Polgar, eds., *Culture, Natality and Family Planning* (Chapel Hill: Carolina Population Center, 1976), pp. 53–54.

21. Although the Hindu Marriage Act of 1955 made polygyny illegal, this law is not well enforced and the practice continues, particularly in rural areas.

22. J. Goody, *Production and Reproduction: A Comparative Study of the Domestic Domain* (Cambridge: Cambridge University Press, 1976), p. 68.

23. See the reviews of the relevant literature in P. Kolenda, "Region, Caste, and Family Structure: A Comparative Study of the Indian 'Joint' Family," in M. Singer and B. Cohn, eds., *Structure and Change in Indian Society* (Chicago: Aldine, 1968). For a more current bibliography of published sources on the changing Indian family, see my "South Asia," in G. Soliday, ed., *History of the Family and Kinship: A Select International Bibliography* (Millwood, N.Y.: Kraus International Publications, 1980), pp. 223–231.

24. H. Orenstein and M. Micklin, "The Hindu Joint Family: the Norms and the Numbers," *Pacific Affairs* 39 (1966–67): 314–325.

25. For discussions of the issues involved in the use of the Indian Censuses for the study of the family, see A. M. Shah, *The Household Dimension of the Family in India* (Berkeley: University of California Press, 1974), pp. 133–138, 145–148; Orenstein and Micklin, "Hindu Joint Family," pp. 347–349 and passim; T. Kessinger, *Vilyatpur: 1848–1968* (Berkeley: University of California Press, 1974), pp. 178–184.

26. Kolenda, "Region, Caste," pp. 339–396. See also her "Regional Differences in Indian Family Structures," in R. I. Crane, ed., *Regions and Regionalism in South Asian Studies* (Durham: Duke University Program in Comparative Studies of Southern Asia, 1967).

27. See the references cited for table 4.10.

28. H. M. Marulasiddaiah, *Old People of Makunti* (Dharwar: Karnatak University, 1969), p. 101.

29. Ibid.

30. Shah, "Household Dimension," pp. 69–71.

31. R. K. Mukherjee, *West Bengal Family Structures: 1946–1966* (Delhi, MacMillan, 1977), pp. 29–31.

32. Delhi School of Social Work, *A Study of the Aged in Delhi* (Delhi: University of Delhi, 1977), p. 78.

33. Marulasiddaiah, *Old People*, p. 113.

34. Delhi School, *Aged in Delhi*, p. 243.

35. Marulasiddaiah, *Old People*, p. 113.

36. Delhi School, *Aged in Delhi*, pp. 78–80.

37. Philip Hauser, "Aging and World-Wide Population Change," in Binstock and Shanas, eds., *Handbook of Aging*, p. 81. See also D. Cowgill, "A Theory of Aging in Cross-Cultural Perspective," in Cowgill and Holmes, eds., *Aging and Modernization*, p. 9.

38. S. B. Mukherjee, *The Age Distribution of the Indian Population: A Reconstruction for the States and Territories, 1881–1961* (Honolulu: East-West Center, 1976), pp. 139–145. See also the more general discussions of the relationship between fertility and the aging of populations in E. A. Wrigley, *Population and History* (London: World University Library, 1969) and P. Laslett, "The History of Aging and The Aged," in *Family Life and Illicit Love in Earlier Generations* (Cambridge: Cambridge University Press, 1977), pp. 175–176.

39. Census of India, 1971.

40. J. Connell, *et al.*, *Migration from Rural Areas: The Evidence From Village Studies* (Delhi: Oxford University Press, 1976), p. 180.

41. Ibid., p. 42.

42. Wyon and Gordon, *Khanna Study*, p. 214.

CHAPTER FIVE—GROWING OLD IN THE QUATTROCENTO*

DAVID HERLIHY

W ide contrasts, whether in the distribution of wealth, the enjoyment of privilege, or the exercise of power, divided the
societies of medieval and Renaissance Italy. But in one respect, as the
moralists of the age constantly reiterated, all men were equal: they
were all growing older. In the phrase of Bernardine of Siena, they
were together moving toward that state of old age which all men
wished to attain, and all regretted when it was upon them.[1] The art
especially of the late Middle Ages, Alberto Tenenti instructs us,
shows an acute awareness of the passage of time and the relentless
approach of death.[2] Many writers, both of the Middle Ages and the
Renaissance, have left us comment and counsel on the experience of
growing old and the divisions of life through which men must pass.
To illustrate these abundant speculations, we may take as fairly
typical Dante's conceptions of the ages of man, as expressed in the
Convivio.[3] Here as frequently, Dante summarizes much earlier
wisdom and was a teacher of influence for the generations which
followed.[4]

   To the great Florentine poet, life has the form of a soaring arc,
ascending to its apex at age thirty-five, and then steeply descending.
The arc has four principal divisions. Adolescence, the first stage,
extends from birth to the twenty-fifth year. Then follows *gioventute*,
full manhood, the prime of one's earthly existence, which extends for
twenty years, past its high point at age thirty-five to its end ten years
later. It was appropriate, Dante instructs us, that Christ, the perfect
man, chose to die in the full flower of his manhood, in the
thirty-fourth year of his life. With the forty-fifth year, old age
commences; and like adolescence, which in some ways it resembles,
it lasts for twenty-five years, until age seventy. The fourth age,
decrepitude, which Dante calls *senio*, has no certain limits, but
typically lasts for ten years, more or less. So, said Dante, Christ the

*This article was originally published as "Veillir à Florence au Quattrocento," *Annales
E.S.C.* XXIV, pp. 1328–1352. Reprinted by permission of the author.

perfect man, had violence not cut short his span of years, would surely have died, like Plato, at the age of eighty-one.

The comments on aging, offered by sensitive men such as Dante, are revealing and priceless, but today they are not the only way by which we can investigate the course of life in this distant world. From the thirteenth century, the Italian cities were undertaking surveys and censuses of their populations, in an effort to marshal effectively their fiscal resources. Some of these records have survived, and by the fifteenth century, they have become particularly detailed and massive.[5] Although redacted for tax officials and not for demographers, sociologists, or historians, these great censuses — if carefully used — can still cast a flood of light over Italian society. They promise us information we cannot hope to obtain for any other region of contemporary Europe. These venerable documents further invite, on the part of the historian, the use of novel techniques. Today, electronic computers can manipulate these huge statistical compilations with incredible speed and accuracy and nearly unlimited flexibility. They can reduce the labor of months to minutes, and allow the historian to put questions to the documents he could never have asked a generation ago.

In this paper we should like to investigate the course of life in one particular Italian community: the city of Florence in 1427. In that year, the Florentine commune undertook to count all its people and to assess their wealth. The tax officials placed within their purview the city, the countryside and subject territories, which then included the greater part of the province of Tuscany. This survey, the justly famous Catasto, included some 60,000 families, and upwards of 260,000 people. A substantial part of these data is now available in machine-readable form, and is deposited at the Data, Program and Library Service of the University of Wisconsin. We shall here consider only a part of this survey, the some 40,000 residents of the city. Specifically, we should like to examine three of the great events — births, marriages, and deaths — which punctuated the lives of the Florentines as they passed their span of years. The analysis here can be only brief and partial, and we shall dispense with the strings of numbers which are the rich, if not always delectable, fruit of computer analysis. But in spite of such restrictions, these remarks may yet offer a rough view of what it was like to grow, to marry, to have children, and to meet with death in the fifteenth century.

In the twelve months preceding the final redaction of the census, more than one thousand babies were born in the city and lived long enough to be registered with their families, with a recorded age of less than one year.[6] Who were the parents of these babies, and in what sort of family were these new arrivals welcomed and reared? One remarkable fact is the small average size of the urban household. The new babies had, on the average, only slightly more than two older brothers and sisters.[7] Further, for all households in the city, the average size was only 3.8 persons, excluding servants.[8] Within the city, it was relatively unusual for married brothers to live together in the same household, or for married sons to remain with their fathers. The most common urban household was formed, in other words, not by joint or combined families, but by the conjugal couple living alone with their children and, with some frequency, a widowed parent or a bachelor brother. This was, we might add, much in contrast with the rural communities, where combined households are encountered with far greater frequency than in the city.[9]

Perhaps still more remarkable are the ages of the new parents. The mothers of these new babies were quite young. The average of their recorded ages is 26.5 years, and half the babies were born to mothers at age 24 or younger.[10] Much in contrast, the age of the fathers was quite advanced—38.5 years. For this thousand pair of new parents, the average difference between father and mother was twelve years. In the fifteenth century, when death came so early to men, this represented no small segment of their ration of life. In many families, there was as much or nearly as much difference in age between father and mother as between mother and baby.

The small size of most urban households and the large age differential between the parents profoundly affected, we would suggest, the character of the family and the milieu in which the children were raised. The advanced age of the father diminished the influence he could exert upon the internal life of his home, especially the education of his children and the formation of their moral and cultural attitudes. Most Florentine fathers were already past the apex of life at the time they assumed the responsibility for their babies. As older and established men, many of them were preoccupied with affairs of business or of government, and had not the time, and perhaps not the vigor, to involve themselves deeply in domestic concerns. Leon Battista Alberti, for example, in the *Books on the Family* written only a few years after the redaction of the *Catasto*, urged that such matters be left exclusively to the mother.[11] Moreover, most Florentine fathers would not live long enough to see their sons pass through the age of adolescence. To judge from the thinning of the age pyramid, life expectancy at age thirty-eight was only about seventeen years.[12] Little wonder that the songs of the Florentine carnival, which marvelously mirror the society of the times, include one for masqueraders depicting sons who have lost their fathers.[13]

These same factors, on the other hand, which tended to make the father a distant figure to his children, greatly enhanced the importance of the wife and mother within the family, and magnified the influence she could exert upon her offspring. In the joint or combined household, the absence, illness, or death of a married male is apt to shift responsibility for his children primarily upon another male, a married brother or father. In the small, conjugal household, that responsibility can pass only to the wife. Younger, more vigorous, present, and destined for longer contact with her children, the wife was thus in a position to exert stronger influence upon their cultural formation than could her older, occupied, and, frequently, absent husband. Moreover, the older husband usually had not been her personal choice; the young wife and mother was cut off by years and experience from her husband's world. It was difficult for a sense of true partnership to develop between them. Never, says the principal character in Alberti's *Books on the Family*, tell your secrets to your wife.[14] In these circumstances, the young mother was likely to lavish her interest, attention, and deepest emotional commitment upon her children. Viewed in another way, the great age difference between the father and his children attenuated the direct influence which he could exert upon his growing family. Within the household, the mother was the principal channel by which the values of the older generation were transmitted to help shape the culture of the new. Inevitably, the mother filtered, according to her own feminine tastes and interests, what she received—and what she passed on.

Strong feminine influence does seem apparent in a new consciousness of childhood and in the development of new ideas concerning child rearing and education, in which the Quattrocento is so rich. One of the first landmarks in the new pedagogy is the *Libro del Governo di Cura Familiare*, written between 1400 and 1405 by the Florentine Dominican, later cardinal, Giovanni Dominici.[15] Giovanni was himself raised by a widowed mother, as his father had died before his birth. He directed his essay to the lady, Bartolomea Alberti, who, like his own mother, was trying to raise her children alone, during the exile of her husband. Many of the works containing educational counsel—those written, for example, by Antoninus of Florence, by Savonarola, by the Neapolitan poet Giovanni Pontano—are directed to women, with the clear implication that the spiritual and moral formation of the child must be their principal responsibility.[16] Vittorino da Feltre, perhaps the most famous of the fifteenth-century pedagogues, was, according to a contemporary biographer, strongly influenced by his mother; at his deathbed he asked to be buried by her side.[17]

A society in which the children, including the boys, are formed primarily by women may understandably show certain pronounced cultural characteristics. It is not likely, for example, to develop a strong military tradition. Giovanni Dominici wants the Florentine mother not even to allow her boys to play with toy swords or daggers. He warns her that the use of such toys may lamentably turn the boy into a soldier; elsewhere he remarks that the commonwealth needed soldiers about as much as the universe needed demons to torment the damned.[18] On the other hand, such a society is more likely to place a high value on elegance in dress, polished manners, social grace, and high esthetic sensibilities. If we are to believe Dominici's colorful picture of child rearing at Florence, the mothers dressed their children, even their boys, in elegant clothes, showered beautiful toys upon them, insisted that their manners be refined and pretty and even, to the friar's grave displeasure, taught their little boys how to dance with girls. "Now what do you gain and what do you accomplish," he inquires of the mother, "by holding [your children] all day in your lap, kissing them and licking them with the tongue, singing songs to them and telling them untrue fables, frightening them with the Thirty Witches, teasing them, playing hide and seek, and taking every care in making them beautiful, plump, happy, smiling and content in all sensuality."[19] In Castiglione's later, famous portrait of the courtier, one of his characters remarks that the arts of the courtier, the gentleman of the Renaissance, were primarily devised for the pleasing of women.[20] If Florentine society of the Quattrocento is any measure, the gentleman was directed toward these tastes and skills not initially by the women he encountered late in life, but through his childhood training, through the woman who reared him and could form him according to her own conceptions of ideal manhood.

The second of the three vital events we are here considering is marriage, and here again, cold figures and averages reveal distinctive patterns which in turn carry, we would suggest, important cultural implications. Girls married extremely young. Based on seventy-three marriages contracted at Florence in 1427-1428, the average age of first marriage for girls was only 17.6 years.[21] Half the girls were 16 and under when they were given in marriage, and their most usual age was only 15. By 20, fully 91 percent of the 375 girls recorded in the census were married. The fate and future of the vast majority of young women were thus decided before they attained the age of 20. For males, we cannot for technical reasons rigorously distinguish first marriages from later marriages.[22] In all marriages, the average age of the grooms was nearly 34 years, and the average age difference between them and their brides was 13 years.[23] For the more than 6000 married couples in the entire urban population for whom ages of both spouses are given, the husbands were again older than their wives by an average of 13 years.[24] In only 1 percent of the households were the married couples the same age, and in only 2 percent were the wives older than their husbands.[25]

Moreover, for technical reasons, it is not usually possible to distinguish in the declarations men who never married from childless widowers. But of men in their late forties and fifties, about 10 percent appear without wives or children, and most of these men were undoubtedly permanent bachelors.[26]

Late marriage for men conformed exactly with the counsel of contemporary moralists. Leon Battista Alberti, for example, in his *Books on the Family*, strongly advised against marriage for men before the age of 25, as full virility was not then attained.[27] In the following century, the poet Ludovico Ariosto, who wrote a sententious essay on marriage, similarly recommended that men should marry only after age 30, and that the bride should be ten to twelve years younger than her spouse.[28] A lady in a novella by the Sienese Pietro Fortini observed that the brains of young men remained soft until the age of 30, and that men in their twenties made poor lovers—she didn't consider their possibilities as fathers.[29]

Not only moral opinion, but economic conditions strongly dissuaded the urban male from marrying young, and some of them from marrying at all. The richer families, fearing the division of their properties, showed the utmost caution in allowing their young men to marry. They further hoped that delay would bring a larger dowry or a more advantageous family connection. "Don't hesitate to delay [in marrying]," Giovanni Morelli, a Florentine domestic chronicler, advised his descendants, "if you think . . . you can improve your estate. . . ."[30] But even among the humble classes, the support of a wife and household required a degree of economic independence which was difficult to achieve before the middle and late twenties.

Late marriages for men had certain pronounced effects upon the society and social customs of the city. It created a nearly desperate competition among the fathers to find suitable husbands for their daughters. Because of the thinning of the age pyramid, there were more girls in their teens than men in their thirties, and many young girls thus had statistically no chance of finding a husband. Already Dante noted that the birth of a daughter struck terror into the heart of her father.[31] This intense competition on the marriage market drove the age of marriage for girls downward, and the size of their dowries up—both beyond reasonable measure, according to the contemporary moralists.[32] Some fathers, recognizing the odds against them, chose to lavish beautiful clothes and extravagant dowries on their pretty daughters, while their homely or unhealthy—and now deprived—sisters languished without hope of winning a husband. Bernardine of Siena, astute observer of the mores of his times, denounced such practices in unminced language: "Thus [he says] many parents, who are unable to provide enormous dowries to their daughters, keep them at home sterile—and would that they stayed virgins and modest girls. And what is more cruel, if they should have three or four daughters whom they are unable to endow according to their wish, they give in marriage one or two of the prettiest ones with the largest dowries. The others, sometimes misshapen, lame or blind, or in some way deformed, they give to a convent, as if they were the scum and the vomit of the world. Would that they were offering them to God, and not to the devil. . . ."[33] At the Florentine carnival, the masks of nuns sing that they were placed in convents when too young and too immature to assess their fate; in their song, they curse their fathers.[34]

Urban society was thus marked by the presence of large numbers of unmarried adult males. Between the ages 18 and 32 only a quarter of the males—1,183 out of 4,456—certainly were or had been married.[35] In evaluating the moral and social effects of this pronounced reluctance to marry, we can do no better than consider once more the comments of Bernardine of Siena. According to the saint, these unattached men would not leave women alone; they hounded and harrassed with their improper solicitations not only single girls, but also widows and married women.[36] Numerous novelle, dating from this epoch, include as stock characters an aging husband, pretty young wife, and importunate young men eager to seduce her. Reluctance to marry created fertile grounds for the practice of prostitution and for still other moral enormities, to use Bernardine's phrase. To return again to the friar's words: ". . . from this the horrible and detestable vice of sodomy is generated, nourished and receives a terrible increment. . . . When young men are captured by this pestilential stain, they are hardly ever cured, scarcely or belatedly or not at all do they allow themselves to be joined in wedlock. If by chance they take a wife, they either abuse her or they do not love her; and for that reason they do not procreate children."[37] Still according to the friar, it was more dangerous for young boys than for young girls to walk the streets of the city, for fear of being accosted and forcibly molested.[38] The Tuscan towns, and Florence chief among them, were notorious among contemporaries for the prevalence of sodomy.[39] From late marriages or no marriages for males and the vices which seemed to accompany it, Bernardine was convinced that the population of the world was falling. "From this," he says, "it is manifest to all that the procreation of children is ceasing. . . ."[40]

With marriage and within marriage, our figures also reveal remarkable contrasts between rich and poor families. The sons of the rich married later in life, and the daughters of the rich earlier, than their poorer neighbors. The age difference between husband and wife averages some 14 years among the richest families and 11 among the poorest.[41] Moreover, the permanent bachelor was a figure more familiar to richer households than to poorer. In regard to their sons, the more affluent families approached marriage more cautiously and, in regard to their daughers, more desperately, than the families which were poor.[42] But if the poor married in relatively greater numbers, within marriage the women of the most disadvantaged classes were remarkably barren. Of children born to the poorest mothers in 1426-1427, only 13 percent had a brother or sister less than two years of age, while over 54 percent of those born to the richest mothers had a sibling in that range of years.[43] It was clearly unusual for poor women to have a baby every year, or even every other year. To judge from the ratio between married women and their children four years of age and under, the richest mothers had three babies for every two born to the poorest.[44] There is little doubt that married couples in Florentine society exerted some sort of strong control over their own fertility. Bernardine of Siena claimed that of 1,000 marriages, 999 were of the devil, because of the practice of what he considered to be unnatural acts within them.[45] Those who were poor in the world's goods were also poor in children. The aristocracy of Florence, barely maintaining its own numbers within the barren city, rested upon social classes which were constantly diminishing over the generations, and had constantly to be replaced through fresh recruitment, primarily from the countryside.

We can now consider the third vital event, and the final punctuation in the lives of the Florentines, their deaths. Death was everywhere in the fifteenth century, but of all vital events it is the most difficult to measure. Its usual result was an expunging from the records, a silence, upon which estimates of mortality cannot safety rest. Still, we have some information as to the dead at Florence in 1427. In the year following the redaction of the Catasto, the census officials cancelled from the declarations 341 persons for reason of death. This figure is probably only a fourth of the true numbers who died, and it is especially defective for women and for the poor. It may be worth noting, however, that half the reported deaths were of people 30 years of age or under. This suggests that one out of two babies born never reached the apex of life. We can also form a judgment concerning life expectancy from the age pyramid, but unfortunately many factors other than mortalities influenced its shape. For what it may be worth, the apparent life expectancy would be 28 years.[46]

To judge from the distribution of reported deaths, one out of three babies who survived the first weeks of life would be dead by age 15, but if he reached age 25 his chances of surviving noticeably improved. Of those who reached the prime of life at age 25, some four out of five would still be alive at age 45. With the advent of old age, coming in Dante's estimation at the forty-fifth year, death once more rapidly reduced the numbers of the aging. More than one-half the males alive at age 45 would die during the span of old age. Of those lucky, or unlucky enough to reach decrepitude at age 70, two out of three would be cut down in the following decade.

In contemporary writings we can find literary counterparts to these grim figures, and Bernardine of Siena has again left us one of the most vivid portrayals of the aging process. "When you surpass 18 years," he instructs us in a sermon, "then you are vigorous, fresh, joyous, happy, and this is called the flower of your life, and it lasts for you until 30 years. For all the time that you remain alive, no time is more lovely and joyous than this one, and therefore David calls it the flower."[47] The saint goes on to describe the subsequent ills of aging. Twilight begins to fall after age 30, and after age 40 you are visited by unwelcome ambassadors—Messere Canuto, Lord Whitehead, and the Lords Hardening and Drying Up. As an old man, you grow stooped, and you lose your vision and your teeth. To return to the friar's words: "If he reaches seventy or eighty years, he trembles and shakes the head, and he acts like this." At this point, the great preacher, for the instruction of his audience, apparently gave an imitation of a trembling old man. In another work, Bernardine compiles for us an extended tract on the seven spiritual ills, seven corporal ills, and the seven, what he calls experimental, ills of aging.[48] Bernardine was of course professionally committed to point out the miseries of life, to save his hearers from worldly lusts, but even in the secular literature, in the *novelle* and the carnival songs, old age and old men are treated with slight dignity. The brilliant society of the Quattrocento, so much in love with beauty and elegance, did not find much satisfaction in the prospect of growing old.

In paring so quickly the numbers of the aging, death helped shape the character of Florentine society in distinctive ways. That society was extraordinarily young. One-half the population was twenty-two years or younger in age. In the richest households, one-half the population was sixteen or under. This reflected the greater fertility of the richest classes, and also their tendency to place more of their older children, especially their girls, in religion.[49] The young, moreover, pressed hard upon the thinning ranks of the aging, and rapidly replaced them in positions of influence and of power. The gifted man was given his main chance early in life, and early passed from the scene. The pace of life thus seems to have quickened, as all men raced with death. The rapid replacement of leaders in all fields of urban culture helped assure careers for creative men and a hearing for what they had to say. One other factor contributed to that remarkable achievement of Renaissance Florence, to its ability to recruit for itself and for history such an array of talented men. The city families with the exception only of the rich were poor producers of children. To maintain their numbers, the city arts and professions had to stay open to new men from the countryside and smaller towns, and even from foreign lands, and these men brought with them new talents, new skills, and new ideas. The very barrenness of urban families assured room in the urban professions for men such as Coluccio Salutati, Leonardo Bruni, Poggio Bracciolini, Ficino, Poliziano, Masaccio, Leonardo da Vinci, and many other gifted immigrants who added to the splendor of Renaissance culture.

Finally, death tended to limit the restraints which the older generation could exert upon the exuberance and vitality, as well as the extravagance and the recklessness, of the young. Here again, a critical factor in shaping the social life of the city, and indirectly its culture, was the advanced age at which most men became fathers. The average age differential of thirty-eight years separating fathers from their children meant that the generation of the fathers was already declining in numbers and vitality before their children reached adulthood. The weak and fading voice of the fathers assured that the culture of the city would be the product preeminently of the very young, largely unaided, and largely unimpeded, by the counsels of the aged.

We have thus surveyed a Florentine lifetime and have tried to suggest ways in which the vital events which marked it worked to influence urban society and culture. Although these comments have been rapid and many tentative, perhaps they may at least show that our appreciation of the Renaissance can be deepened by a vigorous and thorough reconstruction of what it was like to grow up and grow old in the fifteenth century. From a still broader point of view, is there not also a humane value and interest in learning more about this, the most common of all human experiences? For we too, in the time we have spent considering the aging Florentines, have grown a little older.

NOTES

1. *S. Bernardini senensis Opera omnia*, VII (Florence: Ad Claras Aquas, 1959), p. 253. "Huc maxime anhelabas, huc pervenire optabas, huc non posse pertingere formidabas; quo, cum perveneris, ingemiscis... Senes fieri volunt omnes, senex esse vult nemo." On Bernardine of Siena and his social commentary, which we shall cite frequently in this paper, see most recently Iris Origo, *The World of San Bernardino* (New York: Harcourt, Brace and World, 1962). On growing old in the Renaissance period, see the recent perceptive article by Creighton Gilbert, "When Did a Man in the Renaissance Grow Old?" *Studies in the Renaissance*, 14 (1967): 7-32.

2. *Il senso della morte e l'amore della vita nel Rinascimento (Francia e Italia)* (Turin: G. Einaudi, 1957). Although largely concerned with iconography, Tenenti also provides a rich survey of attitudes towards old age and death manifested in the literature of the times.

3. *Convivio*, IV, xxiv. *Le opere di Dante. Testo critico della Società Dantesca Italiana*, 2nd ed. (Florence, nella sede della società, 1960), pp. 279–93.

4. Dante's division of four "ages of man," analogous to the seasons of the year, is the simplest of several traditional conceptions concerning the periods of life. For other divisions, see for example the great thirteenth-century encyclopedia of Vincent of Beauvais, *Vincentius Bellovacensis Speculum naturale* (Graz: Akademische Druck- und Verlagsanstalt, 1964), Book 31, cap. 75, pp. 2348–2349. "De gradibus aetatum." Following Isidore of Seville, Vincent gives six ages: *infantia* (to 7 years), *pueritia* (to 14), *adolescentia* (to 28), *iuventus* (to 50), *gravitas* (to 72), and *senium* (to death). Vincent also cites Avicenna's division into four ages: *adolescentia* (to 32), *aetas pulcritudinis* (to 35 or 40), *senectus* (to 60), and *senium*. For a more popular expression of this fourfold division in the period of the Renaissance, compare the carnival song by Antonio Alamanni, "Trionfo dell' età dell'uomo," *Canti carnascialeschi del Rinascimento*, in Charles S. Singleton, ed., Scrittori d'Italia, 159 (Bari: G. Laterza e figli, 1936), p. 240. We also possess, from the Middle Ages and the Renaissance, a rich tradition of medical literature, giving advice on how to delay the physical deterioration of old age. See, for example, *Fratris Rogeri Bacon De retardatione accidentium senectutis cum aliis opusculis de rebus medicinalibus*, ed. A. G. Little and E. Withington (British Society of Franciscan Studies, Publications, 14 (Oxford: Clarendon Press, 1928, republished 1966). There is an English translation by Richard Browne, *The Cure of Old Age and the Preservation of Youth* (London, 1683); Arnaldus of Villanuova, *The Conservation of Youth and Defense of Old Age*, trans. Jonas Drummond (Woodstock, Vt.: The Elm Tree Press, 1912); and for the fifteenth century, Marsilio Ficino, "De vita libri tres," *Marsilio Ficino florentino Opera omnia*, I (Turin: Bottena d'Erasmo, 1958), pp. 491–547.

5. Among the earliest surviving *estimi*, dating from the late thirteenth century, are those of Perugia, Orvieto, Prato, and Macerata in the Marches of Ancona. On the nature of the direct tax system which these surveys served, see E. Fiumi, "L'imposta diretta nei comuni medioevali della Toscana," *Studi in onore di Armando Sapori*, I (Milan: Istituto Editoriale Cisalpino, 1957), pp. 329–353; my own "Direct and Indirect Taxation in Tuscan Urban Finance, ca. 1200–1400," *Finances et comptabilité urbaines du XIIIe au XVIIe siècle* (Brussels: Centre "Pro Civitate," 1964), pp. 385–440. For the tax surveys of

Perugia, see G. Mira, "I catasti e gli estimi perugini del XIII. secolo," *Economia e Storia*, I (1955), 76–84. For Orvieto, see E. Carpentier, *Une ville devant la peste. Orvieto et la peste noire de 1348* (Paris: S.E.V.P.E.N. 1962), p. 16, and G. Pardi, "Il catasto d'Orvieto d'anno 1292," *Bollettino della Società Umbra di Storia Patria*, II (1896): 255–320. For Macerata, R. Foglietti, *Il Catasto di Macerata del 1268* (Macerata, 1881). For Florence and Siena, U. Sorbi, *Aspetti della struttura o principali modalità di stime dei catasti senese e fiorentino del XIV e XV secolo*, 2nd ed. (Florence: Vallecchi, 1962), and Elio Conti, *I catasti agrari della repubblica fiorentina e il catasto particellare toscano (secoli XIV-XIX)*, La formazione della struttura agraria moderna nel contado fiorentino, III, pt. 1, sect. 1 (Rome: Istituto Storico Italiano per il Medio Evo, 1966).

6. Of babies less than one year of age, the *Catasto* records 1,005. Between July 1427 and June 1428, 785 newborn babies were added to the declarations, but this list of additions is probably not complete.

7. In exact figures, the babies born in 1426–1427 had an average of 2.23 older brothers and sisters; those born in 1427–1428 had an average of 2.54.

8. Servants were required to make their own declarations and thus do not appear in the declarations of their employers; slaves, however, while not officially considered to be *bocche* or deductible members of the household, were declared as property owned and are thus included in the count. The census includes 20,116 men, 17,304 women, and 23 persons whose sex is not stated.

9. At Arezzo, for example, in 1427, scarcely one household in 10 was multiple, in the sense of including several generations or several couples, but in the countryside, one household in five was of this type. Combined households included only 19 percent of the inhabitants of the city of Arezzo, but 35 percent of the rural population. On the Tuscan hearth, see now David Herlihy and Christiane Klapisch-Zuber, *Les Toscans et leurs familles. Une étude du catasto florentin de 1427*. (Paris: Editions de l'Ecole des Hautes Etudes en Sciences Sociales, 1978), pp. 469–511.

10. As the babies were entered in the *Catasto* during the year following their births, the average age for mothers would be between 25.5 and 26.5 years. For the 785 babies added in 1427–1428, the average age of the mother was 25.6 years—nearly identical with what it had been the year before. For these babies, the average age of the father was 37.97 years.

11. *Libri della famiglia*, in C. Grayson, ed., *Opere volgari*, Scrittori d'Italia, 218 (Bari; G. Laterza, 1960), p. 216. "Perché a me parea non piccolo incarico provedere alle necessità entro in casa, bisognando a me non raro avermi fuori tra gli uomini in maggiori faccende . . . guadagnare e acquistare di fuori, poi del resto entro in casa quelle tutte le cose minori lascialle a cura della donna mia . . . a me parrebbe ancora biasimo tenermi chiuso in casa tra le femine. . . ."

12. The number of males in the population age 38 and older was 5,498. Life expectancies based on a single census would be precise only if the birth and death rates were stable for all the years considered and if the population was not gaining or losing members through immigration or emigration.

13. Cf. J. A. Symonds, *Renaissance in Italy: Italian Literature*, I (New York: H. Holt, 1888), p. 389.

14. *Libri della famiglia*, *Opere volgari*, p. 219. "Solo e' libri e le scritture mei e de' miei passati a me piacque e allora e poi sempre avere in modo rinchiuse che mai la donna le potesse non tanto leggere, ma né vedere. . . .'"

15. *Regola del governo di cura familiare compilata dal Beato Giovanni Dominici fiorentino*, ed. Donato Salvi (Florence: A. Garinei, 1860). English translation by A. B. Coté, *On the*

Education of Children (Washington, D. C.: The Catholic University of America, 1927).

16. The pedagogical works of all these writers are discussed by Augustin Rösler, *Erziehungslehre und die übrigen pädagogischen Leistungen Italiens im 15. Jahrhundert* (Freiburg im Breisgau; Herder, 1894), especially pp. 67 ff. For Pontano, see his Latin poem, "Ad uxorem de liberis educandis," *Ioannis Ioviani Pontani Carmina, ecloghe, elegie, liriche*, ed. Johannes Oeschger, Scrittori d'Italia, 198 (Bari: G. Laterza, 1948), pp. 144–147.

17. Rösler, *Erziehungslehre*, p. 103.

18. *Cura familiare*, p. 146. "Comperandoli la spaduccia, o vero la daga, sarà nato a' soldati." Ibid., p. 180: "E se dicessi: pure la repubblica ha di ciò bisogno, dico ch' ella ha bisogno di manigoldi, e l'universo ha bisogno di demoni che tormentino i dannati . . . ."

19. Ibid., p. 151. "Or come ben guadagni e lavori, tutto 'l di tenergli in collo, baciargli, e con la lingua leccare, cantare lor canzone, narrare bugiarde favole, far paura con trentavecchie, ingannare, con essi fare a capo nascondere, e tutta sollecitudine porre in fargli belli, grassi, lieti, ridenti e secondo la sensualità in tutto contenti?"

20. "Do you not see that the cause of all gracious exercises that give us pleasure is to be assigned to women alone? Who learns to dance gracefully for any reason except to please women? Who devotes himself to the sweetness of music for any other reason? Who attempts to compose verses, at least in the vernacular, unless to express sentiments inspired by women?" The words are attributed to Cesare Gonzaga. Baldesar Castiglione, *The Book of the Courier*, trans. Charles S. Singleton (Garden City, New York: Doubleday, 1959), pp. 257–258.

21. Between July 1427 and June 1428, seventy-three girls with ages stated were cancelled from their fathers' declarations and entered into those of their husbands. The fact that they were still under their fathers' authority and were not accorded the title of *mona* shows that these were first marriages for the girls.

22. The marital status of men in the *Catasto* is almost never explicitly stated but must be deduced by the presence of a wife or children in the household.

23. Based on seventy-six grooms. The average age of the brides, including widows who were remarrying, was 20.33 years, and the average age difference was 13.63 years.

24. For 6,104 married males, the average age difference was 12.94 years. For 6,110 women, the average difference was 12.73 years. The slight difference in the number of married men and women is attributable to the death of wives during the year 1427–1428 and the remarriage of their husbands, which means that the husband was recorded with more than one wife in the declaration.

25. Of the 6,110 married women, 5,896 were younger than their husbands, 80 were of the same age, and 135 were older.

26. In the age interval 48 to 52, out of 859 men, 717 (83.47 percent) were married, and 42 (4.89 percent) were certainly widowers. Of the men, 100 (11.64 percent) were thus of unknown status, either childless widowers or, more likely, bachelors.

27. *Opere volgari*, p. 109. "A tutti prima che XXV pare che sia dannoso accostare le gioventù volenterosa e fervente a simile opera, ove ella spenga quella vampa e calore della età, più atto a statuire e confermare se stessi che a procreare altrui."

28. *Le satire di Lodovico Ariosto*, ed. Cirillo Berardi (Campobasso: G. Colitti, 1918), Satira V, 11. 187–189, p. 127. "Di dieci anni o di dodici, se fai / Per mio consiglio, fia di te minore, / Di pari o di più età non la tor mai . . ." and 11. 193–195, "Però vorrei che' l sposo avesse i suoi / Trent'anni, quella età che 'l furor cessa, / Presto al voler, presto al pentirsi poi."

29. *Novelle di Pietro Fortini senese*, ed. T. Rughi (Milan, 1923), p. 133. "Ma io di ciò non mi maraviglio, perchè non hanno ancora fermo il cervello, perchè fino a tanto che l'omo non passa trenta anni non è in perfetta età; però una donna non deverebbe mai eleggersi per suo amante un simil giovinastro . . . Ma un giovine di trenta fino a quaranta se s'abbatte al' amore d'una fanciulla lo serva fino che gli ha vita . . .''

30. Giovanni di Pagolo Morelli, *Ricordi*, ed. Vittore Branca (Florence: Le Monnier, 1956), p. 207. "Ma abbi riguardo di non ti disavvantagiare però pell' affrettarti: vo' dire che se tu pensassi per indugiarti insino in trenta anni avere migliorato tuo istato in che che atto si fusse, per modo da valerne molto di meglio, indugia . . .''

31. *Paradiso*, Canto XV, 103–105. "Non faceva, nascendo, ancor paura / la figlia al padre; ché 'l tempo e la dote / non fuggien quinci e quindi la misura.''

32. Giovanni Morelli urges his descendants to see to it that their daughers are not made to marry before the age of fifteen. *Ricordi*, p. 207. "Se lasci fanciulle femmine, fa ch' elle non si maritino se non hanno anni quindici compiuti . . .''

33. *Opera omnia*, II, pp. 82–83. "Similiter multi parentes, qui non valent immensas dotes tradere filiabus, in domo steriles, non propter Deum, retinent illas, et utinam virgines et pudicas! Et quod crudelius est, si quando tres vel quatuor filias habent, ad vota non valentes dotare illas, unam vel duas formosiores cum dotibus maximis nuptui tradunt; reliquas vero, quandoque distortas, claudas seu caecas sive quocumque modo deformes, quasi spumam vel vomitum saeculi, monasterio tradunt; illas, utinam Domino, non diabolo dedicantes!''

34. Singleton, ed. *Canti carnascialeschi*, p. 44, no. 33. "Siamo state in penitenza, / in digiuni e in affanni; / avam poca conoscenza / quand' entrammo in questi panni: / or che siam mature d'anni, / conosciamo il nostr' errore . . . / Maladisco il padre meo / che cosi tener mi vuole!''

35. Of these 86 were widowers. But as mentioned above, it is unfortunately not possible to distinguish childless widowers from single men; still, the former category could only have been small.

36. *Opera omnia*, II, 83. ". . . solutis iuvenibus atque viris nec propter predictas causas coniugio copulatis puellisque grandaevis in domibus male servatis, quot enormia sequantur potius eligo operire silentio quam aperire sermone. Non solum puellae, sed nec relinquitur vidua neque nupta quin vesetur molestiis, crucietur angustiis et importunitatibus opprimatur ab iis qui perseverant innupti . . .''

37. Ibid. "Sed super omnia iam praedicta, horrenda atque detestanda sodomia ex his generatur, nutritur atque suscipit terribile incrementum . . . Cumque capti fuerint iuvenes hac pestifera labe, vix umquam curantur, vix et tarde vel numquam coniugio se copulari permittunt. Si casu uxorem suscipiant, vel illa abutuntur vel non diligunt eam; propterea non generant filios . . .''

38. *Prediche volgari di San Bernardino da Siena*, ed. Luciano Banchi, III (Siena: Tip. edit. all' inseq. di S. Bernardino, 1884), p. 270, referring to Siena. "Oimmè, a che se' tu condotta, città di Siena! . . . non si può mandare uno fanciulletto per le strade, che elli non sia preso per forza e traviato, poichè ella è si condotta! Sapete che vi dico? Riparare si vuole. O donne, fate che voi non mandiate più attorno i vostri figliuoli: mandate le vostre figliuole, chè non v' è pericolo niuno, se voi le mandate fra tali genti. Elle non vi saranno contaminate di nulla . . .''

39. According to Bernardine, Genoa excluded by statute all Tuscan teachers, because of their reputation for being sodomites. *Le prediche volgari*, ed. Ciro Cannarozzi, O.F.M., II (Florence, 1958), p. 103. "A Genova è uno statuto che niuno toscano può essere maestro di scuola solo per tal caso. O Toscana, che corna t'è questa, che è una

confusione di noi per tutto 'l mondo." For a reference to the Florentines as being addicted to sodomy, see *Novelle di Pietro Fortini*, p. 64, "Che mi farò fiorentino? no, perchè li loro vizi sono tali che le donne non li possono patir di vedere, che dicano sono loro nemici, che di non voler vedere in viso le donne stanno al paragone co' lucchesi."

40. *Opera omnia*, II, 82. "Ex his omnibus manifeste apparet quod cessat generatio filiorum . . ."

41. For 405 married women in households with a tax estimate of more than 3,200 florins, the average age difference with their husbands was 14.37 years. For 2,200 women in households with no tax assessment, the difference was 10.97 years.

42. For example, in the poorest households (those with no tax assessment), 36.59 percent (146 out of 399) of the men in the age interval 23 to 27 were married, but only 20.29 percent of men in the richest households (3,201 and more florins assessment), or 28 out of 138, were married. Girls, on the other hand, married younger in the richer households than in the poorer. In the richest, the average age of first marriage for women was 15.70 years (based on ten marriages) and 26.33 (based on nine) in the poorest.

43. Of 312 babies born in the poorest households, 69 (22.12 percent) had no brothers or sisters, 20 (6.41 percent) had a brother or sister less than one year of age, and 24 (7.69 percent) had a brother or sister between one and two. In the richest households, out of 81 babies, only 12 (14.81 percent) had no brothers or sisters, 21 (25.93 percent) had a brother or sister less than one year, and 23 (28.40 percent) had a brother or sister between one and two years.

44. The child-woman ratio, or the ratio between married women between the ages 15 and 44 and their children age 0 to 4, was 101.31 in the poorest households (1,628 children, 1,607 married women) and 149.58 in the richest (528 children, 455 married women). For all women within the age range 15 to 44, the ratio was 84.35 (1,930 women) in the poorest and 116.04 (455 women) in the richest households.

45. *Prediche volgari*, ed. Banchi, II, 95. "Io ho uno grandissimo dubbio di voi, che io mi credo che se ne salvino tanti pochi di quegli che sono in istato di matrimonio, che de' mille, novecento novantanove credo che sia matrimonio di diavolo." Compare ibid. III, 271. "Cosi dico anco a le donne, le quali so' cagione che i figliuoli che hanno già conceputi, si vengono a perdere. Peggio, chè anco s' di quelle che aoperano che non possono generare; e se n'hanno generati, in corpo gli disperdono. Voi (a chi toca, dico) sête più iniqui che non son e' micidiali. . . . Vedi che tu se' cagione che il mondo manchi, come il sodomitto: da te a lui non è differenzia niuna."

46. The exact figures are 27.1 years for men and 28.2 for women.

47. *Prediche volgari*, ed. Banchi, III, 365. "Quando tu giògni colà in su' diciotto anni, allora tu sei gagliardo, fresco, giocondo, allegro, e quello si chiama el fiore de la tua età, e durati insino a trenta anni. Tutto il tempo che tu stai in questa vita, non è più bello e giocondo che quello; e però il chiama Davit el fiore."

48. De calamitatibus et miseriis humanae vitae et maxime senectutis, *Opera omnia*, VII, 243–62.

49. The tendency of the richest classes to place more of their girls in religion seems manifest in the sex ratios of the population. In the richest households, the ratio was 120.23 for the population aged 0 to 13, but then jumps to a very high 157.04 for those aged 14 to 59. The loss of girls seems primarily attributable to the putting of girls into convents. In the poorest households, the ratio shows no such jump. It is 115.59 for the ages 0 to 13, and 114.17 for those aged 14 to 59.

CHAPTER SIX — A WIDOWS' ASYLUM OF THE RENAISSANCE: THE ORBATELLO OF FLORENCE*

RICHARD C. TREXLER

O ur contemporary attitudes toward the elderly are potent mixtures of historical myths and conventional classifications. In the good old days, we would like to believe, the organic or kin family took care of its own; historians know, on the contrary, that early modern European welfare institutions interned thousands upon thousands of disadvantaged persons including elderly parents. The asylum is a modern discovery, we are told, a product of heartless statism which is the inexorable enemy of kin affections;[1] this article will show that, in fact, communal asylums existed in Renaissance Florence whose intent and function was to maintain and augment nuclear families. If we have trouble thinking of the state as a benevolent father, finally, we encounter as much difficulty in considering the elderly as sexual creatures; the story I tell demands, on the contrary, that we examine the care of elderly women as part of the history of women. Historical reveries, misconstrued concepts of the family, and an asexual approach to the elderly in history, are the problems which the study of the widows' home of Orbatello addresses.

Built after 1370 by a merchant who envisioned some four or five dozen old women praying his soul into heaven in the lonely comfort of stately individual quarters, the great asylum of Orbatello passed at the turn of the century to the tutelage of the commune of Florence, which revised its function and population in the light of the total welfare needs of the city. What was that historical context? First, through its guilds and other agencies, the city government administered numerous hospitals and homes filled with dependents without functioning fathers. The commune called itself these dependents' "father" and, like any father, it aimed to marry the

*I should like to thank Christiane Klapisch-Zuber and Sarah Elbert for reading and discussing this paper.

younger part of that population when it came of age while providing long-term care in hospitals for single surviving elders.

The commune was not just a father to those in institutions, however, but also to its own servants or *familia*. As early as 1378 the Florentine government not only saw to its familiars' hospital bills, but through an as-yet-unstudied retirement system kept its "sons" from begging and thus in their nuclear families once they left communal service; so that, in the law's words, the fathers of government would not be ashamed and dishonored.[2] Thus both the rhetoric and institutions of the time show a complex relationship between the kin family and the family of the commune, each informing the concept and actuality of the other, both supported by the union of male masters and servants we call patronal government.

All elders are not created equal; contextualizing Orbatello involves understanding the particular state of Florentine women which the commune addressed as it reshaped the asylum. First, the Florentine marriage pattern insured that, on an average, older husbands died when their wives were still fairly young; in a society where wealth was controlled by men, this meant that caring for the elderly usually involved caring for women.[3] Next, these youngish widows, their ranks swollen by women "widowed" by runaway husbands, usually had children to care for, and the females among them were again the most enduring problem. Wealthy widows might profit from the special investment fund which the fourteenth-century commune, ever the father, had instituted to prevent widows' pauperization and thus their desertion of children, and the daughters of wealthy men might survive with honor in half a hundred urban nunneries.[4] That left the mass of poor widows and their daughters, the latter unable to enter nunneries and also difficult to marry, especially once they lost their "honor." It is this world of nunneries, of superfeminine foundling homes whose girls, unable to find spouses, grew old among ever-new classes of "innocents;" of desperate mothers in the streets hoping to land a position as some man's servant, nurse, or lover; of the public brothels and "shops" which were often their ultimate recourse; and of young girls in families who cultivated their own desperation at ever marrying, that, taken together, so forcefully argues for viewing the problem of the Florentine elderly as sororal.[5]

Orbatello would be used by the commune to attack one aspect of this immense problem in a highly creative fashion: it would be an asylum where widows and their children would live together. Different from the charities of neighboring Venice, where the care of widows generally remained a parishional obligation,[6] different also from the nunneries and beguinages of Europe, where religious persons and the occasional converted laywomen lived out their lives in community, and different as well from the monasteries and hospitals which provided occasional rental properties to the old,[7] the Orbatello of Florence was a secular establishment providing free housing for large numbers of older laywomen in common life. It may have been the only widow's asylum in Europe, yet Orbatello was more: this was a house whose matrons took in mother-led families, preserving these family segments and creating new solidarities.[8]

The stage is thus set for a dramatic confrontation of two types of paternalistic poor care, that intended to preserve family segments and that which sought to care, like a father, for those who had none. Our study is about a house for women run largely by them, and about how this institution faltered when its matrons were attacked by parentless children who defied mothering. The history of Orbatello through the sixteenth century was part of a crisis history of the Renaissance Florentine female.

THE FOUNDATION

Located to this day in the northeast section of Florence in the parish of San Piero Maggiore and in the ward of the Keys, Orbatello was founded by Niccolò di Jacopo degli Alberti, perhaps the richest man in Europe, familiar of princes and head of Florence's premier banking establishment. About two-thirds built between April 1370 and September 24, 1376, the date of his testament, Alberti's Orbatello was finished and filled by his son Antonio after the father's death on August 7, 1377, and before summer 1378, when a crowd of Ciompi attacked the place and its allegedly "whoring" inhabitants.[9] After Antonio Alberti's expulsion from the city in 1400, the commune turned the asylum over to the Parte Guelfa for administration, a position that organization of Florence's finest families kept till the eighteenth century. We gain an idea of its cloistered state, complete with church, from an illumination done in the first half of the fifteenth century (Plate 1); of its total walled structure during the sixteenth century, focus of our study, from the Bonsignori city map of 1584 (Plate 2); of its internal design from an eighteenth-century plan of the Orbatello which preserves the founder's basic architecture (Plate 3). Alongside terrain where, as Niccolò had wanted, "the inhabitants can promenade and accomplish seemly exercise," were three rows of houses, the two nearest the church on a "lower street" whose single units were numbered 1 through 20 in the sixteenth century, the third on the "upper street" with units numbered 21 through 29, which was the last house in Orbatello at that time.[10]

For all the abstract coldness of the plan, examination of the separate apartments reveals units designed for intimate life experience. Each of these houses was divided between an upper and lower floor (hereafter "s" and "i"), as a 1431 document explains, each apartment being partly divided by an internal wall.[11] Sixteenth-century documents make it clear that a *sala* or livingroom was on the kitchen side of the partition (4 on the plan), a *camera* or bedroom being on the other side (6)[12] The terminology indicates the domestic intention even if that was not always maintained in practice. Some of the houses also had a *palcuccio* or loft above the second floor where a single person lived, but we do not know how intimate the relations

PLATE 1. *Codice Rustici, Seminario Maggiore, Florence.*

between that person and those on the second floor had to be.[13] The staircases shown on the plan, however, indicate that the residents of the ground and second floors could live apart from each other.

PLATE 2. *Nova pulcherrimae civitatis Florentiae Topographia* (detail).

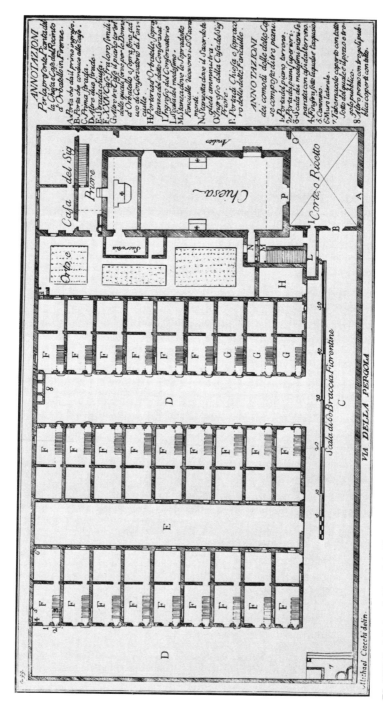

PLATE 3. Michael Ciocchi, Plan in 1754. in G. Richa, *Notizie Storiche delle Chiese Fiorentine* I (Florence, 1754), at p. 298.

THE PARTE GUELFA AND ORBATELLO

For most of the first century of its stewardship, the only surviving Parte records regarding Orbatello are legislative rather than deliberative in nature, dealing with general objectives and guidelines rather than with the day-to-day administration of the asylum. In 1511 precise administrative records begin, and they continue with that precision until around 1550. What the legislative records of the fifteenth century do tell us in no uncertain terms is that the Parte corruptly used the Alberti funds to finance its own affairs instead of Orbatello's.[14] They tell us that the Parte had not established the lay administration which the founder had mandated, but had thrust upon the church rector all the day-to-day financial and social responsibilities.[15] Finally, these legislative records give us our first detailed idea of the composition of the house, both ideally and in reality.

A 1461 Parte declamation comes to the point:

While it is clear from the words of the testator and from his houses that they were intended for persons of good social status who by some bad fortune have become Shamed Poor, [they have been taken by] a truly brutish bunch who are unsuited [to them].[16]

The Parte captains who described this situation in 1461 pointed directly at the types of brutes they did not want in Orbatello. "Slave women, who whenever they enter disquiet and perturb the whole house, [and] Corsican women . . . usually have different customs, and this [variety] is not suitable in such a pious place."[17] These legal and geographical disqualifications for entry remained in force through the remainder of the period, in 1520 taking on a racial taint when the captains spelled out the colors they did not want there.[18] In 1509, meanwhile, the Parte introduced a fiscal qualification which it could never enforce: from then on, it said, only those persons could enter whose ascendants had been subject to taxes in the city for at least 25 years.[19]

The captains of 1461 also addressed another axis of population control, the matter of men. "The places are badly distributed, and in one and the same house men and women are mixed together," they complained. The solutions were two, the first of which was already on the books, and simply needed reiteration: no male relative (usually a son, grandson, or nephew) twelve years of age or over could live with his kin in Orbatello. The second was apparently new: no unrelated man and woman could reside together in the house.[20] While both rules had significant moral intentions, the former is

important from a demographic point of view as well, for it established
the classical model of young males' movement out of Orbatello: from
no later than 1461, the Parte had an established policy of expelling
boys once they reached twelve years of age.

No such policy pertained to adolescent girls. Indeed the "girls of
Orbatello," as nubile females were soon called as a group, were
expected to remain there until they married, at which time they
would be helped by a dowry subvention from the Parte. In 1504 a new
ordinance required that these girls live in Orbatello for five
continuous years before claiming that dowry.[21] Such was the general
administrative policy toward young girls.

The *mulieres Orbatelli*, finally, were presumably in Orbatello for
life: the Parte offered no aid for widows to remarry, and none seems
to have done so. The chastity of these women was expected,
whatever the reality. Boys would leave before they seduced girls or
women, but girls would stay, the Parte regulations seem to assume,
to be schooled in abstinence even while the matrons prepared them
for marriage. Ideally, the house was without sexual activity.

THE POPULATION OF ORBATELLO

On certain feast days during the year, the Parte Guelfa provided
a stipend of seven shillings for each "soul" in Orbatello. The total
alms on any such feast, combined with two official Florentine
censuses, tell us how many people lived in Orbatello during the first
two-thirds of the sixteenth century:

TABLE 6.1
General Population[22]

1511	1512	1513	1518	1519	1520	1521	1522	1552	1562
203	195	193	221	254	248	221	259	154	178

Alone among our documents, the census of 1552 gives us a
precise idea of the distribution of the souls among the residences, and
tells us who these souls were. There were thirty houses in that year,
the last appearing in the Parte records for the first time in 1549, and
the census taker occasionally distinguished between those living on
the first and second floors: there was an average of 2.6 persons on
each floor and 5.1 persons in each house.[23] The total population of
1552 was, however, unrepresentatively small, and the more
representative largest population figure of 259 in 1522, distributed
among twenty-nine houses, yields an average of 8.9 souls in each
house and 4.5 on each floor.

The census taker distinguished between children and adults in Orbatello in 1552 by naming the latter but only counting the former. Thus the 11 males among the 154 residents were not named, they obviously being those boys less than twelve years of age who could live there.[24] This omission of name allows us by a process of elimination to determine the young female component of the house as well. Our counter named all the heads of the 30 hearths plus 66 other women, 62 percent of the residents in all. These 96 women were further identified as follows: 86 were called "mone" or adult women ("domne" or "donna" in the Latin sources); two others had the prefix "la" before their name, indicating nubile unmarried women; there was one "suora," (an elderly *pinzochera* leading a saintly life), one woman living with the priest, and six women with no title or designation. The 47 unnamed females were evidently dependents of those who were named, both of the 30 heads of hearths and of the other named women living in those hearths. The preponderance of 47 unnamed girls over only 11 unnamed boys is explained by boys twelve years of age or over having to leave Orbatello; we may therefore suggest that of the girls, some 36 were that age or beyond, only 11 being cohorts of the same number of boys. Finally we should point out that 58 children living with 96 women has its own significance: that meant that there was only child per floor, and only 1.6 children for every mature woman in the house. This was a predominantly older population of women.

How old? Before pursuing that question, let us recall that to be "old" in traditional European society meant to be over 40 years of age, a literary convention quite in keeping with actual life expectancy. Further, we must recall that bearing children was hazardous in this age, so that whatever ages we find among this population will be significant partly in relation to their generational passivity or activity.[25] That having been said, we must admit that none of our sources gives us any exact fashion of determining the age of the women of Orbatello. The 68 years of the mona Piera we meet in the 1427 *Catasto*, the one sexagenarian who gave her age when she matriculated, the 35 and 40 years of two women involved in a sex scandal in 1559 are suggestive of the age range, but scarcely of any calculable value.[26] To get a clearer idea of the age profile, we must proceed in other fashions. The stated ages of the children entering Orbatello will help, as will a study of the longevity of particular women in Orbatello.

Since the boys of Orbatello had to leave on their twelfth birthday, the average 6.7 years of 15 such boys is less significant than that of the girls, 77 percent of the 1552 young population in any case. Nineteen girls who entered Orbatello with their mothers between 1511 and

1530 averaged 9.6 years when they entered while 21 other young females giving their age who were not accompanied by their mothers had a similar average age of 10 years in the same 20 year period.

These ages, taken from the licenses to enter Orbatello conceded by the Parte during that time, permit us to make a rough calculation of the ages of the mothers who accompanied many of the children once we recall the peculiar Florentine marriage pattern. At the end of the fifteenth century, women with an average age of 21 years married men much older than they, in 1427 that age gap being 18 years for women of the social condition we shall find in Orbatello![27] This meant that women were widowed at a relatively early age. Take a typical woman entering Orbatello: she would have borne her first child at age 22 and, assuming that she had one child each year and entered Orbatello promptly after being widowed, she would have been approximately 42 years of age when she entered with her average 10 year old. We may go one step further, hypothesizing an average age of 47 for those many mothers whose daughters were dowered by the Parte after the family had been there for five years.[28] Thus there were certainly some premenopausal adults in Orbatello, even if we could find no case of a woman marrying after entering there as an adult. But among the 157 donne we can identify in the records between 1511 and 1530, the 39 whose children lived with them quickly passed that landmark. Almost all the other donne, we shall find, were older than these mothers.

Let us first concentrate on the women called "donne." We noticed that in the census of 1552 such women made up almost all those whose names were given, and the same is true for the females mentioned in the Parte records from 1511 to 1530: once the children are eliminated, almost all the other females, 157 in all, were called "donna," and they were mostly laywomen who had been or were still married. This was the case not only with the 43 among them who were identified as widows, but with most of those donne whose proper name is followed in the records by the Latin genitive of a male name, such as "domna Maria Bartholomei": whenever we can identify this male through another source, he almost invariably turns out to be the husband of the woman and not her father.[29] The fact that females without the appellation "donna" before their names regularly follow their Christian names with the term "the daughter of," whereas donne do so only when they also say that they are "a one-time wife and now widow," is significant; the donnas had almost all been married.

We may quickly add: "and mostly widowed." To be certain, donna Lodovica of Ferrara's Savonese husband had fled her and his

10-year-old daughter Maddalena, but he was not dead; donna Lucrezia, with her 14-year-old daughter Francesca and 7-year-old son Giovanmaria, "does not live with her husband," but she evidently had one.[30] Nineteen donne among the 39 in Orbatello between 1511 and 1530 with their children were not named as widows, and there were definitely some wives among them. But 2 of these 19 had children with them who were themselves called "donne," and one of them was herself called a widow.[31] It is altogether probable that this widow's mother, like most of the donnas whose genitive male we can identify, was also a widow. It is in this period, in fact, that Orbatello was first identified as a place where "poor widows without a house are received."[32]

In contemporary Florence there was a nunnery of San Niccolò whose death books have survived, from which I elsewhere calculated that its celibate population, comparable to the women of Orbatello who, as we see, had survived the childbearing years, had a life-expectancy of 42 years.[33] Orbatello was in every respect, therefore, an old women's home, but, like the nunnery, a certain proportion of its population had not only defied the odds of general life expectancy, but had even gone beyond the life expectancy of about 60 years for those who reached menopause.[34] These women were the matrons of Orbatello, their very longevity claiming our attention as it gave them authority among their colleagues. Let us look at two biographies.

Twice-widowed donna Antonia was the longest resident of Orbatello we know. Antonia entered the house in 1513 with her three children: Silvestra (age 12), Goro (13) and Lisabetta (eight months old). It was Antonia's mother-in-law donna Cucca who accepted the four into apartment 13-i, and as part of the same transaction, Cucca also took in her own daughter Maddalena with the latter's sons, Geri (7) and Domenico (5).[35] Antonia must have lived at Orbatello throughout the 1520s, for in 1530 she returned to Orbatello's apartment 7-s with one Pasquino, probably her grandson, from the hospital of the porters of Florence, where all the women had lived during the siege of Florence while Orbatello was garrisoned with troops.[36] Those 17 years since her matriculation would prove less than half her total stay at Orbatello, however. For in 1549 Antonia was still living in apartment 7, now with an unmarried girl who may have been caring for the matriarch in her old age.[37] The following year the Parte captains inspecting Orbatello queried "four old widows of commodious presence" on the state of the house, and few women could have given the perspective which Antonia may have afforded, for in 1549 she had been in Orbatello for 36 years.[38] Recalling that she had been twice widowed when she first entered Orbatello, we may be sure that this matron had now passed her seventieth birthday. She had probably died by 1552. In the census of that year, someone else was living upstairs in apartment 7.

Then consider the rich history of Maddalena the widow of Piero di Meo Muchini of Novoli in the Mugello north of Florence, the youngest of the long-term residents we can trace. She must have entered Orbatello before 1510, so as to justify the Parte's dowry paid her daughter Maria in 1515.[39] In 1513 Maddalena accepted as her companion an apparently unrelated 18-year-old girl from Strada south of Florence, and that girl's presence may explain why in 1519 the Parte was so insistent that Maddalena's overage son leave her apartment and Orbatello instantly.[40] In the meantime Maddalena had married off another daughter, Lucrezia, with the Parte's help (1517), and she must subsequently have bowed to the threat of expulsion and sent her son packing, for Maddalena was living in apartment 17-i in 1522 with another woman, about 12 years after she had entered.[41] Maddalena must have been well beyond 50 years of age. These biographies indicate therefore that a substantial number of elderly women lived in Orbatello a good part of their adult lives and—a point to which we shall return—that many of them lived in the same apartment for years on end.

Where had these women come from? They were not, first of all, mostly natives as the Parte regulation of 1509 wished to make them, but to a significant extent came from outside Florence. If we examine the provenance of the dead husbands or rare fathers of the 58 donne among the 157 mentioned in Parte records from 1511 to 1530 who listed that information, we find that only four said they came from the city. Three others were from distant places outside the dominion of Florence, two from Naples and one from Bruges. The remaining 51 women, that is their husbands or fathers, came from the dominion. A majority of them came not from the nearby *contado* but from the more distant *distretto*, with no noticeable locative concentration. The attention recent authors have drawn to such dominion women, often "bathed . . . with tears . . ., coming toward the city with their tiny children, some hanging from their necks, some carried in their arms," springs to mind.[42] At least one-third of the donne of Orbatello came from the countryside.

A completely distinct source confirms this finding, and suggests that a majority of these outsiders came more or less directly to the Orbatello rather than entering after a lengthy sojourn in the city. From 1500 to 1517, the Parte notary Bartolomeo Leoni recorded in one of his registers 74 marriages which had been partially dowered by his masters.[43] Twenty of the girls' fathers, who were all deceased, were identified by their origins, and all were originally from the dominion rather than from Florence, again indicating that a minimum of 27 percent of the girls were not Florentines. It is when we turn to the new husbands of these same girls, however, that we begin to suspect that several of the latter had come directly to Orbatello. Twenty-four of the husbands, about one-third of them, were themselves identified as stemming from outside the city. Now, only 5 of this group of 24 were also said to *live* in the city, their parish of residence being given, and 3 of these 5 were natives of distant Lyon, Genoa, and Bologna. Only 2 husbands from the Florentine dominion were said to also live in the city, therefore, and thus only they were possibly of the type who in Florentine records listed their native area but had actually lived in the city for some time. We may look at the matter from another angle: of the 19 husbands from outside the city who do not have any Florentine residence given, all but 1 had origins in the dominion. Since the scribe otherwise scrupulously included the parish of residence in the city, there can be no doubt that practically none of the husbands from that dominion had a Florentine residence; they came to Orbatello from their homelands, married one of the "girls of Orbatello," and returned home.

Why then were there so many grooms from the countryside, almost all making such quick trips to the city? One simple, arguable, but perhaps less probable explanation would be that the £ 50 dowry assistance normally provided by the Parte to its girls made these girls attractive. The more probable explanation runs like this: many of these dominion girls had come almost directly to Orbatello from their homelands. Under the supervision of their elders, they had preserved their "pudica honesta" in Orbatello as they would have had trouble doing if they or their mothers had worked in the city as domestics. They were thus in a moral and financial position after five years to contract an honorable marriage, occasionally, be it noted, with the boy back home.[44] Whatever may be the truth of the matter, we have discovered one further element about the asylum of Orbatello: girls not only came to it from the countryside, but returned to the countryside from Florence. The Orbatello favored a counter-migration from the city to the countryside.

A final vital statistic about the *miserabili vergognosi* of Orbatello is their social condition of occupation and wealth. First, the occupations of 79 distinct fathers or prematriculation husbands were compiled from the dowry records of 1500 to 1517, and from the Parte deliberations of 1511 to 1530. In table 2 I add for future reference the occupations of the husbands of the girls who married after their mandatory residence in Orbatello:

TABLE 6.2
Occupations of Fathers and Husbands of the Women of Orbatello

	MERCHANT INDUS-TRIALISTS	WEAVERS	DYERS	WOOL WORKERS[45]	CHISELERS	MASONS	METAL WORKERS	LEATHER WORKERS
Pre-Orbatello	2	6	3	16	3	4	4	3
New Husbands	4	13	2	16	0	1	5	0

	SHOE AND HATMAKERS	EYEGLASS MAKERS	WOOD WORKERS	SPICERS	BUTCHERS	BAKERS	POULTERERS	USED-CLOTHES PEDDLERS
Pre-Orbatello	11	3	4	2	1	2	0	2
New Husbands	4	1	1	1	0	2	1	0

	HOSTELRY	MILLERS	AGRI-CULTURAL WORKERS	BARBERS	WRITERS	PAINTERS	TAX COLLECTORS
Pre-Orbatello	0	4	5	1	1	1	1
New Husbands	2	2	6	1	0	0	0

Two points seem worth making about these occupations. First, only five in the lot of seventy-nine were farm laborers; the women did not come from a peasant background. Second, the Florentine industrial occupations were as important as the land was insignificant: one in five of these men had labored in Florence or its immediate environs as a salaried woolworker, while one in nine had been in the economically superior position of dyer or weaver in the wool or silk industry.

We have in Orbatello, then, a population roughly one-third of which came from the dominion of Florence, another third whose husbands or fathers had been part of Florence's industrial labor force, and a final third whose husbands and fathers had been artisans not involved in the wool and silk industries. Not surprisingly, the daughters and wives of the Florentine elite of merchant-industrialists rarely landed in Orbatello[46] and there is almost no indication of eventual occupations of the women themselves.

A vital question of social origins is that of wealth, and another source of information leaves no doubt that the women did not come from the penniless, destitute population so often encountered among domestics. We know the total makeup of thirty-seven of the dowries which the notary Leoni recorded between 1500 and 1517, and they turn out on inspection to be small but not unusual for girls with fathers in the range of occupations we have documented.[47] They ranged first of all from 15½ to 52½ florins (£ 64 to £ 215), but the more significant figure is the contribution the girl herself ("or rather her mother," one document clarifies) made to the dowry.[48] While not one girl seems to have drawn her part from the commune's dowry investment fund, a sure indication of these girls' relative poverty, the average girl's contribution to her dowry, including money and goods, was a respectable 18 florins, £ 3 (£ 4, s. 2 per florin):

TABLE 6.3
Dowries of the Girls of Orbatello, 1500–1517, in £

AVERAGE DOWRY	PARTE CONTRIBUTION	ALL OTHERS' CONTRIBUTIONS	DAUGHTERS' CONTRIBUTIONS	THIRD PARTIES' CONTRIBUTIONS[49]
134, s. 8	50, s. 4(37.4%)	84, s. 4(62.6%)	76, s. 16(57.1%)	7, s. 10(5.5%)

The thirty-seven dowries averaged in this table include all those dowries which can safely be designated "total," and every one of them includes some contribution by the girl; I could find no certain case of a girl whose total dowry was constituted by the Parte.[50] The girls of Orbatello therefore usually had mothers or relatives who made a significant contribution toward their marriage. This was a population which might be miserable, but was not destitute.

MAKING ORBATELLO WORK

The Orbatellan administrative records of the first half of the sixteenth century leave the reader with two strong impressions. The first is that there was no civil war in the house: not one recorded conflict or case of violence of the type so common in the Florentine nunneries! Second, mobility within Orbatello was remarkably limited. Only 22 of the 157 donnas named in the comprehensive Parte records from 1511 to 1530 showed up in two different apartments, and none lived in more. Since few donnas seem to have vacated Orbatello willingly and not many more unwillingly, it seems safe to estimate that five of six donnas stayed in one place until they died. The picture is no different for children, who almost never moved from one apartment to another without their relatives; 5 of the 22 women who moved took children with them, comparable to that proportion of the donne in the home with children. There can be little doubt that with all its vicissitudes, Orbatello worked, and the question is why.

Despite itself, the Parte is part of any answer. It placed a pillory in the courtyard "to give example . . . [and] spectacle to all the . . . women," and a priest in the rectory who was charged among other things with "holding the women in peace and restraining them from perpetrating bad behavior or violence either inside or outside."[51] Rules and punishment were the more likely to be heeded because the Parte captains were replaced every six months: with their own civic clientele to please, each new set of officials had good reason to "empty and disencumber" apartments so they could then exercise their pro rata right to refill them.[52] Yet a countervailing consideration worked in the women's interest. Orbatello existed to intern dependent families, and expelling them only created more public beggars, to the dishonor of the Parte. So this organization compromised with its own strict rules, and in effect allowed the women to run their asylum on a day-to-day basis. It was the matrons who governed Orbatello by manipulation of the rules.

The force of their leadership can first be surmised in the repeated practice of staggered matriculations, by which an individual moved in, to be only later officially followed by her child or sister or other hearth member.[53] Yet it is improbable that these second matriculants had actually been abandoned for a time by their mothers or sisters, but rather it seems that they entered surreptitiously, with the connivance of the elders, to then obtain official admission when the census allowed. Whatever the truth of this matter, such staggered admissions had the evident effect of maintaining a coherent and limited group of kin networks in the asylum. If a woman wanting to matriculate into Orbatello would do a Parte official a favor by accepting as her charge an unattached girl whose relations that official had to please, that same woman once established in the house became part of a decision-making corps who actually approved changes in Orbatello's living arrangements. Living *familiariter* in Orbatello, we find, included moving in with the consent of the person already inhabiting an apartment: both had to "be content" with the arrangement.[54] Women "offered" to welcome newcomers to their quarters, and in the case of one girl named Felicia, we even catch a glimpse of the *mulieres Orbatelli* described as a decision-making corporation.[55]

In 1549 the Parte discovered Felicia living in the house without license, and apparently moved to expel her. Yet it soon reconsidered, for the captains found, in their suggestive language, that Felicia had been "received by the *mulieres* of the said place" six years or more earlier.[56] These women, the Parte formulation continues, had themselves decided that the girl was "poor and seemly," and the Parte thus decided to go along with the corporate judgment to keep her. They justified their action in now giving Felicia six years tenure in Orbatello (and thus the right to dowry aid) by noting that the girl presently lived with the widow Antonia who, "led by mercy," had "received" her into her apartment, and who now "offered" to "retain" her in the future. The matter was settled. Over the course of six years the *mulieres Orbatelli* had individually and apparently corporately conspired to conceal Felicia's presence from the visiting captains and perhaps even from the priest; that did not deter the Parte from accepting their opinion, and bowing to their solidarity.

The matrons of Orbatello seem to have been quite as resourceful in manipulating the moral guidelines of the asylum, aided by an often weak and indecisive Parte. Time and again that organization decreed the expulsion of women "to preserve seemliness in their houses of Orbatello," and just as regularly "drunkards and troublemakers" of every kind still lived in their apartments months and even years later.[57] No norm was more timeworn than the prohibition against foreign women and slaves, yet the Parte not uncommonly revoked or prorogued its application, for it was clear that some of these women were acceptable to the matrons and, indeed, that they sometimes were stabilizing forces in Orbatello.[58] In March 1512, for example, the dark-skinned donna Caterina, the slave donnà Apollonia, and donna Lucia daughter of Bernardina of Barbary received expulsion notices because of their origins and conditions. Yet a year and a half later donna Lucia was not only still living in her accustomed apartment; the Parte actually assigned her the custody of the *contado* girl Camilla, in other words made her responsible for the girl's upbringing. The Parte's, and surely the other matrons' confidence in Lucia, was well placed. In 1521 they had the pleasure of seeing Camilla led into matrimony.[59]

The women seem to have been quite as unruffled by the occasional signs of prostitution in the house, from the earliest Ciompi defamation of 1378 to the 1530 evidence of a nest of ladies led by an Alberti and staffed by the likes of Lena the Grand and Caterina the Bean.[60] These and other women who sinned and stayed could not have persevered without the tolerance and protection of the established women of the house. No judgment is possible or desirable on the moral condition of the house, but it is quite plausible that the matrons would have been more upset by the likes of donna Barbera, who set up permanent residence in Orbatello with her husband and thus prevented other women from getting their relatives admitted to the asylum,[61] than they were with the sexual torts which dot the pages of the record. In the light of all this, the protection and commiseration shown those despairing women whose sons were supposed to leave because they had reached their twelfth birthday, hardly needs mention. Boys as old as eighteen years hung on with their mothers, clearly the beneficiaries of a corporate stance of the matrons.[62]

Orbatello owed some of its evident stability to the self-administration of its matrons. As far as is known, these women left no ledgers. There is no evidence that they exercised any formal administrative duties involving record keeping. But the suggestion that the older women acted as a corporate body in accepting members; that the Parte relied on them for an assessment of the condition of the house; that they as well as the men were capable of "staging" matriculations, perhaps in part by managing available space for unlicensed sisters and their children; that the matrons controlled access to and from the cloister of Orbatello; as we shall see: all this points to a consensus system of administration of a type which received no press from the male writers of the age. Contemporaries repeated the story of Cornelia Gracchi and her Florentine counterpart Alessandra de' Bardi, of course—those exemplary individual widows and abandoned wives who performed wonders of family administration because they were "more men than women." But these male writers had nothing good to say about women in groups. The Orbatello however provides some evidence that widows, while certainly profiting from their past marital experience, confronted the new and unique life-experience of Orbatello with creative energy, an energy all the more compelling because of the maladministration of the Parte Guelfa.

Thus Luigi Passerini was surely right that the women of Orbatello helped each other in their infirmities, and the widows who took in the lame girl Caterina in 1522 and those who welcomed the widow Maria of the Leg are examples of such solidarity.[63] Yet it was a practical human administration we see at work in the asylum, and not mindless maternalism. If the women were willing to accept, they could also expel or isolate when that was advisable. The matrons must have been the ones who in 1546 told the captains that Bartolomea of Romagnola could not be left with donna Lucrezia: the latter was old and sick, while Bartolomea may have been mentally ill. Someone of such "poor judgment and [so] contentious" needed to be isolated, and the Parte moved Bartolomea into a separate residence near the gate so as to avoid the "scandal" which threatened.[64]

This female organization was predominantly familial in nature. The women of Orbatello said by their actions what the Parte never specifically stated in its statutes: Orbatello's widows preserved family solidarities, and we have already sketched the biographies of some of these widows catering over the years to a series of younger relatives. Many of these were their own children, and we counted 39 donne with their children among the 157 donne in the records between 1511 and 1530. Ten grandmothers with their grandchildren can be discerned in the same records, several maternal and paternal aunts united with a small army of nephews and nieces, and sisters living with each other. We have seen that a few children with no relatives entered Orbatello, and one of the donnas acted as if she were a funnel for strange children, accepting first one set of siblings and then another.[65] There should be absolute clarity that many widows lived with each other with no children, and moved from one house to the other to form more perfect unions.[66] Yet when widows did not live together but rather accepted the younger generation or two generations, the chances were overwhelming that they would be their relatives.

When apartment 28-s changed hands in 1518 and 1519, the human variety of Orbatello could be seen in its microcosm. On November 13, 1518, the Parte successfully expelled two widows with all their children and *familia* "pro honestate Orbatelli."[67] Had their nefarious behavior been denounced by the *pinzochera* suora

Margherita, who lived in the loft above the apartment? We are not sure, but the good sister may have bitten off more than she could chew. Three days after the expulsion the Parte captains gave donna Domenica Valva, widow of a wool spinner, permission to move into 28-s below the saintly elder Margherita. Donna Domenica came from apartment 5-s to her new home . . . with six children![68] Suora Margherita moved out less than three months later, going to apartment 1-s, perhaps to keep a pious eye on who came and went from this sometimes noisy, but rarely violent asylum.[69]

Driven by the practical need for a livable and durable environment, therefore, the women of Orbatello succeeded where the Parte itself would have failed. Yet there was another powerful motivation behind this success, and that was the productive activity within the asylum itself. The specific activity in Orbatello was rearing legitimate girls for marriage, and here again, the record speaks for itself. Between 1500 and 1517, the Parte sponsored an annual average of 4.4 girls of Orbatello in marriage, 74 of the asylum's children being aided in all.[70] We have seen that their mothers provided important additions to the £ 50 dowry the Parte furnished the girl, and from the list of the new husbands' occupations (table 2) as well as from their origins in city and countryside, it is clear that the mothers attracted solid working husbands.[71] Very few of the girls became servants in nunneries and none seems to have entered the twilight zone of domestic service or the brothels.[72]

The matrons must have been pleased and gratified when, on any given Sunday or feast day, weddings were celebrated in the asylum church before them, Parte representatives, and the rector.[73] For a minimum of five years these girls had lived in Orbatello with their mother or other relative, and those elders now saw their training, financial aid, and spouse-searching pay off. The girls had entered Orbatello as legitimate offspring, and they now left *pudica et honesta* to rear another generation free, at least on the girl's side, of the stain of bastardy. The matrons' activities made them part of the reproductive activities of the city at large. Orbatello was a village of hope for its inhabitants, and of honor for the Parte and commune.

The commune of Florence played the father to legions of girls who had none, providing dowries for an overwhelmingly illegitimate population of foundlings, slaves, and servant girls. Here in Orbatello the £ 50 went to "honorable" girls. A proven friend of the nuclear family by its dowries to bastards, the commune here protected and augmented legitimacy. In part through such support from the patronal commune, sentiment for and the sacrality of the nuclear family might grow apace in and around Orbatello, that model of a female culture whose elders provided both the caring and warmth men said proper to the "frivolous sex," and the "gravity" they reserved to themselves.

THE INVASION OF THE INNOCENTS

In the decades after 1550, a fundamental change took place in the population, life, and function of Orbatello. The change is reflected in the breakdown of the notarial consistency, and it is mirrored as well in the inability of subsequent scribes to keep track of a population whose mobility within Orbatello had enormously accelerated. In 1636 one scribe thought he had devised a way of "knowing and encountering in a second in what houses the said women lived, how and when [since 1588] they had entered, so as to put an end to disorders,"[74] and the scribe of the successive Book of the Women of Orbatello, though recognizing that "because of the necessary, continued changing of rooms, one cannot easily fix the numbers of the rooms assigned to the women who enter Orbatello one after the other," tried again.[75] Both failed. Mobility by this time was beyond control, for the house had been invaded by the girls and women of the foundling home of the Innocenti.[76]

To understand the full implications of this invasion, we must first pause to examine the larger problem of women in Florentine society, which was ultimately responsible for this mutation. The background to that problem was indicated at the beginning of this article: the property laws favoring men, the Florentine marriage pattern creating widows at an early age, the high dowries, the constant flow of female migrants driven into the city by war and famine; these and many other factors affected different women in different ways. Finally, we pointed to the demographic upswing which started around 1470. Now we must gauge these factors' impact on Florentine institutions for women. Let there be no mistake: the mass of unwanted females in the Florentine population at the end of the fifteenth and in the following century was a phenomenal demographic and moral fact, and no want of contemporaries raged at a "scandal" for which they knew no precedent.[77]

The explosion of the Florentine nunneries was the most tangible institutional evidence of this crisis, for between 1470 and 1550 the number of religious houses for women doubled and their population had grown to the point where in mid-sixteenth century, some 13 percent of the total female population of Florence lived behind their walls![78] This was the "scandal" which perhaps most outraged the good citizens of Florence, for the nuns of Florence, we remember, were recruited from the "good families" of the city. These roughly 3,000 women entered warehouses their fathers could afford, unlike the mere 250 souls who inhabited Orbatello. We must turn again to the poor females.

Founded in an age of low population, Orbatello eased the plight of one segment of this mass, the elderly widows with their children and younger relatives, a communal resource of legitimate parentage held together by familial bonds. Yet a smaller part of Orbatello's population, though at times protected by the matrons, was not welcomed by the Parte, women we may characterize as having other commitments than to Orbatello. Slaves and foreigners made up part of this group, ladies who knew only a mother if any parent. Still-active women who refused to live continuously in Orbatello constituted another part, those like donna Lucia of Decomano whom the Parte allowed out for a month to "take care of her business," like donna Brigida of the same Decomano, who went to Livorno to stay with the Medici captain of that town, like donna Maria who lived in Orbatello while being an agent for a nunnery.[79]

A third order of women appeared in Orbatello at the very end of our period, and hinted at the avalanche to come. These were single women who were the daughters of communal servants. With one possible exception, neither the daughters nor wives of servants of any governmental body, including the Parte Guelfa, had come to Orbatello until suddenly, in mid-sixteenth century, the government started to find homes in Orbatello for daughters of communal familiars who could not find a husband. The daughter of a squire of the meat office entered Orbatello in 1547, followed by the daughter of an official of the Monte di Pietà.[80] The Parte also found room for the female cook of the government at this time.[81]

The significance of these straws in the wind around 1550 is that some of these governmental assignments were the few single girls without relatives in Orbatello—and *with* ties to the *familia* of the government. These girls' links were to the outside and not the inside, and it was that characteristic which would alter the house's population. The two different caritative family structures of the Florentine state were about to collide.

The irresistible force would come from the foundling home of the Innocenti, after the nunneries and Orbatello the third Florentine institution housing unwanted females. Opened in 1445 by the Florentine silk guild which administered it, this home for abandoned children soon found that despite promised dowries, its girls were unmarriable. Older girls filled up both the Innocenti and another foundling home limited to such an older clientele.[82] The Italian Wars from 1494 to 1530 further stimulated the population of the Innocenti into a frightful spiral which defied the house's horrendous mortality rate.

Simultaneously the streets of Florence filled with legions of displaced and deprived women who sold sex to preserve body and soul. Prostitution had left the brothel, and spread to other areas, including a large concentration near Orbatello.[83] Who can doubt that the older girls of Innocenti made their pittance in these brothels? This dreary catalogue of the crises of the contemporary female seemed to peak in the masses of young children, in the majority female, who had survived infancy but were too young to sell their bodies, so begged in the streets. Duke Cosimo insisted that these victims too were human beings when he began to deal with the scourge in the 1540s. Homes for these *abbandonati*, one for males but three for females between the ages of three and ten, were established and in the census of 1562 can be found warehousing hundreds of children.[84]

Yet where would *they* go when *that* abstract age of exit was reached? The ability of the Florentines to create rational welfare institutions based on vital statistics was undoubted, and the festive representations of the age delighted in presenting these abstract entities: the San Giovanni festival of 1545 showed its audience 70 pairs of little boys and 70 pairs of adolescent boys, 40 pairs of girls ten years or less and 80 pairs of girls looking for husbands.[85] Could one doubt that the republic or the principate was a loving father, the legions of such abstractly divided human beings the sentimental favorites of the patronal state? It was not for want of mind or sentiment, but because of the clamorous demographic problems of the age that, in this unjust society, the support systems of the Florentine welfare state started to buckle. That "firm and solid column" of the Innocenti approached financial collapse, its worthy structures bulging with so many unwanted girls that they had "reached the point of becoming insupportable," in the hapless administrator's words.[86] By 1580 the sixteen hundred children, up from twelve hundred in 1552, could be held no more. The Innocenti declared bankruptcy, sent all its boys aged 12 to 16 to the galleys and forced large numbers of young women into the streets.[87] It was at this point that the women of the Innocenti, girls with no fathers but the state, made their first sudden appearance among the inhabitants of Orbatello.

A document of 1585 makes clear that the "women of the Innocenti" were being put in Orbatello, and creating "scandals." Young *setaioli* or silk merchants came to see their favorites, and the *Innocentine*, with no reason to be beholden to either the priest or women of Orbatello, brought them into their rooms. The Parte did what little it could. It insisted that these new arrivals were subject to the priest just like the established residents, and it set up a group of "the older and venerable women" of Orbatello to guard the entrance to the cloister: the girls would come out rather than the men going in.[88] Yet what more was to be done? The girls were subjects of the *setaioli*, the women of Orbatello responded to the Parte Guelfa; a conflict of competence was unavoidable. The girls of Innocenti were illegitimate, the women and girls of Orbatello mostly legitimate. The former had no family and were known by their mother, the latter had a colleague who was a relative, and knew their dead fathers. Finally, there were so many of the new arrivals. The merest glance at the Book of the Women of Orbatello started in 1636 shows that perhaps one in two of the women who came to Orbatello after 1588 and was still alive in 1636 had come from the Innocenti.[89] Doubtless that figure must be clearly understood: since the girls of the Innocenti may have been younger when they entered than the average widow of Orbatello, more of them would have been alive in 1636. Yet there can be no doubt that as they jammed into the houses near the gate of Orbatello, they changed that venerable institution.

From the time of its foundation in 1370 well into the eighteenth century, the Orbatello played a significant role in the total Florentine welfare effort. Though Florence had no written master plan for care of the aged, Orbatello had provided a refuge for widows and abandoned wives, and had functioned to preserve the integrity of mother-led family units. The female crisis of the sixteenth century significantly affected that function, even if widows remained a feature of Orbatello for generations to come. For a society of widows had met one of illegitimate girls, and the ultimate fate of Orbatello was to lie with the young rather than the old.

The Innocenti no less than the Orbatello was a creation of that sense of family moderns often evoke from the past without truly understanding. In two senses. It was the rational creation of a commune which conceived of itself as a father to all, but it was also a creation of the bastards' fathers, *their* "solid and firm" support. For without the Innocenti, these men's own family honor would have perished from the defamations of their lovers, forced to kill or abandon the children of honorable fathers. *Then* how would these same fathers have married their own, legitimate, daughters? The abstract welfare institutions of Florence, no less than the family-centered asylum of Orbatello, protected the family.

In the eighteenth century, Orbatello served as a forced residence for girls pregnant out of wedlock, for "women in secret labor." The contemporary Giuseppe Richa waxed pious over that latest function of the ancient house, saying without saying what block "H" of Orbatello did. It was used ". . . for endangered girls, being destined to save not less their honor, than the life of the creatures with whom they were pregnant."[90]

Richa meant that the girls might have killed the children if not supervised, and would have shamed their families if their pregnancy had been public knowledge.[91] Orbatello continued to guard the family. Perhaps in that age, the descendants of our sixteenth-century widows played the policewoman who preserved life, or perhaps there were those elder midwives in Orbatello who eliminated the unwanted, to-be-anonymous infants.

There is pathos in the contrast between the Renaissance and the Enlightenment matron in Orbatello. In the early sixteenth century, this asylum had made the later life of many widows one of hope and contribution to future generations, perhaps the only island in Europe where a female community preserved family units and prepared new ones. All this without being midwives. In the eighteenth century, however, the matrons of Orbatello were surely midwives, bringing new life into the world from imprisoned girls who were not Orbatello's but the state's. Even while birthing, the widow of this Orbatello was severed from her history. She was a technician of the Tuscan state, creating the reality and ideology of the modern nuclear family.

A Renaissance asylum where for centuries widows were communally encouraged to stay with and rear their children adds to our knowledge of preindustrial old-age dependency. It questions not only the general idea that the traditional family sufficed as a welfare institution for the elderly, but the specific one that historically, state asylums have compromised kin family solidarities. Orbatello's history suggests that in early modern Europe we view the care of the female elderly in the context of a competition for funds and attention between widow-led kin families and the "family of the state," those dependent on government as an abstract but supportive father. The female elderly were not privileged within Florence's operative if unwritten policy for this world of dependents; hence the Orbatello proved vulnerable when the internment of masses of illegitimate girls proved politically and socially more imperative than the care of the elderly and their legitimate children. Issues implicit in this eclipse of an old women's institution—the functions of the female elderly in society and their claims on municipal assistance—are not confined to early modern Florence.

NOTES

1. D. Rothman, *The Discovery of the Asylum* (Boston: Little, Brown, 1971), examining nineteenth-century America.

2. *Archivio di Stato, Firenze (ASF), Provvisioni*, 66, ff. 37r–38r (June 12, 1378); 136, ff. 15rv (Apr. 22, 1445). See further ibid., 119, f. 268v (Nov. 27, 1428); 120, f. 401r (1429); 121, f. 168r (1431); 122, f. 156v (1431); 125, f. 193v (1434 Florentine style/1435 modern style); 143, ff. 250r–251v (Oct. 30, 1452); 153, f. 160r (Oct. 27, 1462); 166, f. 266r (1470); 185, ff. 37rv (1495). Also *Statuta Populi et Communis Florentiae* II (Fribourg, 1778), 352f; G. Brucker, "The Ciompi Revolution," in N. Rubinstein, ed., *Florentine Studies* (London: Faber and Faber, 1968), p. 324, n. 2; B. Varchi, *Storia Fiorentina* (Florence: Salani, 1963), bk. VI, ch. 11.

3. The marriage pattern is studied in D. Herlihy and C. Klapisch-Zuber, *Les Toscans et leurs Familles* (Paris: E.H.E.S.S. [Ecole des Hautes études en Sciences Sociales] 1978), 323f, 393–404, 488. See also C. de La Roncière, "Pauvres et Pauvreté à Florence au XIVe siècle," in M. Mollat, ed., *Études sur l'Histoire de la Pauvreté (Moyen Age-16e siècle)*, (Paris: C.N.R.S. [Centre Nationale de la Recerche Scientifique] 1974), pp. 666–669.

4. R. Trexler, "Une Table Florentine d'Espérance de Vie," *Annales E.S.C.* XXVI (1971): 138; *ASF, Prov.*, 113, f. 229v (Dec. 13, 1423). R. Trexler, "Le Célibat à la Fin du Moyen Age: les Religieuses de Florence," *Annales E.S.C.*, XXVII (1972): 1329–1350.

5. C. Klapisch-Zuber, "Célibat et Service Féminins dans la Florence du XVe siècle," *Annales de Démographie Historique 1981*, 289–302. R. Trexler, "The Foundlings of Florence, 1395–1455," *History of Childhood Quarterly* I (1973): 259–284, and my "La Prostitution Florentine au XVe siècle: Patronages et clientèles," *Annales E.S.C.* XXXVI (1981): 983–1015.

6. B. Pullan, *Rich and Poor in Renaissance Venice* (Cambridge, Mass.: Harvard University Press, 1971), pp. 253, 425. R. Mueller, "Charitable Institutions, the Jewish Community, and Venetian Society," *Studi Veneziani* XIV (1972): 54, says many Venetian hospitals were reserved for widows; I could not verify this.

7. See R. Trexler, "Une Table Florentine," p. 138, for monasteries with quarters for the elderly. A mid-fifteenth-century description of the male and female branches of the great hospital of S. Maria Nuova shows them providing such cottages: "E apresso a' detti spedali vi sono case molte belle nelle quali v'abitano donne vechie e huomini vechi"; *Codice Rustici, Seminario Maggiore, Firenze*, f. 50v.

8. N. Zemon Davis could find no cases of subsidized housing outside hospitals and beguinages except for the early-sixteenth-century Fuggerei (Augsburg) for elderly workers; *Society and Culture in Early Modern France* (Stanford: Stanford University Press, 1975), 281.

9. The testament is in L. Passerini, *Gli Alberti di Firenze*, 2 vols. (Florence: Tip. M. Cellini, 1869), II, 156–185 (hereafter "T"); G. Richa's description of an Alberti testament is untrustworthy; *Notizie Istoriche delle Chiese Fiorentine* I (Florence: P.G. Viviani, 1754), 296. A document of 1425 shows the house was finished before the apartments were filled; *ASF, Parte Guelfa, numeri rossi* (hereafter *PGR*), 6, ff. 31v–33r (Mar. 5). The Ciompi reference is in *Diario d'Anonimo Fiorentino dall'anno 1358 al 1389*, in A. Gherardi, ed., *Cronache dei Secoli XIII e XIV* (Florence: Tip. M. Cellini, 1876), 365.

10. T, 161. For the street distinctions see *PGR*, 16, ff. 62r, 117r–154v. Houses 4–11, 13, 14, and 20 (*PGR*, 16, f. 122v) are on the prior or lower street in the 1540s. "No. 29 supra, videlicet in ultima domo"; *PGR*, 13, f. 63v. Houses 23–25 and a later house 30 are on the upper street in the 1540s. Records of assignments to designated houses start in 1511.

11. *PGR*, 27, f. 14r ("Beni della Parte, 1431").

12. E.g. *PGR*, 16, f. 123r (May 15, 1549).

13. The documents are sparing of information on actual living arrangements. Note this description of Nov. 15, 1550: "Tutte le habitante in dete case, che sono a numero xxviiii. Et in ciascheduna habita almancho 2 famigle: una in terreno et l'altra in palcho. Et alchuna casetta in è che ha el palchuccio dove habita una persona sola"; *PG, numeri neri* (hereafter *PGN*), 698, no. 13. There is one hint of more than one loft per house, a document speaking of the "primo palcuccio di sopra" of 21-s; *PGR*, 14, ff. 12v–13r.

14. E.g. *PGR*, 4, ff. 47v–48v (Parte statutes of 1420); 6, ff. 31v–33r (Mar. 5, 1424/25); 7, f. 50r (July 14, 1447); 9, f. 57v (Jan. 14, 1459/60); 9, ff. 36r, 61v–62r, 66v, 76v (1461, 1509).

15. T, 158, 163ff. "Sacristam et rectorem et gubernatorem dicte ecclesie et habitantium," the priest was required to prepare inventories "de bonis ecclesie et domibus eiusdem"; *PGR*, 11, f. 193r (Feb. 13, 1514).

16. "Il quale chiaramente et per le parole del testatore et per le habitationi d'esso più ornato et meglio aconcie, che a quella tanto bruta gente non si conviene, s'intende essere suto facto per persone di buona conditione, per alcuna mala fortuna divenuti vergognosi miserabili"; *PGR*, 9, f. 61v (Mar. 19, 1460/61). On the difference between "the poor" and the "miserable poor," and on the legal status of the *vergognosi*, see De La Roncière, "Pauvres," 685–704; R. Trexler, "Charity and the Defense of Urban Elites in the Italian Communes," in F. Jaher, ed., *The Rich, the Well Born, and the Powerful* (Urbana: University of Illinois, 1973), 67–74.

17. *PGR*, f. 61v (Mar. 19, 1460/61).

18. On "ghesse o bigie" or "nere" see *PGR*, 12, ff. 232r, 234v (Jan.).

19. Vs. persons "di diverse sangue et costumi et forestieri"; *PGR*, 9, f. 36v (Jan. 17).

20. *PGR*, 9, f. 61v (Mar. 19); further *PGR*, 12, f. 3r (Mar. 5, 1517/18); 13, f. 13v.

21. This was to prevent fraud; *PGR*, 9, f. 30v (Feb. 2); further 13, ff. 211v, 213v, 230r, 233r (1520–22), for the "girls of Orbatello."

22. The payments were made per "persona sive anima" on the following feasts: Annunciation, Easter, All Saints, and Christmas. They were gathered from *PGR*, 11–13. The census figures of 1552 and 1562 are respectively in *ASF, Miscellanea Medicea*, 223, ff. 151v–153v (hereafter "C"), and ibid., 224, f. 119r. All these figures exclude the priest.

23. The pollster divided houses 22 and 24's floors by a line. For no. 30, see *PGR*, 16, f. 140v.

24. No males other than the priest were named in the census, perhaps indicating that no other male adults lived there. Note that in the 1562 census, there were 174 females but only 4 males excluding the priest.

25. On aging in Florentine society, see the article by David Herlihy in the present volume. Also C. Gilbert, "When Did a Man in the Renaissance Grow Old?" *Studies in the Renaissance* XIV (1967), 7–32; K. McKenzie, "Antonio Pucci on Old Age," *Speculum* XV (1940): 160–185.

26. The 60 year old was donna Mea, widow of Domenico of Sesto; *PGR*, 11, f. 93r. The 1559 case is in *PGN*, 707, no. 104 (Mar. 11).

27. A. Molho and J. Kirshner, "The Dowry Fund and the Marriage Market in Early Quattrocento Florence," *Journal of Modern History* L (1978): 433; Herlihy and Klapisch-Zuber, *Toscans*, 207; Klapisch-Zuber, "Célibat," n. 21.

28. This would apply only after 1504, of course, when that requirement was introduced.

29. "Domna Juliana Tomasii Bartolomei de Businis" (*PGR*, 13, f. 184r) is actually "domna Juliana vidua uxor olim Tomasii Bartolomei Businis"; *PGR*, 12, ff. 217rv. "Domna Agnioletta Antonii gualchieroni" (*PGR*, 13, f. 159r) is really "domna Angioleta vidua uxor olim Antonii gualcherarii"; ibid., f. 63v. "Domna Magdelena Pieri Muchini (*PGR*, 11, f. 176v) is "domna Magdelena vidua uxor olim Pieri Muchini; *PGR*, 13, f. 186v. Several other cases of this type emerge from a comparison of C to *PGR*, 16.

30. Respectively *PGR*, 11, ff. 23r, 155v.

31. Donna Angela is the mother of "domna Margherita vidua uxor olim Rafaelis battilani"; *PGR*, 12, f. 71v.

32. "Illud vero, quod Orbatellus nuncupatur, in quo pauperculae viduae domo carentes recipiuntur"; Mariano Ughi (fl. 1518), cited in Richa, *Notizie*, I, 297.

33. Trexler, "Célibat," 1344.

34. D. Herlihy calculated a life-expectancy of 15.5 years for a 45-year-old woman of Pistoia in early fifteenth century; *Medieval and Renaissance Pistoia* (New Haven: Yale University Press, 1967), 287.

35. *PGR*, 11, f. 155v. Silvestra married with the help of the Parte in 1518; *PGR*, 12, f. 195v.

36. *PGR*, 14, ff. 12v–13r. Silvestra's husband was Bartolomeo di Pasquino; their son could have been our Pasquino. On the Orbatello full of troops, and the "hospitali portitorum situato in via S. Galli, in quo hospitali ad presentem habitent mulieres solite habitare in domibus Orbatelli," see ibid., f. 3r (March 23, 1529/30).

37. *PGR*, 16, f. 142r.

38. "A maggior parte vi sono entrate col partito, et sono vedove povere co lloro figluole et nipote et qualche nipote maschio minori d'anni 12, et di assai honesta aria. Et vi è infra l'altre quatro vedove vecchie et di commoda presenza. Le quale, chiamate in disparte et dimandate dei costumi e i portamenti delle altre . . ."; *PGN*, 698, no. 13 (Nov. 15, 1550).

39. *ASF, notarile antecosimiano*, Leoni 140(1500–1517) f. 142v. (hereafter, Leoni).

40. *PGR*, 11, f. 176v; ibid., 12, f. 112r.

41. Leoni, f. 147v; *PGR*, 13, f. 168v.

42. See nos. 3, 5. The quote is from Giovanni Cavalcanti's description of events in 1440; cited in my "Foundlings," 266.

43. Leoni. Samuel Cohn was kind enough to bring this volume to my attention.

44. For a girl's father and her new husband both from the Mugello: Leoni, f. 41v; from S. Maria Contigiono: ibid., f. 101r; from the Casentino: ibid., f. 120v. The *pudica honestas* (*PGR*, 9, f. 30v [Feb. 2, 1503/04]) possible at Orbatello may be compared to the many girls of the Innocenti sprung from mothers who were domestics; Trexler, "Foundlings," 270f.

45. Included are *battilani, pettinatori, purgatori,* and *schardassieri.*

46. Single individuals of the following families were encountered: Biscioni, Busini, Cardini, Gerini, Gori, Migliori, Redditi, Ricciardi, and Schiatti. There were two Medici women and two Alberti, for whom see below.

47. See Molho and Kirshner, "Dowry Fund," 418, for comparisons. Herlihy and Klapisch-Zuber characterize households with a taxable estate of from 10 to 100 florins as "de fortune médiocres"; *Toscans*, 287.

48. Leoni, f. 105r. In the following I use a conversion rate of £ 4, shillings 2 per florin, that used in the midst of the period 1500–1517 by the Parte authorities.

49. The third parties contributing in 8 cases were the Buonomini di San Martino who catered to the *poveri vergognosi* (3 X), the confraternity of the wool weavers (1 X), the hospital of S. Maria Nuova (1 X), and three private individuals.

50. There are four cases where the wording would indicate a whole dowry, but they had to be eliminated because of the notary's evolving terminology, which made these cases more probably *pro parte dotis* than *pro dote*.

51. *PGN*, 707, no. 104 (Mar. 11, 1558/59); 795, f. 34r (Mar. 27, 1625).

52. *PGR*, 13, f. 197v. Cases *pro computo* are in *PGR*, 11, f. 92v (Oct. 13, 1512); f. 143v (May 27, 1513); 14, ff. 12v–13r (Aug. 19, 1530).

53. Thus the widow donna Costanzia entered Oct. 11, 1519, her 12-year-old daughter Candida joined her July 19, 1520; *PGR*, 12, f. 177v; 13, f. 37v. Donna Diamante, who on Aug. 17, 1521 moved into 25 s with her daughter Andrea (*PGR*, 13, f. 139v), took in her daughter Caterina on Apr. 15, 1522 with the approval of the Parte; ibid., f. 191r. The case of sisters is in *PGR*, 14, ff. 12v–13r.

54. "Et hoc comune, que sint contente"; *PGR*, 11, f. 76v. On "familial life," *PGR*, 15, f. 78v. The deal with the Parte is in *PGR*, 16, f. 140v (Nov. 6, 1549). "Custody" of a girl by her grandmother is at *PGR*, 16, f. 123r.

55. For "offering," see the deal above and Felicia below.

56. "Et quod ipsa est pauper et honesta, propter que fuit recepta a mulieribus dicti loci. Et quod hodie degit et habitat una cum domna Antonia vidua . . ., et que domna, misericordia ducta, ipsam recepit in eius habitatione, et obtulit se fuisse et esse paratam ipsam retinere etiam in futurum"; *PGR*, 16, f. 117r (Mar. 27, 1549).

57. See *inter alia PGR*, 11, ff. 113r, 139r, 153r, 163r, 171rv, 222r; 12, f. 76r; 16, f. 152v.

58. One case of revocation is in *PGR*, 12, f. 234v (Jan. 18, 1519/20).

59. *PGR*, 11, ff. 58r, 178v; *PGR*, 13, f. 214v.

60. *PGR*, 14, f. 12r.

61. *PGR*, 13, f. 170r (Jan. 28, 1521/22).

62. Cases of overage boys staying on are in *PGR*, 11, ff. 59r, 60r, 139r, 153r, 163r; 12, f. 112r; 13, f. 31r; 14, f. 12r.

63. Passerini in the introduction to T, 155; *PGR*, 13, f. 178v; 16, f. 26r.

64. "Attento qualiter domna Bartolomea de Romandiola, que habitat in Orbatello et in domo segnata no. xi et una cum domna Laurenza vetula ac egrota, est persona levis et modici iuditii ac riscoza, ita quod habitando et stando in societate facile esset quod deveniri et quod deveniret ad aliquid scandalum"; *PGR*, 16, f. 33v (Dec. 22).

65. Donna Cosa took the boy and girl of a shoemaker into her apartment 28 i in Feb. 1521, and in the following August accepted into the same apartment two daughters of a wool beater; *PGR*, 13, ff. 88v, 141v.

66. Single donnas entering and moving about, are the most common fact in these records.

67. *PGR*, 12, f. 76r.

68. The children ranged from a girl of 17 to a boy of 3 years of age; ibid.

69. Apartment 1-s was at the gate; *PGR*, 12, f. 98v.

70. Computations based on Leoni. Parte controls over qualifications are in *PGR*, 11, f. 171v (1513); 13, ff. 122r, 197r (1521–1522); 14, f. 119r (1532).

71. The distribution between, in, and outside the city is described above. Leoni recorded the city parishes of 55 grooms, most well removed from Orbatello. The largest contingent came from S. Lorenzo (17), from the wool workers' parishes of S. Frediano

and S. Maria in Verzaia (8), followed by the nearby large parishes of S. Ambrogio (7) and Orbatello's own S. Piero Maggiore (6).

72. Two girls became servants in nunneries, one became a nun in the convent of converted prostitutes; PGR, 11, f. 238v; 15, f. 166r; 16, ff. 75r, 123v.

73. On the celebrations, see PGR, 14, f. 3r (Mar. 23, 1529/30). The standard meal for the attending captains is recorded at PGR, 11, f. 221r. None of Leoni's notarial records refers to marriages infra missarum solemnia, and occasionally the rector was not even present; Leoni, ff. 53v, 105v. C. Klapisch-Zuber emphasizes the meager role of priests and church at marriages: "Zacharie, ou le Père Évincé. Les Rites Nuptiaux Toscans entre Giotto et le Concile de Trente," Annales E.S.C. XXXIV (1979): 1216–1243. The brides generally did not move out of Orbatello until the grooms had collected the entire dowry owed them; the two exceptions are in Leoni, f. 144v.

74. Archivio degli Innocenti, Firenze (AIF), XLVII, 7, f. 1r.

75. AIF, XLVII, 8, f. 1r.

76. Note that both of these volumes are now in the Archive of the foundling home of the Innocenti, which took over responsibility for Orbatello in the eighteenth century.

77. See my "Prostitution," and my "Infanticide in Florence: New Sources and First Results," History of Childhood Quarterly I (1973), 98–116, and for the cultural implications my Public Life in Renaissance Florence (New York: Academic Press, 1980), chs. 11–14.

78. Trexler, "Célibat," 1333–1347.

79. Donna Lucia d'Antonio da Decomano entered on Aug. 22, 1513 into apartment 13-i; PGR, 11, f. 164v. On Oct. 11, 1519 she was permitted to absent herself the following February, her room to be held for her; PGR, 12, f. 177v. Brigida di Biagio "possit ire et stare Liburnum cum Bernardo Alamanni de Medicis ibidem capitano, et quod eius habitatio eidem domne preseveritur"; PGR, 11, f. 194v (Mar. 4, 1513/14). The fattoressa Maria of the nunnery of the Murate is recorded in C.

80. PGR, 16, ff. 62r, 142r. The possible exception is one donna Maria, but it seems that her husband rather than she was a "buco o quoqui dominorum," i.e., of the Signoria of Florence. She entered apartment 19-s with her four children in 1513; PGR, 11, f. 118v (Feb. 26).

81. Donna Nanna "cuocha di palazzo" is mentioned in C.

82. See my "Foundlings." A decision of 1483 to place the grown population as servants in Florentine families was abandoned, perhaps because of the sexual abuses associated with such placements; G. Bruscoli, Lo Spedale di S. Maria degli Innocenti di Firenze (Florence: Ariani, 1900), 16, 49.

83. Trexler, "Prostitution." The suspicion that this brothel area was supported by "girls of Orbatello" could not be confirmed in the sources. According to P. Battara, the largest concentration of licensed prostitutes in 1552 was in the Via de' Pilastri near Orbatello; La Popolazione di Firenze a metà del '500 (Florence: Rinascimento del Libro, 1935), 18. This is wrong because of noncounting of the public brothels.

84. In the masculine house 95, in the three female houses 346 youngsters; ASF, Misc. Medicea, 224, ff. 4r, 13r, 69r, 87v.

85. Text of the description in M. Plaisance, "La Politique Culturelle de Côme Ier et les Fêtes Annuelles à Florence de 1541 à 1550," in J. Jacquot et E. Konigson, Les Fêtes de la Renaissance III (Paris: C.N.R.S., 1975), 150. These groups were contingents in a representation of the Slaughter of the Innocents, and the decision to represent age and sex groups separately, rather than in the family groups proper to the Slaughter, is a

stunning example of Florentine abstractiveness. Not surprisingly, the one other group in this same representation was "26 pairs of widows." Could this contingent have come from the Orbatello?

86. Bruscoli, *Spedale*, 63.

87. Ibid., 66. The numbers are in Battara, *Popolazione*, 28. An admittedly late document of 1642 through its breakdown of the females in this population gives an impression of the load from those of advanced age:

Milking	188	From 12 to 20 ·	198
Below 7 years	324	From 20 to 40	177
From 7 to 12	140	Older than 40	141
		(of which 10 were 86 years old).	

According to our source, the girls, "because all were kept in the convent, little by little start to live like animals. For now the girls sleep eight to a bed, and there are only 690 of them. Think what it will be like when the 300 [at nurse] return"; *Biblioteca Nazionale, Firenze, fondo principale*, II. iv. 370, f. 12r (Oct. 31, 1642, and undated, 1647).

88. "Disordini causati dalle donne degl'Innocenti cavate di là, et mandate in Orbatello, quali non vogliono stare a obedienza del prete, intromettono giovani setaiuoli et altri bottegai nella clausura. . . ." The Orbatello now seemed "Più presto luogo poco honesto, che ecclesiastico et pio. . . . " The recommendation was that "si metta alla porta nelle stanze contigue di quelle vechie più venerande, perchè possino et debbino chiamare quelle che son volute dalli settaiuoli, o altri, presente le dette vecchie"; *PGN*, 751, f. 70rv (Jan. 17).

89. Thus the third oldest living resident of Orbatello was Maria della Licia delli Innocenti, who entered in 1588, the fifth was Albiera della Ginevra delli Innocenti, who entered in 1591, the seventh was Agnola di Agnola delli Innocenti, who entered in 1592, etc.; *AIF*, XLVII, 7, at the years.

90. Richa, *Notizie*, I, 298, publishing this volume in 1754. Note also that in Plate 3, the first three houses' upstairs are used for girls as well. Passerini noted the gradual decline of the widows in Orbatello and the increasing number of girls, till in 1861 it was converted into a hospital for syphilitic women and an office for the city's prostitution regulators; introduction to T, 155f.

91. The evasive language was typical of contemporary literature; Trexler, "Infanticide," p. 98–116.

CHAPTER SEVEN — OLD AGE AND WITCHCRAFT IN EARLY MODERN EUROPE*

EDWARD BEVER

INTRODUCTION

W itch! The word conjures in our minds an image from Disney: an evil, ugly, old woman in a black cape and peaked cap astride a broomstick, soaring across a harvest moon. She occupies a marginal place in our thoughts, one of the thousand imaginary dangers frightening to children but meaningful to adults only as a literary relic of a bygone age. If we think of her at all, we can only wonder that for thousands of years our ancestors credited cantakerous old crones with dreadful magical powers and persecuted them with a steadily increasing vehemence that culminated in the great witch craze of the sixteenth and seventeenth centuries. Across Europe, millions of women were suspected of witchcraft, hundreds of thousands were arrested, and scores of thousands were tortured and burned in a frenzy of hatred that left us the phrase "witch-hunt" to describe the senseless persecution of innocent scapegoats.[1]

Historians have long sought to understand the source of the fear and anger fueling early modern Europe's witch-hunts. Their explanations have focused on the institutional imperatives of inquisitorial investigations, Catholic and Protestant doctrines and rivalries, the enormous suffering and anxiety created by European economic and political expansion, and the particular social dislocations within small communities accompanying modernization. In general, interest has shifted from the institutional and intellectual foundations to the socio-economic, from the broad evolution of European civilization to specific changes in social roles and cultural stereotypes. Recent studies, drawing heavily on the insights of anthropologists, have begun to reveal the place of the witch within her local community. They have shown that ugliness, while

*I should like to thank Professors Theodore K. Rabb, Natalie Z. Davis, and H.C. Erik Midelfort, as well as my colleagues Maureen Callahan, James Amelang, Christine Lunardini, and Andrew Barnes for their insightful criticisms and helpful advice.

theoretically a characteristic of witches, in practice played little part in accusations and almost none in convictions.[2] On the other hand, evilness, or perceived evilness anyway, stood at the center of local fears. Theologians and jurists may have railed against all practitioners of magic, but villagers patronized "white witches" — "wise women" and "cunning men" — while denouncing only those people they felt were an immediate threat.[3] That witches were generally female was and remains beyond question. The roots of this misogyny have long puzzled scholars, and have received much attention, especially since the rise of the women's movement and the consequent increase of interest in women's history.[4]

The importance of age remains less clear. Its place in our image is definite, and several recent studies have suggested that "friction with the older inhabitants who . . . made demands on younger village families" constituted a central mechanism leading to accusations; witchcraft fears were "a mother-in-law problem that had got totally out of hand."[5] However, due to haphazard record keeping by the infant bureaucracies of early modern Europe, hard data concerning age are scanty. Furthermore, these hypotheses have been advanced as parts of much larger works, limiting their authors' ability to trace the relationship between age and witchcraft systematically and connect it to current knowledge of historical gerontology. In order to evaluate and refine these recent hypotheses, we will examine, first, the role of age in the early modern literature on witchcraft; second, its place in historical treatments of the subject; and, third, the relevant psychological and sociological insights into old age offered by recent work in the fields of gerontology and history.

EARLY MODERN VIEWS OF THE RELATIONSHIP BETWEEN OLD AGE AND WITCHCRAFT

"It has . . . lately come to Our ears," pontificated Innocent VIII in a Bull dated 1484:

that . . . many persons of both sexes . . . have abandoned themselves to devils . . . and by . . . incantations, spells, and conjurations . . . have slain infants yet in the mother's womb . . . have blasted the produce of the earth . . . [they] afflict and torment men and women . . . as well as animals . . . with terrible and piteous pains . . . hinder men from performing the sexual act and women from conceiving . . . [and] over and above this they blasphemously renounce that Faith which is theirs by the Sacrament of Baptism.[6]

Convinced of the threat posed by this "heretical depravity," the Pope affirmed the right of the inquisitors Heinrich Institoris and Jacob Sprenger to carry out an investigation in western Germany with the full cooperation of all officials, lay and ecclesiastical. Their activities marked the opening of the great early modern witch-hunt.

Institoris and Sprenger, members of the Dominican order and Masters of Theology, undertook their investigation with zeal. Not only did they interview, interrogate, torture, and burn numerous suspected witches, but also they produced a legal manual for witch-hunters and judges, the *Malleus Maleficarum*. In it, they drew together strands of thought already converging in the late medieval period: concern over popular heresies, disapproval of all magic outside the framework of traditional church ritual, and distrust of women.[7] Most of what they wrote had already been expressed in papal pronouncements, theological tracts, and inquisitor's manuals, but the two Dominicans assembled it all in one volume and linked the theoretical formulations to practical examples drawn from their own experiences. The *Malleus* was not the first discussion of witchcraft, but it was the most comprehensive to date and the most authoritative long afterward.

Unlike our Disney image, the witches discussed by Institoris and Sprenger were not distinguished by their advanced age. Their witches, like ours, were evil, for according to the two Dominicans, witches made an explicit pact with the Devil, the Prince of Evil. Theirs, like ours, were magically powerful, for through the pact they exchanged homage to the Devil for his help in working minor miracles. Theirs, like ours, were generally female, for "there was a defect in the formation of the first woman, since she was formed with a bent rib . . . And . . . through this defect she is an imperfect animal, weak" in "both in mind and body," subject to "inordinate affections and passions," and slave to her "insatiable" lusts.[8] But their witches, unlike ours, were not necessarily old. Older women, they felt, were "concerned for worldly profit," and most often became witches after suffering "grievous losses in their temporal possessions."[9] In contrast, "young women, more given to bodily lusts" generally became witches to satisfy "their carnal desires and the pleasures of the flesh," or to avenge themselves after having "been corrupted, and . . . [then] scorned by their lovers." While "in actual practice" the Devil tempted "the wicked more than the good," he was "more eager . . . to tempt the good than the wicked," and consequently tried "all the harder to seduce . . . the more saintly virgins and girls." While he perhaps found worldly wise older women easier to recruit, Institoris and Sprenger's Devil preferred young girls.

The *Malleus Maleficarum* provoked a storm of controversy that continued for over a century and a half. A host of derivative works appeared, defending its emphasis on witches' powers, elaborating on its discussion of the Sabbaths where homage was rendered to the Devil, and repeating its call for the greatest severity in judging these cases.[10] A plethora of short, popular pamphlets recounting the "shocking deeds and actions" attributed to witches in various localities and describing the bloody retribution exacted by the authorities circulated as well. These hard-line documents naturally had no interest in limiting the age range of potential suspects, which could only have lessened the public's sense of urgency.

In fact, as time went by, the defenders of the *Malleus* tradition insisted more and more firmly that the Devil's disciples could be any age.[11] Their explicitness resulted not from any new interest in age on their own part, though, but from their desire to refute an argument raised by their opponents, those who disbelieved some aspects of the witchcraft described in the *Malleus* and urged some degree of moderation toward suspected witches.

Almost as soon as Institoris and Sprenger's book appeared, dissenting voices had been raised, creating a more moderate tradition which insisted that God, not witches or the Devil, was the true source of all events, and that any apparently magical effect was merely "a fantasy or appearance that the Devil arouses in the thoughts or memory of men."[12] The argument for the primacy of God rested on the Book of Job, with its message that man must accept suffering as a manifestation of God's will and not second guess Him by constructing explanations or apportioning blame. The assertion that magic was illusory continued a tradition grounded in the tenth-century *Canon Episcopi*, which stated that the "wicked women" who believed that they flew at night with the Godess Diana were "seduced by illusions and phantasms of the Devil."[13] Few authors championed the moderate tradition, and fewer still developed it in a consistent or encompassing form. Most accepted the possibility of some true miracles, and many demanded severe punishment of convicted witches for their evil intentions, but the moderates' work did form the starting point for the eventual rejection of witchcraft beliefs.

Opposition to the hard-line tradition of the *Malleus Maleficarum* received a tremendous boost from the publication in 1563 of *De Praestigiis Daemonum*, written by Johann Weyer. Student of the renowned doctor and magician Cornelius Agrippa, later court physician to the tolerant Duke of Cleves, Weyer was a "survivor from the civilized days of Erasmus."[14] While he strongly denounced magicians "who are male and *use* the devil," Weyer urged leniency toward witches, females "*used by* the devil."[15] He based his argument for leniency on an innovative combination of the moderate theological tradition and insights into the psychology of witches first put forward around 1550 by the Italians Arnaldo Albertini and Jerome Cardan.[16] Albertine called witches "mostly old women who can find no lovers" and said people who believed in their powers were "mostly foolish old women and infirm men such as melancholics, crazy, maniacal boys and stupid rustics and paupers." Cardan described witches as "miserable women . . . emaciated, deformed . . . pallid, showing in their faces black bile and melancholy." He ascribed their visions and magical experiences to the "black bile, which arises partly from food and drink and air and grief and . . . poverty, partly from the heavens (stars), and partly from association with other crazy folk." Nonetheless, both he and Albertini advocated harsh penalties for witches, and Weyer's innovation was to use psychological arguments in defense of toleration. Through a "blanket use of Cardano's diagnosis of melancholia," Weyer argued that witches' supposed activities were merely the "follies of old women."[17] Women in general, and especially old women, "think they can perform many . . . wicked acts," but their "imagination . . . and the torture of melancholy makes them only fancy they have caused all sorts of evil." Governments should not, he concluded, "impose heavy penalties on [these] perplexed, poor old women."

Weyer's book, published in German and French in 1567, renewed the European debate about witchcraft, and brought a torrent of abuse upon his head. Theologians and lawyers of all confessions and nationalities joined in denouncing him, and Jean Bodin composed a stinging rebuttal which he appended to his widely used handbook for witch-hunters, *De la demonomanie*. Venturing "even into his rival's own professional field of medicine," Bodin argued that according to contemporary medical theory, "women are naturally cold and wet," a condition "directly contrary to adust melancholy."[18] He and the others insisted that witches were not "merely deluded 'melancholic' old ladies," but servants of "the enemy of the human race."

At the time, Bodin's arguments prevailed, for his book appeared at the high point of the persecutions. Weyer's arguments did find a following, however, and after a long period of dormancy eventually won general acceptance. Reginald Scott, in his *Discoverie of Witchcraft*, published in 1584, 1651, and 1665, insisted "that the glorie and power of God be not so abridged and abased as to be thrust into the hand or lip of a lewd old woman," and that, "the vanitie of . . . [witches'] confessions" came from their "base and simple education . . . the extremitie of their age giving them leave to dote . . . their humor melancholicall . . . and full of imagination."[19] Another Englishman, George Gifford, went beyond Weyer's psychological insight by emphasizing the sociological process causing accusations to be made. In two tracts, published in 1587 and 1593, he laid "bare the interweaving of gossip, fear, and tension" behind many accusations:

Some woman doth fall out bitterly with her neighbor: there followeth some great hurt . . . There is a suspicion conceived . . . Great fame is spread of the matter. Mother W. is a witch . . . Well, Mother W. doth begin to be very odious and terrible unto many . . . Shortly after an other falleth sicke and doth pine . . . Everyone sayth now that Mother W. is a witch in deede . . . It is out of all doubt.[20]

Neither these books nor the few others which agreed with them exercised much influence when they first appeared, but the severe persecutions over the following half century caused so much turmoil and suffering, even to the governing classes, that by the late seventeenth century many leaders were ready to heed them. Early Enlightenment thinkers repeated and expanded their criticisms, emphasizing the unreliability not just of old women, but of peasants in general. In 1654 Cyrano de Bergerac discounted the "brainless caprices of an ignorant villager . . . the crack-brained head of a ridiculous Shepard."[21] Turning his acid pen to an old woman's story, he observed:

She was old: age had weakened her reason. Age makes one gossipy: she invented this story to amuse her neighbors. Age weakens the sight: she mistook a Hare for a Cat. Age makes one afraid: she thought she saw fifty instead of one.[22]

Other writers approached the problem more dispassionately, but expressed "the same middle-class contempt for the rustic."[23] By showing magical beliefs to be the "mental rubbish of peasant credulity and feminine hysteria," opponents of the witch persecutions were able to reduce once universally held ideas to mere "old wives' tales."[24]

Emphasis on the witches' old age, then, came not from the witch-hunters, but from their opponents. Striving to portray witchcraft as a medical instead of moral problem, the product of *dementia* rather than diabolism, they included age along with sex and class to heighten the plausibility of their point of view. Discrediting the beliefs as "feminine hysteria" was simple; the overwhelming majority of witches were women, and this argument merely stood on its head the witch-hunters' contention that women's temperament made them especially vulnerable to the Devil's temptations. Ridiculing "peasant credulity" was equally effective as widening social divisions distanced the urbane elite from the superstitious peasantry. But the source of the argument concerning age is less clear.

Were witch suspects generally old? The skeptics' testimony is unambiguous, but their bias makes it unreliable. A number of proponents of the hunts accepted the claim, but many others denied it. Institoris and Sprenger's statement that "in actual practice" the Devil "tempted the wicked more than the good" and consequently tried "harder to seduce . . . virgins and girls" implied that older, more experienced women more often responded to his advances.[25] But the implication is oblique, the examples of witches they and other witch-hunters discussed were of diverse ages, and nowhere in the *Malleus Maleficarum* did the Dominicans mention directly a special association between witchcraft and old age.

Unless they simply made them up, the skeptics must have derived their ideas about old age and witchcraft from one or both of two sources: popular images of old women and witchcraft and actual observation of suspected witches. Evidence about each is scanty and unreliable, but what does exist suggests that old women were especially suspect as witches, and because of this they stood trial more often than any other comparable group.

Sources on late medieval popular culture untarnished by elite influences are extremely scarce, so any attempt to reconstruct the common people's image of witches and old women must proceed indirectly. Anthropologists have noted that "older women" are especially "vulnerable to charges of sorcery" in a great many societies, because "across cultures and with age they seem to become more domineering, more agentic, and less willing to trade submission for security."[26] Latin and Germanic old women shared this vulnerability, for among these peoples, civilized and barbarian alike, the image "of the *old witch*" was "common," although by no means exclusive.[27] Satiric writers during the Renaissance revived the classical literary image of "the old woman" as "always more or less a sorceress," a revival which seems to have provoked little dissent.[28] A German pamphlet from the late sixteenth century quoted "the old saying, 'What the Devil can't do himself, he does through an old woman.' "[29] While we do not know if this "old saying" was actually older than the *Malleus Maleficarum* (written almost a century earlier), just as we do not know if Renaissance writers adopted their image with any regard for its contemporary applicability, these fragments do suggest that early modern Europeans, like many other peoples, particularly associated old women with witchcraft. Without believing that only old women were witches, they appear to have thought that old women were especially likely to be witches; in literature as in folklore, "the old woman and the witch were often looked upon as one."[30]

Since World War Two, a number of historians have collected numerical information on witch suspects' ages. While limited by the fact that "we have little reliable data about the exact ages of . . . people . . . accused of witchcraft,"[31] their results support what many skeptics themselves claimed, that direct experience with witch trials led them to the conclusion that witches were mostly old women (see Appendix). The proportion of known ages above fifty ranged from a low of 42 percent among the accused at Salem, Massachusetts, to a high of 90 percent at Basel. The low figure probably reflects the particular circumstances of the Salem trials; during similar large-scale panics in Germany "age and sex barriers crumbled until anyone . . . could be accused."[32] The high figures probably reflect a systematic bias toward the noteworthy over the ordinary in the unsystematic records kept by many of early modern Europe's fledgling bureaucracies. Allowing for wide regional and circumstantial variation, it seems safe to conclude that suspects over fifty constituted between half and three-quarters of the accused witches. Since this age group amounted to less than 20 percent of the population, the extent to which it was overrepresented is obvious.[33] A substantial minority of suspects were under twenty, and some suspects were middle-aged, but it seems that the skeptics were justified in asserting that most witches were old.

Many historians assumed that this was the case long before attempts had been made to validate it empirically. They adopted along with the skeptic's observation about suspects' advanced age their conclusions about its implications: that witch beliefs were simply the victimization of "foolish old women" by their neighbors and by their own "humor melancholicall." They have not, however, merely repeated these observations, but have constantly expanded them, tying them into the ever-growing corpus of psychological, sociological, and anthropological knowledge. Before considering the relevance of advances in modern and historical gerontology to the problem of witch beliefs and persecutions, we must first examine what this work has revealed.

HISTORICAL VIEWS OF THE RELATIONSHIP BETWEEN OLD AGE AND EARLY MODERN WITCHCRAFT

Historians have investigated witchcraft beliefs and trials since the eighteenth century. Until recently, however, they generally discussed age only incidentally, if at all. The degree of emphasis placed on age reflected less an explicit consideration of its importance thàn an implicit adjustment to each historian's general perspective on witchcraft and the trials. Thus Henry Charles Lea, a nineteenth-century rationalist, accepted the enlightened tradition of Weyer and Scot. "This witch-madness was essentially a disease of the imagination," he wrote in his *History of the Inquisition.*[34] "If some old crone repaid ill treatment with a curse, and the cow of the offender happened to die . . . she was marked as a witch." In contrast, Jules Michelet, a nineteenth-century romantic, portrayed witchcraft as a perversion of "the genius peculiar to woman and her temperament" brought about by the savage persecutions of the male Christian clergy, which feared the "High-Priestess of Nature" as "a menacing rival," and drove her to "*hate God.*" Champion of feminine wisdom, Michelet made no reference to melancholic old ladies. Montague Summers, representative of a third, religious, tradition, believed that a Devil's conspiracy actually existed, that "witches were a vast political movement . . . a world plot against civilization." Like Michelet, Summers had no particular interest in portraying witches as old.

Few subsequent writers have chosen to take the leap with Summers, but Michelet's tradition received powerful stimulus in the 1920s from Margaret Murray's *The Witch Cult in Western Europe.*[35] Several historians have roundly criticized her work since, but it still has a following among ethnologists, folklorists, psychologists, and occultists. Her vision of witchcraft as a surviving pagan cult has been demolished, but historians have themselves become more aware of the ubiquity and importance of local "wise women" and "cunning men" in medieval peasant communities.[36] The age distribution of these people, whose role of diviner-healer-magician stretches back beyond antiquity, has never been investigated. Popular images of such people, in the past as well as now, suggest that they were often old.

Most professional historians have worked in a tradition more influenced by Lea and other rationalists than by the other two perspectives. They have adopted and elaborated both the psychological and the sociological lines of reasoning first put forward in the sixteenth century, portraying the trials as the scapegoating mechanism of a troubled society, while explaining uncoerced confessions as evidence of some sort of mental defect. In "The European Witch-Craze," Hugh Trevor-Roper argued that "the witch-craze was created out of a social situation": when "Christian Europe came into conflict with social groups it could not assimilate," their "defense of their own identity was seen . . . as heresy."[37] Fear of heretics led churchmen to create the witch stereotype, and "the stereotype, once established . . . became 'subjective reality' to hysterical women." Under the pressure of religious conflict, fear became panic, and "the persecution extended from old women, the ordinary victims of village hatred, to educated judges and clergy . . . the elite of society." The dual role of the old woman was scapegoat and hysteric; her susceptibility to culturally structured delusions made her a lightning rod for society's discontents.

Writing a few years before Trevor-Roper, the medical historian Sona Rosa Burstein produced an essay entitled "Aspects of the Psychopathology of Old Age Revealed in Witchcraft Cases of the Sixteenth and Seventeenth Centuries." Despite her very different interests and point of view, particularly her more sophisticated psychological knowledge, her conclusions about old age and witchcraft were not all that different from the social historian's. On the one hand, "their very appearance, behavior, and tormented bad temper" made "these old women ready scapegoats for a sick and oppressed society."[38] On the other hand, "the prevalent beliefs in witchcraft provided ready-made molds for the fancies of any sick or unhappy mind seeking satisfaction in the delusional transformation of reality." In place of Trevor-Roper's vague references to "sexual hysteria" and "psychopathic persons," Burstein compared early modern descriptions of witches to the modern diagnosis of senile psychosis. Discussing mumbling, lack of appreciation of personal danger, and excessive irritability, she asserted, "these and other related traits become familiar to the point of monotony in any intensive reading of the original [English] witchcraft data." While aware that "what is regarded a psychopathological behavior now may have been normal in other times and conditions," she concluded that "the striking problem . . . is that of a twofold antisocial psychopathy—of society against old women and of old women against society."

Only one historian has seriously questioned the view of self-proclaimed witches as somehow demented. Carlo Ginzburg found records in northern Italy of an actual cult which believed that its members, while in a trance state, flew out of their bodies to do battle against evil witches attempting to destroy the harvest. Accepting that "many witches . . . and people possessed by devils" could have been "epileptics" or "hysterical," he argued that with his group, the *benadanti*:

we are faced with phenomena which cannot be reduced to the field of pathology: partly from statistical reasons (faced with such a large number of "sick" people we would have to shift the boundary between sickness and health), and especially because the supposed hallucinations . . . have a precise cultural consistency . . .[39]

Denying the appropriateness of pathological explanations, he called the *benadanti's* experiences "a specific form of popular religion or a special brand of deviate mysticism."

Ginzburg's work is known outside his native Italy, but its influence has been relatively limited. Until recently only short sections had been translated into English, and only one major work, Jeffrey Russell's *Witchcraft in the Middle Ages*, has Ginzburg's findings incorporated into its central theme. During one generation, between 1610 and 1640, the pressure of inquisitorial trials transformed the *benadanti*, in their own view as well as their community's, from a group dedicated to defending the local harvest to a sect of "Devil-worshipping witches."[40] Russell proclaimed that "no firmer bit of evidence has ever been presented that witchcraft existed," and used it along with a great deal of more questionable evidence in an account of medieval witchcraft that depicts it as a disjointed series of licentious, antiestablishment heresies.[41] He has been justifiably criticized for his reluctance to differentiate fact from fantasy in evaluating medieval sources, but his vision of witchcraft as orgiastic counter-religions ironically led him away from Ginzburg's most radical assertion: that accused persons should not be regarded as psychologically deficient individuals even if they regarded themselves as witches. While Russell explicitly insisted that "it will not do to assume that witches were on the whole mentally ill," he described witchcraft as, " a form of nihilism . . . demanded by mentally and emotionally unstable people," "the deterioration of mental order in a time of social crisis."[42] In fact the explanatory scheme underlying his discussion of "witchcraft and the medieval mind" follows closely the rationalist tradition: "Terrified by changes in a cosmos that was not supposed to change, some people were driven to embrace witchcraft; others were driven by the same terrors to irrational fear of witchcraft."[43]

Two other historians have paid particular attention to the psychology of witch suspects, especially those who accepted their own guilt. In "The Psychology of Lorraine Witchcraft Suspects," Etienne Delcambre observed that "a fairly large number of those accused . . . were people of ill reputation and slight desirability: thieves, swindlers, fornicators, incestuous, sexual perverts, rapists, procurers, people without religion and blasphemers, poisoners, and above all quarrelsome or bad-tempered persons."[44] An "important number" of these people, "prompted by their social milieu or by the peremptory tones of their judges, truly believed themselves to be witches." Delcambre viewed this belief as a form of pathology: "some had been victims of such hallucinations even before being arrested; others became so in the course of their trial." Only "the better-balanced defendants . . . kept wholly conscious of their innocence to the end." Because "the faith of our ancestors was more spontaneous and more alive than that of even our most devout contemporaries," many people with guilty consciences could be pressured by cultural expectations or inquisitorial personalities into "denouncing themselves, as well as their presumed accomplices," believing "that they were obeying the commands of their conscience."

In The *World of the Witches*, Julio Caro Baroja carried Delcambre's psychological insights one step further by speculating how a woman could come to see herself as a witch even without external pressure:

[Some] initial failure of her life as a woman . . . drives her to use improper means to achieve her ends, although this does not always involve the work of the Devil . . . as she grows older, and no longer has any strong sensual desires . . . her only satisfaction is to see younger women go the same way as she, living a life of false or inverted values. For them evil becomes good; the crooked, straight. What is public loses its importance, and what is private . . . becomes significant.[45]

Despite its lack of empirical grounding and psychological sophistication, this description sketches a plausible process by which women, as they got older, became witches, rejecting the moral commands of their society, and in turn being rejected by it. Usually "middle-aged or old," these "unfortunate sick people . . . were put to death . . . because nobody knew what was wrong with them."

Delcambre and Caro Baroja's psychological insights have affected the work of many other historians, but most have concentrated their own efforts on elaborating the sociocultural process of scapegoating. Several local and regional studies have appeared which, inspired and informed by the work of anthropologists in contemporary primitive societies, offer a close look at the witch suspect's place in her community. Age is just one of the factors they have found to have been influential in shaping this relationship.

In a comprehensive survey of the occult in early modern England, *Religion and the Decline of Magic*, Keith Thomas centered his discussion of witchcraft on "the helpless old woman who had fallen out with the rest of the community."[46] Adopting the perspective of social anthropology, he regarded this alienation as a gradual process of ostracism by the small, tight communities unable to assimilate nonconformists. Thomas asserted that "the most common situation" bringing enmity to a head "was that in which the victim . . . had been guilty of a breach of charity or neighborliness, by turning away an old woman who had come . . . to beg or borrow some food or drink." If the old woman "had recourse to malignant threats in her extremity" and later some "personal misfortune" befell the ungenerous villager "for which no natural explanation was immediately forthcoming," the old woman was presumed to be a witch. These conflicts occurred more and more frequently in the early modern village because "the old tradition of mutual charity and help was being eroded by such new economic developments as land hunger, the rise in prices, the development of agricultural specialization and the growth of towns and commercial values . . . accompanied by the disappearance of some of the old mechanisms for resolving village conflicts . . . provided by manorial courts and religious guilds."

Thomas's student Alan Macfarlane shared the same basic vision of witchcraft, but stressed the importance of "tensions between the generations" in his local study of Essex county, *Witchcraft in Tudor and Stuart England*.[47] Older people "by their very presence, made demands on younger village families," and older women who "tended to be more intimately connected with various village groups . . . [and] who borrowed and lent" more than their men, were particularly likely to provoke conflicts over charity. During the "change from a 'neighbourly,' highly integrated and mutually interdependent village society, to a more independent one" younger, better off villagers used witchcraft accusations as "a clever way of reversing the guilt, of transferring it from the person who had failed in his social obligation . . . to the person who had made him fail." Witch denunciations were "hostility and guilt . . . projected . . . on to" an inconvenient old woman.

In his regional study *Witch-hunting in Southwest Germany*, Erik Midelfort focused on the social forces causing the mass panics which engulfed entire localities and victimized large portions of their populations, male as well as female, young as well as old. He detailed how these panics grew out of "accusations . . . aimed at the stereotyped examples of old, secluded, peculiar women," when "denunciations spread . . . from tortured suspects until a hundred or more persons were implicated."[48] Since several accusations were needed to justify an indictment, the panics tended to sweep up "the people of notoriously bad reputation . . . and . . . the better known men and women of a town." Noting that due to changing marriage patterns the number of "old and unattached women" was probably on the rise, he hypothesized that "unmarried women would have appeared as a seditious element . . . until society learned to adjust to the new family patterns." What began as a functional mechanism "deliniating the social threshold of eccentricity" by this "socially indigestible group," became a beserk machinery "that . . . could destroy all sense of community, and all inhabitants as well."

Paul Boyer and Stephen Nissenbaum's intensive study of the Salem witch trials, *Salem Possessed*, provided strong confirmation of both the linkage between limited suspicions and mass panics and the view of these panics as manifestations of social stress. After carefully reconstructing the intensifying conflict between the leading families of Salem town, a commercial seaport, and Salem village, an agricultural community, they showed that the village leaders were slowly losing power to the town's elite.[49] After several girls began acting as if possessed, the villagers aimed accusations at people identified with the new commercial order, at first marginal, stereotypical suspects, and then more prominent people, although they never actually accused their primary enemies, the heads of the dominant family in the town. While advanced age was not a notable characteristic of the accused, nor was torture needed to broaden the accusations, Boyer and Nissenbaum's work reveals the social basis and mechanisms of the scapegoating process. "Unable to relieve their frustrations politically . . . [the accusers] fell back on a . . . more archaic strategy: they treated those who threatened them . . . as an aggregate of morally defective individuals."

William Monter studied the small and medium-sized trials in the Franco-Swiss borderland and found in *Witchcraft in France and Switzerland* that trials there combined elements of the German situation Midelfort examined, the English patterns elucidated by Thomas and MacFarlane, and the French evidence uncovered by Delcambre.[50] Noting "how often these accused witches were elderly widows or spinsters," he argued that, "accusations can best be understood as projections of patriarchal social fears onto . . . de-fenseless and . . . isolated women." In addition, since "older women who lived apart from direct patriarchal control were unable to revenge their numerous injuries" through "physical violence . . . or law courts . . . they had only magical revenge." He mentioned that this magical revenge could have been effective "since their victims also believed that magic worked," and ascribed confessed participation in Sabbaths in part to drugs old women used "to introduce . . . some excitement into their monotonous and wretched lives." Yet he left these two ideas relatively undeveloped, and his account struck a balance between the sociological and psychological explanations of the scapegoating process: some witches were the "victims" of "panics"; others "were sincerely persuaded of their guilt" because they had "attempted to practice black magic."

Each of these interpretations offers important insights into the psychological and sociological roots of the witchcraft persecutions first identified by the early modern opponents of the trials. Although the individual perspectives diverge and in some cases conflict, they are not as incompatible as they first appear. Together, they suggest that witch denunciations manifested a severe conflict of interest between relatively poor old women and better off, younger villagers. Unable to fend for themselves, the old women demanded help from their neighbors, and resorted to magical "substitute action" when their benefactors began to chafe under the burden.[51] The younger villagers believed in the efficacy of such magic themselves, and saw its employment as an attempt to circumvent or overturn the patriarchal hierarchy which made middle-aged men heads of households and the final authorities within the villages. Once fear and suspicion had arisen, villagers blamed these supposed witches for all manner of inexplicable problems until, guided by an elite obsessed by demonological fears, they transformed individual cantankerous old women into the vangard of Satan's "fifth column . . . on earth."[52] And some of these old crones, bitter, melancholy, or drugged, embraced the "collective hallucination," and fantasized demons, Sabbaths, and a whole fairy tale world of magical conflicts and visionary experiences.

These discussions of early modern witchcraft have added tremendous subtley and sophistication to the basic insights of the rationalist tradition. Yet, in following that tradition, they depict witchcraft as a pathological phenomenon, a combination of psychopathology and socio-pathology. The crucial processes were scapegoating and self-delusion; the central mechanism was projection. Frustrated by failures they could not comprehend, accusers projected "hostility and guilt" and "patriarchial social fears" onto helpless old women, some of whom projected their own hostility into chance events and their own orgiastic fantasies onto a cold and unresponsive world.[53] Old women were cast as witches because they were burdensome, vulnerable, and disturbed: mostly they were the passive victims of society's distress; occasionally they were the pathetic perpetrators of illusory crimes. The overall impression left by the recent historical literature remains that witch beliefs manifested "a twofold antisocial psychopathy—of society against old women and of old women against society."

THE RELATIONSHIP BETWEEN OLD AGE AND EARLY MODERN WITCHCRAFT IN VIEW OF HISTORICAL GERONTOLOGY

Gerontology, as a distinct field of inquiry, has only just left its infancy. Psychologists and medical doctors long neglected the problems of advanced age, and even today their general theories have not kept up with increased understanding of particular aspects of the aging process. Historians, too, have only begun recently to approach old age as an independent topic for research, and have just started to look beyond the evolution of learned medical doctrines to the social and cultural realities of old peoples' lives. Nevertheless, gerontologists have produced enough literature in the past few decades that it is now possible to discuss the last stage of life from a scientific viewpont. Historical works on the subject are still few and far between, but have uncovered enough information to hint at the outlines of old age in past times. Before we can consider the role of advanced age in early modern witchcraft, we must know something about old age itself at that time, its boundaries and internal development.

One boundary of old age is obvious: death. When it generally occurred and how its timing affected old age, however, is not so obvious, and historians have recently reevaluated their views on the basis of a more sophisticated appraisal of the demographic record. Earlier, they had assumed that because the average life span was around thirty years, few people lived long enough to experience old age, and "the truly aged were few in numbers."[54] But this view overlooked the statistical influence of extremely high mortality among infants and children, which makes measures of life expectancy at birth unrepresentative of the experience of people who survived childhood. A person who lived to twenty could expect to reach the early fifties, while a person who reached sixty could reasonably hope to survive into the seventies. "A good many people did live to experience old age," and so "the elderly were about, at all levels of society . . . in considerable numbers." Typically, people above sixty made up between 5 and 10 percent of early modern populations, while those above forty represented fully a quarter of their communities. Life may have been nasty and brutal, but it does not seem to have been quite as short as once thought.

The other boundary of old age is harder to identify, both functionally and chronologically. Menopause, retirement, and "incipient decrepitude" have all been proposed as the crucial transitional process, while the ages suggested during the early modern period ranged between forty and sixty-five.[55] Women were commonly supposed to age sooner than men, and menopause, which occurred around forty, often served as the boundary. While this demarcation certainly slighted older women, who were "still likely to be healthy" well after menopause, three considerations recommend it for our purposes.[56] First, a woman's reproductive potential was more central to her status then than now; second, because of the rigors of childbirth and motherhood, women often appeared old early; and third, witch accusations became much more frequent precisely at this age. Accepting forty, menopause, as the beginning of female old age will simplify our discussion of witchcraft and gerontology without doing violence to the historical reality.

Early modern Europeans, like most other peoples, did not regard old age as a uniform stage of life, but instead subdivided it into two or more periods distinguished by both psychophysical attributes and sociocultural expectations. Some of these schemas had as many as five separate substages, but the simplest and probably most common differentiated between two.[57] As part of a popular seven-stage division of life, two stages were assigned to the old: "old age" proper and the "the crooked age." This simple division parallels that found among primitive peoples, who generally distinguish between "elders," whom they regard with respect and endow with authority, and the "overaged" or "already dead," whom they often neglect or even abandon. A similar attitude among early modern Europeans was conveyed by the association of the planet Jupiter, named for the Greco-Roman King of the Gods, while the elderly period, and Saturn, the tyrant Jupiter overthrew, with the last period of life. Indeed, "men in their forties and fifties . . . 'grave and staid men . . . above the levities of youth, and beneath the dotages of old age' " most often held the highest positions of authority and power, and could remain eminent into their sixties and beyond.[58] But at a certain point, they became "fit for nothing" except playing with their grandchildren; the last stage of life was "second childishness and mere oblivion, sans teeth, sans eyes, sans taste, sans everything."

The witchcraft prosecutions involved two related but distinct components: fear of a diabolical conspiracy and anger over attempts to inflict harm magically. The educated elite expressed the greatest concern about diabolism, participation in the Devil's conspiracy. In contrast, the peasantry cared far more about the effects of *maleficium*, the infliction of harm, particularly through magic. The two aspects were linked at the time by the theologians' conviction that any magic had to involve the cooperation of evil spirits, and hence indicated a pact with the Devil. Both aspects can and have been evaluated in terms of modern psychology, but their differences make it useful to consider their relationship to gerontology separately.

According to the witch-hunters' theories, the Devil had embarked on a massive campaign to recruit witches by offering material rewards and magical powers to people who agreed to renounce God and swear allegiance to him. Once recruited, they would be transported periodically to Sabbaths, where they would eat, drink, dance, copulate, and worship their diabolic master through various obscene rites. Inquisitors and magistrates tortured numerous suspects into confessing such activities, and most confessions can be ascribed to this coercion. Nevertheless, a number of people freely confessed to having participated, and their confessions cannot be explained so simply.[59] For example, Magdelena Horn, an "old woman from Cannstadt," in Württemberg confessed in 1565 that the Devil tempted her "day and night."[60] She claimed that he was "black, and had black clothes," and helped her do "so many bad things to animals and people, that she couldn't describe them all." The magistrates investigated the incidents she did discuss, and found that the people had indeed suffered the harms she claimed to have inflicted, although no one had thought to link her with them. "Furthermore," the magistrates reported, "she has been to the dances, especially on the Feuerbacher meadow, many times, and occasionally with her daughter . . . and others, whom she can't or doesn't want to name." The magistrates could not, of course, check the veracity of this claim, and we can never know why she made it. But we can consider the possibilities.

The first and most straightforward possibility is that Magdelena actually went to demonic dances. Unfortunately, no attempt to prove that such events took place has stood up to close scrutiny. Murray's and Russell's works are flawed by their authors' credulous use of evidence, while Ginzberg's investigation revealed only that a group of magical fertility warriors existed, whose self-conception turned diabolic only under the intense pressure of inquisitorial stereotyping.[61] Groups of people did come together to practice ritual magic and probably for other illicit purposes as well, but whether even small, isolated groups practiced anything approaching the Devil-worshipping witchcraft described by the demonologists remains in doubt.

A second and more likely possibility is some sort of senile or schizophrenic pathology. Among modern old people "manic-depressive psychoses . . . can develop a schizophrenic course" involving delusions and hallucinations strongly reminiscent of supposed witch experiences.[62] One clinician recently reported on a seventy-five-year-old schizophrenic woman who

becomes desultory in thinking, suspicious and irritable. . . . she . . . sees animals, people, and silent scenes in their entire reality. She feels hypnotized . . . by . . . ether waves . . . and during the night, she is "pumped" by a male member of the "air-waves group" . . . She hears voices giving her orders . . . and expressing what she was going to think.

The parallels with Magdelena's story are clear, but one caution must be introduced. Early modern Europeans were aware of nondiabolical mental disorders and often distinguished them from witchcraft. In Württemberg, for example, officials treated several other cases similar to Magdelena's as medical rather than moral problems, even though they were prosecuting other people as witches around the same time. Age would seem to be an important factor here, for older schizophrenics, despite strong delusions and hallucinations, often remain "unusually emotionally well preserved, and do not show typical schizophrenic autism."[63] Thus, older schizophrenics may have been more vulnerable to witchcraft charges because they displayed fewer of the symptoms officials could use to identify them as pathological.

A third likely source of diabolic experiences, and again one particularly relevant to older people, was use of witches' salves, hallucinogenic compounds based on plants found in the woods and fields of Europe. One group of modern German researchers prepared a seventeenth-century recipe, anointed themselves, and "fell into a twenty-four hour sleep in which they dreamed of wild rides, frenzied dancing, and other weird adventures of the type connected with medieval orgies."[64] Numerous reports, both early modern and more recent, recount similar experiences. Culturally formed expectations naturally influence these drug-induced experiences, but the basic sensations, such as flight, result directly from the biochemical effects of the active ingredients. Significantly, most of the plants used—belladonna, henbane, mandrake, and *Datura*—contain alkaloids to which older peoples' nervous systems are particularly sensitive. Unlike the youth-oriented drug culture of the 1960s, early modern drug users may have tended to be older people. In any case, the drugs used have a stronger effect on the old than the young.

A fourth and final source of free confessions of diabolic activity lay in some people's acceptance of the argument that a tendency to do bad things and think bad thoughts signified allegiance to the Devil. Without suggesting that they consciously rendered him homage or attended sabbaths, these people did recognize retrospectively that a pattern of bad behavior amounted to the same thing. As Delcambre pointed out, "for [our ancestors], the world beyond was no metaphysical concept, but a concrete reality."[65] Delcambre himself noted that many suspects had disreputable backgrounds, though he regarded their innocence as self-evident. Those who confessed freely, however, seem to have disagreed. Whatever the validity of the specific accusations of diabolism, they seem to have accepted them as representative of a legitimate indictment. Magdelena, for example, may have been neither schizophrenic nor a drug user, but simply a person who perceived her own evil thoughts as the work of the Devil, and fabricated stories of the "dances" to bring her confession regarding real misdeeds into line with the expectations of her examiners.

Real misdeeds were of far greater concern to the common people than diabolic dances or hallucinogenic trips. This difference was revealed most clearly in the small-scale prosecutions involving one to five suspects. Of twenty-five denunciations contained in twenty-seven such cases sampled from the two hundred supervised by Württemberg's *Oberrat*, or High Council, between 1550 and 1750, the overwhelming majority concerned specific harms people believed witches had caused. Only two alleged attendance at witch dances; one, diabolical behavior; three, ritual magic; one, sex with the Devil; and one, membership in a witch's family.[66] In contrast, seventeen denunciations concerned specific harms attributed to the accused witches. Seven alleged bewitching, magical injury from ill-will; six, poisoning, which was still regarded as a quasi-magical process; two, harming animals; and one, killing a newborn baby.[67] Thus, more than two-thirds of these investigations were of people perceived to be an immediate threat to members of the community; fear of diabolism led the elite to provide the legal framework for the prosecutions, but specific denunciations came mostly from commoners angered over *maleficium*. As numerous historians have emphasized, the basic scenario of village-level accusations was some manifestation of hostility followed by some unexpected misfortune. In England, a poor woman's tendency to "chide and threaten" most often led to trouble.[68] On the Continent, grounds for denunciation were more diverse, but still centered on "negative personality traits," "a reputation as a bad neighbor."

Only one historian, Sona Burstein, has attempted systematically to link these "negative personality traits" to the psychology of old age. As we have seen, she called the witch stereotype "a recognizable pattern of senile psychosis," and cited as evidence "neglected appearance, forgetfulness, confused and agitated behavior, incomprehension of personal danger, and a variety of antisocial psychopathies ranging from mild suspiciousness to homicide."[69] However, several considerations make her thesis questionable. To begin with, a substantial minority of suspects were children, adolescents, and middle-aged adults. Even among the older women who formed the majority, ages were rather evenly distributed between forty and eighty, which makes it unlikely that most suspects could have been exhibiting symptoms of advanced senility.

Furthermore, Burstein only systematically documented mumbling, "lack of comprehension of immediate . . . danger," and irritability as having been widely noted among suspects. None of these symptoms is inherently psychotic. All can accompany acute mental disorders, but they also occur to mild degrees in people who are fairly well adjusted, especially in situations of stress, which tend to exaggerate normal behavior patterns and provoke abnormal reactions. Some of Burstein's examples were clearly pathological, but we cannot simply assume that everyone who exhibited some of the symptoms had acute senile psychosis.

In fact, the most important of the symptoms Burstein listed, excessive irritability, is closely identified with an earlier stage of old age. Fears of *maleficium* were central to village-level suspicions, and a tendency to "chide and threaten" or act as a "bad neighbor" were the signs which identified a particular person as the agent responsible for misfortune. In our culture, "emotional lability, lack of stability . . . short-circuit reactions . . . fanaticism and querulous tendencies . . . occur more frequently toward the fiftieth year and during the fifties than the sixties."[70] Members of both sexes may suffer from frequent depression during these years, and "needs stemming from insecurity and threat" increase in importance. The attendant "anxiety . . . is especially important as a generator of defensive and handicapping behavior patterns."[71] Drawing on their wealth of memories, the elderly rely increasingly on "past experience . . . and attitude rather than analysis" in making decisions.[72] Inevitable "differences in what time has taught lead to perennial clashes . . . between youth and age." Many people begin to show a "lack of concern about the social situation, a lessened influence of everyday social controls, and a dominance of self-concern."[73] While the fifties are not as uniformly bleak as this discussion makes them sound, of course, characteristics associated with this phase of old age seem more related to the charges supporting witchcraft accusations than the decrepitude of advanced senility.

Information on how early modern older people behaved is scanty. But what does exist suggests that some elderly people then exhibited many of the same problem behaviors as their contemporary counterparts—and preindustrial society was at least as ready to generalize from instances of troublesome behavior as modern society is. Since "the old were to rule" and "the young were to serve," early modern culture insisted on respect for the "ripeness of judgement . . . prudence, temperance, continency . . . and fuller and more certain knowledge of God" of the elderly.[74] But this enforced respect coexisted with "intense and bitter satire" through which the young lamented and lampooned the "undesirable changes in personality" brought by age.[75] One typical early modern commentator observed that "in our old age . . . we may see . . . sin and lusts . . . which we saw not before.[76] He described the elderly as "covetous . . . fearful . . . touchy, peevish, angry, and forward . . . unteachable . . . hard to please . . . full of complaints . . . suspicious . . . and apt to surmise, suspect and fear the worst." Humoral theory linked old age and melancholy, which made people "easy prey for the Devil, who 'moves the phantasy by mediation of the humors.' "[77] These "distinctly negative undertones" were even found "in the attitudes of the elderly toward their own aging," which often created in them "a continuing anxiety."[78] "Old age," as Simone de Beauvoir observed, is "a fact that runs throughout history arousing a certain number of identical reactions."

The basis of the negative personality changes which often develop early in old age, especially those in women, have traditionally been linked to the menopause, the deactivation of the reproductive system. During this transition, which occurs as late as fifty in modern women but happened around a decade earlier in early modern women, the ovaries cease producing hormones.[79] Since the body's functioning depends on a delicate hormonal balance, "their removal requires considerable readjustment." In particular, the "loss of the estrogen-pituitary gonadotropic hormone balance affects" a woman's "whole physical mechanism on all levels of control." Victorian doctors ascribed to this physiologic turmoil " 'morbid irrationality' . . . 'minor forms of hysteria' . . . melancholia, and the impulses to drink spirits, to steal, and perchance, to murder." But while the menopause is unquestionably related to heightened nervousness and irritability in some women, more recent work has revealed that the great majority of women have at most minor problems during the physiologic adjustments, and most of these "are culturally induced."[80] Estrogen replacement therapy has shown that "the only symptoms . . . uniquely characteristic of the menopausal period are hot flashes . . . and genital atrophy."[81]

A recent medical discussion of the subject observed that "since the menopause consists of a natural physiologic process, it has no psychodynamic etiology.[82] However, the menopause . . . can and frequently does serve as a stimulus for emotional distress." The menopause "is only one part" of a "transition made during a period of fifteen to twenty years" referred to as the climacteric.[83] In both modern men and modern women "midlife stresses are a result of a combination of personal, family, social, and biological variables." In women, the climacteric begins a few years before the end of menstruation, and in both sexes it tapers off slowly as adjustments are made not only to the end of reproductive potency (though "andropause" is not universal, it occurs when it does because of a decline in interest rather than a physiologic loss of ability), but also to the start of physical and mental decay, the loss or modification of social status, and the nearing of inevitable death. This combination of changes, affecting a person's self-definition on all levels from the biological to the metaphysical, causes the intensification of negative personality traits in modern elderly people discussed previously.

Since the early modern elderly manifested many of the same behaviors, was witchlike behavior simply an expression of the stresses experienced during the climacteric, combined with a new inability of the witch-hunting society to cope with the manifestations of this life crisis? This hypothesis appears attractive, but must be evaluated in view of two weaknesses.

First of all, how can the substantial minority of suspects under forty be reconciled with such a view? This objection is not critical, however, since the behaviors and attitudes associated with the climacteric are by no means unique to elderly people. Personalities do not change fundamentally during it; at most people come to resemble "a caricature of their younger selves at their emotional worst."[84] Some younger people are far more hostile than most of the elderly ever become, and this is particularly true of adolescents, who, significantly, figured prominently among younger suspects. In fact, the climacteric "bears many physiological and emotional similarities to puberty: both are times of hormone realignment and physiologic upheaval, and both may result in the production of physical or emotional symptoms."[85]

The second weakness cannot be dealt with as easily. Among modern elderly people, the climacteric is a temporary, transitional period of stress followed by a time of greater adjustment and calm. Indeed, "after menopause," modern "women have the easiest time in terms of physical and emotional symptomology."[86] Yet the records of suspects' ages generally show a steady rate of accusation from forty on, allowing for the decline in numbers in older age brackets. From the aggregate statistics we cannot determine whether the behaviors associated with the climacteric and witch denunciations occurred less regularly or for a more protracted period in the early modern women. Since the climacteric is defined by sociocultural factors more than biological ones, either pattern could have obtained. But consideration of both the usual development of witchcraft suspicions and the sociocultural situation of elderly women suggests the second possibility.

Witchcraft cases typically involved a long period of suspicion before an accusation could be made and accepted. "Suspicions gradually built up in a village," and except during mass panics, an accusation was unlikely to be accepted in court unless it was supported by a history of suspect incidents.[87] No one has yet calculated the average time lag involved, but evidence supporting an accusation often extended back well beyond a decade. Agatha Stosser, an elderly woman from Sulz in Württemberg, for example, was first accused by an incarcerated suspect in 1630. She was arrested and investigated for bewitching animals in 1645, but let off because "no matter how much one repeated the accusations against her, she stuck firmly to her conviction" that she was innocent. Fourteen years later, though, she was convicted of a long list of charges accumulated over the intervening period. First accused at forty-four, she was finally burned at seventy-three.

Why did women like Agatha continue to provoke suspicion for so long? The answer lies both in the pressures on early modern elderly women and in their response to them. Women, especially elderly, lower-class women, were during this period in a double bind: if they were in a position of relative security, they possessed little authority, while if they had independent responsibility, they were unlikely to have much security. This is a dilemma perhaps inherent to life, but for these women the contrasts were especially stark. Elderly women in early modern villages had many reasons to act like witches.

Most women lived as dependents in households headed by men. Daughters were normally subordinate to their fathers, servants to their employers, spinsters to their brothers, wives to their husbands, and widows to their sons.[88] Some women, especially widows, escaped this predicament, but they, as we shall see, had formidable problems of their own. For the most part, by the sixteenth century "the patriarchal family . . . was paramount."[89] Among their Germanic and Latin ancestors, women had been subordinate to their men, but this subordination was tempered by some property rights and the protection of extended kinship ties. "The feudal system . . . gradually curtailed the property rights of women," and "lowered their status." By the early modern period, "the power of the husband to enforce obedience to his will by threats, blows, and confinement . . . was rarely questioned." Women were reduced to "complete . . . subordination."

The gradual reduction of women's status was not only legal and social, but cultural and psychological as well. Many men and women shared a "belief in the biological inferiority of women," considering them, "the weaker vessell, of a frail heart, inconstant, and with a word soon stirred to wrath."[90] Women in the sixteenth and seventeenth centuries were exhorted to be "docile and submissive . . . silent . . . and at all times submissive to men." This ideal has found favor among many men throughout history, but the contemporaneous legal and social developments in early modern Europe lent it particular force.

The later years of life were especially stressful for women because of the widespread system of contractual retirement.[91] During the Middle Ages, many lords insisted that their peasants set an age at which men would hand over control of their farms to their sons in exchange for a promise of support. The system continued, via individual family arrangements, into the early modern period, as aging peasants often found it difficult to maintain their lands. The retired parents lived within the household or in a special outbuilding, but in either case, one contemporary observed, "they were often not treated the way they should be."[92] There was "an underlying hostility towards" them, "and a reluctance to devote much of society's limited resources to them." But even if the younger generation fulfilled its material obligations, elderly women still lost their place at the center of domestic activity. While older men might continue to exercise public functions, older women had virtually no role other than informal advisor and critic, "wise woman" and witch.

The intent of the European retirement system was to increase production within the male sphere of farm activity, but it had at least as much impact on women's lives since they tended to marry younger, live longer, and, as widows, retire as soon as a son came of age.[93] Traditionally, a propertied widow might strike a favorable bargain in a remarriage; in the sixteenth and seventeenth centuries this avenue was blocked as a new marriage pattern arose in response to overpopulation. Age-at-marriage rose, and remarriage, especially for women, was discouraged, sometimes violently. A young woman lucky enough to marry a well-off widower could easily find herself a ward of her stepson for her last decades. The other point of view in this relationship has been preserved in fairy tales about children's fear of their stepmother, who was often explicitly identified as a witch. But the relationship could be just as hard on the woman, at least in its later phases when roles were reversed. As a contemporary observer noted, "no prison can be more irksome to a parent than a son's or daughter's house."[94]

Most independent women were widows with minor children or without any children due to infertility, death, or migration. Many women lost their husbands at a relatively young age, and enjoyed control of a household at least temporarily.[95] But for this independence and responsibility they paid a heavy price. A woman could earn only a fraction of a man's wage, and "the jobs available to these [widowed] women . . . were notoriously poorly paid."[96] Hence, they could not live on their earnings alone. Widows' names "predominate" on charity rolls, and "they often sent their children off to charitable institutions, or to fend for themselves." Even without dependents, though, "relief for the elderly was a low priority, and in the villages it could be bitterly resented." Furthermore, even if they were relatively well off, widows' traditional property and other legal rights dwindled between the fourteenth and eighteenth centuries as lawyers devised ways to circumvent archaic practices.[97] Whether they lived from charity and poor relief or struggled to keep alive a farmstead or shop, women who exercised independence and commanded authority generally did so in the face of numerous and formidable obstacles.

In addition to these problems related to dependence and insecurity, elderly women in both positions suffered from some common complaints. First of all was sexual frustration.[98] By the seventeenth century opportunities for remarriage were rare. Sexual urges in the postmenopausal were "condemned as both disgusting and unhealthy" by "universal agreement." While people in the upper strata of society enjoyed some latitude, in general, "the aged were to refrain from sexual competition . . . Lust in the elderly was an infallible occasion for ridicule and censure." These legal and cultural barriers definitely hindered sexual activity, but they could not eliminate the desire for it. According to modern studies of sexuality, menopause tends to heighten rather than depress women's sexuality.[99] "There is no time limit drawn by the advancing years to female sexuality," and, freed from the psychic burden of fertility, women "frequently manifest increased levels of sexual activity." Strong sexuality in women obsessed many of the proponents of witch-hunting; Institoris and Sprenger asserted (inconsistently) that "all witchcraft comes from carnal lust, which is in women insatiable." Barred from remarriage and discouraged from promiscuity, elderly women were frustrated at exactly the point in life when sex lost its responsibility. Cultural norms inhibited recognition of these bodily desires and hindered their fulfillment, but elementary psychology suggests that they could not eliminate them. The net result was probably similar to the predicament of modern elderly women who, "deprived of normal sexual outlets . . . exhaust themselves . . . in conscious or unconscious effort to dissipate their accumulated . . . sexual tensions."

Another development creating new frustrations for the elderly, male as well as female, was the rise of religious and legal bureaucracies. Village elders had always had a great deal of influence over village affairs, for in the peasants' oral culture they were the testators "who controlled access to the past."[100] During the early modern period the clerical and lay elites proliferated, pushed increasingly into matters once the concern only of local leaders, and introduced codified prescriptions to replace local traditions.

All of these negative developments were exacerbated by the demographic and economic trends of the sixteenth and seventeenth centuries.[101] During the second half of the sixteenth century, when the trials became widespread, real wages were falling, the land was filling up, and food prices were soaring. The trials peaked in the first half of the next century, when the European economy stagnated and in many places declined. In the second half of the seventeenth century and into the eighteenth, the economy recovered and the prosecutions of elderly women for witchcraft tapered off.

Early modern elderly women clearly felt a variety of pressures which made increased levels of irritability, hostility and aggression understandable. Most were completely subordinate to males, and many had lost even their limited authority within the domestic sphere to younger women. Those who enjoyed independence lost as much as they gained, for its price was generally economic insecurity, legal weakness, and social marginality. And for most elderly women, limitations on remarriage and sanctions against sex frustrated their normal sexuality, while the subordination of local communities to centralized bureaucracies undermined the social value of their memories and judgment.

But we cannot understand the roots of witchlike behavior simply by listing the pressures on elderly women. Elderly women today suffer from many similar problems—limited opportunities for sex, lack of a challenging social role, and economic insecurity—but the most widely-noted problem among them is depression, not aggression.[102] We need also to understand the attractions of witchcraft; why some early modern elderly women accepted and even cultivated socially disapproved attitudes and behavior patterns.

The basic attraction of witchlike behaviors was that they worked. While its intellectual foundations may have been faulty and some of its practices ineffectual, witchcraft could endow an elderly woman (or anyone) with considerable power in a village setting. A witch's armory contained numerous natural weapons whose effectiveness has never been in doubt, although their significance has generally been slighted.[103] Poison, arson, and the aphrodisiac and anti-aphrodisiac qualities of tastes and smells could obviously be used to inflict harm or influence behavior. Furthermore, because belief in curses was so widely shared, "the formal imprecation could be a powerful weapon . . . it could strike terror into the hearts of the credulous and the guilty."[104] This terror was not inconsequential, for the fear and anxiety curses and other magical attacks caused could, in fact, create or contribute to real maladies. "Many observers have noticed how the inhabitants of modern primitive societies can afflict their enemies with aches and pains, vomiting and insomnia, by sheer suggestion; and the dramatic, even fatal, effect of the voodoo curse . . . is well authenticated." Such ailments did not just threaten "the credulous and the guilty," for all people are vulnerable to the connection between the psychic and somatic dimensions of health. According to "most investigators and clinicians . . . psychosocial factors influence the onset and course of all illnesses."[105] Psychosomatic problems not only make people think they are sick, they make them sick, sometimes alone and often in combination with other agents. A poor elderly woman in a closely knit peasant community had good reason to manifest behaviors and attitudes geared to intimidate and punish through interpersonal pressure. A reputation as a witch no doubt added to resentment of her already burdensome existence, but in many cases it was the only alternative to passive acceptance of a miserable fate.

For elderly people to actively enforce respect and obedience was hardly unusual. In primitive societies "their security has been more often an achievement than an endowment," an achievement gained less through "the manipulation of things" than "the adjustment to and manipulation of people."[106] Anthropologists have long been aware that "in virtually all preliterate societies aged persons . . . especially women . . . derive considerable advantage from the practice of magic." Recent historical studies of the early modern period have shown that "if . . . the elderly retained authority, it was because of the material resources at their disposal," and the present study suggests that these material "levers of power" could be supplemented or replaced by magical ones. Beset by numerous socioeconomic problems and hampered by equally numerous sociocultural restrictions, many elderly women had to rely heavily on their traditional source of influence: "force of personality and knowledge of human nature."[107] If they found it necessary to prolong and even intensify the unpleasant attributes we associate with the menopause and climacteric, this was the price they had to pay for the increased respect and obedience they could command. Considering the pressures of their situations, it was a reasonable bargain. At least, until the magistrates arrived.

CONCLUSION

Our Disney image of the witch as an old woman reflects historical reality. It continues a tradition found among many primitive peoples, and in European culture as well, that particularly associates old women and witchcraft. Independent of the demonologists' theories, early modern Europeans suspected and tried older women more often than any other comparable group in society. The demonologists' opponents, convinced that the fears were distorted and exaggerated, emphasized age as well as sex and class to belittle the beliefs behind the persecutions. Long unheeded, their arguments eventually won the day, transformed diabolism into *dementia*, a moral problem into a medical one, and the trials came to an end.

Historians have placed different degrees of emphasis on the role of age in witch suspicions, but the dominant tradition has been a continuation and elaboration of the views originated by the early modern opponents of the trials. Regarding the prosecutions as a twofold pathology, rationalist scholars have examined the psychological roots of self-denunciation and the sociological roots of accusations made by others. Concentrating more on the latter aspects, they have depicted the trials as a combination of demonological fears among the educated and generational, economic, and gender-based tensions within villages and towns. In an atmosphere pervaded by hardship and fear, people were all too ready to find scapegoats onto whom they could project their anger and hostility. Some old women, burdensome and vulnerable, defiantly or compliantly adopted the very attitudes and behaviors for which they were vilified, and hallucinated the fantastic experiences concocted by their enemies. Through repetition and torture, suspicions and accusations proliferated until the stereotype of the eccentric old woman broke down, accusations against magistrates and their relatives became frequent, and the elite came to its senses and abandoned the witch ideology.

Consideration of the psychology of old age as well as the sociocultural situation of elderly women in early modern Europe suggests that the rationalist tradition, while it has added much to our knowledge of the witchcraft persecutions, has neglected the role of the suspected witches in witch beliefs. The elite's fear of a diabolic conspiracy does seem to have combined misunderstandings of group magic, drug experiences, schizophrenic delusions, and its own metaphorical conception of sin and guilt. But fears of *maleficium*, the heart of village suspicions, reflected the real patterns of behavior which expressed real needs and could have real results. Some women really acted like witches, really hurt other people, and really came to accept that in so doing they were performing the Devil's work. Either totally subordinate to men or precariously independent, women, especially as they reached old age, found themselves beset by socioeconomic problems and frustrated by sociocultural restrictions. At an age when irritable and other socially disruptive behaviors are likely to emerge anyway, some elderly women accepted and even cultivated them in order to enforce respect and obedience.

The demonologists, of course, blew the problem posed by these women all out of proportion, for their work was part of an ambitious program to systemize Christian morality and impose it on society.[108] The late medieval clergy spent a great deal of effort on evaluating lay activities in religious terms, and the civil bureaucracies which grew tremendously during the early modern period cooperated in enforcing adherence to the resulting ethical codes. The witch trials, like the Stalinist purges, were an attempt at socio-demographic engineering. The middle-aged and elderly male elites were determined to eradicate the truly wicked people and educate the rest, to remold human nature in the image of God's word and according to His desires. Many villagers and townspeople were willing to collaborate in order to rid themselves of their burdensome and threatening neighbors. Elderly women naturally bore the brunt of this effort, for they depended most on " 'neighborly' highly integrated and mutually interdependent village society," and were therefore its most aggressive defenders.[109]

One final point deserves consideration before we close, one which has only recently begun to receive the attention it deserves. What were the effects of the witch hunts, particularly on their principal victims, elderly women? Most older accounts ended on a note of relieved discontinuity, implying that for all their horror and violence, the main result of the trials was to discredit magical beliefs by taking them to their extreme. More recent historians have linked the witch trials to the sociocultural transition to the modern world; by permitting communal obligations to be repudiated, accusations resolved "fundamental questions as to the nature and structure of the social order . . . on the side of individual freedom."[110] Individualism, especially individual accumulation of wealth, was insured, and care of the poor and elderly had to be restructured to reflect this new irresponsibility.

These were certainly important effects of the trials, but were they the only ones? What of the hundreds of thousands of elderly women who were suspected, accused, investigated, tortured, and burned? Were the ones who survived changed? We cannot answer this question with any certainty, but we can suggest a hypothesis. According to the *Malleus Maleficarum* and other accounts from around 1500, people, especially women, of all ages were suspected and punished. During the mass panics around 1600, the number of men and children rose significantly, and only after the mid-century "crisis of confidence" did the persecutions settle in on old women.[111] Among the sampled suspects from Württemberg, anyway, four of six aged seventy or older were accused after 1660, while the median age of suspects appears to have been between sixty and seventy, considerably higher than the median for the period of the trials as a whole. Historians have learned from anthropologists to regard witch accusations as "a highly effective means of social control."[112] But this characterization is actually rather an understatement in the case of early modern Europe. These trials were not simply a means of control, an attempt to "contain" diabolism. Instead, they represented an attempt to restructure European social demography and transform popular culture, to "roll back" the Devil's dominion. Every student of subsequent European history knows that they failed to eradicate the truly wicked people and reform the rest, but short of that goal, they may well have had an important impact. During the late Middle Ages, women were characterized as bawdy, aggressive, and domineering.[113] In extreme form, these were the attributes ascribed to witches. By the nineteenth century, the stereotype of women had changed completely. They were expected to be asexual, passive, and submissive. How accurately these images reflected social and psychological reality is not known, but they suggest a dramatic shift in attitudes and behavior. Certainly there were many forces during the intervening centuries contributing to the changing status of women in Western society, but the witch hunts, protracted, brutal, and pervasive, would seem to have been a primary cause.

Thus, both late medieval witch-hunters and their Enlightenment critics may have been right. When the *Malleus* was written, witchlike behavior may well have been fairly widely diffused in the population, although strongest among elderly women. Two centuries later, though, only decrepit, senile old crones would risk ostracism, torture, imprisonment, and death by cursing their neighbors or boasting of their diabolical contacts. This hypothesis is only a hypothesis, and must await evaluation in light of future research into women's roles and mentalities in the past. But it suggests that the witch trials had a profound impact on the behavior and attitudes of early modern elderly women and their descendants.

Appendix

AUTHOR	PLACE	# < 50 YEARS OLD	# > 50 YEARS OLD	% > 50 YEARS OLD
Villette	Dept. Nord	23	24	51
Demos	Salem, Mass.	69	49	42
Monter	Basel	1	9	90
	Freiburg	2	7	78
	Geneva	24	71	75
	Valangin	2	7	78
	Val de Travers	6	12	66
	Total	35	106	75
Macfarlane	Essex	2	13	87
Bever	Württemberg	13	16	55
Muchembled	Cambrésis	6	7	54

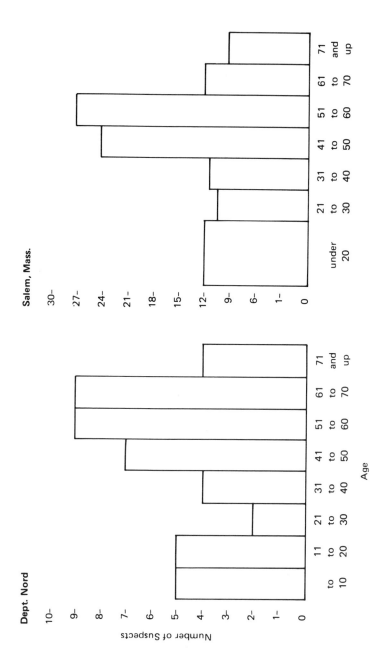

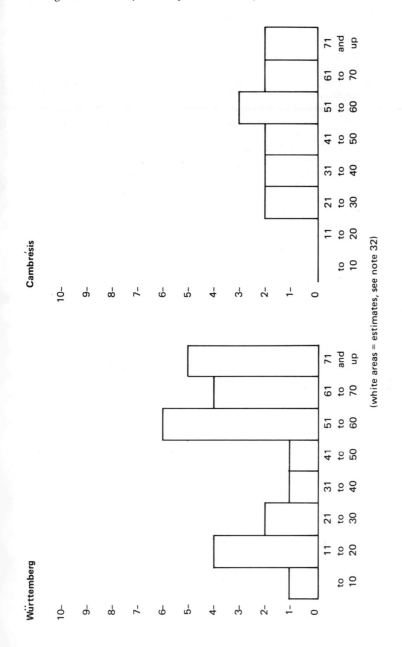

(white areas = estimates, see note 32)

NOTES

1. Estimates of the number of Europeans accused and executed vary widely and are all based on little more than guesswork. Alan Kors and Edward Peters, in the "Introduction" to their *Witchcraft in European History 1100–1700: A Documentary History* (Philadelphia: University of Pennsylvania Press, 1972), p. 13, place the number executed between 50,000 and 500,000, while William Bossenbrook, in *The German Mind* (Detroit: Wayne State University Press, 1961), p. 198, says that about 1,000,000 were killed in Germany alone. Numbers accused or convicted would be more useful in judging the impact of the trials on the population as a whole, but these are even harder to estimate. In any event, the witch-hunts involved a huge number of people; a significant proportion of the European population must have been touched by them, at least indirectly.

2. Alan Macfarlane, *Witchcraft in Tudor and Stuart England* (New York: Harper & Row, 1970), p. 158.

3. Ibid., p. 129; Richard Kieckhefer, *European Witch Trials* (Berkeley: University of California Press, 1976), p. 103.

4. Most studies have found the proportion of women to have been 75 percent or more. See Macfarlane, *Witchcraft*, p. 160; H.C. Erik Midelfort, *Witch Hunting in Southwest Germany* (Stanford: Stanford University Press, 1972), pp. 179–181; E. William Monter, *Witchcraft in France and Switzerland* (Ithaca: Cornell University Press, 1976), pp. 119–120. A more general study of women and witchcraft is Gabriele Becker, et al., *Aus der Zeit der Versweiflung: Sur Genese und Aktualität des Hexenbildes* (Frankfort a.M.: Suhrkamp, 1977).

5. Macfarlane, *Witchcraft*, p. 163; Midelfort, *Witch Hunting*, p. 183.

6. "The Bull of Innocent VIII," in *The Malleus Maleficarum of Heinrich Kramer and James Sprenger*, trans. and ed. Montague Summers (New York: Dover, 1971), reprint of 1928, p. xliii, hereafter *Malleus*.

7. Norman Cohn, *Europe's Inner Demons* (London: Sussex University Press, 1975), p. xi; Edward Peters, *The Magician, the Witch, and the Law* (Philadelphia: University of Pennsylvania Press, 1978), pp. 167–168; Sydney Anglo, "Evident Authority and Authoritative Evidence: The *Malleus Maleficarum*," in Sydney Anglo, ed.,*The Damned Art*, (London: Routledge & Kegan Paul, 1977), pp. 8, 14.

8. *Malleus*, Summers, pp. 44–47.

9. Ibid., pp. 96–97.

10. Henry Charles Lea, *Materials Toward a History of Witchcraft*, 3 vols., ed. Arthur Howland (Philadelphia: University of Pennsylvania Press, 1939), esp. vol. I, pp. 260–416, vol. 2, pp. 435–754. The quote is from *Warhafftige unnd Erschreckliche Thatten un handlungen der Lxii Hexen und Unholden so zu Wisenstaig/mit dem Brandt gericht worden seindt* (no place: no publisher, 1563), title page.

11. Hugh Trevor-Roper, "The European Witch-Craze of the Sixteenth and Seventeenth Centuries," in *The European Witch Craze of the Sixteenth and Seventeenth Centuries and Other Essays* (New York: Harper & Row, 1956), p. 146.

12. Trevor-Roper, *European Witch Craze*, pp. 130–132; Midelfort, *Witch Hunting*, pp. 34–56. The quote is from Ulrich Molitor, *Von Hexen und Unholden: Ein Christlicher/nutzlicher/und zu disen unsern gefahrlichen Zeiten notwendiger Bericht/auss Gottes wort/Geistlichen unnd Weltlicher Rechten/ auch sunst allerley Historien gezogen*, trans. (from Latin) Conrad Lautenbach (no place: no publisher, 1575, rpt. and trans. of 1489), p. 51.

13. Jeffrey Burton Russell, *Witchcraft in the Middle Ages* (Ithaca: Cornell University Press, 1972), p. 76.

14. Trevor-Roper, *European Witch Craze*, pp. 146–147.

15. Christopher Baxter, "Johann Weyer's *De Praestigiis Daemonum:* Unsystematic Psychopathology," in Anglo, *Damned Art*, p. 61.

16. Lea, *Materials*, II, pp. 450 (Albertini), 446–447 (Cardan). Both these writers were reviving ideas expressed two centuries before by Peter of Abano, a medieval physician at the University of Padua. See Trevor-Roper, *European Witch Craze*, p. 131.

17. Baxter, *Praestigiis*, p. 68; Johann Weyer, "De Praestigiis Daemonum (1563)," trans. excerpts in *European Witchcraft*, ed. E. William Monter (New York: John Wiley & Sons, 1969), pp. 46, 44, 39–40, hereafter *European Witchcraft*.

18. The evaluation of Bodin's argument is Monter's in his introduction to Jean Bodin, "Demonamanie des Sorciers," trans. excerpts in *European Witchcraft*, p. 47; quotes from Bodin, pp. 50–51; " 'melancholic' old ladies" is from Trevor-Roper, *European Witch Craze*, p. 146.

19. Sydney Anglo, "Reginald Scott's *Discoverie of Witchcraft:* Scepticism and Sadduceeism," in Anglo, *Damned Art*, p. 108.

20. Alan Macfarlane, "A Tudor Anthropologist: George Gifford's *Discourse* and *Dialogue*," in Anglo, *Damned Art*, p. 145; Gifford quoted in Sona Rosa Burstein, "Aspects of the Psychopathology of Old Age Revealed in Witchcraft Cases of the Sixteenth and Seventeenth Centuries," *British Medical Bulletin*, 6, (1–2) (1949); p. 66.

21. Cyrano de Bergerac, "A Letter Against Witches (1654)," trans. excerpts in *European Witchcraft*, p. 114.

22. Ibid., p. 115.

23. Monter's introduction to Malebranche, "Recherche de la Vérité (1674)," trans. excerpts in *European Witchcraft*, p. 121.

24. Trevor-Roper, *European Witch Craze*, pp. 92, 116.

25. *Malleus*, Summers, pp. 96–97.

26. David Gutman, "The Cross-Cultural Perspective: Notes Toward a Comparative Psychology of Aging," in James Birren and Warner Schau, eds., *Handbook of the Psychology of Aging*, (New York: Van Nostrand Reinhold, 1977), p. 309.

27. Julio Caro Baroja, *The World of the Witches*, trans. O.N.V. Glendinning (Chicago: University of Chicago Press, 1964) pp. 48, 39.

28. Jacques Bailbé, "La Thème de la Vieille Femme dans la Poésie Satirique du Seizième et du Debut du Dix-Septième Siècles," *Bibliothèque de Humanisme et Renaissance*, vol. 26 (1964), p. 110; Simone de Beauvoir, *The Coming of Age*, trans. Patrick O'Brian (New York: G.P. Putnam's Sons, 1972) pp. 136, 146, 155.

29. *Newe Zeitung aus Berneburgk/Schrecklich und abschewlich zu horen und zu lesen/Von dreyen Alten Teuffels Bulerin/Hexin oder Zauberinnen/* . . . (no place: "eine Liebhaber der Warheit," 1580), p. 8.

30. de Beauvoir, *Coming of Age*, p. 150.

31. Monter, *European Witchcraft*, p. 122.

32. Midelfort, *Witch Hunting*, p. 194; in my own research, I found the information in summaries in archival indices wildly inaccurate, (the median age contained in *Archivsreperatorium A 209* in the Hauptstaatsarchiv Stüttgart was 11!). The information contained in the documents themselves was more accurate, but incidental information, primarily number and ages of children, suggested that middle-aged suspects' ages tended to be omitted more often.

33. This is a very generous estimate. See Henry Kamen, *The Iron Century* (New York: Praeger, 1971) p. 15, and Peter Laslett, *The World We Have Lost* (New York: Charles Scribner's Sons, 1965), p. 103.

34. Lea quoted by George Lincoln Burr in his "Introduction" to Lea's *Materials*, I , p. xxxi; Jules Michelet, *Satanism and Witchcraft*, trans. A.R. Allinson (New York: Citadel, 1969, rpt. of 1939) pp. viii, x, xiv; Summer's "Introduction to 1928 Edition" of the *Malleus*, p. xviii.

35. Margaret Murray, *The Witch-Cult in Western Europe* (Oxford, 1921). For criticisms of her thesis, see G.L. Burr, review article in *American Historical Review*, xxvii, no. 4 (1922), pp. 780–783; C.L. Ewen, *Some Witchcraft Criticisms: A Plea for the Blue Pencil* (No place, 1938); Elliot Rose, *A Rose for a Goat* (Toronto, 1962).

36. Macfarlane, "A Tudor Anthropologist," pp. 115–130; Richard Horsley, "Who Were the Witches? The Social Roles of the Accused in European Witch Trials," *Journal of Interdisciplinary History*, IX(4) (Spring 1979): 697; Keith Thomas, *Religion and the Decline of Magic* (New York: Charles Scribner's Sons, 1971), pp. 212–252.

37. Trevor-Roper, *European Witch Craze*, pp. 183, 190.

38. Burstein, "Psychopathology," pp. 69–70; Trevor-Roper, *European Witch Craze*, pp. 125, 190.

39. Carlo Ginzburg, "I benandanti: Richerche sulla stregoneria e sui culti agrari tra Cinquencento e seicento," trans. excerpts in *European Witchcraft*, p. 163.

40. Cohn, *Inner Demons*, p. 123.

41. Russell, *Witchcraft*, pp. 41–42, 20–24, 127–132, 141–142, 218, 289; for a stinging critique, see Cohn, *Inner Demons*, pp. 121–125, 223–234.

42. Russell, *Witchcraft*, pp. 273, 278, 270.

43. Ibid., p. 271.

44. Etienne Delcambre, "The Psychology of Lorraine Witchcraft Suspects," trans. excerpts in *European Witchcraft*, pp. 105, 108–109.

45. Baroja, *World of Witches*, pp. 256–257.

46. Thomas, *Decline of Magic*, pp. 553, 530, 557, 563.

47. Macfarlane, "A Tudor Anthropologist," pp. 163–164, 161, 196–197.

48. Midelfort, *Witch Hunting*, pp. 187, 195, 185, 191.

49. Paul Boyer and Stephen Nissenbaum, *Salem Possessed: The Social Origins of Witchcraft* (Cambridge, Mass.: Harvard University Press, 1974) pp. 39, 87, 30–31, 190, 145–146, 109.

50. Monter, "Recherche," pp. 10, 124, 196–200.

51. Thomas, *Decline of Magic*, p. 510.

52. Trevor-Roper, *European Witch Craze*, p. 96; Robert Mandrou, *Introduction to Modern France, 1500–1640: An Essay in Historical Psychology*, trans. R.E. Hallmark (New York: Harper & Row, 1975), p. 228.

53. Macfarlane, *Witchcraft in Tudor and Stuart England*, p. 196; Monter, "Recherche," p. 124; Burstein, "Psychopathology," p. 76.

54. For the older view, see Marvin Koller, *Social Gerontology* (New York: Random House, 1968), p. 68; de Beauvoir, *Coming of Age*, pp. 140–141; Keith Thomas, "Age and Authority in Early Modern England," in *Proceedings of the British Academy* 62 (1976): 212, 233. For life expectancies after childhood, see Laslett, *World We Have Lost*, p. 93; Louise Tilly and Joan Scott, *Women, Work, and Family* (New York: Holt, Rinehart & Winston, 1978), p. 28. For quotes see Stephen Smith, "Growing Old in Early Stuart England," in *Albion* 7, no. 2 (Summer, 1976): 126; Peter Stearns, *Old Age in European Society: the Case of France* (New York: Holmes & Meier, 1976), p. 19. For proportions of the population in different age strata, see Kamen, *Iron Century*, p. 15; Laslett, *World We Have Lost*, p. 103;

John Demos, "Old Age in Early New England," in John Demos and Sarane Boocock, eds., *Turning Points: Historical and Sociological Essays on the Family* (Chicago: University of Chicago Press, 1978), special supplement to *American Journal of Sociology* 84 (1978), p. 254.

55. For the functional proposals, see Peter Stearns, "Old Women: Some Historical Observations," in *Journal of Family History*, 5(1) (Spring 1980): 45; Janet Roebuck, "When Does Old Age Begin? The Evolution of the English Definition," in *Journal of Social History* 12(3) (Spring, 1979): 419–421; Thomas, "Age," p. 237. For the chronological proposals, see Stearns, *Old Age*, pp. 16, 24; Demos, "Old Age," p. 249; Thomas, "Age," p. 240.

56. Stearns, "Old Women," p. 46. For importance of appearance, see Richard Grant, "Concepts of Aging: An Historical Review," in *Perspectives in Biology and Medicine*, 6 (Summer, 1963): 444.

57. On early modern subdivisions, see Smith, "Growing Old," pp. 128–130. For primitive attitudes, see David Hackett Fischer, *Growing Old in America* (New York: Oxford University Press, 1977), pp. 8–9; de Beauvoir, *Coming of Age*, p. 51; Leo Simmons, *The Role of the Aged in Primitive Society* (New Haven: Yale University Press, 1945), p. 81.

58. Lawrence Stone, "Walking Over Grandma," in *New York Review of Books*, XXIV (8) (May 12, 1977): 10; Smith, "Growing Old," pp. 130, 126; Thomas, "Age," pp. 211–212. Stone includes a passage from Shakespeare's *As You Like It*, the final quote.

59. George Rosen, *Madness in Society: Chapters in the Historical Sociology of Mental Illness* (Chicago: University of Chicago Press, 1968), p. 6.

60. Württemberg Hauptstaatsarchiv Stuttgart (hereinafter HSAS), A209, Bsl, 719.

61. See above, pp. 159–160. One example of group magic is contained in HSAS, A209, Bsl, 525.

62. On modern elderly schizophrenics, including quoted case, see Werner Janzarik, "Diagnostic and Nosological Aspects of Mental Disorder in Old Age," in Richard Williams et al., eds., *Processes of Aging: Social and Psychological Perspectives*, I (New York: Atherton Press, 1963), p. 398. On early modern awareness of natural mental disorders, see Rosen, *Madness*, pp. 15, 17, 240; HSAS, A209, Bsls, 546, 1924, 1789.

63. Erik Strömgren, "Epidemiology of Old-Age Psychiatric Disorders," in Williams, *Processes of Aging*, II, p. 140.

64. The experiment was conducted by Professor William Erich Peukert and a report is quoted along with many similar descriptions in Michael Harner, "Hallucinogens in European Witchcraft," in Michael Harner, ed., *Hallucinogens and Shamanism* (London: Oxford University Press, 1973), pp. 125–150, esp. p. 139. For the biochemical basis of the sensation of flight, see Harner, "Hallucinogens and Shamanism: The Question of a Trans-Cultural Experience," in Harner, pp. 151–154. The reason to believe that this (South American) material is applicable is that the active ingredients in European hallucinogens block nerve transmissions in the peripheral nervous system as well as the central nervous system, thus creating a sense of disembodiment; see Oakley Ray, *Drugs, Society, and Human Behavior* (St. Louis: C.V. Mosby, 1978) p. 381. On the particular sensitivity of old people, see Vladimir Frolkis, "Aging of the Autonomic Nervous System," in Birren and Schau, *Handbook of the Psychology of Aging*, p. 186.

65. See above, pp. 160–161 and note 44.

66. These figures are based on a partial and preliminary assessment of a sample to be incorporated into Chapter 4 of my forthcoming dissertation, "Witchcraft and Shamanism in Early Modern Württemberg," Princeton University. Because of multiple

denunciations and difficult handwriting, it may differ somewhat from my final assessment. However, the uncertain cases are few enough that these figures are substantially accurate. The raw data are contained in HSAS, A209, Bsls, 2099, 1789, 767, 546, 851a.

67. HSAS, A209, Bsls, 1787, 2096, 449, 767, 1780, 434, 782, 1884a, 852, 873, 1223, 1431, 1486, 8, 1856, 1881. See caution, note 66.

68. Reginald Scot, quoted in Burstein, "Psychopathology," p. 69; Monter, *Witchcraft*, pp. 134–136.

69. Burstein, "Psychopathology," pp. 69, 65.

70. Janzarik, "Aspects of Mental Disorder," pp. 391–392.

71. Eric Pfeiffer, "Psychopathology & Social Pathology," in Birren and Schau, *Handbook*, p. 653; Raymond Kuhlen, "Developmental Changes in Motivation During the Adult Years," in Bernice Neugarten, ed., *Middle Age and Aging* (Chicago: University of Chicago Press, 1968), pp. 115, 124.

72. Harold Geist, *The Psychological Aspects of the Aging Process with Sociological Implications* (St. Louis: Warren Green, 1968), p. 34; Koller, *Social Gerontology*, pp. 49–50.

73. Marian Yarrow, "Appraising Environment," in Williams, *Processes of Aging*, p. 202.

74. Thomas, "Age," p. 207; Smith, "Growing Old," p. 134; Fischer, *Growing Old*, pp. 17–18.

75. Fischer, *Growing Old*, p. 16; Smith, "Growing Old," p. 132.

76. Demos, "Old Age," pp. 252, 251, quoting William Bridge. See also Thomas, "Age," pp. 244–245; Rosen, *Madness*, p. 233.

77. Rosen, *Madness*, pp. 236–238.

78. Demos, "Old Age," p. 263; Fischer, *Growing Old*, p. 72; de Beauvoir, *Coming of Age*, p. 92.

79. On early modern age of menopause, see Laslett, *World*, p. 101; Tilly and Scott, *Women, Work*, p. 28. For the physiology, see Elizabeth Parker, *The Seven Ages of Woman*, ed. Evelyn Breck (Baltimore: Johns Hopkins University Press, 1960), pp. 477–478. Victorian attitudes are discussed in Janice Delaney et al., *The Curse: A Cultural History of Menstruation* (New York: E.P. Dutton, 1976), pp. 186–188.

80. Delaney, *The Curse*, pp. 188, 179; Parker, *Seven Ages*, pp. 469, 480–488, 491; Malkah Notman, "Midlife Concerns of Women: Implications of the Menopause," *American Journal of Psychiatry*, 136, no. 10 (October, 1979): 1271; Judith Posner, "It's All in Your Head: Feminist and Medical Models of Menopause (Strange Bedfellows)," *Sex Roles* 5, no. 2 (1979): 183; Paula Weideger, *Menstruation and Menopause: The Physiology and Psychology, the Myth and the Reality* (New York: Knopf, 1976), pp. 201, 203.

81. Kenneth Ryan, "Conference Summary," in Kenneth Ryan and Don Gibson, eds., *Menopause and Aging*, Department of Health, Education, and Welfare Publication # (NIH) 73-319 (1971), p. 3.

82. E. James McCranie, "Psychodynamics of the Menopause," Robert Greenblatt, et al., eds., *The Menopausal Syndrome* (New York: Medcom Press, 1974), p. 85.

83. Weldeger, *Menstruation and Menopause*, pp. 196–197; Notman, "Midlife Concerns," p. 12270; Kuhlen, "Developmental Changes," pp. 124–128. On male sexuality, see de Beauvoir, *Coming of Age*, p. 27.

84. Ryan, *Menopause and Aging*, p. 3.

85. See appendix; Weideger, *Menstruation and Menopause*, pp. 199, 201.

86. Stearns, *Old Age*, p. 37; quote from Weideger, *Menstruation and Menopause*, p. 201.

87. Macfarlane, *Witchcraft in Tudor and Stuart England*, p. 160; HSAS, A209, Bsl, 1884a.

88. Tilly and Scott, *Women, Work*, pp. 31–32.

89. Willystine Goodsell, *A History of the Family as a Social and Educational Institution* (New York: Macmillan, 1915) p. 264, 199–201, 182–183, 219–220, 264, 243–245, 301–304. On Roman women, see de Beauvoir, *Coming of Age*, p. 115. See also Lawrence Stone, "The Rise of the Family in Early Modern England: The Patriarchal Stage," in Charles Rosenberg, ed., *The Family in History* (Philadelphia: University of Pennsylvania Press, 1975), pp. 14, 25, 33, 35, 49, 50; David Sabean, "Aspects of Kinship Behavior and Property in Rural Western Europe before 1800," in Jack Goody et al., eds., *Family and Inheritance: Rural Society in Western Europe 1200–1800* (Cambridge: Cambridge University Press, 1976), pp. 108–109; Ingeborg Weber-Kellermann, *Die deutsche Familie: Versuch einer Sozialgeschichte* (Frankfort a.M.: Sushrkamp, 1974), pp. 26–28.

90. Lawrence Stone, *The Family, Sex, and Marriage in England 1500–1800* (New York: Harper & Row, 1977), pp. 356–357; Stone, "Rise," pp. 52–53. See also Alan Anderson and Raymond Gordon, "Witchcraft and the Status of Women—the Case of England," *British Journal of Sociology* 29 no. 2, (June, 1978): 173–174.

91. "Evidence" of this system is "widespread," although "not . . . universal," Jack Goody, "Inheritance, Property, and Women: Some Comparative Considerations," in Goody et al., eds., *Family and Inheritance*, p. 29. For the origins of this system, see Michael Mitterauer, "Der Mythos von der vorindustrieller Grossfamilie," and "Familienwirtschaft und Alternversorgung," in Michael Mitterauer and Reinhard Siedler, eds., *Vom Patriarchat zur Partnerschaft: Zum Strukturwandel der Familie* (Munich: C.H. Beck, 1977) pp. 57, 195–197. Note that the exact rate of retirement in the early modern period has not been determined; it would be interesting to the following argument if it increased, but this is not known.

92. Lutz Berkner, "The Stem Family and the Developmental Cycle of the Peasant Household: An Eighteenth-Century Austrian Example," in Michael Gordon, ed., *The American Family in Social-Historical Perspective* (New York: St. Martin's Press, 1973), p. 38; Thomas, "Age," p. 237. On the psychological stresses of retirement in general, see also Stearns, *Old Age*, p. 44; de Beauvoir, *Coming of Age*, p. 130–131; Mitterauer, "Alternversorgung," p. 198. On women's loss of status, see Sabean, *Kinship Behavior*, p. 109; Reuben Hill, "Social Theory and Family Development," in Jean Cuisenier, ed., *The Family Life Cycle in European Societies* (The Hague: Mositon, 1977), p. 13. On elderly males' status potential, see Thomas, "Age," p. 209, Simmons, *Role of the Aged*, pp. 130, 174; de Beauvoir, *Coming of Age*, p. 85.

93. On the problems of stepmothers and older widows, see Mitterauer, "Mythos," pp. 52, 60, and "Alternversorgung," p. 199; Stearns, *Old Age*, p. 121; Berkner, "Stem," pp. 40, 55, n'. 20; Laslett, *World*, p. 95; Cicely Howell, "Peasant Inheritance Customs in the Midlands, 1280–1700," in Goody, et al., eds., *Family and Inheritance*, p. 143. On the importance of new marriage patterns, see Midelfort, *Witch Hunting*, pp. 184–185; Natalie Z. Davis, "The Reasons of Misrule," in *Society and Culture in Early Modern France* (Stanford: Stanford University Press, 1975), p. 105–106.

94. Stone, "Grandma," p. 10.

95. Lutz Berkner, "Inheritance, Land Tenure, and Peasant Family Structure: a German Regional Comparison," in Goody et al., eds., *Family and Inheritance*, p. 78; Peter Laslett, *Family Life and Illicit Love in Earlier Generations* (Cambridge: Cambridge University Press, 1977), pp. 198–199.

96. Stone, "Rise," p. 50; Tilly and Scott, *Women, Work*, pp. 51, 29; Thomas, "Age," p. 242; Stone, *Family*, p. 195; Stearns, *Old Age*, pp. 22, 32; Fischer, *Growing Old*, p. 62.

97. Stone, "Rise," p. 50; Goodsell, *History of the Family*, pp. 220, 304.

98. See above, note 93; Stearns, *Old Age*, p. 30; William Goode, "Family Cycle and Theory Construction," in *Family Life Cycle*, p. 72; Thomas, "Age," p. 243. On the limited success of cultural barriers, see Stone, *Family*, p. 609.

99. William Masters and Virginia Johnson, "Human Sexual Response: The Aging Female and the Aging Male," in Neugarten, ed., *Middle Age and Aging*, pp. 271–275; *Malleus*, p. 47; for the inconsistency, see above, pp. 171–172.

100. Rudolf Tartler, "The Older Person in Family, Community, and Society," in Williams, *Processes of Aging*, II, p. 63; Thomas, "Age," pp. 233, 246; de Beauvoir, *Coming of Age*, pp. 71–72.

101. B.H. Slicher van Bath, *The Agrarian History of Europe*, trans. Olive Ordish (London: Edward Arnold, 1963). In addition, during this period, the proportion of old people in the population probably was higher than before or after until the twentieth century. See Stearns, *Old Age*, p. 20; Laslett, *Family*, p. 192; Philip Hauser, "Aging and World-Wide Population Change," in Robert Binstock and Ethel Shanas, eds., *Handbook of Aging and the Social Sciences* (New York: Van Nostrand Reinhold, 1976), p. 66.

102. Pfeiffer, *Psychopathology*, p. 653.

103. Monter hints at the possible effectiveness of witchcraft above, p.   see also Peters, *Magician*, pp. 116–117.

104. Thomas, *Decline*, pp. 510–511; John Davenport, *Aphrodisiacs and Anti-Aphrodisiacs* (New York: Award Books, 1970), pp. 135, 157, 163.

105. Armand Nicoli, ed., *The Harvard Guide to Modern Psychiatry* (Cambridge: Belknap Press, 1978) p. 325. See also Freedman and Kaplan, eds., *Comprehensive Textbook of Psychiatry* (Baltimore: Williams & Williams, 1967), p. 1039; Alberto Seguin, *Introduction to Psychosomatic Medicine* (New York: International University Press, 1950), p. 19.

106. Simmons, *Role of the Aged*, pp. 82, 175; Thomas, "Age," p. 247; Stone, *Family*, p. 199; Tilly and Scott, *Women, Work*, pp. 53–56.

107. Margaret Mead quoted by Jack Goody, "Cross-Cultural Perspective," *Family and Inheritance*, p. 311.

108. On late medieval theology as related to popular culture, see M.D. Chenu, *Nature, Man, and Society in the Twelfth Century* (Chicago: University of Chicago Press, 1968) pp. 223–224. On the rise of the bureaucracy, see Theodore K. Rabb, *The Struggle for Stability in Early Modern Europe* (New York: Oxford University Press, 1975), pp. 60–61; for its relationship to moral imperialism, see Robert Moore, *The Origins of European Dissent* (New York: St. Martin's Press, 1977), p. 278. The theme of the imposition of elite values on popular culture as a stimulus behind the witch trials has recently been expounded by Robert Muchembled, in both his *La Sorcière au Village (XVe–XVIIIe siècle)* (Juilliard/Gallimard, 1979) and a collaborative volume he prepared with Marie-Sylvie Dupont-Bouchat and Willem Frÿhoff, *Prophètes et Sorciers dans Les Pays-Bas XVIe–XVIIIe siècle* (Hachette, 1978). Unfortunately, both these works became available to me too late to be incorporated into the discussion of witch historiography in section 3.

109. Macfarlane, *Witchcraft in Tudor and Stuart England*, p. 197.

110. Boyer and Nissenbaum, *Salem Possessed*, p. 105. See also Macfarlane, pp. 204–206; Thomas, *Decline*, pp. 581–582.

111. Midelfort, *Witch Hunting*, p. 195.

112. Horsley, "Who Were the Witches?," p. 713.

113. Natalie Z. Davis, "Women on Top," in *Society and Culture*, pp. 124–125.

CHAPTER EIGHT—GROWING OLD IN AN AGE OF TRANSITION

STEVEN R. SMITH

Society's perception of its older members depends on a variety of factors, such as the proportion of elderly, the range of retirement possibilities, housing patterns, religious attitudes and beliefs, and the broad ideals of family and community. All of these factors are subject to change, and with these changes come different attitudes about aging and the aged. This paper raises the question of whether the social perception of the elderly altered significantly in seventeenth-century England. The century involved great change overall, not only in politics but also in aspects of popular outlook and family life. On the other hand, we are learning that attitudes toward the elderly can be remarkably immune to changes in other areas of a society, even other features of family life. Hence the particular interest of applying the test of change to old age in seventeenth-century England.

In 1651, Alice Wandesford, the twenty-four-year-old daughter of Christopher Wandesford, Yorkshire gentleman and onetime Lord Deputy in Ireland, married William Thornton. Her first child was born on August 27, 1652, and died the same day. Over the next fifteen years, she gave birth to eight other children, five of whom lived only a few months or less. Her childbearing years ended with the death of her husband in 1668 when he was 44. She lived on until the age of eighty, surviving all of her children except one daughter.[1]

The life of Alice Thornton was not typical of the lives of seventeenth-century women, but certain facets of her life allow her to serve as an example of family life more than three hundred years ago. She was not typical in that she was better off economically than most of her contemporaries and she was literate; we know her life because she recorded it in an autobiography, something rare for a woman in that era. But she did have much in common with other women of the seventeenth century. She married at just about the average age of marriage; she produced children regularly and her children died regularly. She was a deeply religious woman, seeing the hand of God in all of her misfortunes as well as her good fortune. When her children died, she praised God and searched her life to understand what God wanted for her. In recording the deaths of her parents and of her husband, she noted the rituals of death, emphasizing the religious attitudes of the dying persons, their confessions, their patience, their exhortations to the survivors, and their final blessings. Alice Thornton also lived a long time and faced the problems and joys of old age, though, typically, her autobiography contains few references to the process of growing old.

Alice Thornton lived in an age of great change, though she and most of her contemporaries would have been unaware of the transitional nature of the age and would more likely have thought in terms of the final age and the coming apocalypse. Looking back, historians have seen the entire early modern period and especially the seventeenth century as one of the great ages of transition. It was a time when a more modern economic system was emerging; when divine right monarchy in England was replaced by a more modern and limited government; when one of the great migrations of history took place and the New World began to take shape; when scientific discoveries and theories were developing and a new Newtonian world view was replacing the ancient view. The religious upheavals of the sixteenth century brought not only new ideas about man's relationship with God, but new ideas about life and death as well. Protestantism, especially in its Calvinist form, emphasized life in this world rather than the late medieval fascination with life in the next world. By sweeping away the doctrine of Purgatory and the obligations of the living to the dead, Protestantism opened up new possibilities and initiated a more modern frame of mind.[2]

Family relationships were also changing during the early modern period. Lawrence Stone has amassed a great deal of evidence showing that during the seventeenth century a new type of family was emerging in England. The modern family was nuclear, with strong affective ties among its members. A new sense of individualism and a desire for personal privacy accompanied these changes. While the nuclear family seems always to have been a feature of English life, the changes of the early modern era may have weakened ties with family lineages and communities.[3] Family changes were related to the other fundamental shifts of the period, especially the decline of the patriarchal idea and the growing sense of economic individualism.

Did all of the changes of this era have much effect on the elderly? Did the emergence of new family relationships affect the position of the elderly? Were they treated any differently by their children or by other younger people? Was this age of transition an important one in the history of aging?

While the position of the elderly must always be viewed in the context of the family, other factors are important. One of these factors influencing opinions is the proportion of aged in the general population. There seems to have been little change in this factor in the seventeenth century; throughout the century, age distribution in England was skewed toward youth. While the rapid growth rate of the early part of the century slowed around 1650, the population remained youthful. Because life expectancy at birth was quite low (somewhere in the late twenties or early thirties), it has often been assumed that few people lived to enjoy or to suffer old age. Today we live in an era of long life expectancy and many do live to be seventy or older. We also live in an age fascinated by statistics, while the seventeenth century was little concerned about such matters and many people were not sure of their correct age. Yet the limited evidence available suggests that a fair number of people did live to be sixty or older.

One crude method of determining the proportion of elderly in the past is to examine the lives of notables whose birth and death dates are more likely to be known. Using three volumes of the popular *Who's Who in History* series yields some interesting results, suggesting changes over a period of three hundred years. Of the 118 persons listed in the sixteenth-century volume whose ages at death could be determined, less than half (42.4 percent) lived to be sixty, though about one-third survived to seventy or older. In the seventeenth century, almost two-thirds were sixty or older at the time of death and more than one-third were past seventy. In the eighteenth century, more than three-fourths (77.4 percent) lived to sixty and almost half to the age of seventy. While these percentages say little about the general population, they do provide a comparison. Of course, many of those listed in these volumes held offices for which long experience might have been a prerequisite. For example, the average age at death of the nine seventeenth-century Archbishops of Canterbury was seventy-three, but the average age at appointment was sixty. Of the thirty-one secretaries of state whose ages at appointment could be determined, thirteen were fifty or older when they assumed the responsibilities of that position: the average age at appointment was forty-six and the median age was forty-eight. Older persons also held prominent positions in local government: for example, in the late sixteenth century, the average age for town councillors in Oxford was fifty and for aldermen, sixty-one.[4] Thus, not only did many live into old age, but many were quite capable of performing important responsibilities long after the age of fifty.

While no accurate figures for the age distribution of the larger population exist, the best estimates indicate that many people did live to be sixty or more. Gregory King, a pioneer demographer, surveyed the population in 1695 and estimated that about one out of every ten people was sixty or older. Since his figures also put the average age at twenty-seven, seventeenth-century England was clearly a youthful society, but the most significant difference between the seventeenth and twentieth centuries is the different proportions of middle-aged persons. King estimated that 25.9 percent of the population was between the ages of thirty and fifty-nine; the comparable figure for 1961 was 40.4 percent. Of course, King's figures were estimates; where actual statistics can be compiled, different percentages emerge showing regional variations. In Chilvers Coton in 1684, 6.7 percent were sixty or older, and, in Litchfield, 8.1 percent in 1695. E. A. Wrigley's study of Colyton, Devonshire, demonstrated the impact of infant mortality on the age distribution. There, approximately half of those who lived to the age of 25 and married lived to the age of sixty and about one-fourth survived to the age of seventy.[5]

In the seventeenth century, perhaps 30 percent of all children born died in infancy; this was by far the most significant factor affecting age distribution and life expectancy. Another factor was the age at marriage; this plus the lack of effective contraceptive devices meant that women started producing children later then than now, but continued until a later age. Thus in the nuclear family, the age range of the offspring might be great and parents would likely be in their forties when the last children were born. For example, had Alice Thornton's first and last children survived, there would have been fifteen years separating them, and had her husband not died, the gap between first and last might have been even greater as more children would probably have been born.

While the proportion of older persons in an advanced industrialized society is higher than in preindustrial historical societies, the possibility of surviving has always existed; statistical comparisons often distort this fact. In the seventeenth century, if a person managed to get through the dangerous years of childhood, he had a reasonably good chance of living into old age. Of course, illnesses and injuries always presented dangers and childbirth was a real threat to women. The poor quality of medical treatment and the level of medical knowledge meant that there was little defense or possibility of cure. Poverty was another factor affecting longevity; both living conditions and diet were substandard according to twentieth-century criteria. But if one could escape direst poverty and serious illness, the chances of survival into old age were fairly good.

Culture was more important than sheer demography in shaping a distinctive preindustrial old age. Historians of old age have perhaps unduly neglected religion as a factor that not only profoundly influenced the elderly themselves, in preindustrial Europe, but also helped integrate them with the culture of other age groups. We know of course of the secularization of the past two centuries, but it remains to tie our knowledge of the role of religion before modern times with the position of old people.

Early modern Englishmen lived in a world of Christianity, and their approach to life was molded by religion. It could be argued that the strength of religion was due in part to the high death rates and the inability of medicine to cure illness; certainly most people, as Alice Thornton, would have seen the hand of God in almost everything and would have found religion comforting in the face of death and suffering. Religion helped determine the nature of the family as well as the nature of the state. Society's attitudes towards old age and old people were influenced by Christian ideas. The Fifth Commandment to honor parents and all persons in authority or of great age was taken seriously, reinforced by sermons, catechisms, and domestic manuals. Patriarchalism, based on biblical injunction and example was a very powerful force in the early part of the century. Much of the literature on old age is to be found in sermons and religious manuals, not in scientific studies and sociological treatises.

Yet many of the basic ideas about old age can be traced back to classical, not Christian, origins. Like the ancient Greeks, seventeenth-century men accepted the notion that all of life is divided into definite stages. Twentieth-century psychologists also see life as organized into stages or periods of development; Erik Erikson's eight stages of psychosocial development are perhaps the best known. But such modern psychological concepts differ from the ancient scheme in that they are determined by development, not chronological age. The scheme which early modern Englishmen had inherited from the past was based on age, though certain personality traits were associated with each stage. While there were numerous methods of dividing life, the most common number of ages of life was seven, a number thought to represent fullness.

Henry Cuffe's *The Differences of the Ages of Man's Life* defined a stage of life as a "period or term of man's life wherein his natural complexion and temperature naturally and of its own accord is evidently changed." This definition accorded with traditional medical thought that the body lost its moisture and warmth as it grew older. Cuffe also tied the seven stages of life to the seven planets, providing a cosmological link between the individual and the universe. The first age, Infancy, which lasted for the first seven years of life, was controlled by the Moon. The second, Childhood, was dominated by

Mercury. The third, which lasted from fifteen to twenty-one, was under the influence of Venus. Youth, from twenty-two to thirty-four, was controlled by the Sun, while Manhood, from thirty-five to fifty, was dominated by warlike Mars. The sixth, Old Age, lasted from fifty to sixty-two and was under Jupiter's influence. The final stage, which Cuffe named Crooked Age, lasted from sixty-two until death and was controlled by Saturn.[6]

It was not unusual to distinguish several phases of old age. Simon Goulart, a French Protestant theologian whose popular and comprehensive account of aging was translated into English as *The Wise Vieillard, or Old Man,* posited three different phases. The first lasted from fifty to sixty-five, "when a man is yet lusty, strong, and youthful" and may continue to be of service. In the next phase, "old men may be fit to be counsellors of estate and directors and governors of families," but after eighty, they are "fit for nothing" with the exception of conversation and the enjoyment of their grandchildren. Dr. John Smith, whose *Portrait of Old Age* went through several editions, also found three stages of old age, but he specified no ages. The first was described as "crude, green, and while it is yet in the beginning," men could still do useful work. The next, "full, mature, or ripe," usually meant retirement from active work, but not physical decay. The final phase, Smith described as "extreme, sickly, decrepit, evergrowing old age.'"[7] It is interesting that the first stage of old age was described as "green," "lusty," and "youthful"; this stage seems really to have referred to a period of full maturity.

As suggested by Cuffe's definition of life's stages, physical characteristics changed with advancing age. Francis Bacon provided a good description of those changes in his *The History of Life and Death,* a supposedly scientific study of the process of aging. Bacon said that in old age, the skin was dry and wrinkled instead of moist and smooth as in youth; the flesh was hard rather than tender; digestion poor rather than good; the bowels dry instead of soft and moist; the muscles trembling and weak rather than steady and strong; the hair gray or missing, not full of color. Old age meant discomfort and weakness for every aspect of the body. Another writer, John Pechey, in *A Collection of Chronical Diseases,* told old people that they could expect frequent attacks of gout, especially if they overindulged in wine and food or failed to get sufficient exercise. His rather discouraging account reminded the elderly that they were weaker than younger persons and therefore more susceptible to illness since they could not purify the blood nor handle the humors as well as the young.[8]

Physical discomforts were only part of the process of aging. The traditional ages of man were each assigned personality traits; those generally associated with old age, particularly the last phase, were undesirable and were not unlike some of the popular misconceptions still held in the twentieth century. Robert Burton's *The Anatomy of Melancholy* listed aging as one of the main causes of unhappiness, especially for those who had lived active lives and then retired with little or nothing to do. Coldness and dryness, the two physical characteristics of old age, were also symptoms of melancholy. Cuffe thought of old people as being excessively talkative, though he pointed out that they talked a lot in order to pass on to younger people the wisdom gained from long experience. He said that old people were "jealously suspicious" but only because of their knowledge of human nature. They also tended to be possessive and wanted to hold on to all those things which help to sustain life. John Smith thought of old age as a time when both understanding and willpower were reduced, and cited the biblical example of Solomon, who was so weak in his old age that he allowed his wives to turn him from God. Goulart also listed the negative features, concluding that old age was a time when people became "weak and feeble . . . in everything they do and take in hand."[9]

The negative side of old age was also reflected in the drama of the era. William Shakespeare's Old Capulet is an example of a silly old man, calling for his sword when a crutch would have been more appropriate. But in *As You Like It*, Old Adam, almost eighty years old, was sympathetically portrayed as a man of strength despite his years; this was attributed to good living in youth. *King Lear*, perhaps Shakespeare's most famous old man, shows old age in its many facets and might have served as a warning to those who were thinking of retiring. In Ben Jonson's *Bartholomew's Fair*, Zeal-of-the-Land Busy-Body embodied Puritanism and old age, both of which were treated irreverently. While the dramatists of the late sixteenth and early seventeenth centuries depicted old age in a variety of conditions, by the late seventeenth century, drama focused almost exclusively on the negative features. Restoration comedies were full of old men and old women who were generally bewildered and victimized by younger characters. Seemingly, old people were associated with the discarded values of the past, and the glorification of youth reflected the Restoration era's rebellion against the earlier constricting morality.[10]

Just as the dramatists of the early seventeenth century had some good things to say about old people, the authors of domestic manuals and religious tracts found some positive features. Goulart thought that the greatest benefit of old age was "ripeness of judgement." That, combined with "prudence, temperance, continency" and a more complete knowledge of God, fitted old men to be statesmen. Goulart also pointed out that the Bible teaches respect for age and that ancient Hebrew society accorded old people special honor and respect. He even thought that old people have an easier time with illness because they had had so much experience with it and because suffering seemed natural to them. Moreover, as the body grew weak, the mind could remain active. Finally, old pople were free from the "desires and lusts of young men" and from all the problems and vexations which accompany sexual and social activity. Goulart offered comforting examples of old soldiers who had defeated young ones in battle and of blind persons who had been useful to society.[11]

John Reading had perhaps the best answer for those who emphasized the negative side of aging. Admitting that many thought of the elderly as "forward, pettish, hasty, malicious, dispraising the present, praising the ages past, self-opinionated, forgetful and the like," he pointed out that these are characteristics of people of all ages. An old grouch had probably been a young grouch. All in all, he thought that old age was a good thing because it carried with it wisdom and intellectual vigor. It also allowed people to give up the "many noisome affections which loaded up our youth" and freed men from false vanity. The nearness of death also gave people a better "view of the most blessed estate of heaven," which was a better future than that faced by most young people. He reminded old people of their obligations to set good examples for others and to behave in a manner which would earn the respect of the young. Old people should always be careful not to criticize youth unjustifiably; quiet examples would accomplish more.[12]

The general obligation of older people to instruct younger generations were often specified in the domestic manuals of the era. Seventeenth-century religious thought emphasized duty as an integral part of the community of the godly, with specific responsibilities for each stage of life. Robert Abbot's *A Christian Family Builded by God* listed six of the most important duties of the aged. First, they must be sober and moderate, especially in their diet. Secondly, they must be "seemly, modest, and gracious in their carriage" in order to provide models for others. Thirdly, they must avoid lust, pride, covetousness, and all other sins associated with youth. Fourthly, they must be "sound in the faith" since they had lived long enough to learn the teachings of Christianity and to receive Christ as their savior. Next, they ought to be charitable. Finally, they must be patient, for the trials and illnesses of old age would bring much suffering, but also put them near their reward. [13]

The apparent closeness of death—which for religious writers was not a defeat or end, but a victory and a beginning—was a theme of much of the religious literature about and for the aged. The question of death's desirability was an old one for Christian writers; while all agreed that death was not something to be feared and that there is a natural desire to maintain life, the question of whether a person should, by artificial means, attempt to prolong life caused some disagreement. Why some people lived longer than others was also a puzzle. In an era when death was commonplace, not only because of the high mortality rates, but also because it usually took place at home in a family setting, such problems may have been of more immediate concern than in the twentieth century. The seventeenth century provided no new answers, but relied on ancient wisdom.

The most common view was that expressed by Richard Allestree, a popular religious writer. His *A Discourse Concerning the Period of Human Life: Whether Mutable or Immutable* opened with the traditional Christian view that the cause of death and suffering is sin. He argued that God has the unquestioned authority to set an arbitrary number of years of life for any particular person, yet he said that there is a "common period of human life" which varies from time to time and from place to place. For seventeenth-century England, he thought that this "common period" of life was about seventy or eighty years. As determinants of the lengths of particular lives, Allestree suggested that a person's life-span could be lengthened or reduced according to circumstances. While God made the final decision, His decision would be influenced by what a person did with his life. It might be "shortened by our intemperance, or neglect of the means; and be extended by our good managery and religious manner of living." Righteousness was much more important than any medicine or other artificial means, which Allestree regarded as generally ineffective. James Cole, a London merchant who wrote a treatise on death, agreed with Allestree. He suggested that God is like the man who uses the bellows to blow air into an organ; he starts the organ and can stop it at any time, yet the quality of music is in the hands of the person at the keyboard just as the quality of life is determined by individuals. [14]

The question of how long one would live was an ancient one. [15] Perhaps since the beginning of mankind, people have been concerned with this problem and have sought the answer in magic and science as well as religion. In the early modern era, many turned to astrology to find out how long they would live, though this method was rejected by religion since it made heavenly bodies the determiners of destiny rather than God. William Lilly, one of the seventeenth century's prominent astrologers, said that he was often asked to predict the date of someone's death, but thought such prediction imprudent.[16] In addition to astrology, certain signs could be used to tell if death was near. For example, if a sick person often turned his face to the wall, it was a bad sign. To determine whether a person would live for another year, a drop of blood could be placed in a barrel of water; if the whole drop sank to the bottom, the person had at least another year to live, but if the blood diffused in the water, he had less.[17]

Physical characteristics could also point to long life. Men who looked more like their mothers than their fathers would live long lives, as would children born to young parents. Bacon thought that children conceived in the morning when parents were "not too lusty and wanton" lived longer than others. He also reported that hairy legs and red hair were signs of longevity. Others thought that the lines on the forehead could predict long life; if the three lines representing Mercury, Jupiter, and Saturn were close together, the person would live until the age of seventy. Sir Thomas Browne, a physician and deeply religious writer, said that it was commonly believed that dreams about death or dead friends were signs of imminent death. He also thought that just prior to death, a person's appearance would change and the dying person would resemble some close relative. Alice Thornton was not surprised when her husband died since he had dreamed a few months earlier that he had only forty-seven more days to live.[18]

Clearly, none of these methods of determining the length of life was consistent with the Christian principle that righteousness was the surest way of extending life and that licentiousness was the surest way of shortening it. Theologians might have been divided on the wisdom of using medical means to extend life, but early-seventeenth-century Englishmen were interested in such methods and many writers offered advice to them. Bacon's *History of Life and Death* was based on the assumption that "age is a great but slow dryer" and that anything which slowed down the drying process would promote longevity. A cool climate would help since coolness retarded drying out. The body's "spirits" should be kept thick; several potions were recommended for that purpose. Deep breathing and proper diet would aid in preserving the spirits. A good emotional attitude and positive outlook were helpful, while anger, fear, and envy could shorten life. Deep breathing was essential, but only in moderation, since too much air would dry out the internal organs.

The best air was the cool, clean air of caves, but if living in a cave were impossible, painting or oiling the skin and wearing linen clothes would protect the body's moisture. If a cool climate were impractical, cool baths would keep the blood at the desired temperature. The body must also be kept firm, since firm substances are less susceptible to decay than soft ones. Solid foods and special exercises were useful in preserving physical fitness. Bacon recommended specific foods and drinks which he thought would help prolong life. Many other books were available similar to Bacon's; almost all of them accepted the traditional view of aging as a process of drying out.[19]

Those who did manage to avoid the drying-out process and survive to great ages were much admired. One of the most famous of the very old men was Thomas Par, who was reported to have been 152 years old when he died in 1635. Following his death, William Harvey, perhaps the century's most distinguished physician, examined Par's body and found that all of the internal organs were in good condition with the exception of the heart. Par had died shortly after moving to London and Harvey thought that had the old man continued to live in the countryside, where the air was fresh and pure, he might have lived even longer. Harvey also reported that "the organs of generation were healthy" and that Par had been sexually active until the age of 140. Later in the century, certain places with favorable climates were thought to be conducive to long life. A report to the London Philosophical Society in 1684 listed a number of persons over 100 in northern England and attributed this to the diet of mountain residents. The parish of Barfreston had a reputation as one of the healthiest in Kent. When the parson there died at the age of 96 in 1700, the funeral service was conducted by an 87-year-old priest and the sermon preached by one who was 82. Several people over 100 attended the funeral. Of course, the ages of all these people might well have been exaggerated; a society which admired old age and in which numerical exactness was not a virtue might very well add years to the true ages of persons. Thomas Fuller, in his 1639 history of the crusades, suggested that just as the size of armies was often inflated, ages were too. He thought that this was especially true after the age of 70: "many old men use to set the clock of their age too fast . . . growing ten years in a twelve month, are presently four-score, yea within a year or two after, climb up to a hundred." One is reminded of David Hackett Fischer's finding that colonial Americans were more prone to exaggerate than to minimize their ages, when they lied in any direction.[20]

At the heart of the admiration of old age was the patriarchal ideal of the seventeenth century. The father was the head of the household and the governor of all who lived therein. Children and young people were continually admonished to obey and respect their parents and a well-governed household was one which respected parental authority. The Fifth Commandment was extended from parents to all those in positions of authority. Many of those positions were held by older persons even though seventeenth-century England was a youthful society. While the country was far from being a gerontocracy, age meant experience and at least the possibility of wisdom. Coupled with the traditional respect for old age and the authority of the Fifth Commandment was the notion that young people and children were wild, unseasoned, and animal-like, in constant need of supervision and guidance. While the obligation of obedience was especially aimed at children, it extended into later life. Parents should always be regarded as superiors, and filial obligation included complete maintenance of aged parents if necessary. One writer suggested that children should even turn to begging if they could not support their parents in any other way.[21]

Respect for old age may well be typical of all preindustrial societies,[22] but it may also be more an ideal than a reality. Certainly in seventeenth-century England, the aged did not always receive the degree of respect they thought they deserved. This lack of respect and its causes were discussed at length by the Earl of Clarendon in *A Dialogue Between A, an Old Courtier; B, an Old Lawyer; C, an Old Soldier; D, an Old Country Gentleman; and E, an Old Alderman*. The five old men, all over seventy, thought that their own era was far worse than earlier times, whether those times were the Age of Solomon or the years of their own youth. The lawyer thought that youth were so unworthy that he proposed limiting offices of authority to those fifty or older. His friends agreed. All five suggested causes for what they saw as a new problem, generally blaming education and poor parental guidance.[23]

Complaints about the treatment of old people can also be found in popular ballads and tales. The story of the old man of Monmouth, which dates from the Middle Ages, was still popular in the seventeenth century. This unfortunate old man transferred his property to his married son with the understanding that his son would take care of him in his old age. At first the old man was accorded due honor and respect. He was first seated at the head of the table, but gradually was moved down and eventually reduced to remaining on a couch behind the door where he was covered with an old sackcloth. When he died and was buried, his grandson asked for the sackcloth telling his father that "it shall serve to cover you as it did my old grandfather." Another story told of an aged couple, who, when too old and feeble to work, traveled a hundred miles to seek help from their wealthy son. When he turned them down, his own children murdered him in order to get his property; they in turn were killed by a greedy cousin.[24] Such stories as these illustrate the idea that God would punish those ungrateful children who failed to meet the needs of their parents.

Actual relationships between aged parents and their children can never be fully known. Some insight can be obtained from the diaries and other autobiographical material, though diarists were often silent on such matters or, if the diary was intended for others, presented an ideal picture. Ralph Josselin's revealing diary is something of an exception. He remained in close touch with his children after they left home. His diary recorded their illnesses and news of them regularly. His children also visited their parents regularly and the old nuclear family sometimes gathered on special occasions such as Christmas. His children were concerned about his health, and, when at the age of sixty-six, Josselin was seriously ill, they hurried to his bedside and remained for a week. Josselin and his wife also visited in the homes of his married children from time to time and his grandchildren stayed with them on several occasions.[25] Another diarist, Henry Newcome, also kept in close touch with his children, though the relationships were not always happy. His second son, Daniel, was a continuing problem. When at the age of fifty, the elder Newcome was planning the education of his youngest son, he noted his wish that "it may please God to take Daniel off me." After Daniel's death at the age of thirty-three, Newcome assumed responsibility for his infant grandson; though at the age of fifty-seven, he was not pleased with that obligation.[26]

Josselin and Newcome were both ministers and neither required any assistance in their old age from their children. Both remained active in the ministry, but Josselin gave up working on his farm several years before his death. Such retirement from active farm work was not unusual in the countryside. Many old men turned over active management of the land to their oldest son, though as in the case of the old man of Monmouth, such arrangements did not always prove to be satisfactory. The agreement between Henry Martindale, a Lancastershire farmer, and his son Thomas was typical. When he was about sixty years old, the elder Martindale entered into an agreement with Thomas whereby the father retained half of his house and, in return for an annual payment, Thomas received the land and the other half of the house.[27] Many artisans and shop owners also turned over responsibilities to their children, but in both town and country, retirement in a society with limited economic resources was not always possible and many were forced to work until death. This was especially true for those without children willing or able to support them. The Elizabethan Poor Law and private charities did provide some support for the aged, but such facilities were able to care for only a small proportion of the elderly.[28]

Even those with children who could support them preferred to live in separate households as long as possible. Three-generation huseholds were very exceptional in early modern England; indeed the large extended family seems to have been rare in English history.[29] The investigations of historical sociologist Peter Laslett show that there were in fact a variety of living arrangements for the elderly and that these were influenced by such factors as the relatively late age at marriage, the tendency of widowers to remarry more often than widows, and the maintenance of the traditional nuclear family over a longer period of time than is common now. Laslett's conclusion is that most old people remained where they were even after the marriage of some or all of their children or the death of a spouse. The general rule was that once a person was the head of a household, he would remain such for as long as possible.[30]

In some cases, an unmarried child would remain at home to care for the parents. For example, when Henry Newcome made his will in 1695, two months before his death at the age of sixty-eight, he left the bulk of his estate to his wife for herself and their unmarried daughter, Rose, "who I know will not leave her in her old age and great infirmities."[31] At his wife's death, Rose would receive three-fifths of the remainder of the estate. Because widowers often remarried, they might well have young children or young wives to take care of them. Sometimes, remarriage was for the purpose of obtaining someone to take care of the old man. In describing the life of Samuel Fairclough, a Puritan minister, Samuel Clarke noted that when he was about seventy, Fairclough "was forced to marry (a third time) an aged gentlewoman to be his nurse." Prior to this marriage, Fairclough had lived with one of his married daughters in a very crowded household and apparently was happy to get out of her home. When Phineas Pett, a shipbuilder, married for the third time at the age of sixty-eight, he was seeking more than companionship and nursing. His wife was pregnant when she died nine months after their wedding.[32] While Pett failed to establish a new family, many did succeed.

In sum, materials from seventeenth-century England (while they certainly illustrate the now commonplace historical conclusion that old age in practice could be less rosy than it was in theory in preindustrial Europe) suggest the important family roles that the elderly could retain. Furthermore, the translation of patriarchalism into actual family relationships was not seriously dislodged, as far as old people were concerned, by 1700. Though the weakening of patriarchal theory signaled a shift in opinion, the position of old people did not change in terms of work patterns or living arrangements. Changes in patriarchalism may long have been selective, affecting other groups in society more directly and immediately than the elderly themselves. Thus younger people developed more autonomy, and the ties of affection between parents and children became stronger.[33] In the long run this development might weaken relationships between parents and their adult children. If, at the same time, society was rejecting the values of an earlier generation associated with Puritanism, the Commonwealth, and a rigid morality, the perception of the elderly—and the views old people held of their own changing society—would have altered as well. Yet this change, too, was very gradual, and became more apparent in the eighteenth century than in the seventeenth.

Certainly there was no alteration of the traditional pattern of household arrangement for old persons, since the tradition of remaining in the role of head of household as long as one was economically and physically able to do so continued. A change in opinion is not obvious in the popular literature of the seventeenth century; patriarchalism remained the ideal. Any significant change in attitudes would more likely have occurred with changes in the age distribution; that is, the increasing proportion of middle-aged persons and the decreasing proportion of young persons. Ancient ideas about life retained their hold on popular mentality: that life is divided into stages, that aging is a process of drying out, that old people are to be honored and respected. Christian thought continued to emphasize that old age is the result of righteousness and a special reward from God which puts a person nearer death but better able to accept the suffering of this world. Old people still had the duty of setting good examples for the young, and the young were still obligated to follow those examples. A mutuality of dependence remained; Henry Newcome was unhappy when he had the financial responsibility for his grandson thrust on him, but he was comforted by the knowledge that his daughter would take care of his widow.

Such was the pattern throughout the seventeenth century. Where the pattern was disturbed by premature death of children or economic inability or indifference, the poorhouses, parish officials, private charities, and neighbors were available. But mixed with the pattern of mutual dependence was a sense of independence. In a world which saw the traditional familial and economic relationships change fundamentally, the elderly retained basically the position they had long held; perhaps their independence grew at the expense of mutual dependence, but any great transformation awaited a later century.

NOTES

1. Alice Thornton, *The Autobiography of Mrs. Alice Thornton of East Newton, Co. York*, ed. Charles Jackson (Surtees Society, XLII, 1873), pp. 87, 91–94, 96, 124, 125, 140, 148, 151.

2. Theodore Spencer, *Death and Elizabethan Tragedy; a Study of Convention and Opinion in the Elizabeth Drama* (Cambridge, Mass.: Harvard University Press, 1936), pp. 36, 47, 54–55, 66–110. See also Nancy Lee Beaty, *The Craft of Dying: The Literary Tradition of the Ars Moriendi in England* (New Haven: Yale University Press, 1970).

3. Lawrence Stone, *The Family, Sex and Marriage in England 1500–1800* (New York: Harper & Row, 1977); see also Philippe Ariès, *Centuries of Childhood*, trans. Robert Baldick (London: Jonathan Cape, 1962).

4. C.R.N. Routh, *England, 1485–1603*, vol. 2; C.P. Hill, *England, 1603–1714*, vol. 3, and G. Treasure, *The Eighteenth Century*, vol. 4 of *Who's Who in History*, ed. C.R.N. Routh (Oxford: Basil Blackwell, 1965); Carl I. Hammer, Jr., "Anatomy of an Oligarchy: The Oxford Town Council in the Fifteenth and Sixteenth Century," *Journal of British Studies* 18 (1978): 1–27; *Dictionary of National Biography* was used to determine certain ages.

5. Peter Laslett, *The World We Have Lost* (London: Methuen and Company, 1965), pp. 103, 98–99; Laslett, *Family Life and Illicit Love in Earlier Generations: Essays in Historical Sociology* (Cambridge: Cambridge University Press, 1977), p. 188.

6. Henry Cuffe, *The Difference in the Ages of Man's Life* (London, 1626), pp. 113, 114–121; see also Ariès's, *Centuries of Childhood*, pp. 18–19.

7. Simon Goulart, *The Wise Vieillard, or Old Man* (London, 1621), pp. 24–25; Dr. John Smith, *The Portrait of Old Age* 2nd ed. (London, 1666), p. 10.

8. Francis Bacon, *The History of Life and Death* (London, 1638), pp. 275–282; John Pechey, *A Collection of Chronical Diseases* (London, 1692), pp. 86, 114–115.

9. Robert Burton, *The Anatomy of Melancholy, What It Is* 4th ed. (Oxford, 1632), pp. 59, 31; Cuffe, *Ages*, pp. 131–132; Smith, *Portrait*, pp. 39, 38; Goulart, *Old Man*, p. 24.

10. Hallet Smith, "Bare Ruined Choirs: Shakespearean Variations on the Theme of Old Age," *The Huntington Library Quarterly* 39 (1976): 241–247; Elisabeth Mignon, *Crabbed Age and Youth: the Old Men and Women in the Restoration Comedy of Manners* (Durham, N.C.: Duke University Press, 1947) pp. 3–21.

11. Goulart, *Old Man*, pp. 87–93, 46–50, 53–62.

12. John Reading, *The Old Man's Staff; Two Sermons Showing the Only Way to a Comfortable Old Age* (London, 1621), pp. 10–15, 23–26, 29–34.

13. Robert Abbot, *A Christian Family Builded by God, Directing All Governors of Families How to Act* (London, 1653), pp. 12–16.

14. [Richard Allestree], *A Discourse Concerning the Period of Human Life: Whether Mutable or Immutable* (London, 1677), pp. 55, 56, 63, 78, 82, 99, 116–117; James Cole, *Of Death, A True Description* (London, 1629), pp. 68–84. See also Samuel Gardiner, *The Devotions of the Dying Man, That Desireth to Die Well* (London, 1627) and Richard Baxter, *A Christian Directory* (London, 1673).

15. Gerald J. Gruman, *A History of Ideas About the Prolongation of Life; the Evolution of Prolongevity Hypotheses to 1800*, Transactions of the American Philosophical Society, new series, Vol. 56, part 9 (Philadelphia: American Philosophical Society, 1966), pp. 15–16.

16. Keith Thomas, *Religion and the Decline of Magic* (New York: Charles Scribner's Sons, 1971), pp. 315–316, 358, 90.

17. *The Boke of Knowledge: Whether a Sicke Person Being in Peril Shall Live or Die* (London, 1555?).

18. Bacon, *Life and Death*, pp. 62, 113, 120, 121; Allan Chapman, "Astrological Medicine," in *Health, Medicine and Mortality in the Sixteenth Century*, ed. Charles Webster (Cambridge, 1979), p. 292; Sir Thomas Browne, *A Letter to a Friend Upon Occasion of the Death of His Intimate Friend* in *The Prose of Sir Thomas Browne*, ed. Norman J. Endicott (New York: W.W. Norton, 1967), pp. 352, 355; Thornton, *Autobiography*, pp. 169, 172–176.

19. Bacon, *History*, pp. 112, 149–156, 173, 183–189, 197, 203; Arnaldus de Villa Nova, *Here is a New Book, Called the Defense of Age and Recovery of Youth* (London, 1540); George Starkey, *Via and Vitam, Being a Short and Sure Way to a Long Life* (London, 1661); Leonardus Lessius, *Hygiasticon; or, the Right Course of Preserving Life and Health into Extreme Old Age* 2nd ed. (Cambridge, 1634); *The Old Man's Dietarie*, trans. Thomas Newton (London, 1586).

20. John Taylor, *The Old, Old, Very Old Man; or, the Age and Long Life of Thomas Par* (London, 1635); William Harvey, *The Anatomical Examination of the Body of Thomas Par* in *The Works of William Harvey, M.D.* (London, 1858), pp. 587–592; L., "A Letter Written to Mr. H.O. Concerning Some Very Aged Persons in the North of England," *Philosophical Transactions* 14 (London, 1684); Alan Everitt, *New Avenues in English Local History* (Leicester, 1970), p. 7; Thomas Fuller, *The History of the Holy War* (London, 1639), p. 261; David Hackett Fischer, *Growing Old in America* (New York: Oxford University Press, 1978).

21. Abbot, *Christian Family*, pp. 49–51; Baxter, *Christian Directory*, p. 551; Robert Cleaver, *A Godly Form of Household Government* (London, 1603), p. 547.

22. Leo W. Simmons, "Aging in Preindustrial Societies," in *Handbook of Social Gerontology; Societal Aspects of Aging*, ed. Clark Tibbets (Chicago: University of Chicago Press, 1960), pp. 62–91.

23. Edward Hyde, Earl of Clarendon, *A Dialogue Between A, an Old Courtier; B, an Old Lawyer; C, an Old Soldier; D, an Old Country Gentleman; and E, an Old Alderman* in *A Collection of Several Tracts of . . . Clarendon* (London, 1727), pp. 288–308.

24. *Pasquil Jests* in *Shakespeare Jest Books*, ed. W.C. Hazlitt (London, 1854), III, p. 61; *A Most Excellent New Ballad of an Old Man and His Wife* (London, n.d.); for the older version, see Alan Macfarlane, *The Origins of English Individualism; The Family, Property and Social Transition* (New York: Cambridge University Press, 1978), p. 142.

25. Macfarlane, *The Family Life of Ralph Josselin, a Seventeenth Century Clergyman: An Essay in Historical Anthropology* (Cambridge: Cambridge University Press, 1970), pp. 113–117.

26. Henry Newcome, *The Autobiography of Henry Newcome*, (Chetham Society Remains, XXVII, Manchester, 1852), pp. 181–184, 215, 217, 228, 229.

27. Adam Martindale, *The Life of Adam Martindale*, ed. Richard Parkinson (Chetham Society Remains, IV, Manchester, 1845), pp. 32–33.

28. Keith Thomas, "Age and Authority in Early Modern England," *Proceedings of the British Academy* 62 (1976): 240–242.

29. Laslett, *World*, pp. 90–96. See also Laslett, "Mean Household Size in England Since the Sixteenth Century" in *Household and Family in Past Time*, ed. Laslett (Cambridge: Cambridge University Press, 1972).

30. Laslett, *Family Life*, pp. 196–207.

31. *Newcome*, pp. 284–286.

32. Samuel Clarke, *The Lives of Sundry Eminent Persons* (London, 1683), II, 176. Phineas Pett, *The Autobiography of Phineas Pett*, ed. W.G. Perrin, Navy Records Society, 51 (London: Navy Records Society, 1918), pp. 168, 171.

33. J.H. Plumb, "The New World of Children in Eighteenth Century England," *Past & Present* 67 (1975); Stone, *The Family*; Ariès, *Childhood*.

CHAPTER NINE—OLD AGE IN THE RURAL FAMILY OF ENLIGHTENED PROVENCE*

DAVID G. TROYANSKY

O ne way of discovering a society's view of old age is to read what its writers had to say about it: how preachers, philosophers, and physicians discussed the aging of body and mind, how playwrights and poets depicted aged characters, how political economists and social theorists explained the roles of generations.[1] The historian of eighteenth-century France has no shortage of cultural sources. Their existence is itself remarkable and indicates contemporary interest in old age; how that interest was expressed reveals even more.[2]

Religious and philosophical texts of the seventeenth and eighteenth centuries provide the most comprehensive view of old age, ranging from baroque warnings that the aged should turn away from the world in preparation for death ("*retraite*" as "retreat") to Enlightenment recommendations that they should remain in the world in order to guide future generations ("*retraite*" as "retirement"). One frequently reprinted text of the seventeenth century that urged sinners to repent described old age as "the worst time of life" and the behavior of old people as "cowardly, negligent, slothful, frigid, coarse, defective, trembling, accompanied by sorrow and *ennui*." A book of piety written for widows referred to the flesh (male and female alike) as "the old man" and urged its mortification.[3] Death overshadowed life both demographically and theologically. Nevertheless, the eighteenth century saw the development of a contrary philosophical position, based primarily upon Cicero's *De*

*An earlier draft of this paper was delivered to the seminar of Prof. Michel Vovelle of the Université de Provence, Aix-en-Provence, in November 1980. The author would like to thank M. Vovelle for his generous guidance both in matters of local research and broader conceptual issues and the members of the seminar for their congenial and critical response. He would also like to express his gratitude to Brandeis University for the Sachar grant which permitted him to begin this study and to the Camargo Foundation whose hospitality permitted him to complete it. Finally, a word of thanks to M. Heckenroth, mayor of Eguilles, and to the archivists of the Archives Départementales des Bouches-du-Rhône, Dépôt d'Aix-en-Provence.

Senectute. The notion of a virile old age replaced that of a time spent solely in preparation for death.[4] Such a favor was extended to women by Madame de Lambert.[5]

Once old age was viewed in a favorable or vital light it became appropriate to ask how to attain it and still avoid its physical infirmities. Scientists borrowing much from the medicine of the Italian Renaissance gave some answers. Translations and reprints of the *Trattato della vita sobria* of Luigi Cornaro found a growing readership among those who chose not to turn from the world. Almanacs devoted pages to reports of longevity with increasing regularity in the 1750s and 1760s.[6] The *Histoire naturelle de l'homme* of Buffon had sparked a series of works analyzing physiological decline, among them the article on old age in the *Encyclopédie*. By the turn of the nineteenth century the new formulations of P.J.G. Cabanis, Xavier Bichat, P.J.B. Esparron, and Philippe Pinel marked a significant change in medical consideration of the ages of life.[7]

Alongside the new medical perception one can detect a change in literary treatment of the aged. Jean-Jacques Rousseau himself suggested that French comedy had accustomed society to confuse the ridiculous old fool (*barbon*) of the stage with the aged man in the street. As if in response, men of the theater treated the aged with growing respect in the later eighteenth century, elevating the status of the head of the family in the *drame bourgeois* and praising the elderly to an even more sentimental extreme on the Revolutionary stage.[8]

Social and economic theoreticians argued that society owed the aged respect and support. Condorcet was the most famous of those who suggested old age pensions, but his was only one plan among dozens. Proposals based upon eighteenth-century sentiment, a belief in a social debt to the aged, and age-specific tables of life expectancy found their way into the offices of the Comité de Mendicité of 1790–1791 and subsequently to the Archives Nationales.[9]

The social historian, when confronted with such a change in the image of old age, may justifiably ask for an explanation. What was it about eighteenth-century France that stimulated such an interest? Why the emphasis on long life, the value of experience, or the need for old age insurance? Surely such an interest in old age made sense during the Enlightenment, a time of dechristianization, humanitarianism, and the rise of *bourgeois* domesticity. But an explanation requires a look at old age in society in a more specific context.

An initial hypothesis explaining the interest in old age is suggested by the present situation in the "developed" world where populations have aged and continue to age to such a degree that social planners see wrinkled disaster ahead.[10] Yet it would be a mistake to transpose twentieth-century aging, a result of falling fertility, to the eighteenth century, when demographic movements were less uniform and only comprehensible in regional terms. Moreover, while the demographic historian is interested in the *aging of* populations, the social historian is interested in the *aged in* a population. René Baehrel found, for example, that the aging of Provence in the seventeenth and early eighteenth centuries was followed by a rapid rejuvenation of the population after 1725. Such demographic trends may be closely correlated with price movements and productivity curves, but they offer little information about old people themselves.[11]

Nevertheless, a decline in mortality would have had important consequences for them. For while a fall in childhood mortality causes a rejuvenation of the population, a simultaneous fall in mortality at all ages can significantly lengthen life expectancy, making old age a "problem" for a youthful population—the more so if the generations are forced to compete for resources. Survival beyond the marriage of children, so rare in earlier generations, put a strain on the family. And though falling mortality did not lead to any definitive aging over the long term—in fact its effect was rejuvenation—it would have tested the society in a way that it had not often been tested before.[12]

But mortality is not aging, and it is difficult to discuss biological aging in historical terms: the climacteric, unlike baptism, marriage, and burial, never found its way into the parish register. Creighton Gilbert estimates that Renaissance artists reached old age at forty-five to fifty, while Robert Favre indicates that old age came much later for writers of the Enlightenment and suggests that personal experience was responsible for their interest in old age.[13] Yet Arthur Young's encounter with a peasant woman who "at no great distance, might have been taken for sixty or seventy, her figure was so bent, and her face so furrowed and hardened by labour—but she said she was only twenty-eight," forcefully attests to class and sex differences that complicate any statements about biological aging in an entire society.[14]

If biological aging is beyond the historian's scope, however, one ought to consider how people of the eighteenth century defined old age in social terms. For many, old age came with the marriage of children, a phenomenon of family and household.[15] To take just one unexceptional literary example, in a story of Louis-Sébastien Mercier, the father of the heroine is called by name until the heroine's marriage. Thereafter he is simply the old man. Two pages later he is dead.[16] The coming of age of one generation brought on the old age of another.

Late marriage, a long period of fertility, and short life expectancy combined to make old age a relatively brief affair, rarely involving a third adult generation;[17] but retirement (when taken) was gradual, perhaps keeping pace with biological time. And in a society in which few people could retire on lifetime annuities (*rentes viagères*) and in which pensions were reserved for soldiers, artists, and courtiers (by no means necessarily elderly), retirement depended upon the family. It was not a bureaucratic arrangement between an individual of a prescribed age and an institution but a notarized act between a retiring individual and his children, who granted his pension. It did not depend solely upon the age of the person retiring but upon his relations with his successors. Frequently, the generations agreed upon a pension against transmission of the patrimony in the marriage contract of the child. Sometimes they drew up a separate act at a later date. Testaments could be used to strengthen one's position before death and thereafter to protect the old age of a widowed spouse.

Gerontologists have called the forced inactivity of the aged a social death that precedes biological death. If today's social death is characterized by a contradiction between a slower biological aging and a more sudden retirement, decided by employer or state rather than family, the older social death was characterized by a network of concerns, sometimes adverse, sometimes supportive. The timing of retirement involved the interests of a household: the marriage of children and the transmission of property. The social historian of aging and the aged must look to the household.[18]

Investigation at the household level will not offer a complete explanation for changes in the society's projected image of old age but should contribute to one. Household patterns of respect and neglect, authority and dependence, evolved slowly; yet, they would have been perturbed by seemingly minor demographic shifts. Survival of the aged would have created unexpected problems in a household that was used to being ruled by one person. Increased life expectancy would have placed more and more households in unfamiliar territory, leaving the aged in an earthly purgatory of weak affective bonds. A new awareness of their plight is evidenced by literary sources. That plight was not new, but it may have grown more common.

Provence serves as a suitable region of study. A land of Roman law, it placed property relations in the hands of the father and his chosen successor.[19] Moreover, the high rate of coresidence of parents and married children provides a precise physical setting for the succession of generations.[20] What follows is a study of the life of parents after the marriage of children in a Provençal village in the eighteenth century. A sample population of parents alive at the signing of their children's marriage contracts was traced through the notarial archives until the parents' deaths were announced in the parish register.[21]

Clearly some of the old people of the village were left out. Where property and profession define the subject, the propertyless and professionless do not appear. Where succession defines the sample, the childless and the unmarried are absent. The very rich will generally be disregarded; the floating poor will not appear.[22] Nevertheless, a study of that part of the aged population that owned land or practiced a profession will serve as a significant starting point for a history of the aged of *ancien régime* France because it was the old age of such people that would serve for some social theorists as the model of how things "naturally" worked.[23]

The farming *bourg* of Eguilles, perched on a hill surrounded by fields producing grain, grapes, and olives, numbered 2,333 inhabitants in 1765.[24] Despite its proximity to Aix-en-Provence (10 km.) where the Boyer d'Eguilles family owned an *hôtel* (now the museum of natural history), the village was socially and economically isolated. *Eguiléen* married *Eguiléenne* and stayed put, transmitting land or profession from generation to generation. Even the plague that devastated Marseilles in 1720 left Eguilles untouched.[25] The only outside influence that seems to have affected it was the dechristianization that swept Provence in the eighteenth century. Eguilles too experienced a decline in piety. Inheritance and property arrangements stand out in the secularized testament while requests for masses disappear. Concern for earthly reality overrode questions of the soul.[26]

At the beginning of the eighteenth century virtually every testament notarized in Eguilles had opened with the remark that death comes without warning to young and old alike. By the 1740s that sentiment appeared in only 13 percent of the total. Then it disappeared completely.[27] Death was still certain, but its hour had become more predictable. People of Eguilles had realized that surviving childhood enormously improved one's chances of reaching old age. Anyone who lived to acquire property and the authority that went with it had a good chance of holding on for a long time. The shift in perception reflects more secular attitudes, but it may reflect also a new or newly realized demographic framework.

How the elderly fared as new demographic and religious frameworks confronted the village environment may be assessed in terms of the exercise of authority and the fulfillment of social functions. But even aside from any change in numbers and attitudes, the village environment was ambivalent with regard to the aged. In theory they were deserving of respect. In practice the interaction of social functions, family politics, and emotional bonds made things a bit more complicated.

According to the nineteenth-century historian of the family Charles de Ribbe, authority bred respect, and respect guaranteed support in old age. After a reading of family registers (*livres de raison*) kept by noble and bourgeois fathers, he delightedly reported that chapters were often entitled "Memoirs of the births of children that it has pleased God to give to my son"—evidence that the grandfather ran the house.[28] Although the *livre de raison* is not a likely place to find records of family conflict, the head of the family (*chef de famille*) was legally the absolute ruler of his Provençal household.

In theory a widow could inherit her late husband's role, and the notarial archives include examples of widows wielding considerable power over their children. But such phenomena were exceptions in male-dominated Provence. Aged fathers, and a few mothers, signed contracts along with their adult children. Children under their parents' authority had to be emancipated by notarial act in order to sign for themselves. This relinquishment of parental authority, though relatively uncommon and normally involving sons leaving the village, is indicative of power relations, as it occurred in the presence of notables and amid considerable feudal pomp.[29]

On November 16, 1745, Jean Reynier emancipated two younger sons, his eldest having died and left four daughters and a son behind. Before the ceremony took place, the father convinced the notable witnesses that he had not been "seduced" into the act. The sons knelt before their father, their hands in his; then the father bade them rise, symbolizing their freedom from his authority. In the same document, Jean Reynier gave them his house, stable, attic, and cellar along with specified furniture. Each would receive a bed and linen. But the father retained the use of a furnished apartment of his choice in the house and storage for the rest of his life.

The role of the community in protecting authority in the family indicates that public status and power were at stake in control of the household. Indeed the head of the family had the right to exercise his power outside the household in the municipal council. The records of that body permit a view of village authority.

An analysis of attendance on annual election days, the best attended meetings of the council, for the years 1716–1788 yields 203 different persons of whom only 69 showed up more than four times.[30] Every family head had the right to vote, this being one of the reasons that nostalgic historians of the nineteenth century wrote of a patriarchal village democracy in the *ancien régime*. But clearly not everyone bothered. The council was not representative of the village, as those who attended regularly were the local notables, the large landowners and the surgeons.[31] Nor was it patriarchal, for the aged retired from the council. Of the 69 persons who attended more than four times, the dates of death of 41 have been recovered. Only 7 of them participated in an election within the year of death, and only 1 elected official actually died in office. An average period of over seven years passed between last ballot cast and death. There was no institutional framework for retirement; a man decided to stop attending and was succeeded by a son or nephew. Thus, local affairs were governed by a council of middle-aged notables, not a council of elders.[32]

There remained, however, the possibility of movement to another post upon retirement from the council. In Provence, it was said that after the council one moved to the hospital—*"Après lou capeiroun, l'Espitau"*—either as administrator or as patient.[33] L'Hôpital Notre Dame de la Miséricorde was founded in 1743 by Pierre Giraud, *bourgeois d'Eguilles*, who ordered that the parish priest, current consuls, and specially elected rectors administer it.[34] It has been suggested by one historian of Provence that the role of rector was filled by an aged consul.[35] But such was not the case in eighteenth-century Eguilles; indeed old age was the reason for which one rector was relieved of his post.[36]

If the aged did not run the hospital, one might find them as inmates. But the extant records of patients point mainly to orphan girls. Moreover, while a few people may have gone to the hospital to die, those who did not die very shortly after admittance were sent home.[37] The nearest large hospital was the Hôpital Saint-Jacques in Aix, where the aged might find asylum along with orphans, incurables, and beggars.[38]

For a time there was an old age home in Eguilles. Founded by the Seigneur d'Eguilles, the Hospice Sainte-Cathérine is mentioned in his testament (February 20, 1767); he prescribed that the poor old men and women in the *hospice* at the time of his death always be provided with the same lodging, clothing, food, and care. In naming his son as heir he asked that care for the aged poor continue.

Such assistance was an old form of charity that was on the wane. Not generalized welfare, it was clearly not to be counted upon by all the aged of Eguilles.[39] Moreover, medical care was not to be trusted either. The rectors of the hospital reported (October 13, 1771) that people, upon falling ill, avoided the hospital "under the pretext that they had no confidence in the surgeon." And if patients expressed reservations about the surgeon, surgeons in turn expressed reservations about the patients. On May 27, 1776, it was announced that no surgeon wanted to visit them. Consequently the officers decided to choose as surgeon of the hospital "Sr. Aubert . . . since he is the oldest surgeon of the place and he offers to perform this service with all the zeal and all the charity of which he is capable." If not trusted by everyone, at least the oldest surgeon in town was respected by his colleagues on the council.

Faith in the aged surgeon would eventually be superseded by faith in the old family doctor. What of other venerable sages? It is often said that in preliterate societies such faith in the wisdom, or at least the memory, of the aged in general is of great importance. In semiliterate Eguilles a long memory played a role in court testimony involving customary boundaries and rights of passage through certain fields.[40] Mathieu and Louis Joye claimed in a suit against Mathieu Artaud in 1744 that "since time immemorial man and beast had passed in the land and meadow concerned."[41] They gathered expert witnesses aged 85, 82, 80, 73, 73, 85, 57, 60, 58, 48, 46, 43, 41, 38, and 43. Pierre Giraud, "townsman aged about 85 years," remembered practices of the past seventy years, but his competence did not derive solely from age; he was the same influential man who had founded the hospital the previous year. And even if his words constituted the wisdom of the aged, they were only testimony. Moreover, in a village where a clerk took notes at council meetings, where orders from either the monarchy or the Parlement de Provence came in printed form, where the curé was dutiful in recording baptisms, marriages, and burials, and where contracts and testaments were carefully written by notaries, there was little room left for illiterate memory.

Records of public life have yielded glimpses of the aged. The elderly have retired from office; they have not gone to the hospital in great numbers, only a few to the hospice when granted charity by the seigneur; they have been called upon only occasionally to remember the past. One must seek them out where they have gone. One must look into the household.

A census of 1765 counted 2,333 inhabitants of Eguilles living in 397 households. How they were actually arranged is unknown as no detailed census exists from before 1810. Nevertheless, the 1810 census gives an approximation of the eighteenth-century household structure.[42] Ages of all except one of the 2,566 residents are given:

AGE	MALE	PERCENT	FEMALE	PERCENT
0–25	629	48.7	639	50.2
26–59	524	40.6	493	38.7
60–91	138	10.7	142	11.1
	1,291	100	1,274	100

A young population, about half of it 25 years of age or less, it included a relatively high number of survivors: 10.9 percent aged 60 and over.

That senior group evidently played a significant role in the village economy. Of the 319 persons whose professions are indicated in the census, 68 were at least sixty years old; 15 of 49 large landholders, 27 of 101 smaller farmers, 2 of 6 masons, 2 of 3 carders, 1 of 2 blacksmiths, 1 of 2 priests, both cloth weavers, the *entrepreneur*, lawyer, mayor, rural policeman, tax collector, and plasterer. Whether they all still actively pursued their careers in 1810 is unknown. However, they were all identified by profession and, priests aside, their sons were generally not. Such a barrier to professional advancement of the young would have been more significant than the turnover of seats on the ill-attended municipal council.

Conspicuous sexagenarian participation in the work force indicates activity in old age but equally implies a fear of dependence. It may have been unwise to test the respect owed by a generation coming to power. Peasant proverbs certainly made that point. But the barrier that protected the aged demanded a psychological price, for it undoubtedly tended to estrange them.

That barrier was characteristic of the stem-family system. Certainly the theme of ambiguity, visible in the community, extends to family arrangements where conflicting individual interests of those coming of age and those growing old might undermine the unity of the household both economically and emotionally. The care with which rights and obligations were apportioned within the stem-family indicates an awareness of potential seeds of discord.

In Eguilles the aged were commonly present in rather complex households. The census lists individuals by district (*isle*), grouped by lines of descent. Except for the 216 residents of the hamlet of Les Figons, 106 of whom were named Alexis, the inhabitants can be grouped in Laslett-type households that, necessarily, only approximate the actual situation. The number of individuals (type 1) and nonfamilial groups (type 2) is small. The number of nuclear family households (type 3) is probably a maximum, while the extended and multiple family households (types 4 and 5) are minimal (the total number of households is undoubtedly high).

TYPE	NUMBER	AVERAGE	PERCENT
1	35–68	52	9.4
2	9–19	14	2.5
3	348–397	373	67.7
4	54–74	64	11.6
5	37–58	48	8.7
		551	99.9

While most households were nuclear, 20 percent comprised three generations at one moment in 1810, thus indicating a common experience in the developmental cycle of the household. Such phenomena are found elsewhere in Provence, where coresidence of parents and married childen is frequently encountered in the marriage contract.[43]

The consequences of the coresidence clause can be seen in the situation of the elderly:

Marital Status and Household Situation of Those Aged 60+

MARITAL STATUS	HOUSEHOLD SITUATION	MALE	FEMALE
Never Married	Living Alone	9	5
	With Others	7	7
		16	12
Married	Living with Spouse	23	20
	+Unmarried Children	46	25
	+Married Children	26	24
		95	69
Widowed	Living Alone	1	12
	With Unmarried Children	5	19
	With Married Children	19	27
	With Others	2	3
		27	61
	Total	138	142

If those under age sixty are included, then Eguilles had 45–46 live-in grandfathers and 60–63 live-in grandmothers in 1810. When aunts and uncles and relations outside the household are considered, it becomes clear that the aged were a familiar sight. And widows were a more familiar sight than widowers; more men than women coped with aging by remarrying.[44]

The historical study of the household has often tended to emphasize the continuity of holdings, treating individuals as impediments to the smooth flow of succession. But the very detours that property took make the study of individuals incumbent upon the historian of old age. The dynamics of the household derived not only from what parents parted with but also from what they retained or demanded. Aging in the household economy can be witnessed in the various notarized acts — e.g., marriage contracts, gifts, and testaments — that spelled out responsibilities of individual household members.

The marriage of children normally provided the first opportunity for fathers and mothers to look to their old age. The marriage contract foreshadowed the future course of the household, making gifts and promising subsequent ones in return for support in retirement. Four hundred and ninety-one marriages were registered in the parish of Eguilles in the period 1741–1770. Not every marriage recorded in the parish register involved a notarized contract, but most did. A comparison of the records of the town's two notaries indicates little difference between them. The figures that follow are derived from one *étude*, which registered 223 marriages — almost half.[45] The 223 contracts mentioned 522 parents; i.e. an average of 2.34 parents per contract. Only 11 contracts pertained to marriages where all four parents were dead. As each household was created it had to coexist with the elders. Sometimes tensions developed — the more so perhaps when two or more couples resided together. And one half of the contracts stipulated coresidence of parents and married children.

Coresidence, of course, did not imply a break in the living situation. The contract did not join two generations that had been living apart; rather, it extended the life of a household beyond a date at which its unity had been threatened. It also introduced a new member, signifying possible shifts in alliance.[46]

The new alliance joined two families of equal status, the wife bringing the dowry and the husband the property. But in the day-to-day fact of coresidence, the husband's family took precedence. Literary sources may suggest that either son or daughter could be the "consolation of old age," and some exceptional daughters did play that role in Eguilles. But 90 percent of the marriage contracts that stipulated coresidence did so for the husband's parents. One looked to a son for support in old age.

In cases of coresidence the dowry was given to the father of the groom. On February 4, 1743, farm laborer Joseph Arquier accepted the dowry of his daughter-in-law Marianne Marroc and gave his son part of an orchard. He housed the married couple, promising to feed and care for them and any children they might have. Arquier literally promised to retire (*retirer*) the couple, thus expressing his control. And when the contract looked ahead to the possibility of a separation of generations, there was no question of a challenge to patriarchal authority. The dowry would be returned to the departing couple and the father would provide his son with land and vineyard, wheat and wine, a furnished room, clothes, and tools. The separation clause did not loose all ties. One father would give his son 1,000 *livres*, some land, and the second floor of his house.[47] Others also provided houses.[48]

Most marriage contracts outlined a future transmission of the patrimony. On August 10, 1761, Jean Baptiste Davin and Marguérite Pelenqui stated the conditions of their son Jean François Davin's marriage to Clère Aillaud. The father agreed to house the couple, and the mother offered a gift (*donation entre vifs*) of a house upon her own and her husband's death; the only condition was that Jean François house his brother until he too should marry. Antoine Artaud, a maker of pails, took in a new couple on November 10, 1755, and provided them with one room. Upon the parents' death the younger couple would receive two more rooms.

Normally the father would promise transmission of most of the patrimony upon his death while reserving some portion for his surviving widow. The contract of Luc Roure's marriage to Cathérine Goujet on September 11, 1747, included Luc's father's promise of a house upon his death under condition that Luc provide his widowed mother with a pension of wheat and wine at each harvest, a room in his house or elsewhere, and a place in the cellar. The same sort of arrangement would have been made for the second wife of the father, perhaps more urgently as the son's notion of responsibility might be somewhat weaker than it had been for his own mother.[49]

When the groom's own mother was widowed, she looked after her own future, usually guided by her husband's testament. When Thomé Jaloux, shepherd of Puyricard, married Marianne Figuière on November 26, 1741, the bride brought a dowry of 350 *livres*. But the contract went into much greater detail about Jaloux's widowed mother Jeanne Audran, who gave her son some land, a vineyard, and furniture in token of her "friendship" (*amitié*) for him. Thomé promised in return "to feed and care for her as his equal in health as well as sickness."

When a couple married late, they looked to their own old age. When widower and widow remarried, the husband set forth his wife's pension in their marriage contract (January 7, 1770). He specified dates for annual supply of wheat, wine, oil, and salt. "She will still have the use of the kitchen and a room, both on the ground floor of the house."

In cases of great longevity, three and even four generations entered into negotiations. Ten of the 223 marriages mentioned the presence of grandparents; two involved two grandparents. One included a great grandmother. On May 2, 1742, Elisabeth Davin received a wedding gift of a house from her great grandmother Marie Giraud. This was doubly exceptional, as the house came from the bride's side. But the old woman reserved the use of the house for herself and her daughter Magdeleine Dumas for the rest of their lives. That would not be long, as Giraud died on June 2 and Dumas had died in April, between the first draft of the contract and its completion. Meanwhile, the couple, in more traditional fashion, was to be housed by the father of the groom.

Great grandmothers were rare; the norm was no more than two coexisting adult generations, and their overlap could be short-lived. Perhaps the most extreme literary example of the rapid succession of generations occurs in Rétif de la Bretonne's *La vie de mon père*. Upon the death of the father Pierre Rétif, the son Edmond is told by the father of his fiancée, "You will be my son . . . bless you both! You will be the consolation of my old age."[50] On the morrow, the marriage was celebrated before the body of the dead Pierre.

In similar fashion on April 12, 1770, a marriage contract for Marguérite Gues and her husband, a wool carder from the Dauphiné, who had married without contract three years before, was drawn up before her father's deathbed. The sequence of events was generally not so fast, but this period of time was critical for the household. It was the time of greatest strain, for it forced the aging parents to consider stepping aside. They had to look ahead to retirement and death.

An average of 10.6 years passed between the marriage contract of children and the death of parents, 9.8 for those involved in coresidence. During this period, aged parents saw fit to insure support in retirement by a variety of notarized acts. Shepherd Martin Cheiland, married since September 5, 1734, eventually came into control of his father Estienne's land. But it was not until November 15, 1754 that Estienne handed it over in an act that recognized that Martin had already been in *de facto* possession of it for several years. Estienne, "finding himself at an advanced age, no longer able to support himself," had Martin promise to pay him an annual pension of 36 *livres* in monthly payments of 3 *livres* as well as 5 *mierolles* (one *mierolle* = sixty liters) of wine at every harvest.

A notarized gift expressed gratitude for assistance and expectation of its continuing. On August 9, 1752, François Armieou presented some land to his son-in-law Mathieu Girard "in order to give a tangible sign of his friendship." Evidently to ensure the continuing friendship of his son-in-law, Armieou stipulated that possession would be taken "immediately after the death of said Armieou and no sooner." Seven years later his testament mentioned that one daughter and her husband Girard, one widowed daughter, and his wife were all living with him. Three weeks later he was dead. Four years afterwards the daughters split their inheritance while reaffirming their obligation to care for their mother.

Retirement normally meant occupation of a particular room in the house; wealth permitting, however, the parent, after welcoming the couple, might move to another house. Widowed shepherd Jean Baptiste Armieu housed daughter Marguérite and son-in-law Louis Aron on May 7, 1742. But on March 26, 1743, he bought part of another house and a barnyard. A transaction of November 9, 1745 shows that he and the couple were no longer living together. Five years later he was dead at the reported age of seventy-seven.

In Provence the head of the family normally chose one principal heir, but division of holdings was an option. Division of the patrimony entailed division of the burden of support of aged parents. On April 18, 1758, François Artaud, a large landholder (*ménager*), split his land and houses between two married sons. After taking possession of the houses, the sons would collect rent from the tenants and pay Artaud 75 *livres* each annually. Payments continued until the father's death on May 6, 1767.[51]

A married son might, after a separation from his parents, return with his own family to live with his widowed mother. In 1739 Antoine Arquier married and left home. On October 23, 1754, Thérèse Bourc declared that her son Antoine had recently come with his wife and family to live with her and had brought with him furniture and other belongings. There followed a two-page list of furniture and utensils. The mother died on January 24, 1757 at the recorded age of 85. The son had returned, no doubt, to help her in her old age and perhaps also, though he was not a principal heir, to insure himself of some share of the inheritance. To sort out these and other motivations would be impossible.

Financial obligations within the family were precisely spelled out. A receipt of August 25, 1751 given to Jean Baptiste Artaud by Rose Salen, his widowed mother, reviewed their recent financial dealings. He owed her a large pension and paid part of it in goods and services. She thought that fifty *livres* should pay for the hospitality he had shown her in her first five months of widowhood. Later that year, no longer residing with him, she sent her brother to collect a further installment of the pension. A year and a half later the son made an additional payment, and so forth until she died nine years later.[52]

Sometimes a grandparent would settle property on a grandchild. Such was the case with Jean Reynier, whose son Jean Estienne had died and who found himself looking after his grandson Joseph (Jean's younger sons were emancipated a year earlier; see above). While the grandfather was too old to work and his grandson too young, the land that would eventually be passed on to the boy was leased for six years to a local muleteer, Louis Davin, who was obliged to bring part of the harvest of his work to the old man as a pension (May 23, 1746).

The same kind of obligation was undertaken by Louis Girard on September 12, 1761. He was given rights by Thérèze Marroc to land, vineyard, olive trees, meadow, and other trees for two years; it obliged him to deliver to her house half of the harvest of "grapes, wine, almonds, and other fruits in their season." Thus, sharecropping for the one was an old age pension for the other. Sharecropping arrangements involved a house as well as land. On October 11, 1751, Elizabeth Abeille of Aix rented out land and country house in Puyricard. She would receive in Aix half of the yield of the land while maintaining the use of a room and the kitchen in Puyricard.

Divestment within the family might involve travel. On September 29, 1759, Imbert Perrin wrote the itinerary of his retirement in passing the patrimony down to his sons Antoine and Joseph. Nominally each would care for him six months out of the year. But until Joseph married, Antoine would house him while Joseph contributed 30 *livres* to his support.

Support came in many forms. In a contract that has a modern ring to it, Agnès Cauvet, widow of Jacques Martin, received a pension when her husband's property was divided between their two sons. Not only did she receive food, housing, and clothing, but also payment of such medical expenses as she might incur.[53]

Widows could band together, as did mother and daughter-in-law, the widows of a father-son pair of masons in neighboring Ventabren, on June 13, 1755. The elder thanked her daughter-in-law for the care she had shown and offered her the use of the house and the fruits of the land as long as she did not remarry. A young widow might, however, return to her own family. Magdeleine Salen Goujet did just that on April 13, 1744. By her late husband's will she received 80 *livres*, including her mourning clothes, from her stepson, whereupon she returned to her father, very likely for the old man's welfare as well as her own.

After the marriage contracts of children and various other donations and arrangements that granted old age pensions, the last opportunity to act on the economy of the household was in the testament.[54] The mere potential to make a will provided leverage in the family. But the act itself could serve as a support in old age. A public rather than secret document (not necessarily dictated from a deathbed), it permitted conditions of inheritance to be stated. Thus, it insured the last days of the testator as well as the widowhood of his spouse.

A young father would have made testamentary provisions for his wife, who promised to raise their children. Their upbringing was the condition of her pension. But when the testator was somewhat older and was dealing directly with his grown-up children, there were no conditions attached to a bequest for the surviving parent except that she not remarry.

In the absence of children, aged siblings became involved. The land of the childless mason Mathieu Baume and his wife, Elizabeth Bonnand, came from his family, the house from hers. Upon his death, she would have the use of the land until her death, when it would be returned to his brothers and sister. The house for its part would be returned immediately to her family, save one room reserved for his sister.[55]

Sometimes the wife, anticipating death, provided for her husband. Magdeleine Arquier requested in her testament of June 6, 1755, that her husband be fed and cared for by their son Lazare Joye. Cathérine Honnorat ordered on March 18, 1766, that her son François Anastay care for his father, Jean Baptiste Anastay.

The testament included recognition of past support. In the course of her testament of May 10, 1750, Elizabeth Alexis thanked her son for a pension that he had paid her for the past two years. And in a very rare act on November 20, 1743, Anne Maurel reduced the pension that her son Louis Marroc was paying her. She would do without half of her promised wheat and some money but would retain the rest of the wheat and three *mierolles* of wine.

The testament also operated outside the family, particularly in the case of aid to servants. For Luc Sextius de Boyer, chevalier d'Argens, the testament was an opportunity to leave 30 *livres* to his mother (a sum she surely did not need) but more importantly a chance to leave an annual pension of 300 *livres* to his domestic servant. Jean Baptiste Brun left 200 *livres* and furniture to his servant Anne Achard but only "in the case that said Achard will be found at his service upon his death."[56]

Such care did not always guarantee a share in the inheritance, as the widow Jeanne Cheiland learned after having taken care of the aged priest Pierre Boyer during his final illness. She was embittered at having received only three articles of worn-out clothing from the priest's nephew. The priest's old age was cared for, but Cheiland's was not.[57]

A more certain form of old age insurance outside the family was the use of *rentes viagères*. Some of the *bourgeois d'Eguilles* resorted to this method. One widow, after being rewarded for care given to Pierre Giraud, loaned out her new wealth and collected eight different pensions in the last ten years of her life.[58] But such techniques were normally limited to the rich and were not by any means specifically designed for old age. They permitted the buyer to be free from the need to work at any age. But for the vast majority of *Eguiléens* the family was the only source of support.

Just how sure could one be of the family? Melchior Gros, a farmer with a lot of wealth to distribute, provided a comfortable pension for his second wife. However, one clause of his bequest is troubling: "She will be permitted to walk in the vineyards, pick and eat grapes from the vines."[59] Gaspard Marroc, in his testament of January 29, 1746, granted the same right to his wife, Jeanne d'Eyme, and the same clause appeared in the contract of Agnès Cauvet mentioned above. Such an act demonstrates the ambiguity of relations between generations in this society. On the one hand it shows a recognition of the sentimental—as well as biological—attachment that an older person had to the land. On the other hand, the need to notarize permission to help oneself to grapes from one's children's field indicates a certain weakness of affective relations.

Care for the aged was a function of family attachments. Yves Castan has suggested a drifting apart of generations in the late seventeenth and eighteenth centuries in neighboring Languedoc.[60] But in any setting one must investigate house-to-house. And only rarely does a source permit the kind of view that Roderick Phillips's archives of the revolutionary family tribunals in Rouen give of households in conflict.[61]

The seigneurial court of Eguilles heard cases of battles between households, but the individual household rarely exposed itself to the law. In-law problems, though, were common. In testimony concerning a nuisance of a mother-in-law, who lived above her married daughter and persisted in pouring water through the cracks in her floor to put out the couple's fire, it was said that her sons-in-law had never set foot in her apartment: separate housing was truly separate.[62]

Testimony about an eighty-year-old man and his sons who fought with the man's son-in-law yields conflicting images of the father. On the one hand he is the powerful patriarch, leading his sons into battle and striking the first blow; on the other hand he is the weak old fool, shouting in the middle of the street, "I'll kill him myself" but "get me a stick so that I can stand."[63] Theater may describe one old man as a respectable patriarch, another as a ridiculous graybeard. In the street the same person could play both roles on the same day. It depended upon who was watching.

If conclusions about individual cases are ambiguous, historical generalizations about affective relations are even more suspect. Nevertheless, some tentative conclusions can be made. The frequent recourse to contract in Eguilles indicates that, although people retired, there was no harmonious course of retirement. Family assistance was not something that was assured without contract, and individual measures resulted from particular attachments and resentments. Eighteenth-century Eguilles was far from a *Gemeinschaft*.

Indeed, what is striking about the old person is his individuality. Except in the case of the religious or guild association, each in decline in the eighteenth century,[64] old age in the *ancien régime* was the time when the individual had outgrown all groups. Baroque texts recognized this fact and saw no solution but retreat. Popular festivals pitted youth groups against aged individuals: aged men in the *charivari*, aged women in the "days of the old woman," a yearly rite symbolizing the end of winter throughout the Mediterranean world.[65]

Yet the cultural élite of Enlightened France refused to take such a dim view of the last years of life. Although the physical order of things had not changed dramatically in the French household, some change in the French consciousness was beginning to render the "traditional" order unacceptable. Perhaps the change is best explained in strictly "intellectual" terms. Nevertheless, eighteenth-century views were views on eighteenth-century reality. Treatment of attitudes remains incomplete without treatment of society.

Longer life expectancy, which forced retirement without a retirement system, may have been a significant influence on the eighteenth-century French image makers' portrayal of the aged as not deserving estrangement. Demographers saw the elderly as a class. Political economists saw assistance to the aged, particularly the aged poor, as a debt owed by society at large. French Revolutionary administrators tried to realize this project, replacing an illusory family "system" with a national bureaucratic scheme.[66] The role of age in Revolutionary festivals, so different from that in traditional ones, made the new order visible. The aged would be the teachers of the French Republic. They would form a didactic chorus in support of national conscription. The Committee of Public Safety would express its gratitude to an entire generation by placing in the rooms of the aged, in the ideal peasant household, banners proclaiming, "Honorable repose after work."[67]

The new system first made its way to Eguilles in the form of a military pension for dependents of soldiers of the Revolutionary army.[68] At a meeting of *29 Ventôse an II*, the Assemblée Générale des Citoyens de la Commune d'Eguilles met to draw up a list of recipients of assistance. Fathers, brothers, and husbands were in the service, but the list accounts most often for sons. Of 148 names of dependents that appear in the list, 139 were parents, 37 of whom were aged sixty and older. An additional 13 were married to sexagenarians, and 1 was a soldier's father residing with his own seventy-seven-year-old father.

Nearly two years later, administrators of the district of Aix sent an order with further details about such assistance to the citizens of Eguilles. Their letter of *9 Frimaire an IV* referred to an enclosed printed order from Paris, dated *23 Brumaire an II*, that prescribed a yearly pension of 50 *livres* for needy parents aged under sixty years and 100 *livres* for those aged sixty or over, infirm, or unable to work.[69] The message had taken some time and at least two régimes to make its way from Paris to Eguilles by way of Aix. But it was, of course, only a temporary measure; the idea of a long-term system encompassing all aged French men and women would take much longer to win out.[70]

NOTES

1. For the literary approach, Simone de Beauvoir, *La vieillesse* (Paris: Gallimard, 1970).

2. A major aspect of the dissertation I am preparing.

3. Antoine Yvan, *La trompette du ciel, qui reveille les pecheurs, et qui les excite puissamment à se convertir à Dieu* (Rouen, undated) pp. 334, 337, 466 (re-edition in Musée Arbaud, Aix-en-Provence); Girard de Villethierry, *La vie des veuves* (Paris: A. Damonneville, 1719).

4. On death, Philippe Ariès, *L'homme devant la mort* (Paris: Seuil, 1977); Pierre Chaunu, *La mort à Paris XVIe, XVIIe, XVIIIe siècles* (Paris: Fayard, 1978); François Lebrun, *Les hommes et la mort en Anjou aux XVIIe et XVIIIe siècles* (Paris: Mouton, 1971); Michel Vovelle, *Piété baroque et déchristianisation en Provence au XVIIIe siècle* (Paris: Plon, 1973) and *Mourir autrefois. Attitudes collectives devant la mort aux XVIIe et XVIIIe siècles* (Paris: Gallimard/Julliard, 1974). For Cicero's text, six French translations of the eighteenth century in the catalogue of the *Bibliothèque Nationale*.

5. La Marquise de Lambert, *Traité de la vieillesse*, in *Oeuvres* (Lausanne: M.-M. Bousquet, 1748).

6. Among other editions of Cornaro, *Conseils pour vivre long-temps* (Paris: J. Le Febvre, 1701). For almanacs, Geneviève Bollème, *Les almanachs populaires aux XVIIe et XVIIIe siècles* (Paris: Mouton, 1969); Lottin, *Almanach des centenaires* (Paris: A.M. Lottin, 1764–1771).

7. Buffon, *Oeuvres complètes* T. IV (Paris: Imprimerie Royale, 1774); Louis de Jaucourt, "Vieillesse," in Denis Diderot *L'Encyclopédie ou Dictionnaire raisonné des sciences, des arts et des métiers* T. XVII (Neufchastel: Samuel Faulche, 1765), pp. 259–260. For discussions of old age elsewhere in the Encyclopedia, see *Table Analytique et raisonnée du Dictionnaire des sciences, arts et métiers* T. II (Amsterdam, 1780). P.J.G. Cabanis, *Rapports du physique et du moral de l'homme* (Paris: Crapart, Caille et Ravier, 1805); Xavier Bichat, *Recherches physiologiques sur la vie et la mort* (Paris: Brosson, Gabon, an viii); P.J.B. Esparron, *Essai sur les âges de l'homme* (Paris: Crapelet, 1803); Philippe Pinel, *Considérations sur la constitution sénile et sur son influence dans les maladies aiguës, Mémoires et observations des Archives générales de médecine, Première année* T. II (Paris: Une Société de médecins, 1823).

8. Jean-Jacques Rousseau, *AM. D'Alembert* (1758), *Oeuvres complètes* (Paris: A. Houssiaux, 1852) T. III, p. 135. For the quintessential *drame bourgeois*, Denis Diderot, *Le père de famille* (Amsterdam, 1758) for Revolutionary sentimentality, L.A. Dorvigny, *L'hospitalité ou le bonheur du vieux père* (Paris: J.B. Colas, an iii).

9. J.A.N. Condorcet, *Esquisse d'un tableau historique des progrès de l'esprit humain* (Paris: Dubuisson, 1864); see also André Jean de la Rocque, *Etablissement d'une caisse générale des épargnes du peuple. . .* (Bruxelles, 1786) and the various plans of Joachim Lafarge. Camille Bloch and Alexandre Tuetey, *Procès-verbaux et rapports du Comité de mendicité de la Constituante 1790–1791* (Paris: Imprimerie Nationale, 1911); and pertinent cartons in *Archives Nationales* F15.

10. See, for example, Gérard-François Dumont, *La France ridée* (Paris: L.G.F. [Librairie Générale Française] Hachette, 1979) or such newspaper articles as Liliane Delwasse, "Alarme: Demain, les vieux," in *Le Monde Dimanche*, 2 nov. 1980, p. iv.

11. For regional demography, Pierre Goubert, *Beauvais et le Beauvaisis 1600–1730* (Paris: S.E.V.P.E.N., 1960) and Lebrun, *Les Hommes et la mort*, René Baehrel, *Une croissance: La Basse Provence rurale (fin 15e–1789)* (Paris: S.E.V.P.E.N., 1961).

12. On falling mortality, Louis Henry, "The Population of France in the Eighteenth Century," in D.V. Glass and D.E.C. Eversley, eds., *Population in History: Essays in Historical Demography* (Chicago: Aldine, 1965).

13. Creighton Gilbert, "When did a man in the Renaissance grow old?" in *Studies in the Renaissance* Vol. 14 (1967); Robert Favre, *La mort dans la littérature et la pensée françaises au siècle des lumières* (Lyon: Presses Universitaries de Lyon, 1978).

14. Arthur Young, *Travels during the Years 1787, 1788, and 1789* (Bury St. Edmund's: W. Richardson, 1792), p. 134.

15. See the articles in Jack Goody et al., eds., *Family and Inheritance* (Cambridge: Cambridge University Press, 1976).

16. Louis-Sébastien Mercier, *Sophie*, in *Contes moraux ou Les hommes comme il y en a peu* (Paris: Pankouke, 1768).

17. Jean Fourastié, "De la vie traditionnelle à la vie 'tertiaire.' Recherches sur le calendrier démographique de l'homme moyen," in *Population*, 14e année, no. 3 (1959); Hervé Lebras, "Parents, grandsparents, bisaieux," in *Population*, 28e année, no. 1 (1973).

18. On social death, Anne-Marie Guillemard, *La retraite: une mort sociale* (Paris: Mouton, 1972); on old age and the household, Peter Laslett, "The History of Aging and the Aged," in Laslett, *Family Life and Illicit Love in Earlier Generations* (Cambridge: Cambridge University Press, 1977).

19. Edouard Baratier, *Histoire de la Provence* (Toulouse: Privat, 1969); Roger Aubenas, *Le Testament en Provence dans l'ancien droit* (Aix-en-Provence: Faculté de Droit, 1927).

20. Alain Collomp, *"Alliance et filiation en Haute Provence au XVIIIe siècle,"* in *Annales: E.S.C.* T. 32 no. 3 (mai-juin 1977):445–477; and *"Maison . . . , famille, en Haute-Provence aux XVIIe et XVIIIe siècles,"* in *Ethnologie française* VIII, 4 (1978):301–320.

21. Notarial archives for Eguilles: *Archives Départementales des Bouches-du-Rhône, Dépôt d'Aix-en-Provence (A.D.,* Aix): 1741–1749, (Notary) Jean-Joseph Carle, Vol. 301 E 486; 1750–1757, (Notary) Jean-Joseph Carle, Vol. 301 E 487; 1757–1764, (Notary) Jean-Joseph Carle, Vol. 301 E 488; 1764–1773, (Notary) Jean-Joseph Carle, Vol. 301 E 489; *Cf.:* 1741–1748, (Notary) Michel-Joseph Séguin, Vol. 301 E 494. Parish register: *Archives Municipales d'Eguilles (A.M.).* Henceforth dates will be given in the text.

22. The Marquis d'Eguilles retired to his château after a conflict in 1763 with the *Parlement de Provence* of which he had been *Président à mortier*; his brother, the Marquis d'Argens, retired to the village after having served as chamberlain to the king of Prussia and having written epistolary novels of some renown. On the Marquis D'Eguilles, Paul Cottin, *Marquis d'Eguilles, Un protégé de Bachaumont –correspondance inédite du Marquis d'Eguilles 1745–1748* (Paris: Revue rétrospective, 1887); among the works of the Marquis d'Argens, *Lettres Juives* (La Haye: P.Paupie, 1736); *Lettres Chinoises* (La Haye: P. Paupie, 1739); *Lettres cabalistiques* (La Haye: P.Paupie, 1741). On the poor, Olwen H. Hufton, *The Poor of Eighteenth-Century France 1750–1789* (Oxford: Oxford Univ. Press, 1974), especially pp. 111–113.

23. The family was supposed to prevent the need for beggary; the Comité de mendicité preferred care at home to care in a hospital.

24. On the agricultural *bourg*, Maurice Agulhon, *"La notion de village en Basse-Provence vers la fin de l'Ancien Régime,"* in *Actes du 90e Congrès national des Sociétés savantes*, Nice, 1965 (Paris, 1966) T. I pp. 277–301; for the census, Edouard Baratier, *La Démographie provençale du 13e au 16e siècle avec chiffres de comparaison pour le 18e siècle* (Paris, 1961).

25. Brigitte Liard, *Les Mentalités collectives et les comportements devant la mort d'après les clauses des testaments dans le pays d'Aix-Eguilles 1680–1789. Thèse de maîtrise, Université d'Aix-Marseille* 1972–73.

26. Ibid; Vovelle, *Piété baroque.* . .

27. *Vovelle, Piété baroque; cf.* Chaunu, *La mort à Paris;* Bernard Vogler, *Trois mémoires sur les testaments à Strasbourg au 18e siècle* (Strasbourg: Société Académique du Bas-Rhin, 1978).

28. Charles de Ribbe, *Les Familles et la société en France avant la Révolution d'après des documents originaux* (Paris: J. Albanel, 1873) p. 53; and his *Le livre de famille* (Tours: A. Mame et fils, 1879).

29. For the decline in the use of the old formulae in upper Provence, Raymond Collier, *La Vie en Haute-Provence de 1600 à 1850* (Digne: Société Scientifique et Littéraire des Alpes-De-Haute-Provence, 1973) pp. 129–130; for his remarks on the emancipation, I thank M.G. Delille.

30. *Délibérations municipales: A.M.*

31. On the oligarchical council, Jean-Pierre Gutton, *La sociabilité villageoise dans l'ancienne France* (Paris: Hachette, 1979).

32. But they were probably older than their medieval ancestors, Marc Bloch, *Feudal Society* (Chicago: University of Chicago Press, 1961), p. 73. For the authority of age in early America, John Demos, "Old Age in Early New England," in Demos and Boocock, eds., *Turning Points: Historical and Sociological Essays on the Family*, Supplement to *American Journal of Sociology* Vol. 84 (Chicago, 1978); and David Hackett Fischer,

Growing Old in America (New York: Oxford University Press, 1978). On the authority of age by class in England, Keith Thomas, *Age and Authority in Early Modern England* (London: Proceedings of the British Academy, 1976).

33. Paul Masson, *Les Bouches-du-Rhône. Encyclopédie Départementale*, T. III (Marseille, 1920): 620.

34. *Registre des délibérations de l'hôpital: A.M.*

35. Masson, *Les Bouches-du-Rhône.*

36. *Registre des délibérations de l'hôpital*, Jan. 14, 1770.

37. Ibid. May 13, 1770.

38. Nicole Sabatier, *L'Hôpital Saint-Jacques d'Aix-en-Provence (1519–1789) Thèse pour le doctorat en droit soutenue le 26 juin 1964, Université d'Aix-Marseille–Faculté de Droit et des Sciences Economiques d'Aix.*

39. On the transition from *charité* to *bienfaisance* in Aix, Cissie C. Fairchilds, *Poverty and Charity in Aix-en-Provence 1640–1789* (Baltimore: Johns Hopkins Univ. Press, 1976).

40. As to literacy, Eguilles fits the pattern of the region on the eve of the Revolution: 30 percent for men, 10 percent for women, Liard, *Les Mentalités collectives*, p. 27. For old age in preliterate societies, Leo Simmons, *The Role of the Aged in Primitive Society* (New Haven: Yale University Press, 1945).

41. *A.D.*, Aix, VI, B 1511 (March 31, 1744).

42. For census of 1765, Baratier, *La Démographie*; for the 1810 census, manuscript in *A.M.*

43. For Laslett types, Laslett, *Household and Family in Past Time* (Cambridge: Cambridge University Press, 1972). On the family in Provence, Michel Vovelle, "Y a-t-il un modèle de la famille méridionale?" in Vovelle, *De la cave au grenier* (Québec: Serge Fleury, 1980) pp. 39–54; on coresidence, two articles by Collomp on the stem family, *Alliance et filiation* and *Maison*; Lutz Berkner, "The Stem Family and the Developmental Cycle of the Peasant Household: an eighteenth-century Austrian example," in *American Historical Review* Vol. 77 (1972).

44. On widowhood, Alain Bideau, "A Demographic and Social Analysis of Widowhood and Remarriage: the Example of the Castellany of Thoissey-en-Dombes, 1670–1840," in *Journal of Family History* Vol. 5, 1 (Spring 1980): 28–43.

45. *Etude* of Jean-Joseph Carle; see note 21 above.

46. On the question of lineage and marriage, Jean-Louis Flandrin, *Familles: parenté, maison, sexualité dans l'ancienne société* (Paris: Hachette, 1976).

47. Marriage contract of Joseph Gros and Thérèze Martin, Feb. 3, 1766.

48. Contracts of Nov. 23, 1744 and Feb. 19, 1753.

49. Marriage contract of Jean Baptiste Marroc, April 23, 1758.

50. Rétif de la Bretonne, *La vie de mon père* (Paris: Classiques Garnier, 1970) pp. 62–63.

51. See receipts of Oct. 18, 1760 and Oct. 31, 1763.

52. See proxy of Oct. 23, 1751 and receipt of March 3, 1753. Died June 22, 1762.

53. *Partage*, Sept. 18, 1766.

54. With almost no exceptions, a *testament nuncupatif*, a public document rather than a secret one. See Liard, *Les mentalités collectives*, and Aubenas, *Le Testament en Provence.*

55. Baume's testament, May 4, 1766.

56. Boyer's testament, Feb. 19, 1762; Brun's testament, Sep. 23, 1762.

57. *Déclaration*, Nov. 10, 1751.

58. Anne Artaud Dumas received payments: April 16, 1746, April 18, 1746, Oct. 21, 1747, Oct. 28, 1747, Nov. 12, 1748, Oct. 9, 1751, Nov. 6, 1751, Nov. 13, 1751, April 15, 1752, and April 15, 1752. She was mentioned in Pierre Giraud's codicil of April 17, 1743; she died Jan. 20, 1757.

59. Gros's testament, Dec. 9, 1756.

60. Yves Castan, *"Pères et fils en Languedoc à l'époque classique,"* in *XVIIe Siècle* Nos. 102–103 (1974): 31–43; and *Honnêteté et relations sociales en Languedoc 1715–1780* (Paris: Plon, 1975).

61. Roderick Phillips, "Women's Emancipation, the Family and Social Change in Eighteenth-Century France," in *Journal of Social History* Vol. 12, no. 4 (Summer 1979): 553–567.

62. *A.D.*, Aix, VI, B 1512 (May 1760).

63. Ibid. VI, B 1511 (May 3, 1746).

64. For their revival, Agulhon, *La sociabilité méridionale* (Aix: Annales de la Faculté des Lettres, 1966).

65. Abel Poitrineau, *"La fête traditionnelle,"* in *Annales Historiques de la Révolution Française* Vol. 47, no. 221 (1975); Natalie Z. Davis, "The Reasons of Misrule: Youth Groups and *Charivaris* in Sixteenth-Century France," in *Past and Present* Vol. 50 (1971): 41–75; Fernand Benoît, *La Provence et le Comtat Venaissin. Arts et traditions populaires* (Avignon: Gallimard, 1976) 3e éd. p. 228.

66. Bloch and Tuetey, *Procès-verbaux*; Fernand Charoy, *L'Assistance aux vieillards, infirmes et incurables en France de 1789 à 1905* (Paris: Thèse pour le doctorat, 1905).

67. Mona Ozouf, *"Symboles et fonctions des âges dans les fêtes de l'époque révolutionnaire,"* in *Annales Historiques de la Révolution Française* Vol. 47, no. 221 (1975) and *La Fête révolutionnaire* (Paris: Gallimard, 1976); Michel Vovelle, *Les Métamorphoses de la fête en Provence de 1750 à 1830* (Paris: Aubier-Flammarion, 1976). For the *levée en masse, Archives Parlementaires. Première série (1787 à 1799) Tome 72*, August 23, 1793 (Paris, 1907) p. 674. For the ideal peasant household, *Commission de l'instruction publique. Architecture rurale. Extrait du registre des arrêtés du comité de Salut public de la Convention nationale, du treizième jour du mois Floréal, l'an deuxième de la République française, une et indivisible. Archives Nationales* F¹⁷ 1281, *dossier* 12; for this reference, I thank Prof. James Leith.

68. *A.M.d'Eguilles.*

69. Ibid.

70. Peter N. Stearns, *Old Age in European Society: the Case of France* (New York: Holmes & Meier, 1976).

CHAPTER TEN—WORK, CHARITY, AND THE ELDERLY IN LATE-NINETEENTH-CENTURY RUSSIA

ADELE LINDENMEYR

T he elderly in late-nineteenth-century Russia grew up in a society overwhelmingly rural, peasant, and agrarian.[1] By the end of the century, however, industrialization and urbanization were eroding the traditional economic and social order at an uneven but accelerating pace. Of all the groups in the Russian population, the elderly there, like the elderly anywhere, probably felt the direct impact of major change least. Yet their experiences, far from being irrelevant or anachronistic, serve as an index of the continuing strength of tradition in Russian society at this time, and a measure of the breadth and depth of economic and social transformations which were revealed to be fundamental and irreversible only to later generations and historians. How, then, did this hitherto overlooked segment of the Russian population live? Did the elderly continue to work, and if so where and in what occupations? What support did society provide to those no longer able to work? And what can one conclude from the patterns of work and assistance about the social and cultural status of the elderly in this period of transition? In most respects, tradition still determined their lives. But the social and economic changes of this time undermined their position and security and, together with the political ferment of the late Imperial period, deflected attention away from their problems and needs. Russian society largely ignored its elderly.

It is difficult to arrive at a satisfactory definition of old age for late Imperial Russia. Definitions based solely on a chronological age group are obviously inadequate; depending on their work, health, and personalities, people age at different rates. However, with even fragmentary information about such factors in Russian society barely available, there is no alternative to the chronological definition. The first census of the Empire (conducted in 1897), the earliest source of direct data on the age composition of the Russian population, defined the elderly as those sixty years of age or older. According to the census about 6.5 million, or 7 percent, of the 93.5 million people in

European Russia belonged to this age group; the majority of them were in their sixties. The difference by sex was relatively slight: 6.8 percent of the male population was sixty or older, compared to 7.1 percent of the female population.[2] While this elderly population may seem small, it should be viewed in light of the rapid population growth of the late Imperial period, when almost half of the European Russian population was under twenty years old.[3] Nor did Russia differ sharply from Western nations at the turn of the century; in France, due to the low birthrate, 13 percent of the population was sixty or older, but only 7.3 percent of the English and Welsh population belonged to this age group.[4] With the considerable demographic change of this period, however, it seems likely that the elderly segment of the Russian population, though probably greater in absolute numbers than in previous generations, was stable or even declining relative to other age groups.

Old age differed little from previous periods of life in one key respect, for most elderly Russians continued to work. The 1897 census, which divided the population into "independents" who supported themselves and "dependents" supported by them—the majority of whom were children—found that over 84 percent of elderly men were self-supporting, although only 18.5 percent of elderly women could be so classified. The proportion of elderly men and women in the entire independent population, slightly more than 13 percent, was almost twice the proportion of elderly people in the entire population.[5] Yet industrialization had little direct impact on these working elderly, as most of them engaged in traditional occupations closely tied to the land, to home, or to crafts.

As in the population as a whole, agriculture remained the principal occupation of the elderly, involving 70 percent of self-supporting men and 27 percent of self-supporting women. For some, particularly those with little or no land, this meant working as hired agricultural laborers. But most of these men and women worked their own land allotments and headed peasant households as the elders of their families and villages. They represented the strong survival of patriarchal customs and multigenerational families in the Russian village.[6] Even when they did not head their households, however, and so were classified as "dependents" by the misleading census definition, elderly peasants continued to work. In all likelihood, most of the almost 2.9 million female elderly dependents in agriculture (and the more than 370,000 men) contributed actively, as they always had, to the economy of the peasant household, as long as their health permitted.[7] *Stariki* and especially *babushki* in the villages performed essential tasks even if they could no longer work in the fields: fetching water, chopping wood, preparing food, cultivating kitchen gardens, rocking cradles and minding children, chickens, and geese. The Granny in Chekhov's story "The Peasants" virtually ran the household while her husband and two daughters-in-law worked in the fields. Out of the entire elderly population of the Empire, then, both self-supporting and supported by others, over two-thirds depended upon the land.

Yet this is relatively low for a society which until recently had been overwhelmingly peasant and agrarian. Considerable numbers of the elderly found work in occupations other than agriculture, though similarly traditional and nonindustrial. Over 13 percent of the female and 4 percent of the male self-supporting population worked in service jobs, the most common occupation after agriculture. Although a few of the men held positions as directors, administrators, or other white-collar workers, most men and women worked in low-paying, menial positions. Two-thirds of the elderly women in this category were domestic servants. Old men also worked as domestic servants, house porters or night watchmen, but almost half in this category supported themselves by unskilled day labor. Other old people found similar service work in religious institutions — the men guarding churches, monasteries or cemeteries, the old women cleaning, selling candles, or preparing Communion wafers. Still others made their living from trade, particularly in food and agricultural products.[8]

Many old people probably combined several such occupations, which varied with the season and their abilities. An old man in the village where the scientist and progressive landowner A.N. Engel'gardt had his estate in the 1870s might have been fairly typical in this respect. A former house serf, deaf and unmarried, Savelich lived in his old age (he has forgotten, as a matter of fact, just how old he is) "like the birds of the air, from day to day, getting by somehow." In summer and autumn the peasants of his village hired him to guard the church; as remuneration each household in turn fed him and paid him five kopecks a night. Once trained as a confectioner in Moscow, Savelich sometimes earned a little extra by making jam for merchant families in the nearby town. In winter he lived on his summer earnings, receiving room in a peasant household in exchange for doing odd jobs. Occasionally he bought a few pounds of sugar to make candy, and sold it in surrounding villages (without bothering to get a peddler's license). Thus supported by part-time work, the old man "always ate poorly, went hungry sometimes," but never resorted to begging.[9]

Another occupation which engaged the elderly had similar ties to tradition and the countryside — *kustar'*, or handicraft industry. For elderly women in particular, some form of domestic textile production could be an important source of income. In 1897 about 6 percent of the self-supporting elderly women worked with cotton, flax, hemp, and other fibers to make yarn, cloth, rope or other materials; most of these women were classified as *kustar'*, i.e. domestic workers. Another 10,700 women were employed in making clothing.[10] Elderly men, too, worked in craft or domestic industries, especially making clothing or articles out of wood, metal, or fibers. More than 52,000 men found work in the construction industry, the majority as carpenters.[11] Such craft industries probably provided a secondary source of income to many other elderly men and women. Factory production, though exerting increasing pressure on craft production at this time, involved few of the elderly. A household investigation of Moscow province in the late 1890s found that in one district 11 percent of male weavers, and 4.5 percent of female weavers, working in factories were over forty-five years of age; but among domestic weavers, 30 percent of the men and 16 percent of the women were over forty-five.[12] In all of European Russia in 1897 only 2.3 percent of the 1,240,700 male factory workers and 1.7 percent of the 264,000 female factory workers were sixty or older.[13]

With the majority of the elderly working in agriculture, and many more supporting themselves in primarily rural craft industries, it would seem that in their old age most Russians either remained in the countryside or returned there. But for a sizable minority, towns offered opportunities for work not available in the villages, especially in service or trade. Russian towns had long attracted large numbers of working-age migrants from the countryside, and this migration intensified with industrialization in the late nineteenth century. Consequently the age composition of the urban and rural populations of European Russia differed, with a much larger proportion of children in the villages and a greater presence of adults between twenty and forty years old in towns. But the 1897 census does not reveal a strong concentration of elderly in rural areas; 6.5 percent of the urban population of European Russia was sixty or older, compared to 7.1 percent of the rural population. On the local level the differences could be greater, but not by much: in the city of Moscow in the second half of the nineteenth century, for example, only about 5 percent of the population was elderly, and in Petersburg less than 4 percent in 1864, while in some rural districts 10 percent or more of the inhabitants was elderly.[14] No clear overall pattern of residence or migration emerges for Russia's elderly. It seems that many tended to move back and forth between town and country in search of work; in fact, the opportunities offered by the village were probably considerably more limited than in the towns. Those elderly no longer able to work were also torn between town and countryside, for each promised different kinds of aid to those in need.

Only a privileged few enjoyed the opportunity to retire to live on a guaranteed income. In the late 1890s, slightly more than 1 percent of the elderly population of the Empire lived on income from their capital and property, and another small group of mostly old women lived on remittances from relatives. Less than 1 percent of the elderly population received pensions.[15] Most pensioners were former employees of the tsarist government, which provided pensions to officials of the civil bureaucracy (who received full pensions after thirty-five years of service) and officers in the military. By the end of the nineteenth century, pension funds also existed for employees of state- and privately owned railroads, managerial employees in some private enterprises, and in thirteen provinces for the employees of the *zemstvos*, the institutions of local self-government.[16] Except for employees of the tsarist government, however, most pension funds had been established too recently to have included many of the elderly at this time; the great majority of working men and women did not receive the protection of pensions until the Soviet period.

For many more aging workers the only alternative was to return to their native village. A great many urban workers—not only in factories but in trade, service, and other urban jobs—as recent migrants from the countryside, retained some link with their village: relatives, or a house and plot of land, or at least a memory.[17] These links could serve as a form of old-age insurance. Some contemporary observers insisted, however, that for the returning worker his home village was only a last refuge in old age and sickness, not a bucolic retreat for comfortable retirement. On the basis of his investigation of workers in Moscow textile factories in the early 1880s, E.M. Dement'ev drew a bleak picture of the prospects awaiting those who managed to reach a usually premature old age:

Where do workers from less healthy occupations, especially workers manufacturing fibrous materials, go after the age of forty?—To the cemetery. But only a few of them die in the factories. Our worker goes "to the homeland" to die. Very often he knows his village only from having heard his father, and from his passport, but it is enough if he knows of the existence of any relative there—he goes "to the homeland." One finds statisticians who will prove, on the basis of absolutely true numbers, the error of our view of the factory and point to the higher mortality in the countryside and the lower mortality in more "cultured centers"—in factories. But zemstvo physicians . . . alone know the true reason for this high mortality: the city and the factory. They know that the very next day after his arrival "in the homeland" the worker returned from the factory will be sitting in their dispensary with all the symptoms of various incurable pulmonary diseases and after a very short time he will be entered in their lists as "died of consumption."[18]

T.E. Startsev, who investigated workers in the Baku oil industry in 1899, similarly claimed that in most cases by forty the worker in industry "turned into an invalid," and left for his home village "not of his own free will," or out of "any poetic nostalgia for it," but out of "severe, deeply prosaic necessity."[19] The theme of an early and bleak old age for factory workers was a common one among such critics, and probably exaggerated. Yet, with the absence of any old age or disability insurance, most factory or urban workers undoubtedly continued to work until physically unable to do so any longer; and thus they returned to their villages and families, often decades after originally leaving, only as additional mouths to feed.

Neither the disabled returning worker, nor the aging peasant who had never left, could count on finding adequate care in his native village. After the abolition of serfdom in 1861 the peasant commune had responsibility both traditionally and legally for the aged and infirm (as well as for orphans and other needy) whose relatives could not care for them.[20] This obligation extended even to members of the commune long absent from it, who had worked in the city or elsewhere; whether they received medical assistance or public relief in the city or returned to the village, the commune was responsible. But given the marginal resources of most peasant families and villages and the pressures of rural overpopulation, communal aid to elderly members was rudimentary and sporadic at best.

They seldom received institutional care, for example.[21] Individual communes usually could not sustain the costs of a permanent almshouse, but the lack of such institutions seems to have resulted from preference and custom as well. An investigation of peasant poor relief in the mid-1890s noted an aversion among the peasantry to charitable institutions, because they deprived the needy of their freedom, and often settled them in some district center, away from their native village. An incident in the Volga province of Samara, reported by a land captain, a local official of the central government, illustrates this aversion:

In the village of Borisoglebsk, in Novouzenskii district, the peasants, by arrangement with the land captain, decided to allocate a certain sum from the revenues of the savings-loan fund to build an asylum for the poor. A good building was built, it was supplied with everything necessary, attendants were employed, and the maintenance of the residents ensured. Despite the fact that more than a few completely decrepit and poor old men and women lived in the district, no one wanted to enter the asylum, and it remained completely empty.[22]

What assistance most communes provided to the needy elderly came in the form of monetary or especially material aid. Sometimes the commune allocated a small monthly grant of a few rubles to a needy old man or woman, or paid a particular household to care for him or her permanently. A particularly common form of aid was "*po ocheredi*"; each household in the village provided food and shelter to a needy old man or woman in turn, while he or she moved from hut to hut, spending a day or week in each. Other forms of communal assistance also involved some kind of collective effort, such as providing grain rations from the communal stores, or collectively working a plot whose harvest went to those in need.[23]

When illness or infirmity made working impossible, most elderly found little security in their native villages. The minimal assistance available to them could even impose additional hardships, as with moving from hut to hut *po ocheredi*. They became a burden on the already limited resources of most peasant families or their communes; in the particularly harsh words of one Russian saying, "poverty in old age is a worm-eaten nut in a rotten shell."[24] Those returning to the village after years of city life encountered difficulties beyond those resulting from the infirmity of old age. As Nikolai Chikildeev in Chekhov's "The Peasants"—a waiter for many years in a Moscow restaurant—discovered when illness forced him to return to his impoverished native village, those used to the relative civilization of even the most backward towns faced a difficult adjustment back to the poverty and ignorance of Russia's isolated villages. Thus a considerable number of those unable to work either remained in the towns or migrated there, if not to find some kind of menial work then to take advantage of the greater opportunities there for charity.

Russian society did not ignore completely the plight of its helpless or solitary elderly. By the end of the nineteenth century, a network of charitable societies and institutions, located largely in towns, supplemented the still prevalent custom of almsgiving. According to the 1897 census over 15,000 elderly men and almost 40,000 elderly women lived in almshouses or other charitable institutions, while over 50,000 men and 96,000 women, or 1.5 percent of the self-supporting old men and almost 12 percent of self-supporting women, lived at home on relief.[25] Of all needy groups the elderly attracted perhaps the greatest sympathy. A woman charity worker in Moscow at the turn of the century described the elderly poor she encountered in her work as follows:

Old workers, men and women: laundresses, charwomen, servants, draymen and others, who have spent their whole lives working, earning pennies, out of which it was impossible to save something for a rainy day, and left in their old age with nowhere to lay their heads. The question of this category of people is resolved very simply: there should be almshouses for them, so that these hard-working people can spend the last years of their lives well-fed and warm, and not die under a hedge.[26]

Unlike younger and more able-bodied needy groups, whom organized charity at this time suspected of willful idleness or moral weakness, the elderly poor seemed truly to deserve the assistance of society. Yet despite such expressions of sympathy for their plight, the particular problems and needs of the elderly poor did not attract any special attention or concern from workers in philanthropy and public relief or society at large.[27]

In fact, whether they found refuge in state or local government old-age homes or, as many more did, received monetary aid from a compassionate philanthropist or private charity, the rudimentary charity available to the elderly in late Imperial Russia did not differ substantially from the charity of previous centuries. Nor can it be viewed as adequate to the existing need for assistance, especially as the number of elderly in need was probably growing as traditional structures like the peasant commune were disintegrating. Monetary or "outdoor" relief was generally given either in the form of one-time grants, often distributed at Easter or Christmas in accordance with an ancient Russian charitable custom, or as periodic grants of a few rubles. Moreover, since most charities were located in towns, the preponderant rural population seldom enjoyed the benefits of organized relief unless they migrated there.[28] The charitable society of the parish of the Andreevskii Cathedral in Petersburg, for example, gave monetary aid to 139 poor people in 1869–1870, of whom 129 were women and 108 over fifty years of age; while only 22 of the recipients were of peasant origin, 41 belonged to the urban artisan estate, 22 were nobles or government officials, and 53 were former soldiers or their families.[29] Charitable organizations themselves often imposed additional limitations on their aid; it was not uncommon for individual charities to restrict their aid to members of one particular religion, or residents of a certain parish (as did the Andreevskii parish society) or other locality.

The institutional aid provided to the elderly reveals most sharply the inadequacy and primitiveness of the relief available to this group. Dating back to the Christianization of Russia in the tenth century, the almshouse, or *bogadel'nia*, was the oldest and still, in the late nineteenth century, most popular form of institutional charitable assistance in Russia.[30] For centuries the *bogadel'nia* offered refuge to all kinds of people in need: not only the aged, but also the sick, the healthy poor, the handicapped, the insane, orphans and foundlings.

Beginning in the eighteenth century, however, and especially from the reign of Catherine the Great (1762–1796), government authorities and private groups established specialized institutions such as orphanages, insane asylums, and workhouses for the able-bodied poor. By default and not by intention, the *bogadel'nia* in the second half of the nineteenth century had become primarily an old-age home, without becoming a specialized institution for the needs of the elderly and still retaining its catchall orientation. In small towns or villages, too, where charitable resources were limited and the number of needy in a particular group too small to justify a special institution, the *bogadel'nia* still housed the needy of all ages and conditions. As late as 1907, for example, in the town of Rybinsk, the institution supported by a local charitable society cared for ten elderly women together with fifty-six orphan boys and girls.[31]

At the end of the nineteenth century, there were about two thousand *bogadel'ni* in European Russia, almost two-thirds of them located in towns. A few housed only men, but most sheltered only women or both sexes, and in homes for both women almost always outnumbered men.[32] A few *bogadel'ni*, mostly located in Petersburg and Moscow, were large, elaborate institutions. Edith Sellers, an English charity worker interested in the elderly, visited several such institutions in the 1890s, including the Widows' Home in Petersburg for six hundred gentry women, located in a former palace; the Petersburg Municipal Almshouse housing 3,800 elderly; and two large, attractive institutions for the "respectable class" in Moscow. She was impressed by what she observed, and judged the homes far superior to the bleak, depressing English workhouse.[33] Most *bogadel'ni* bore little or no resemblance to these institutions in the two capitals, however. The majority housed under twenty-six persons. Although many rural institutions stood half empty, the number of *bogadel'ni* in or close to towns seldom met the need.[34] Overcrowding was a common problem in these institutions; in his unusually frank description in 1908 of the Obukhov *bogadel'nia* near Moscow, the district physician, I. I. Orlov, admitted that the institution, originally built for thirty-six, housed sixty people, the overflow sleeping in the corridors.[35] Often the institutions had long waiting lists, like the home for fifty-five elderly men and women outside of Petersburg, which in 1884 had a waiting list of forty, dating back to 1870.[36]

In the majority of *bogadel'ni* the amenities were few and conditions austere. Financial caution, the uncertainty of revenues (often coming in large part from donations), and the need to accommodate as many needy as possible, pressed the authorities who ran *bogadel'ni*, be they public or private, to economize. Their additional concern that they not coddle the poor or raise them above their station also led them to provide in most cases only the minimum of care: "warm lodgings, a clean bed, simple but nourishing, wholesome food."[37] Thus in most institutions the elderly roomed together in wards. They ate a plain, sometimes meager peasant diet, consisting mostly of bread, potatoes, porridge, and cabbage. In the Obukhov *bogadel'nia* each resident received an average of about three pounds of food per day, and a tea ration sufficient for a glass or two of tea every ten days.[38] Sometimes the elderly residents did not receive even this much. In principle, *bogadel'ni* were supposed to provide full care, but many offered residents only their shelter and a small daily allowance, or a money grant only at Easter and Christmas. Others made no provision at all for the food, clothing, and other daily needs of their residents, who relied on occasional donations to the institution or resorted to begging.[39] Medical care, too, was usually minimal. A few of the large, well-endowed institutions employed their own physicians for the residents; but in most cases, if *bogadel'ni* provided any medical care at all, they relied on the voluntary services of a local physician or the limited free time of the already overworked town or district physician. Although Dr. Orlov visited the Obukhov home when he could, most of the time the nearest medical help for the residents was the local clinic, a four-mile walk away.[40]

Finally, while most residents of *bogadel'ni* received free care, a number of *bogadel'ni* required a monthly fee or a certain sum at the time of entering from some of their residents.[41] Some elderly paid these fees themselves, out of their savings or pensions; others were subsidized by relatives, a private philanthropist, their commune or corporate estate, or a government institution. Those who bought, as it were, their places were usually members of relatively privileged classes. Often they enjoyed at least a private room, and sometimes a personal servant and special food.[42] But class counted even in institutions without such special privileges, as an incident related by another woman volunteer in charge of a small municipal *bogadel'nia* in Moscow illustrates:

During my administration of the *bogadel'nia* an 80-year-old lady died there, daughter of a marshal of the nobility, a graduate of an institute, who had been a governess because her property had all been lost in speculation by a close relative; when she was no longer able to work and all her relatives had died, nothing else was left to her but to rent a corner in a basement, and finally she could not even pay for that. When she was placed in the *bogadel'nia* and I learned her story, I tried as much as possible to lighten her life amidst the vulgar and ignorant old women, but she bore her position with humility and was so good and gentle that her little privileges did not arouse envy, and she exercised a beneficial influence over her fellow residents, weaning them away from swearing.[43]

There remained one final resort—begging—for those elderly who could not work, had no other means of support and found no assistance from family or charity. Begging was still widespread in late nineteenth-century Russia as it had been for centuries. The 1897 census discovered over 250,000 people who declared begging as their principal occupation and almost 40,000 who reported it as a supplementary occupation.[44] Since begging was illegal in the Russian Empire, and punished by imprisonment or exile, the number of those bold enough to report it as their occupation to the census takers probably constituted only a fraction of those who resorted to this ancient pursuit. A disproportionately large number of beggars were elderly; of the more than 250,000 counted by the census, almost 120,000 were men and women sixty or older, or almost 1.5 percent of the entire elderly population.[45]

The causes of begging in late-nineteenth-century Russia and the forms it took varied considerably, creating a multifaceted subculture still little studied by historians.[46] In all likelihood most elderly were compelled to beg by the absence of any other way to keep body and soul together. The shortage of charitable institutions for the elderly as well as for orphans, the disabled, or the incurably ill, was often cited by contemporaries as a principal cause of begging.[47] The Russian common people, and many of the privileged, too, viewed begging as a morally acceptable way of life, and responded to it with generosity and compassion, if not with discrimination as to who was truly deserving, as critics of the custom complained. As one land captain in Viatka province remarked of the peasants there, "Not to give alms to a beggar is considered a sin."[48]

Especially for the elderly who resorted to it, begging was closely tied to the Orthodox religion. Beggars congregated around churches, cemeteries, and monasteries, and in places with holy relics. Many Russians spent the last years of their lives on religious pilgrimages, and begged along the way. Others, equipped with subscription booklets, disguised their begging as the collection of funds for the construction or maintenance of a church somewhere.[49] Religious customs and legends still popular in the late nineteenth century encouraged begging: many Russian merchant families distributed alms every week on a certain day, or every year in commemoration of church or family occasions, while some Russians believed that Christ walked the earth in the form of a wanderer and tested the souls of Christians by asking them for alms.[50]

A particularly vivid picture of begging as a last resort of the elderly is found in Maxim Gorky's autobiographical work *My Childhood*, set in a provincial town in the 1870s. One by one the elderly members of Gorky's family circle ended up on the streets.

Grigory, for decades shop foreman in Gorky's grandfather's dye works and member of his household, turned to begging when blindness made him useful no longer and Gorky's grandfather turned him out. Like many blind or elderly beggars, he found a guide, an old woman who led him around to every house to ask for alms. Eventually impoverishment forced Gorky's once prosperous grandfather, too, to join the town's motley beggar population. However tragic such an end may seem, it was not seen as shameful; as Gorky's grandmother told him, "Christ was a beggar—and all the saints as well."[51]

From the compassion shown to elderly beggars or recipients of charity, one could be tempted to conclude that the elderly enjoyed at least emotional if not material security. Moreover, the 1897 census reveals that the overwhelming majority of elderly Russians had been married, and for a significant number of them—almost two-thirds of the men and over a third of the women—their spouses were still living.[52] Historians have usually assumed that the Russian family included more than two generations and more than one nuclear family, presided over by the patriarch. But recent Soviet work suggests that this pattern might have been far from universal, even before extended peasant family units began to break up after the abolition of serfdom in 1861.[53] Folkloristic evidence on the place of the elderly in the family or society is also ambiguous. Many of the folk sayings in Vladimir Dal's collection express respect for the elderly, their wisdom and experience; but others emphasize the infirmity or senility of the old, such as "Old age is no joy," and "The young grow older and wiser, the old older and foolish."[54]

Although more work in Russian social history remains to be done before questions about the familial and cultural role of the elderly can be answered, the patterns of work and assistance suggest that respect towards the elderly, if it existed, was seldom translated into any special consideration for their problems and needs. The concept of old age as a separate stage in life was lacking; what mattered in Russian society was not years but the ability or inability to work. As long as they could work, the elderly remained useful members of their families and communities, although their work was often menial. Many of those no longer able to work faced destitution, relieved only occasionally by rudimentary aid from commune or charity. In these ways, their situation probably did not differ from that of their grandparents. But with rural overpopulation, factory industry, and urbanization gradually eroding their traditional occupations and marginal status, the elderly in late-nineteenth-century Russia, unlike their grandparents, had lost the stability of a traditional society.

NOTES

1. As late as 1897 only 13 percent of the population was urban, 85 percent belonged to the peasant estate, and 70 percent made its living from agriculture; A.G. Rashin, *Naselenie Rossii za 100 let (1811–1913 gg.)*. *Statisticheskie ocherki (The Population of Russia over 100 Years (1811–1913): Statistical Essays)* (Moscow: Gos. Statisticheskoe Izdatel'stvo, 1956), pp. 98, 262; N.A. Troinitskii, ed., *Pervaia Vseobshchaia Perepis' Naseleniia Rossiiskoi Imperii, 1897 g. Obshchii svod po imperii rezul'tatov razrabotki dannykh pervoi vseobshchei perepisi naseleniia, proizvedennoi 28 ianvaria 1897 goda (The First General Census of the Population of the Russian Empire, 1897: General Collection for the Empire of the Results of the Tabulation of Data of the First General Census of the Population, Conducted on January 28, 1897)*, 2 vols. (St. Petersburg: Tsentral'nyi statisticheskii Komitet, 1905), 2:xlv–xlvi (hereafter cited as *Obshchii svod*).

2. *Obshchii svod*, 1:58; Rashin, *Naselenie*, p. 264. Analysis of the age data of the 1897 census has revealed substantial inaccuracies in age reporting, but these errors do not cause significant distortion when ages are grouped, as with the sixty and older category. See Don Karl Rowney and Edward G. Stockwell, "The Russian Census of 1897: Some Observations on the Age Data," *Slavic Review* (June 1978), pp. 217–227. The sex ratios in older age categories also suggest that the 1897 census undercounted women, particularly those over sixty. A relevant factor may be that in European Russia only 10.5 percent of the women sixty or older were literate. *Obshchii svod*, 1:58.

3. Rashin, *Naselenie*, p. 265.

4. Peter Laslett, "Social Development and Aging," in *Handbook of Aging and the Social Sciences*, ed. Robert H. Binstock and Ethel Shanas (New York: Van Nostrand, 1976), p. 103.

5. Most of the data and other materials used in this article concern European Russia. It was chosen as the geographical focus in order to reduce somewhat the influence of the great ethnic and material diversity of the entire Empire; although European Russia contained many distinct ethnic groups, the majority population by far was Great Russian and Orthodox. But information on occupation and age is not available for European Russia alone. The ageXoccupationXsex table of the 1897 census, covering the entire Empire, is in *Obshchii svod*, 2:236–255. Over sixty different occupational groups, and almost four hundred individual occupations, were delineated. While probably not strictly accurate, the Empire occupational information is useful for comparative purposes, and probably does not differ sharply from European Russia.

6. On the patriarchal nature of the extended peasant family see Peter Czap, Jr., "Marriage and the Peasant Joint Family in the Era of Serfdom," in David L. Ransel, ed., *The Family in Imperial Russia: New Lines of Historical Research* (Urbana: University of Illinois Press, 1978), pp. 103–123, and Anatole Leroy Beaulieu, *The Empire of the Tsars and the Russians*, 3 vols. (New York and London, 1902–1905; reprint ed., New York: AMS Press, 1969), 1:bk. 8, ch. 2. The collection of essays edited by Ransel, virtually the only historical work devoted to the prerevolutionary family, touches on the elderly only in passing.

7. Almost 2.5 million men and over 220,000 women sixty or older were "independents" in agriculture, i.e. heads of households in most cases. *Obshchii svod*, 2:xlvi.

8. Ibid., 2:238–241, 250–255.

9. A.N. Engel'gardt, *Iz derevni: 12 pisem, 1872–1887 (From the Countryside: 12 Letters, 1872–1887)* (Moscow: Gosudarstvennoe Sotsial'no-ekonomicheskoe Izdatel'stvo, 1937), pp. 5–6. As the "work" given to Savelich suggests, there often was no clear boundary between work and charity.

10. *Obshchii svod*, 2:242–249.

11. Ibid.

12. Rashin, *Formirovanie rabochego klassa Rossii: Istoriko-statisticheskie ocherki (The Formation of the Working Class of Russia: Historical-statistical Essays)* (Moscow: Izdatel'stvo sotsial'no-ekonomicheskoi literatury, 1958), pp. 286–287.

13. Ibid., p. 281.

14. Rashin, *Naselenie*, pp. 266–269, 275, 282.

15. *Obshchii svod*, 2:240–241.

16. *Entsiklopedicheskii slovar' (Encyclopedic Dictionary)*, 86 vols. (St. Petersburg: Brokgauz-Efron, 1890–1907), 23:148–157. Social insurance legislation of the 1880s, 1903 and 1912 established accident, illness, and disability protection for some workers, but not old age insurance.

17. On the rural ties of the Russian working class, see Robert Eugene Johnson, "Family Relations and the Rural-Urban Nexus: Patterns in the Hinterland of Moscow, 1880–1900," in Ransel, pp. 263–279.

18. Quoted in Rashin, *Formirovanie*, p. 284.

19. Ibid., p. 285.

20. The legal obligation was asserted in the Statute on Public Assistance, volume 13 of the Law Code of the Russian Empire (1892 ed.), arts. 581 and 582. The Statute asserted that relatives held first responsibility for the needy.

21. E.D. Maksimov, "Soslovnoe prizrenie v Rossii" ("Estate Assistance in Russia"), *Vestnik blagotvoritel'nosti (Charity Herald)* (April 1898), p. 34.

22. Incident cited in Maksimov, *Istoriko-statisticheskii ocherk blagotvoritel'nosti i obshchestvennogo prizreniia v Rossii (Historical-Statistical Outline of Charity and Public Assistance in Russia)* [St. Petersburg, 1895], pp. 126–127. Peasant reluctance to build or use charitable institutions is noted in reports from other provinces as well: see Sobstvennaia ego Imperatorskogo Velichestva Kantseliariia po uchrezhdeniieam Imperatritsy Marii, *Blagotvoritel'nost' v Rossii* (His Imperial Majesty's Own Chancery for the Institutions of Empress Maria, *Charity in Russia*), 2 vols. (St. Petersburg: [Tipo-lit. N.L. Nyrkina, 1907]), appendix to vol. 1 (the investigation of the mid-1890s): 12, 23–24, 26, 29, 40–41.

23. On the various forms of peasant communal assistance see *Blagotvoritel'nost' v Rossii*, 1:102–109.

24. "*Star da nishch, gnil' da svishch.*" Vladimir Dal', *Poslovitsy russkogo naroda (Sayings of the Russian People)*, 3d ed., 7 vols. (St. Petersburg-Moscow: M.O. Vol'f, 1904), 3:73.

25. *Obshchii svod*, 2:240–241.

26. N.K., "Iz nabliudenii sotrudnitsy popechitel'stva" ("From the Observations of a Guardianship Volunteer"), *Trudovaia Pomoshch' (Work Assistance)* (April 1901), p. 472.

27. At their 1910 congress, for example, charity and public relief workers discussed reports on the needs of the crippled, the mentally ill and especially children, but devoted no time at all to the elderly. Vserossiiski Soiuz uchrezhdenii, obshchestv i deiatelei po obshchestvennomu i chastnomu prizreniiu, *Trudy pervogo s"ezda russkikh deiatelei po obshchestvennomu i chastnomu prizreniiu, 8–13 marta 1910 g.* (All-Russian Union of Institutions, Societies and Workers in Public and Private Assistance, *Proceedings of the First Congress of Russian Workers in Public and Private Assistance, 8–13 March 1910)* (St. Petersburg, 1910).

28. *Blagotvoritel'nost' v Rossii*, 1:xliv.

29. "Otchet o deistviiakh Obshchestva vspomozheniia bednym v prikhode An-dreevskogo sobora v S-Peterburge, za 1869/70 g." ("Report on the Operations of the

Society for Aid to the Poor in the Andreevskii Cathedral Parish in St. Petersburg for 1869–70''), *Nuzhda i pomoshch' (Need and Assistance)* (May 1871), pp. 37–39. The social origin of one, evidently, was unknown.

30. V. Stepanov, "Hospices et Maisons de Charité," in Direction Générale de l'Économie Locale du Ministère de l'Intérieur, *L'Assistance Publique et Privée en Russie* (St. Petersburg: Imprimer-ie de L'Académie Impériale des Sciences, 1906), pp. 152–156.

31. *Obzor deiatel'nosti i Otchet o dvizhenii summ . . . Rybinskogo Pokrovsko-Voskresenskogo Obshchestva vspomoshchestvovaniia bednym . . . za 1906 god (Review of the Activity and Report on the Finances . . . of the Rybinsk Pokrovsko-Voskresenskoe Society for Assistance to the Poor . . . for 1906)* (Rybinsk, 1907), p. 16.

32. Stepanov, "Hospices," p. 162; *Blagotvoritel'nost' v Rossii*, 1:193–194. Although based on the same government survey of charity, the figures on *bogadel'ni* differ slightly in these two sources.

33. Edith Sellers, "In Danish and Russian Old-Age Homes," *The Nineteenth Century and After* (October 1902), pp. 650–655.

34. Stepanov, "Hospices," p. 163; *Blagotvoritel'nost' v Rossii*, 1:190.

35. I.I. Orlov, *Dom prizreniia neizlechimo bol'nykh, slepykh i prestarelykh oboego pola v sele Obukhove, Klinskogo uezda, Moskovskoi gubernii (The Home for the Incurably Ill, Blind and Aged of Both Sexes in the Village of Obukhov, Klin District, Moscow Province)* (Moscow: Tovarishchestvo "Pechatnia S.P. Iakovleva," 1903), p. 6.

36. K.I. Myslovskii, *Opisanie doma prizreniia prestarelykh i uvechnykh osnovannogo v g. Petergofe v pamiat' Imperatora Nikolaia I-go, 11 iiunia 1859 goda (A Description of the Home for the Aged and Disabled Founded in Peterhof in Memory of Emperor Nicholas I on June 11, 1859)* (St. Petersburg: Tip. Ed. Treimana, 1884), p. 10.

37. Evgeniia Berkut, "O gorodskikh uchastkovykh popechitel'stvakh v Moskve (Vospominaniia sotrudnitsy)" ("On the City District Guardianships [for the Poor] in Moscow [Reminiscences of a Volunteer]"), *Trudovaia pomoshch'* (March 1903), p. 356. The Obukhov *bogadel'nia*, for example, was not only overcrowded, but also its revenues were diminishing every year and its twenty-year-old building was in desperate need of major repairs; Orlov, *Dom prizreniia*, pp. 7–8.

38. Orlov, *Dom prizreniia*, p. 7.

39. Stepanov, "Hospices," p. 158. About one quarter of the residents of the Obukhov *bogadel'nia* fended for themselves, mostly by begging; Orlov, *Dom prizreniia*, p. 7.

40. Orlov, *Dom prizreniia*, pp. 10–12. It was in almshouses, however, that evidently the first medical study in Russia of aging was carried out, in 1889. Planned by the eminent Russian clinician S.P. Botkin, the study involved a team of physicians in the examination of over two thousand elderly residents of almshouses in Petersburg. The doctors investigated mortality and disease rates for men and women, social and medical factors influencing longevity, and the process of aging itself. D.F. Chebotarev and Yu. K. Duplenko, "On the History of the Home Gerontology Movement," in *Leading Problems of Soviet Gerontology* (Kiev: Institute of Gerontology, 1972), pp. 6–9.

41. *Blagotvoritel'nost' v Rossii*, 1:194.

42. Stepanov, "Hospices," pp. 158–160; Sellers, pp. 650–653.

43. Berkut, "O gorodskikh uchastkovykh popechitel'stvakh," p. 358.

44. Stepanov, "La mendicité en Russie," in *L'Assistance Publique et Privée en Russie*, p. 183.

45. *Obshchii svod*, 2:254–255.

46. Works which capture some of the color and variety of this subculture include I.G. Pryzhov, *Nishchie na sviatoi Rusi: Materialy dlia istorii obshchestvennogo i narodnogo byta v Rossii (Beggars in Holy Rus': Materials for the History of Social and Popular Life in Russia)* (Moscow: Tip. M.I. Smirnovoi, 1862), and A. Levenstim, *Professional'noe nishchenstvo, ego prichiny i formy: Bytovye ocherki (Professional Begging, its Causes and Forms: Sketches of Popular Life)* (St. Petersburg: Tip. M. Stasiulevicha, [1899]).

47. For example by Stepanov in "La mendicité," p. 183.

48. *Blagotvoritel'nost' v Rossii*, 1, appendix:11.

49. Stepanov, "La mendicité," p. 184.

50. Levenstim, pp. 14–16.

51. Maxim Gorky, *My Childhood* (Harmondsworth: Penguin Books, 1966), p. 161.

52. *Obshchii svod*, 1:80.

53. For example, a study of the peasant family in the first half of the nineteenth century in western Siberia suggests that simple, two-generational families were common or even prevalent there. A study of pre-Emancipation Russian towns found that two-generational families predominated in those towns for which sufficient data are available. N.A. Minenko, "Krest'ianskaia sem'ia zapadnoi Sibiri v pervoi polovine XIX veka (chislennost' i struktura)," ("The Peasant Family of Western Siberia in the First Half of the 19th Century"), in M.M. Gromyko and N.A. Minenko, eds., *Iz istorii sem'i i byta sibirskogo krest'ianstva v XVII - nachale XX vv.: Sbornik nauchnykh trudov (From the History of the Family and Life of the Siberian Peasantry in the 17th-Early 20th Centuries: A Collection of Scholarly Works)*, (Novosibirsk: Novosibirskii Gos. Universitet, 1975), pp. 3–29; M.G. Rabinovich, *Ocherki etnografii russkogo feodal'nogo goroda: Gorozhane, ikh obshchestvennyi i domashnii byt (Essays on the Ethnography of the Russian Feudal Town: Townspeople, Their Social and Domestic Life)* (Moscow: Nauka, 1978), pp. 178–191. Rabinovich stresses, however, the great authority of the head of the family.

54. Dal', *Poslovitsy*, 3:72–73.

CHAPTER ELEVEN—HISTORICAL CHANGE IN THE HOUSEHOLD STRUCTURE OF THE ELDERLY IN ECONOMICALLY DEVELOPED SOCIETIES*

DANIEL SCOTT SMITH

S pecifying and understanding the relationships between old people and their families in past societies are challenging and important tasks. Historians have only recently begun to study older populations. Entering a field already explored by other social scientists, they encountered a variety of theoretical discussions relevant to their own inquiries. Characteristically, the historians adopted one or another of these perspectives to design their research and to organize their findings. At the same time, the catholicism and empiricism of the tradition of historical study shaped their works. Time and space were given expansive specifications. To understand the present, historians instinctively sensed that they must go back not a decade or generation but centuries, and that they had to examine the family relationships of the elderly in a diversity of cultures. Historians also attempted to discover a data source that would provide maximal comparability over time and among societies. Research has thus concentrated on the study of family relationships from information on households.

Although historical documentation of the household structure of the elderly remains incomplete at present, contrasting the extant record with the theoretical perspectives can yield insights about both

*Reprinted with permission of Academic Press. The paper originally appeared in *Aging: Stability and Change in the Family*, edited by Robert W. Fogel et al. (New York: Academic Press, 1981), 91–114. The paper was originally presented at a May 1979 Annapolis, Maryland conference sponsored by the Committee on Aging, National Research Council.

The underlying research for the paper was supported by the National Institute on Aging, Grant AG 00350-02. Michel Dahlin, Mark Friedberger, and Janice Reiff assisted in the research on the 1880 and 1900 United States samples. Hans Christian Johansen (Odense University), Andrejs Plakans (Iowa State University), and Ethel Shanas (University of Illinois at Chicago Circle) generously supplied unpublished data for use in this paper.

history and theory. This preliminary assessment is the chief purpose of the paper. The first section outlines three major theoretical notions pertinent to the subject and briefly discusses the categories and problems of interpretation of data on households. The apparent conflicts among the perspectives define what needs to be known empirically; the constructs thus supply a useful heuristic framework. The second part of the essay employs the available historical evidence to fill in the desired framework. Three more realistic propositions emerge to clarify the historical record and to modify the theoretical constructs. The final section of the paper surveys and comments on three important problems suggested by the realistic propositions.

THE THREE PERSPECTIVES

Modernization and Postmodernization

Once upon a time, in traditional societies, people lived in extended families; now they live in nuclear families. In between came (in older versions) the industrial revolution or (in newer terminology) modernization. Old people enjoyed security, status, and power in traditional societies in part because their age made them dominant within their families. Modernization or industrialization involved proletarianization, urbanization, greater geographic and social mobility, and the rise of individualism. These developments destroyed the extended family and the advantaged position of the elderly.

Some versions of this interpretation concentrate on changes that have occurred in the twentieth century in Western societies. Among these are the rising proportion of the population in older age groups, the impact of compulsory retirement, the emergence of mass affluence, and the development of the welfare state as an alternative to the family. This is the postmodernization or advanced-industrial variant of the model.

If this orientation is completely correct, then the comparative situations of the elderly in currently advanced societies should be roughly similar as should their positions in traditional, preindustrial societies. This theory, in short, predicts little variation over space but great change over time.

Demographic Determinism

In all human societies, past and present, mean household size has been remarkably small. Multigenerational households are never universal and, more frequently, comprise only a distinct minority among all households. Demographic constraints—a steep age structure produced by high fertility, large variance in fertility, and high mortality—explain the striking similiarity in household structure in all traditional societies. Since no golden age of the extended family for old people existed, there could not have been a major transition as predicted by the modernization model. The secular decline in vital rates ironically implies that a larger proportion of the population in demographically advanced (low fertility and mortality) societies can enjoy the possibility of an extended family or household. Generally, however, this perspective emphasizes little variation over either time or space.

Cultural Continuity

As a primary group, the family embodies a set of meanings whose definition is extraordinarily important to individuals in all societies. People will maintain a whole range of family practices, regardless of major demographic changes, economic transformations, and ideological revolutions. The nuclear family, for example, does not fit modern societies any better than alternative ways of conceptualizing and organizing family relationships. In the distant past, usually before written records existed, different cultures developed divergent ways of organizing family structure. Although there may be functional reasons why a particular type of family structure evolved in a given society, the important point for this argument is that whatever exists, persists. Family structure is primarily a cultural phenomenon, a set of intimate relationships robustly resistant to change. This perspective thus predicts great variation in household structure over space but little change over time.

Discussion

The first perspective derives from classic sociological theory that has attempted to define and understand, most often by means of dichotomous ideal types, the great transformation under way in Western society since the early nineteenth century. "From extended to nuclear" is the familial analogue of "from status to contract" and "from *Gemeinschaft* to *Gesellschaft*." The demographic emphasis reflects a later orientation in sociology and anthropology: the search for various universal features in human relations, and in human societies and the development of functional explanations to account for the commonalities. With its origins in anthropology and linguistics, the emphasis on cultural continuity is still more recent.

Based on relativistic assumptions about cultures, this orientation uses language to locate universals in the human mind.

No bibliographical citations are provided for these three interpretations, for no scholar would subscribe completely to any of them. Although there is some truth in each position, they are now polemical arguments, more often cited by their opponents than by their proponents; they have become straw men. Not only do competing social science theories reflect different orientations (often ideological in origin) and the distinctive concerns of the times of their formulators; they also provide answers to quite distinct questions and are not, when fully understood, actually competing. The theoretical literature is most significant for identifying the important issues. I hope in this paper to transcend the straw men and resultant pseudocontroversies by explicitly not regarding them seriously as explanations but as constructs that inform us as to what needs explanation. In this case the three perspectives supply an empty matrix that needs to be filled with historical evidence.

Time.   Data from three eras—premodern, modern, and postmodern—are required. Scholars agree that sustained per-capita economic growth is the proper division between the first two periods. The modern versus postmodern distinction is more ambiguous and controversial; the contrast should perhaps be labeled industrial versus advanced industrial. We can avoid this terminological problem for Western societies by comparing the nineteenth century with the era after World War II. Whether this periodization is important for the history of the elderly is, of course, an empirical question.

Cultural Space.   If the modernization perspective requires us to examine change over centuries, the cultural continuity argument informs us that an adequate theory cannot rest on the experience of a single society. Three major cultural family systems may be documented with historical evidence on household structure.

Household structure is a narrower phenomenon than family structure. The latter might be defined through the diversity, frequency, and meaning of interactions between persons biologically or fictively related by blood or marriage. It is difficult and sometimes impossible for the historian to study that expansive definition of family structure. The patterns of coresidence enumerated by census takers and other list makers should not be confused with this broad conception of family structure. Who lives with whom supplies an operationalizable index of family structure. In terms of relative availability of data over time and space, the household must be regarded as the basic building block of the comparative history of the family. Furthermore, sharing living space is not a trivial matter for individuals. The study of household structure is at least as central to larger issues as such possible alternatives as family law, inheritance practices, child-naming patterns, and marriage contracts. Without the index of the household, this paper about the history of the family of the elderly would lack an empirical section.

That data exist does not prove that they have meaning. There is, however, considerable evidence that a correspondence exists between household structure and family structure. My earlier work on Massachusetts has convinced me that a conjugal family system prevailed during the colonial era and became even more pronounced during the nineteenth century. The evidence for this conclusion comes from the range of kin recognized in wills, the names parents gave and did not give their children, and the emphasis on the centrality of marriage in law and in Puritan writings on the family. For example, if men had children, they almost never gave anything in their wills to anyone except their wives and children; a man also did not name a son for his brother, unless the son's uncle had no children. As the culture linked marriage to the economic independence of men, people overwhelmingly lived in conjugal or nuclear households, although taking in a widowed mother was not uncommon. Their writings about the family neglected the subject of household composition; they seemed to have held quite precise ideas about family statuses (what it meant to be a wife, a father, a head of household) and family relationships (husband-wife, parent-child).

The study of household structure involves the interpretation, classification, and analysis of the persons clustered together on listings. It is not always clear if the people listed together lived under one roof, ate together, worked together, or were merely a unit to be taxed by authorities. Slaves, for example, are listed at the bottom of the households of white Marylanders in 1776. A widow in early Massachusetts living in the same house as her married son was sometimes enumerated as a separate head of family if her autonomy had been established in her late husband's will. Although she was a dependent of her son, her rights to that dependence could not be sustained in court. Who lived with whom in the past obviously depends on what was meant by both the enumerators and the enumerated. Historians appear to have been quite careful in using household lists; other sources are usually exploited to determine the meaning behind the lists.

Focusing on the households of the older population has two additional disadvantages. Because of high fertility, old people were relatively scarce in the past. For the era before national census taking one must rely on listings for localities. Thus, only 297 persons over age 64 from five communities are available from *all* of England before 1800. Local listings in the premodern era, as in Maryland in 1776, often do not provide information on relationship to head; kin ties must be inferred from surnames and ages of persons in the household. Finally, since previous research on the history of the household has concentrated on mean size, the data typically are not tabulated by age.[1]

Social gerontologists and historians use different schemes of household classification. The typology of the gerontologists depends on a set of priorities in the coding of family structure. Living with a married child has precedence over all arrangements; living with an unmarried child has precedence over living with another relative (other than spouse), which has precedence over living with an unrelated person, which, finally, has precedence over living alone or, if married, living with a spouse.[2] Historians of the family use the number of marital units in a household to define its structure. The main types are: (1) nuclear—one married couple living with or without unmarried children or a widow(er) living with unmarried children; (2) extended—a nuclear household plus individuals from another marital unit, e.g., a brother or widowed mother of the head; (3) multiple—a household with two or more married couples; (4) no family—a household without a marital unit but containing related persons, e.g., coresident unmarried siblings; and (5) solitary—living alone, sometimes defined to include living with nonkin such as servants or boarders.[3]

Although these household classification schemes are not directly comparable, each distinguishes among the three types of family structures (systems) documented for both normative ideals and actual behavior of people. These types and their historical locales are defined below:

(*a*) *Conjugal.* The married couple defines the family unit, and households in this system have only one marital unit or, on occasion, one couple and another relative, e.g., a widowed mother. The existence of the ideal and the reality of the conjugal family has been attributed to societies in Northwestern Europe.

(*b*) *Stem.* The family line, not marriage, provides the key to kinship. Couples in each generation attempt to preserve the continuity of the "house." Although households ideally contain two married couples (a married parent and a married child), there is only one couple per generation. A widowed mother living with a married child is also consistent with the stem pattern. Although the stem structure existed in parts of Europe, Japan provides the most striking case.

(*c*) *Joint.* The family is a corporate entity including married siblings. A household with an old person would typically have two or more married siblings. A joint understanding of the family may be found in the cultures of Eastern Europe and China.

It is difficult, of course, to define family types in an unequivocal yet comprehensive manner. For some analytical purposes, a set of prerequisites as to inheritance rules, economic activity, etc., might be advantageous; but such elaborate specifications limit comparative analysis to a few cases.[4] The conjugal, stem, and joint types are suited to the subject addressed—the historical evolution of the family structure of the elderly in economically developed societies. Some scholars have argued that conjugal households have predominated in the populations of all societies, while others claim that different forms of domestic organization existed in significant proportions in some cultures. The types and the societies they include provide a genuine problem for empirical historical analysis.

Demographic Variables.   Since demographic factors influence the distribution of household types in a population, we must define three different concepts.

(*a*) *Incidence in the population* is the least desirable indicator. Demographic parameters affect the proportion of households with three generations; with earlier marriage, for example, increasing the possible incidence.[5] Many studies, however, report only a distribution of household types for the entire population.

(*b*) Here *age-specific incidence* refers to the households of persons aged sixty-five and over. Age-specific incidence is more comparable among societies; in a society with earlier marriage, however, old people will be more likely to have only married children. Since coresidence of married old people with their married children is the distinguishing characteristic of nonconjugal family sustems, nuptiality patterns affect the incidence of stem and joint households in the older population.

(*c*) Although *age-specific propensity* is the best measure for assessing rules of behavior, it is often difficult to estimate and is rarely reported. Age-specific propensity measures, for example, the percentage of old people who are grandparents who live with grandchildren. Unfortunately, it is usually not known what proportion of old people have living grandchildren. More frequently the percentage with living children is known or can be indirectly estimated.

THREE REALISTIC PROPOSITIONS

The three perspectives provide the framework of Table 11.1: Cultural Space by Stages of Time. Northwestern Europe, Japan, and Eastern Europe represent the historic areas of conjugal, stem, and joint families, respectively. The preindustrial era, the stage of industrialization, and the current, advanced industrial era delineate the time parameter. Stages of the demographic transition roughly correspond to the time periods; demographic controls must also be introduced for the columns, since these family types also have characteristic patterns of nuptiality.

Realistic Proposition 1.

The best predictor of differences in the household structure of the elderly among economically advanced societies today is the pattern extant before industrialization/urbanization/modernization.

The results for Japan (see table 11.2 and for detail, Appendix, table 11.A-1) provide the most striking support for this contention. Four of five Japanese over age sixty-four lived with their children in 1973 and three in five lived with married children.

Although some historians of the Japanese household stress its small size and simple structure,[6] the idea of the household (*ie* in Japan) conforms to the stem ideal. Although the Japanese ideal differs from Chinese and Indian models, the emphasis is strongly on the continuity of the household over generations. The incidence of the three-generation household in the entire population is much higher in the Tokugawa period (1615-1868) than in premodern Northwestern Europe. The frequency of parent-child coresidence in the 1972 survey of the elderly is so high that one doubts that it could have been still higher in the Tokugawa era.

Both demographically and familially, northwestern Europe in the preindustrial era was unique: late marriage, especially for women, with a high proportion never marrying; higher marital fertility; and a very high proportion of conjugal or nuclear households among all households. Eastern Europe was at the other extreme—very early marriage for both sexes and high proportions of nonnuclear households.[7] Central Europe was probably closer to Northwestern Europe, and Southern Europe to Eastern Europe, albeit with considerable variation among localities within these broad areas.

The results for Europe in the 1950s and 1960s nicely correspond to these traditional differences. The countries with the lowest proportions of old people living with children include Sweden (11

TABLE 11.1
Framework and Evidence for the Historical Study of the Household Structure of the Elderly

VARIABLES	CULTURAL SPACE: TYPE OF FAMILY SYSTEM			DEMOGRAPHIC CHARACTERISTICS
	Conjugal	*Stem*	*Joint*	
A. Periodization: Premodern	(Rural Denmark in 1787, 1801) (England before 1801) (Maryland, 1776)		(Kurland, Latvia, 1797)	High fertility and mortality; small percent of the aged in the population
Modern	(U.S., 1880, 1900) (Preston, England, 1851)		(Poland, 1966) (Yugoslavia, 1969)	Declining mortality and fertility; a somewhat older population
Postmodern	(United States, 1962, 1975) (Britain, 1962) (Denmark, 1962)	(Japan, 1972)		Low fertility and mortality, with 10 percent or more over age sixty-five
B. Historical regions:	Northwestern Europe	Japan	China, Eastern Europe	
C. Distinctive demographic parameters:	Late marriage; low maximum of complex households	Earlier marriage; greater complexity possible, esp. with first-son succession	Earliest marriage; greatest possible complexity	

TABLE 11.2

Summary of Living Arrangements of Population Over Age Sixty-Four

PLACE AND DATE	SAMPLE SIZE	PERCENT WHO HAVE LIVING CHILDREN	PERCENT LIVING WITH:	
			Children	Married Child
United States, 1975 [a]	5,756	82	14	5
1962 [b]	2,442	82	25	10
1952 [c*]	17,661	–	33	
1900 [d]	3,001	85	61.4	26.5
1880 [d]	1,500	–	60.7	25.0
Maryland, whites, 1776 [e]	99	–	58–64	–
Denmark, 1962 [b]	2,446	82	18	4
Rural Denmark, 1801 [f]	464	c. 75	56.0	29.5
Rural Denmark, 1787 [f]	369	–	55.0	28.5
Britain, 1962 [b]	2,500	76	33	12
Preston, Lancashire, 1851 [g]	194	c. 67	68.0	32.5
Preston environs, 1851 [g]	249	–	48.1	18.5
Five places in England, pre-1801 [h]	297	–	46.1	16.5
Postenden, Latvia, 1797 [i]	94	65	41.5	24.2
Sweden, 1956 [j*]	–	–	11	–
West Germany, 1958 [k]	821	80	32	–
Milan, Italy, c. 1958 [j]	1,958	–	41.8	8.3
Poland, 1966 [l]	2,693	86	48	31
Yugoslavia, 1969 [l]	2,645	86	48	38
Israel, Western origin, 1967 [l]	793	–	26	15
Oriental origin	349	–	58	25
Japan, 1972 [m]	–	96	81	60

Sources: [a] Ethel Shanas, "Final Report: National Survey of the Aged," Unpublished report to the Administration on Aging, 1978. Cited by permission of Ethel Shanas, University of Illinois at Chicago Circle.

[b] Ethel Shanas et al., *Old People in Three Industrial Societies* (New York: Atherton Press, 1968), Table VII-1, p. 186.

[c] Peter O. Steiner and Robert Dorfman, *The Economic Status of The Aged* (Berkeley and Los Angeles: Univ. of California Press, 1957), Table 3.6, p. 22.

(*Women married to men under age 65 are excluded from the sample; those living with children who are all under age 21 are counted in the category without children.)

TABLE 11.2 *(Continued)*

Sources: [d]National samples of the noninstitutionalized population in 1880 and 1900. For details on the samples, see Daniel Scott Smith, "A Community-Based Sample of the Older Population from the 1880 and 1900 United States Manuscript Censuses," *Historical Methods* 11 (1978): 67–74.

[e]Gaius M. Brumbaugh, ed., *Maryland Records* (Baltimore: Williams & Williams, 1915). (Data from Prince George's County, I, pp. 1–17; Frederick County, I, pp. 198–232; and Harford County, II, pp. 122–137, 142–193.)

[f]Tabulated from printouts kindly supplied by Hans Christian Johansen, University of Odense. See his essay, "The Position of the Old in the Rural Household in a Traditional Society," in Sune Akerman, Hans Christian Johansen, and David Gaunt, eds., *Chance and Change: Social and Economic Studies in Historical Demography in the Baltic Area,* (Odense, Denmark: Odense Univ. Press, 1978), pp. 122–130.

[g]Michael Anderson, "Household Structure and the Industrial Revolution: Mid-Nineteenth-Century Preston in Comparative Perspective," in Peter Laslett, ed., *Household and Family in Past Time* (Cambridge: Cambridge Univ. Press, 1972), Table 7.8, p. 225.

[h]Peter Laslett, "Societal Development and Aging," in Robert H. Binstock and Ethel Shanas, eds., *Handbook of Aging and the Social Sciences* (New York: Van Nostrand Reinhold, 1976), Table 8, p. 111.

[i]Andrejs Plakans, "The Familial Contexts of Old Age in a Serf Community," (Unpublished paper presented at the Social Science History Association, 1979), Table II, p. 11. Cited by permission.

[j]Ernest W. Burgess, "Family Structure and Relationships," in Z. W. Burgess, ed., *Aging in Western Societies: A Comparative Survey* (Chicago: Univ. of Chicago Press, 1960), p. 282.
(*Sample limited to those aged sixty-seven and over.)

[k]Gerhard Baumert, "Changes in the Family and the Position of Older Persons in Germany," in Clark Tibbitts and Wilma Donahue, eds., *Social and Psychological Aspects of Aging* (New York: Columbia Univ. Press, 1962), Table 2, p. 421.

[l]Ethel Shanas, "Family-Kin Networks and Aging in Cross-Cultural Perspective," *Journal of Marriage and the Family* 35 (1973): Tables 1, 2, p. 507.

[m]Erdman Palmore, *The Honorable Elders: A Cross-Cultural Analysis of Aging in Japan* (Durham, North Carolina: Duke Univ. Press, 1975), Table 4-2, p. 39.

percent), Denmark (18 percent), the United States (25 percent in 1962, 14 percent in 1975), and Great Britain (33 percent). Coresidence of old people with children was distinctly higher in both Poland and Yugoslavia (48 percent in each case). In between, come West Germany (32 percent) and Milan, Italy (42 percent). The differential between older Jews of Western origin (26 percent) and non-Western origin (58 percent) in Israel is also consistent with an emphasis on the continuity of household patterns between the preindustrial era and the present.

Perhaps cultural continuity is not the entire explanation. Current differentials among countries might be attributed to the level of economic development as indexed by per capita income. Housing shortages in the socialist countries of Eastern Europe, the inadequacy of pensions in Japan, or the relative poverty of non-Western-origin Jews in Israel, might also be advanced as explanations. It is naive, however, to believe that people in the non-Western world are merely Westerners with less money and less constituent-oriented governments. The concentration on industrial development in both Eastern Europe and Japan may have been facilitated by the cultural tradition of intergenerational coresidence of old people with their children. The family, to invert C. Wright Mills's classic definition of the sociological imagination, is an institution that can channel public issues into private troubles.[8] The most serious criticism of this proposition is that cross-sectional differentials provide an unreliable basis for making generalizations about historical development; the converse of that argument is also true.

Realistic Proposition 2.

The household structure of the older population changed relatively little during the early and middle phases of modernization and industrialization.

The remarkable similarity between the distribution of household types in rural Denmark in 1781 and 1801 and the United States in both 1880 and 1900 provides the best evidence for this contention. The distinctive household characteristic of the conjugal family system was present in both preindustrial Denmark and the industrial United States; married old people tended to live with unmarried childen, and unmarried (i.e., mostly widowed) old people tended to live with married children (see Appendix table A-1).

Although some scholars have written about the United States in 1900 as if it were a traditional, rural society,[9] nearly every indicator of modernization—urbanization, per capita income growth, fertility decline, and level of literacy—points to a process of rapid change under way already for more than half a century.[10] Rural Denmark in 1787 and 1801 also provides a realistic example of a Western preindustrial society. Nearly half of the heads of families in the entire population were farmers, mainly lease-holding tenants, more than a quarter were cottagers, and about one in eight were artisans.[11] The small sample from Maryland in 1776 is not as adequate, since family relationships had to be inferred and since the slave population is excluded from the tabulation. The standard image of Western preindustrial society also excludes such American innovations as slavery. Not many Americans in 1900 were of Danish origin; but then, the ancestors of many Americans in that year also were not Americans in the eighteenth century.

Realistic Proposition 3.

The household structure of the older population has changed dramatically in the twentieth century in Western societies.

In both 1880 and 1900 more than three in five persons aged sixty-five and over in the United States lived with their children. By 1962 the proportion coresiding with children had dropped to one in four and, by 1975, to one in seven. One may guess that the change in household structure of the elderly in Britain and Denmark is also a twentieth-century development. The twentieth-century timing is consistent with the other major discontinuities in the history of old people—the rising fraction of the aged in the total population, the decline in rates of labor force participation by older men, and the development of welfare policies such as social security. The modern/postmodern or industrial/advanced industrial dichotomy appears to be central to the history of old people in Western societies.[12]

The framework outlined in table 11.1 represents an advance over the limited truth in the three perspectives. Although there has been a before and after in the history of the household structure of the elderly in Western societies,[13] that transition was not coincident with the breakthrough to modern, industrial civilization in the nineteenth century. Although continuity in household structure during that century supports the cultural argument, change finally did occur. Even if a similar massive transition is not inherent in, for example, the Japanese case, it is also true that no culture today is isolated. Western family values have been resisted, but they have also seemed attractive to persons in other cultures.[14]

Still, the labels could be incorrect; perhaps the change should be identified with the particular region, the West, and not with such general categories as postmodern or advanced industrial. The straw man of demographic determinism is just that, representing a confusion of what is significant for the entire population with what is relevant to a small fraction who are old enough to have both married children and grandchildren.

THREE EMPIRICAL PROBLEMS

Table 11.1 is designed to outline the long-run comparative picture and to suggest what work needs to be done. The apparent regularities therein are not unimportant. That 64 percent of Taiwanese who had a married child between the ages of twenty and thirty-nine lived with a married child in 1973 does not seem so surprising.[15] Policymakers concerned with curtailing rapid population growth will find it significant that, historically, fertility changes more easily than family structure. Since research into the history of the elderly is only beginning, I can only outline three important areas in this paper:

(a) the origin and persistence of the distinctive premodern patterns of household structure;

(b) the curvilinear hypothesis that early industrialization and urbanization produced a higher incidence of coresidence of older people and their children;

(c) the mixture of considerations underlying the dramatic decline in the coresidence of the elderly with their children in the United States in the twentieth century.

Premodern Discontinuity and Continuity

Since the characteristic patterns of households are so persistent over time within societies, examples of change therefore become very interesting. Cross-cultural data suggest that nonnuclear household organization does have correlates, being more common in settled agricultural societies than in hunting-and-gathering or urban-technological ones.[16]

Several scholars have uncovered hints of major transitions within the premodern period. Mean household size in Suwa County, Shinano Province, Japan fell sharply from 7.04 to 4.25 between 1671–1700 and 1851–1870. The number of married couples in households with at least one married couple declined from 1.66 to 1.20 over the same interval. In all periods the proportion of three-generation households fluctuated around 30 percent.[17] These trends, not elaborated on by the authors of the study, are consistent with a shift from a joint to stem structure.

The European historical record provides examples of a shift to the northwest European demographic pattern. Monter has documented an upward shift in marriage age in the fascinating case of post-Calvin Geneva.[18] If Geneva shifted from the Southern European regime, the Baltic area appears to have moved from the Eastern European to the Northwest European model during the nineteenth century. The Baltic provinces of Russia in 1897 had non-Russian levels of marital fertility and age at marriage; mean household size was only 4.8.[19] Plakans's work in progress on the soul-revision (fiscal census) of 1797 points to a quite different pattern—very large households (a mean size of 17 persons), early marriage, and nonnuclear household organization.

Two noteworthy points appear in the comparison (see table 11.3) of household structure for persons aged sixty-five and over in the United States in 1900 and people in the same age group located on forty serf estates in Kurland (Latvia) in 1797. In Latvia there were more multiple households and, more surprisingly, a higher proportion of old persons living without kin.[20]

One should not exaggerate the extent of coresidence of old people with their kin in the preindustrial era.[21] A larger fraction of old people in rural Denmark in 1787 and 1801 lived apart from kin than in the United States in 1900. Very high proportions of multiple families were, however, a distinctive feature of serf societies in Eastern Europe and solitary residence was unusual.[22] At present it is unknown whether the abolition of serfdom in Latvia in the 1820s resulted in a nuclear household pattern or a small, kin-based, complex household; the mean size of 4.8 in 1897 is compatible with the predominance of either form.

If one can find hints of change in characteristic household structure within preindustrial societies, the literature is even more rich in illustrations of continuity. The incidence of the complex household in Yugoslavia, including the famous *zadruga*, may be as common in the recent past as the nineteenth century or, for that matter, the medieval period.[23] The Bulgarian village of Dragalevtsy, located on the outskirts of Sofia, provides a particularly striking case of continuity. In 1935 some 60 percent of the households in the village had three or more generations. By 1974, after the abolition of private ownership of farmland and the integration of the population into the economy of the capital, 61 percent had three or more generations.[24]

The continuity in living arrangements may conceal important shifts in the content of family relationships; household structure may be an insensitive index of family structure. Anthropologists have a great advantage over historians, whose respondents are dead, and over survey researchers, who limit their reports to narrowly

TABLE 11.3

Comparison of the Household Structure of the Population Aged Sixty-Five and Over on Forty Serf Estates in Kurland (Latvia) in 1797 and the United States in 1900

(In percent)

TYPE OF HOUSEHOLD	MALES		FEMALES	
	Kurland 1797	U.S.A. 1900	Kurland 1797	U.S.A. 1900
Solitary	15.8	5.8	30.0	8.5
Nuclear	48.8	57.3	25.6	39.2
Extended and No Family	7.4	29.6	22.1	47.2
Multiple	28.0	7.5	22.3	5.2
Sample size	1,177	1,508	945	1,493

Sources: Kurland: Unpublished results furnished by Andrejs Plakans, Department of History, Iowa State University. See Plakans (1978).

United States: National sample of noninstitutionalized population. See Smith (1978).

quantifiable aspects of behavior. The anthropological tradition stresses the interpretation of the meanings underlying behavior. Robert J. Smith studied the Japanese village of Kurusu in 1952 and 1975. By the latter date he reports that "the parents and children of Kurusu obviously feel they rarely understand one another." Despite the vast change in economic life and subtle shifts in the meaning of family relationships, the ideal of intergenerational coresidence persists. A young woman is quoted for the ideal:

It's best for a young couple and the husband's parents to live separately—but not too far apart—until the first baby comes. Then the young couple can move in with the parents. I think the trend to living separately went too far. Now the generations are moving closer together and both children and parents are more willing to adjust and make compromises than they were until recently.[25]

Such views may be merely rationalizations, functional substitutes for "adequate public welfare and pension programs for the elderly."[26] Or they may be persistent value preferences, transcending mundane economic necessities. Although one must not reify the index of household structure into the larger concept of family structure, the preferences of the young woman quoted above are reflected in the actual living arrangements of the elderly in Japan today.

Industrialization and the Curvilinear Hypothesis

In his important study of the Lancashire textile city of Preston, Michael Anderson reversed the modernization argument that associates industrialization with the decline of complex household formation. Coresidence of old people with children in Preston in 1851 was more common than in either the preindustrial period or the present in England. Retaining the moral thrust of the modernization perspective, Anderson argued that coresidence occurred on the basis of calculation rather than norms; older people, particularly widows, were useful in caring for the children of a working mother.[27]

There are several reasons for supposing that old people may have been more likely to live with children and other kin during the nineteenth century. Declining mortality increased the proportion of old people with surviving children. In rural areas where the household was a unit of economic production, separate residence (or separate listing) might have been more common than in cities; in urban-industrial settings, on the other hand, people worked outside the home for employers who were not kin. During the early phases of urban growth, housing was scarce and expensive. Finally, a characteristic of current kinship among the working classes, the close linkage between mothers and daughters, may be part of the urban world of the nineteenth century.[28]

Although inheritance and farm succession structured kinship along male, father-son lines in rural areas, affect was more important in the city.

The evidence currently available for the United States during the nineteenth century does not support the curvilinear interpretation. Data on household headship may be used as a proxy measure for household structure; widows who head their households are less likely to live with married children than widows who are not household heads, and only those listed as heads can live completely alone. The most representative evidence comes from a one-in-five sample of the 1840 Census of Revolutionary War Pensioners.[29] This volume lists both the old person and the household head; headship may thus be ascertained and, if the old person was not the head, one knows if she or he lived with a person who had the same surname. Only 22.5 percent of widows aged seventy-five and over (standardized on the 1900 age-distribution of the over seventy-four population) headed their household in 1840; by 1900 the figure had increased to 28.8 percent. Thus, there was a slight trend toward independent residence among very old widows during the nineteenth century, a shift consistent with a probable tendency of men to leave their property to their widows rather than to their children. The important subject of inheritance practices has not, however, been sufficiently studied.

Rural-urban differentials may also be cautiously used to make inferences about trends. Some 14.2 percent of married old people in places over 2,500 population in 1900 lived with married children, while in rural areas the figure was 17.8 percent. Old unmarried people were more likely to live with their married children—some 32.1 percent in urban areas compared to 39.6 percent in rural places. Since the city drew widowed, single, and kinless old people who had no place or opportunity in rural areas, these slight urban-rural differences should not be emphasized.[30]

More suggestive is the differential in living with married sons in contrast to living with married daughters. Old unmarried people were marginally more likely to live with married daughters in urban areas (20.1 percent) than in rural places (17.2 percent); urban unmarried old people, however, were much less likely to live with married sons (12.1 percent) compared with rural unmarried persons aged sixty-five and over (22.4 percent). Thus the urban shift to the parent-daughter tie was associated with a sharp decrease in coresidence of old people and married sons. This cross-sectional pattern for 1900 is also evident in the comparison of the 1962 national sample with that for 1900. Some 11 percent of unmarried old people in the United States in 1962 (compared with 18 percent in 1900) lived with married daughters, while only 4 percent lived with married sons (contrasted also to 18 percent in 1900.) Since we do not have adequate samples before 1880, we cannot address the specific issue of the effects of the first phase of industrialization and urbanization. No change in household composition occurred, however, in Bertalia, a parish lying outside the city of Bologna, Italy, during its period (1880–1910) of initial urbanization.[31] Although change in the household structure of the elderly during the nineteenth century in the United States was probably slight, the direction of change was consistent with the modernization perspective rather than the curvilinear hypothesis.

The Transformation of the Household Structure of the Elderly in the United States during the Twentieth Century

Although the change in living arrangements of the elderly in the United States has accelerated since 1950,[32] that movement was under way in the first half of the century. The percentage of men aged sixty-five and over living as parent-of-head declined from 16.3 to 10.9 between 1900 and 1940; the figures for women are 34.2 and 23.0 for the two dates. By 1970 only 4.3 percent of men and 12.7 percent of women aged sixty-five and over were living as the parent of a head of household.

The decline in the coresidence of old people and their children was primarily due to changes in the propensity to form these types of households rather than to shifts in demographic structure. The proportion of old persons with no living child has increased only slightly, from 15 percent of women in 1900 to 18 percent of both men and women in 1962. Earlier marriage age and a shorter time span of fertility do imply that old people in recent years are less likely to have an unmarried child with whom they could reside; this is particularly important for married old people who were more likely to live with single rather than married children in 1880 and 1900. The change in the quantity and timing of fertility has, however, only a very small impact on the coresidence of the widowed with children. In 1900 the number of surviving children barely affected the probability of a widowed woman living with a child; some 79 percent of widows aged sixty-five and over with one living child in that year lived with that child, while those widows with five or more living children were coresident with a child in nearly 90 percent of the cases.[33]

Without a decline in the propensity for coresidence, the proportion of households with three generations or more in the entire population would have sharply increased after 1930.[34] The ratio of the population sixty-five and over to the population in the age-groups occupied by their children has risen dramatically. Similarly, the decrease in male labor force participation at older ages (again, particularly marked in the 1930s when participation of men aged sixty-five and over dropped from 58.2 percent to 41.5 percent) would also have increased the frequency of multigenerational households.[35]

Non-gainfully-employed old men in 1900 were distinctly more likely to live as dependents of children than those men who still had occupations. The social security system emerged at precisely the right time to dampen these effects produced by changes in age-structure and labor force participation.

Both social commentators and scholars disagree about the larger implications of the decline in the propensity for old people to live with their children during the twentieth century. In social science, as on Wall Street, there are bulls and bears.[36] Historians aspire to be owls, wisely flying over time, rather than optimistically grazing in the fields of survey research or pessimistically foraging in the forests of classic sociological theory.

The bulls emphasize that old people in the United States today live near and frequently interact with their children; old people are not isolated from kin.[37] Separate residence for old people and their children alleviates the tension and conflicts inherent in sharing space. Intergenerational relationships today are perhaps more harmonious than ever in the past, and social security has reduced the need for generations within a family to struggle over the allocation of income.[38]

The bears speculate differently. While producing tension and conflict, coresidence also generates a more genuine closeness. Furthermore, change in the household structure of the older population is not an isolated development in the American family. The bears can draw connections between that movement and the continuing exponential rise in divorce, the ongoing sexual revolution among teenagers, the rising incidence of primary individuals in all age-groups, and other changes in American family behavior.[39] Bullish critics of this position argue that the "modern" familial glass is still more than half full.[40] The dispute is thus between the bulls who emphasize current cross-sectional patterns and the bears who focus on the direction and extent of recent change.

While this historical owl leans toward the bulls in the short run, he must favor the bears over the long-term future. Perhaps the most significant thing one learns from studying the history of the family is how slowly it changes; a decade or two is but a moment in its glacial evolution. Since the family changes slowly, the owl must be impressed by the rapidity and recent origin of the transformation of the living arrangements of the elderly in the United States. The bulls could, however, invoke a historical explanation for the recent shift: it might be regarded as a consequence of the long-standing conjugal emphasis of the family system of northwestern Europe. Behind that peculiar understanding of the family, however, is a general cultural tendency toward individualism.[41] Thus, the recent change from living-with to living-near may be an ongoing process with living-completely-apart being the ultimate terminus. The middle-aged children of old people today grew up in a society in which a majority of old people lived with children; young persons now are growing up in a society in which a majority of old people live near their children.

The historian may fail in his role as a prophetic owl; he will have ample company. His job narrowly is to figure out what happened in the past and how past patterns compare and relate to the present. To accomplish this task he requires salient data, a technical knowledge of intervening or confounding factors, and a sense of what are the crucial forces for change and continuity. Information on the household structure of the elderly has supplied the first need. Demographic processes—the impact of nuptiality, mortality, and fertility on indices of household composition—are the most important control variables. Modernization in this story provides the irresistible force for change in all human relationships. Cultural preferences for particular definitions of the family make that institution the agent of continuity, an immovable object. When the irresistible force encounters the immovable object, the result, in history as in literature, is a complex, extended drama with an uncertain outcome.

Appendix
TABLE 11.A.1
Historical and Comparative Data on the Living Arrangements of Persons Aged Sixty-Five and Over
(In percent)

	UNITED STATES				DENMARK		
	1975	1962	1900	1880	1962	Rural 1801	Rural 1787
A. MARRIED PERSONS HOUSEHOLD TYPE							
1. With spouse only	84	79	28.6	25.2	82	31.9	29.1
2. With married daughter	2	1	7.4	6.6	1	6.8	3.3
3. With married son		1	8.6	6.6		10.4	9.9
4. With unmarried child	10	15	42.4	44.1	14	35.9	37.1
5. With other relative	4	3	7.5	10.3	0	4.0	4.7
6. With nonkin	2	1	5.6	7.1	3	11.2	16.0
Sample size	3,005	1,335	1,532	757	1,399	251	213
B. UNMARRIED PERSONS HOUSEHOLD TYPE							
1. Living alone	66	48	11.4	9.0	61	8.9	8.3
2. With married daughter	7	11	18.8	20.7	7	13.6	23.7
3. With married son		4	18.7	16.3		30.5	25.6
4. With unmarried child	10	18	27.0	27.2	15	15.5	12.2
5. With other relative	13	12	13.4	11.8	7	8.0	7.0
6. With nonkin	3	6	10.8	15.0	10	23.5	23.1
Sample size	2,751	1,107	1,468	744	1,107	213	156

TABLE 11.A.1 (Continued)

A. MARRIED PERSONS HOUSEHOLD TYPE	BRITAIN Before 1801	BRITAIN 1962	JAPAN 1972	POLAND 1966	YUGOSLAVIA 1969	ISRAEL 1967 Western Origin	ISRAEL 1967 Oriental Origin
1. With spouse only	44	68	15	50	49	82	47
2. With married child	6	5	79	22	33	4	10
3. With unmarried child	43	23	5	19	11	12	41
4. With other relative	7	3	1	3	5		
5. With nonkin		1		6	2	2	2
Sample size	119	1,211	–	1,263	1,392	508	204

B. UNMARRIED PERSONS HOUSEHOLD TYPE	BRITAIN Before 1801	BRITAIN 1962	JAPAN 1972	POLAND 1966	YUGOSLAVIA 1969	ISRAEL 1967 Western Origin	ISRAEL 1967 Oriental Origin
1. Living alone	17	43	9	30	32	50	23
2. With married child	24	19	83	38	44	35	47
3. With unmarried child	21	18	6	16	8	9	21
4. With other relative	38	13	2	9	8		
5. With nonkin	6	6		7	8	6	9
Sample size	178	1,289	–	1,451	1,192	285	145

Sources: See references to Table 2.

NOTES

1. Michael Anderson, "Household Structure and the Industrial Revolution: Mid-Nineteenth-Century Preston in Comparative Perspective," in Peter Laslett, ed., *Household and Family in Past Time* (Cambridge: Cambridge Univ. Press, 1972), pp. 215–236, provides a rare exception.

2. Ethel Shanas, Peter Townsend, Dorothy Wedderburn, Henning Friis, Poul Milhøj, and Jan Stehouwer, *Old People in Three Industrial Societies* (New York: Atherton Press, 1968).

3. Peter Laslett, "Introduction: The History of the Family," in Laslett, ed., *Household and Family*, pp. 28–32.

4. A good general perspective on the subject is provided by Burton Pasternak, *Introduction to Kinship and Social Organization* (Englewood Cliffs, N.J.: Prentice-Hall, 1976). For restrictive definitions, see the example by Michel Verdon, "The Stem Family: Toward a General Theory," *Journal of Interdisciplinary History* 10 (1979): 87–106.

5. Franklin Mendels, "Notes on the Age of Maternity," *Journal of Family History* 3 (1978): 236–250.

6. Chie Nakane, "An Interpretation of the Size and Structure of the Household in Japan over Three Centuries," pp. 517–543; Akira Hayami and Nobuko Uchida, "Size of Household in a Japanese County Throughout the Tokugawa Era," pp. 473–515, both in Laslett, ed., *Household and Family*.

7. John Hajnal, "European Marriage Patterns in Perspective," in D.V. Glass and D.E.C. Eversley, eds., *Population in History* (London: Edward Arnold, 1965), pp. 101–143; Peter Laslett, "Characteristics of the Western Family Considered over Time," *Journal of Family History* 2 (1977): 89–116.

8. C. Wright Mills, *The Sociological Imagination* (New York: Oxford Univ. Press, 1959), p. 8.

9. M.F. Nimkoff, "Changing Family Relationships of Older People in the United States during the last Fifty Years," in Clark Tibbits and Wilma Donahue, eds., *Social and Psychological Aspects of Aging* (New York: Columbia Univ. Press, 1962), pp. 405–414.

10. Richard D. Brown, *Modernization: The Transformation of American Life, 1600–1865* (New York: Hill and Wang, 1976).

11. Hans Christian Johansen, "Some Aspects of Danish Rural Population Structure in 1787," *Scandinavian Economic History Review* 20 (1972): 61–70.

12. W. Andrew Achenbaum and Peter N. Stearns, "Essay: Old Age and Modernization," *Gerontologist* 18 (1978): 307–312.

13. Peter Laslett, "Societal Development and Aging," in Robert H. Binstock and Ethel Shanas, eds., *Handbook of Aging and the Social Sciences* (New York: Van Nostrand Reinhold, 1976), pp. 87–116.

14. William J. Goode, *World Revolution and Family Patterns* (New York: Free Press, 1970). John C. Caldwell, "A Theory of Fertility: From High Plateau to Destabilization," *Population and Development Review* 4 (1978): 553–578; Barbara Alpern Engel, "Mothers and Daughters: Family Patterns and the Female Intelligentsia," in David Ransel, ed., *The Family in Imperial Russia* (Urbana: Univ. of Illinois Press, 1978), pp. 44–59.

15. Ronald Freedman, Baron Moots, Te-Hsiung Sun and Mary Beth Weinberger, "Household Composition and Extended Kinship in Taiwan," *Population Studies* 32 (1978): 65–80.

16. Rae Lesser Blumberg and Robert F. Winch, "Societal Complexity and Familial Complexity: Evidence for the Curvilinear Hypothesis," *American Journal of Sociology* 77 (1972): 898–920.

17. Hayami and Uchida, "Size of Household in a Japanese County," Table 18.2, pp. 487–488.

18. F. William Monter, "Historical Demography and Religious History in Sixteenth-Century Geneva," *Journal of Interdisciplinary History* 9 (1979): 399–427.

19. Ansley J. Coale, Barbara Anderson and Erna Härm, *Human Fertility in Russia Since the Nineteenth Century: The Demographic Transition in a Different Historical Context* (Princeton, New Jersey: Princeton Univ. Press, 1979); Andrejs Plakans, "Familial Structure in the Russian Baltic Provinces: The Nineteenth Century," in Werner Conze, ed., *Sozialgeschichte der Familie in der Neuzeit Europas* (Stuttgart, Germany: Ernst Klett Verlag, 1976), pp. 346–362.

20. Andrejs Plakans, "The Familial Contexts of Old Age in a Serf Community" (Unpublished paper presented at the annual meetings of the Social Science History Association, 1979).

21. Correcting this emphasis on the extended family has been the major theme in the writings of Peter Laslett.

22. Peter Czap, Jr., "Marriage and the Peasant Joint Family in the Era of Serfdom," pp. 103–123 in David Ransel, ed., *The Family in Imperial Russia*.

23. Eugene Hammel, "The Zadruga as Process," pp. 335–374 in Peter Haslett, ed., *Household and Family*; Joel M. Halpern and David Anderson, "The Zadruga: A Century of Change," *Anthropologica* 12 (1970): 83–97.

24. Irwin T. Sanders, "Dragalevtsy Household Members Then (1935) and Now," in H.L. Kostanick, ed., *Population and Migration Trends in Eastern Europe* (Boulder, Colorado: Westview Press, 1977), pp. 125–133.

25. Robert J. Smith, *Kurusu: The Price of Progress in a Japanese Village, 1951–1975* (Stanford, California: Stanford Univ. Press, 1978), pp. 190–191.

26. Toshi Kii, "Aging in Japan: Policy Implications of the Aging Population," Ph.D. dissertation, University of Minnesota, 1976.

27. Michael Anderson, *Family Structure in Nineteenth Century Lancashire* (Cambridge: Cambridge Univ. Press, 1971). Also, see Anderson, "The Impact on the Family Relationships of the Elderly of Changes since Victorian Times in Governmental Income Maintenance Provision," in Ethel Shanas and Marvin B. Sussman, eds., *Family, Bureaucracy, and the Elderly* (Durham, North Carolina: Duke Univ. Press, 1980), pp. 36–59.

28. Dorrian Apple Sweetser, "The Effect of Industrialization on Intergenerational Solidarity," *Rural Sociology* 31 (1966): 156–170; Elisabeth Bott, *Family and Social Network: Roles, Norms, and External Relationships in Ordinary Urban Families* (London: Tavistock Publications, 1971).

29. United States Office of the Census, *A Census of Pensioners for Revolutionary or Military Services* (Washington: Secretary of State, 1841).

30. Janice L. Reiff, Michel R. Dahlin, and Daniel Scott Smith, "Rural Push and Urban Pull: Work and Family Experiences of Older Black Women in Southern Cities, 1880–1900" (Unpublished, 1980).

31. David Kertzer, "The Impact of Urbanization on Household Composition: Implications from an Italian Parish (1880–1910)," *Urban Anthropology* 7 (1978): 1–23.

32. Frances Kobrin, "The Fall in Household Size and the Rise of the Primary Individual in the United States," *Demography* 13 (1976): 127–138, and Kobrin, "The Primary Individual and the Family: Changes in Living Arrangements in the United States since 1940," *Journal of Marriage and the Family* 38 (1976): 233–239.

33. Daniel Scott Smith, "Life Course, Norms, and the Family System of Older Americans in 1900," *Journal of Family History* 4 (1979): 285–298.

34. Kobrin, "The Fall in Household Size."

35. Michael J. Brennan, Philip Taft, and Mark B. Schupack, *The Economics of Age* (New York: W.W. Norton, 1967), p. 19.

36. J.S. Berliner, "Internal Migration: A Comparative Disciplinary View," in A. A. Brown and Egon Neuberger, eds., *Internal Migration: A Comparative Perspective* (New York: Academic Press, 1977), pp. 443–461.

37. Shanas et al., *Old People in Three Industrial Societies*.

38. Anderson, "Family Relationships of the Elderly."

39. Samuel H. Preston and John McDonald, "The Incidence of Divorce within Cohorts of American Marriages Contracted since the Civil War," *Demography* 16 (1979): 1–26; Melvin Zelnik and John F. Kantner, "Sexual and Contraceptive Experience of Young Unmarried Women in the United States, 1976 and 1971," *Family Planning Perspectives* 9, no. 2 (1977): 55–71; Kobrin, "The Primary Individual and the Family."

40. Mary Jo Bane, *Here to Stay: American Families in the Twentieth Century* (New York: Basic Books, 1976).

41. Alan Macfarlane, *The Origin of English Individualism* (Cambridge: Cambridge Univ. Press, 1979).

ABOUT THE CONTRIBUTORS

EDWARD BEVER is a graduate student at Princeton University. He graduated *summa cum laude* in 1975 from Dartmouth College, and received his M.A. in 1978. He completed his dissertation, "Witchcraft and Shamanism in Early Modern Würtemberg," in 1982.

DAVID H. FOWLER is Professor of History at Carnegie-Mellon University, where he teaches courses in American social history. He is editor and joint editor of a number of texts and readings in Western Civilization and American history, most recently *In Search of America*, 2 vols. (New York: Holt-Dryden, 1972). He is currently at work, with Lois Fowler, on a biography of Jane Grey Swisshelm.

LOIS JOSEPHS FOWLER is Professor of English at Carnegie-Mellon University, where she teaches courses in Topical Approaches to Literature, Biography, Victorian Society, Professional Writing, Curriculum Design, and Applied Rhetoric. She has been active in the National Council of Teachers and has served on the Executive Board of the Conference on English Education. Her most recent articles appeared in *College English, Teaching English in the Two-Year College,* and *Future American Colleges*. She is currently working with David Fowler on a biography of Jane Grey Swisshelm, nineteenth century abolitionist, reformer, and journalist.

DAVID HERLIHY is Henry Charles Lea Professor of Medieval History at Harvard University and Master of Mather House. His chief interests are in the social history of the Middle Ages, especially in Italy. Among his principal publications is the computer-assisted analysis of the Florentine *Catasto* (census) of 1427, done in collaboration with Mme Christiane Klapisch-Zuber. Published in 1978, the book is entitled *Les Toscans et leurs familles*. An English translation is in preparation.

LOIS LAMDIN, Associate Dean at Empire State College, is currently on leave to finish her book on the Jewish-American novel. During this time she is also serving as consultant on adult education to CLEO (Compact for Lifelong Educational Opportunity), a consortium of forty-nine Delaware Valley Colleges. Dr. Lamdin's publications include *The Ghetto Reader* (Random House), a Cael monograph on *Interpersonal Competencies in an Institutional Setting*, and a number of journal articles on Victorian writers, Jewish-American novelists, and individualized education.

ADELE LINDENMEYR received her Ph.D. in Russian History from Princeton University and now teaches at Carnegie-Mellon University. She is completing a study of public and private poor relief in late Imperial Russia.

ROBERT J. MAXWELL has done field work in Samoa and among the Tlingit Indians of Alaska, where he studied the circumstances of the aged. His research interests include the management of spatial relationships and the effects of building design on behavior.

PHILIP SILVERMAN is Professor of Anthropology at California State College, Bakersfield. He has done research in rural communities of eastern Canada and among the Lozi of Zambia. In addition to the cross-cultural study of the aged, he is interested in ethnicity and aging, tribal-national relations, and African ethnology.

DANIEL SCOTT SMITH is associate professor of history, University of Illinois at Chicago Circle, associate director of the Family and Community History Center of the Newberry Library, and editor since 1979 of *Historical Methods*. The paper in this volume is an extension of a study of older Americans and their families in 1880 and 1900.

STEVEN R. SMITH is Associate Professor of History at Savannah State College. He is the author of several articles on aspects of social history in early modern England including "The London Apprentices as Seventeenth-Century Adolescents" in *Past & Present* (No. 61, November, 1973) and "Death, Dying and the Elderly in Seventeenth-Century England" in *Aging and the Elderly: Humanistic Perspectives in Gerontology* (Atlantic Highlands, N.J., 1978).

RICHARD C. TREXLER taught Renaissance history at El Paso (UTEP), Los Angeles (Occidental College), and Urbana (UI), before assuming his present post at the State University of New York at Binghamton in 1978. He has specialized in the social history of Florence since his terminal degree at the University of Frankfurt am Main in 1963. The recently published *Public Life in Renaissance Florence* (Academic Press, 1980) synthesized Trexler's research on formal behavior in the Renaissance. The present monograph continues the author's research on the marginal groups of Florentine society, which has led to articles on infanticide, foundlings, adolescents, the shamed poor, nuns, and prostitutes.

DAVID G. TROYANSKY, a graduate of Carleton College, is a Ph.D. candidate in the Program in Comparative History at Brandeis University. He is currently completing a dissertation on old age in eighteenth-century France.

SYLVIA VATUK is Associate Professor of Anthropology and Director of the Gerontology Office, University of Illinois at Chicago Circle. She has carried out anthropological field research in India, focusing on problems of urbanization and changing family and kinship organization, and, most recently, on cultural and social dimensions of aging and the life cycle. She is the author of *Kinship and Urbanization* (University of California, 1972) and of numerous articles in professional journals.

INDEX